AN EXPLORER'S GUIDE

Mexico's Aztec and Maya Empires

AN EXPLORER'S GUIDE

Mexico's Aztec and Maya Empires

Zain Deane

with photographs by the author

FIRST EDITION

The Countryman Press ✷ Woodstock, Vermont

Explorer's Guide Mexico's Aztec & Maya Empires

ISBN 978-1-58157-107-3

Interior photographs by the author unless otherwise specified
Maps by Erin Greb Cartography, © The Countryman Press
Book design by Bodenweber
Composition by PerfecType, Nashville, TN

Published by The Countryman Press, P.O. Box 748, Woodstock, VT 05091

Distributed by W. W. Norton & Company, Inc., 500 Fifth Avenue, New York, NY 10110

Printed in the United States of America

10 9 8 7 6 5 4 3 2 1

I dedicate this book to my father, who has been my strongest and proudest advocate, and to my mother, who has encouraged me from the beginning.

You've made every page possible.

EXPLORE WITH US!

Mexico is a vast, incredibly diverse country that offers virtually every kind of vacation experience, from beach resorts along the coast to colonial Spanish towns to jungle treks. But for all its touristic richness, there is nothing quite like the majesty of Mexico's ancient ruins. There is an enigmatic power to them, an aura and mystique that can only be appreciated when standing at the foot one of their temples. They are the physical remains of cultures that once burst with vitality, mythology, creativity, and ingenuity.

In terms of geography, Mexico's ancient sites can be found predominantly in the central and southern parts of the country, although the north is home to the remains of an enigmatic city-state named Paquimé. As such, our travels will canvass the country, which will provide the added advantage of seeing many sides of cultural, modern-day Mexico.

As far as the tourist is concerned, this geographic spread means two things—or more accurately, two vacation options. First, you can follow this guide around Mexico, visiting a fascinating tapestry of pre-Columbian architecture and cultures; this would entail a lengthy and adventurous trip, and is certainly not what I'd recommend if relaxing by the beach is your priority, or if time is limited. Your other option is to visit one part of Mexico and refer to this guide for what there is to see and do, with an obvious emphasis on pre-Hispanic heritage. While I focus on Tenochtitlán in Mexico City, for example, I also provide plenty of information on lodging, dining, and attractions in the capital. You'll also find details on nearby sites such as Xochicalco and Teotihuacán.

Visiting Mexico has its challenges. Language is a big one for those who don't speak a word of Spanish; food and water can cause problems if you're not careful; crime is a concern in parts of the country; and even altitude and pollution play a role, depending on where you are. No guide can promise a safe, incident-free journey, but the prepared visitor, with a little savvy and a lot of common sense, should be able to enjoy a wonderful and memorable vacation in this country.

Of course, the history of ancient Mexico is the major focus of this book, and I hope it proves a fascinating chronicle of civilizations that flourished before the New World collided with the Old. It is a history rife with conquest, tragedy, heroism, legends, and colorful gods. And it's a testament to a people's scientific and astronomic breakthroughs, artistic achievements, and a religion so complex that a full pantheon of gods governed the fate of kings and peasants alike. You will find great mystery in ancient Mexico, the sudden rise and unexplained collapse of mighty cities, the enigma of vanished peoples, and wondrous relics. And best of all, perhaps, you will find the customs and traditions of the past alive and well in the present.

PRICES

Mexico offers a vacation for every budget, whether you're a backpacker visiting Mexico's ruins by bus and hostel, or enjoying a string of five-star resorts as you fly around the country. Its museums and ruins are affordable for virtually every tourist, and food choices will range from under-a-dollar tacos to restaurants that will challenge the deepest pockets. As for entertainment, the sky, and the water, are the limits.

Because prices are elastic and can vary greatly by region, I've used the following chart when reviewing lodging, dining, attractions, and shopping options around the country. While central Mexico is not subject to seasonal fluctuations in its tourist pricing, the coastal areas certainly have peak seasons, with spikes during major holidays.

Note that prices listed in the book do not include taxes or gratuities. Tipping follows its own customs in Mexico. A taxi driver does not generally expect a tip but will appreciate one all the same. Porters and other hotel staff should be tipped for their services, and at restaurants, a 10 to 15 percent tip is standard. Make sure to check your bill at restaurants, as some include the service charge.

Price Guide

Code	Lodging (double occupancy)	Restaurants (per entrée)	Attractions (per adult)
$	Up to $100	Up to $10	Up to $10
$$	$101–200	$11–25	$11–25
$$$	$201–300	$26–35	$26–50
$$$$	More than $300	More than $35	More than $50

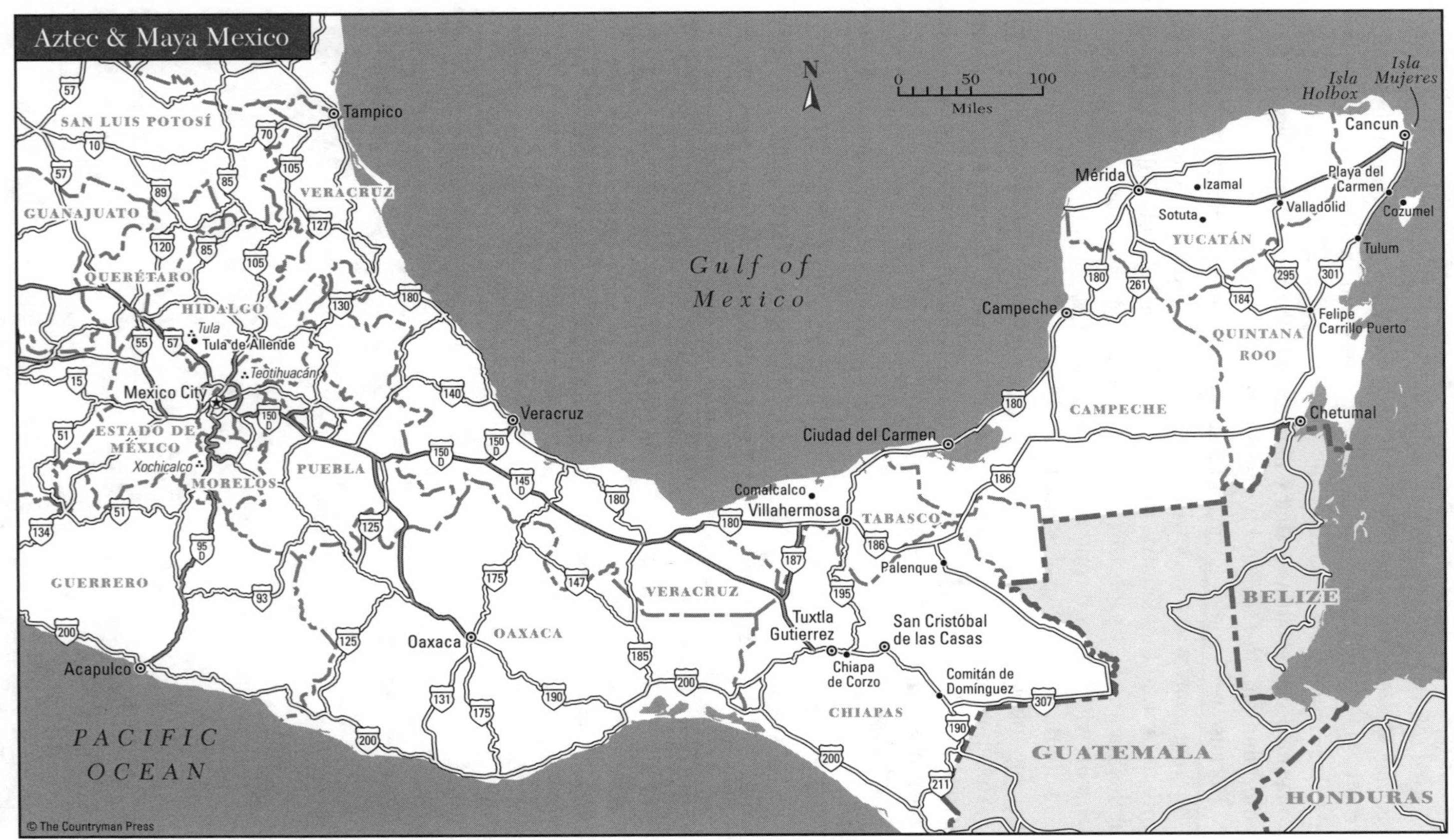
Aztec & Maya Mexico
N
0 50 100
Miles
Gulf of Mexico
PACIFIC OCEAN
SAN LUIS POTOSÍ
GUANAJUATO
QUERÉTARO
HIDALGO
VERACRUZ
ESTADO DE MÉXICO
MORELOS
PUEBLA
GUERRERO
OAXACA
TABASCO
CHIAPAS
CAMPECHE
YUCATÁN
QUINTANA ROO
BELIZE
GUATEMALA
HONDURAS
Tampico
Tula
Tula de Allende
Teotihuacán
Mexico City
Xochicalco
Veracruz
Acapulco
Oaxaca
Comalcalco
Villahermosa
Ciudad del Carmen
Campeche
Mérida
Izamal
Sotuta
Valladolid
Cancun
Isla Holbox
Isla Mujeres
Playa del Carmen
Cozumel
Tulum
Felipe Carrillo Puerto
Chetumal
Palenque
Tuxtla Gutierrez
Chiapa de Corzo
San Cristóbal de las Casas
Comitán de Domínguez
© The Countryman Press

CONTENTS

ACKNOWLEDGMENTS

Every writer owes his or her book to a silent army of people who, in one form or another, help see it to fruition. I wish I could thank everyone who gave their time, effort, and hospitality to introducing me to Mexico's Aztec and Maya empires. But this abbreviated list must suffice.

Special thanks go to Kim Grant, who loved the idea of this book, and Kermit Hummel, who commissioned it. Sylvie Laitre's outstanding service, Mexico Boutique Hotels, was an invaluable resource and asset in virtually every part of my journey in Mexico, and Rocío Martínez Quintal convinced me to visit Holbox. Claire Kunzman introduced me to the efficient and well-run Grupo Posadas.

My friends Sebastian, Maria Cristina, and Javier helped me navigate the wonderful jungle of Mexico City. The tourism board of Yucatán, with the help of Humberto Gómez, helped me discover their unforgettable state, and Mario Arturo Garrido (not to mention Rita and her dad!) showed me the Yucatán I'd never have known on my own (special thanks to Itzel for that). I owe a huge debt of gratitude to Agustín Ballesteros for putting me in touch with Israel Kumul, who was an invaluable asset in Cancún and the Riviera Maya.

In Chiapas, Adriana Alarcón was an incredible host, both knowledgeable and wonderful company throughout my time there. And it was thanks to Sheila, Lourdes, and Wilberth that I got to know Campeche.

To my parents, without whom I would never have become a writer, and my sister, without whom I would never have fallen in love with Mexico. And finally, to Saira, who endures and supports the chaos of my writing.

INTRODUCTION

There are about 40,000 registered archaeological sites in Mexico. Take a moment to absorb that statistic: It's an astounding record of over three thousand years of civilization. Of these sites, *only* 174 are open to the public as of this printing. These range from uninspiring mounds that leave nearly everything to the imagination to towering structures that humble its visitors. Whereas the Aztecs ruled from central Mexico, the Maya empire clustered around the central and southern parts of the country, especially in the Yucatán peninsula, and spanned far beyond Mexico's present-day borders. Before either made their mark, their forerunners settled in Mexico, and left indelible traces of their existence.

The destinations covered in this book represent the most important and impressive Aztec and Maya ruins in Mexico. Many of them are included on the list of Mexico's 27 UNESCO World Heritage Sites (again, an impressive figure). Some are world famous, like the incomparable Chichén Itzá and Teotihuacán. Others, like Mayapan and Tenam Puente, are archaeological gems most often bypassed on the way to more famous sites.

I wrote this book both to help visitors discover Mexico's history and to pay homage to the legacy of the Maya and Aztec empires that have played such a defining role in the early development of the Americas. There is still much we don't know about these people, and our general knowledge has been clouded by Hollywood's focus on bloodthirsty tribal warfare and human sacrifices. Sure, these were prevalent especially in the Aztec era, but so were great scientific and cultural achievements. I've attempted to paint a more complete picture of these civilizations.

In organizing this book, I was cognizant of the very real prospect of archaeological overdose. After all, architecturally, many of these structures follow similar blueprints. For this reason, this guide offers ideas and suggestions for what to see and do while you're exploring these sites. Rather than string together road trips with ten to fifteen ruins on the agenda, the focus is on what each place offers its visitors, both in terms of the star attraction and nearby points of interest. In addition, hotels, restaurants, and other tourist listings have been provided for each destination, allowing visitors to plan their own way through Mexico's Aztec and Maya territory.

However, I must warn readers that this guide does not, in any way, aim to be a complete resource to Maya and Aztec Mexico. I've had to select, out of many, the sights I felt best represented these cultures. I've had to sacrifice some archaeological zones as well as some of my coverage of many destinations to ensure I did justice to the places mentioned herein. In the process, amazing sites—among them Monte Albán, El Tajín, and La Venta—which did not belong directly to these civilizations, have been omitted.

And finally, this book does not stretch beyond Mexico's boundaries, even if the Maya empire certainly did. The magnificence of Tikal, El Mirador, and other cities, must be left for another book.

In the end, I hope I've put together a guide that will give you the information, insight, and tips to help you experience the best of Aztec and Maya Mexico. And above all, I hope to present the full magnitude and glory of two civilizations that helped shape the modern world. Let's walk in the footsteps of once-mighty people who were scientists and priests, warriors and farmers, athletes and scholars, and builders of wonders.

Zain Deane

WHAT'S WHERE IN AZTEC AND MAYA MEXICO

ADMISSION FEES The majority of the archaeological sites and museums in Mexico are a bargain, charging less than $5 (at press time, for example, major attractions such as Tulum and Edzná cost 51 pesos). There are rare exceptions (Chichén Itzá is one), but even so, your archaeological exploration can be done on any budget. Bring cash, however, as many of them don't accept credit cards. You'll have to pay an additional fee (again hovering around the $5 mark) if you want to use a video camera. The vast majority of archaeological sites are open daily 8–5.

AIRPORTS For the purposes of this book, your entry point into Mexico will either be the well-appointed **Benito Juárez International Airport** in Mexico City, from which you can continue on to any other city in the country; **Cancún International Airport**, one of the busiest hubs in the Caribbean, which services most national and international airlines; or the **Manuel Crescencio Rejón International Airport** in Mérida, which services a handful of international flights. More information on each is available in chapter 3.

ARCHITECTURAL STYLES IN THE MAYA WORLD As you explore archaeological Mexico, especially the Maya region, you'll note various architectural styles, such as Río Bec or Puuc. Several sites, such as Tulum, Chichén Itzá, and Edzná, also feature multiple styles, indicative of influence from other cultures and cultural evolution. Here's a quick rundown on what they mean, and where you can find them.

Petén: The Petén region in modern-day Guatemala was a cultural and architectural forge for the Maya of the Classic period, and the Petén style spread far beyond its geographic borders. The heartland of the Petén was Tikal, but its style can be seen in Cobá, Chichén Itzá, Calakmul, and Uxmal, to name a few. Most representative of the Petén was

AN ICONOGRAPHIC MOUNTAIN, OFTEN MISTAKEN FOR REPRESENTATIONS OF CHAAC, THE RAIN GOD, AT MAYAPAN

the construction of temple pyramids of immense size with steep staircases and decorative crests atop its buildings. The Petén predated the Puuc and Río Bec styles covered below, and their architectural style is clearly more rudimentary. But what it lacks in sophistication, it made up for in sheer size.

Puuc: The Puuc style is named for a group of hills found in southwestern Yucatán, and represents the architecture and culture of the Terminal Classic period. The pride of the Puuc is Uxmal, a site that deserves to be on anyone's shortlist of places to visit. Puuc buildings feature an exterior of thin, square-shaped limestone blocks, high, narrow stone vaults, round columns, and elaborate cornices. One of the most distinctive and elaborate characteristics of this style is a detailed "mask" with a hooked nose (sometimes pointing up, sometimes down), and often with flower patterns above the eyes.

Many guides will tell you that these are representations of the rain god, Chaac. In fact, research has shown that they are iconographic mountains representing *witz,* the first mountain in the Maya creation story. You'll find these masks at Chichén Itzá, Uxmal, Kabah, and numerous other sites, indicating the refined Puuc style.

Chenes: South of the Puuc region in present-day Campeche,

Campeche Tourism Board

you'll find a cluster of sites representative of the Chenes style, which flourished in the Classic period. As far as distinguishing features go, you really can't miss the Chenes: portals decorated with fantastically elaborate façades of a giant mouth with jaws wide open, representing the Monster of the Earth (that is, of the Maya Underworld). Chicanná, Hochob, Tabasqueño, and Santa Rosa Xtampak are all fine examples of this remarkable style.

Río Bec: North of the Petén Region in southern Campeche, the Río Bec style developed in the late Classic period and can be found in Xpuhil, Becán, Río Bec, and Calakmul. A word you'll hear often to describe these structures is *fake*, because many of their features are ornamental rather than functional; the most notable of these elements are the often twin tapering towers with steep, narrow steps not really designed for climbing, crowned by a false temple with no rooms within. The function of these false pyramids and temples is believed to be a representation of the twin towers of Tikal.

***Talud-Tablero*:** The classic stepped temple pyramid you find throughout pre-Columbian Mexico is an example of the *talud-tablero,* or slope-and-panel, façade. This is comprised of a

BELOW: TEOTIHUACÁN SHOWCASES THE TALUD-TABLERO STYLE. Mexico Tourism Board

Mexico Tourism Board

THE MAGNIFICENT CASTILLO DE KUKULCÁN AT CHICHÉN ITZÁ

rectangular structure (*tablero*) placed over a sloping panel (*talud*). The style has been associated primarily with Teotihuacán, and is indicative of the widespread influence of the ancient city's culture throughout Mesoamerica.

Toltec: The arrival of the Toltec in the Maya world transformed everything from Maya religion to its structures. Arguably the most impressive building in all of Mexico—the Castillo de Kukulcán at Chichén Itzá—is an example of Toltec influence. Eagle and jaguar motifs; the *tzompantli,* or skull rack; and, above all, representations of the feathered serpent are examples of the Toltec style.

AREA CODE Mexico's country code is 052. The area codes for the regions below can be found in their respective chapters. If you don't have, or haven't activated, international roaming for your cell phone, your best bet to call the United States from Mexico is to buy a Ladatel calling card. These are easily available at convenience stores and shops all over the country and can be used at payphone booths. To call outside the country, dial 00, the country code (1 for the U.S. and Canada), the area code, and the phone number. You can also dial 090 to reach an English-speaking operator for local, collect, or international calls.

ARTS AND CRAFTS Mexico's arts and crafts are incredibly diverse and vary from region to region. While you can get many items just about anywhere, each area has its own arts and crafts tradition and specialty. Here are just a few items to look for as you travel through Aztec and Maya Mexico. You'll find more information on what you can buy in each state in their respective chapters.

Campeche: Campeche has a wonderful tradition of arts and crafts; in particular, look for the Panama hats woven in the town of Bécal, handicrafts made out of bull horns, hammocks from the town of Calkiní, and ceramics from Tepakán.

Central Mexico: One of my favorite handicrafts in all of Mexico is the Calavera de la Catrina (The Elegant Skull), the iconic figure of a female skeleton in a long gown and a feathered hat, often sporting an umbrella. The image, first created by engraver José

Guadalupe Posada in 1913, has become a popular national symbol, and makes for a wonderfully original and authentic keepsake. Also look for handmade Talavera pottery from the town of Puebla.

Chiapas: With the third biggest bed of amber in the world, Chiapas specializes in jewelry made from this typically yellow-hued resin. Also visit Zinacantán for its handwoven textiles.

Quintana Roo: Look for beautiful huipils (traditional handwoven blouses), seashells, and crafts made with conch shells on Mexico's Caribbean coast.

Yucatán: The Yucatán is famous for its hammocks, guayabera shirts, and, if you want to get really authentic, the *makech,* a live, bejeweled beetle that you buy and hang onto your clothing.

BUS TRAVEL I can't say enough about how convenient, safe, affordable, and efficient it is to travel by bus in Mexico, whether you're going across town or cross-country. There are generally three classes of service for long-distance travel.

- Luxury (de lujo) class is like first-class plus, with added benefits including reclining seats and more room. Sometimes you even get refreshments and headphones for the onboard movie.
- First-class (primera clase) buses have air-conditioning, reclining seats, and usually come equipped with a toilet. They are always quicker than local buses covering the same route, as they tend to stick to toll roads and make less stops.
- Second-class (segunda clase) buses stop more frequently, and sometimes service smaller stations in a large city. This class is far more representative of bus travel for laborers and other locals in the countryside, but it's also decent enough to offer you safe and convenient passage to your destination. Many smaller towns offer only second-class bus service.

A terrific resource to coordinate your bus travel around Mexico is **Ticket Bus** (www.ticketbus.com.mx), which is in the process of rebranding itself as **Boletotal**. From this portal you can book travel to just about anywhere in the country. In addition, here are a few bus companies that service different parts of the country.

- **ADO** will likely be the bus service you take most when exploring Maya Mexico, as it covers Quintana Roo, Yucatán, Chiapas, and Campeche. With a variety of options throughout central and southern Mexico, ADO even sells bus passes (www.ado.com.mx).
- **Enlaces Terrestres Nacionales (ETN)** covers

mostly northern and central Mexico (www.etn.com.mx).

- **Estrella de Oro** runs from Mexico City to the Pacific Coast (www.autobus.com.mx/edo).
- **Omnibuses de México** has extensive coverage in northern and central Mexico (www.odm.com.mx).
- **UNO** is ADO's platinum line and covers central and southern Mexico. This is the ideal way to travel overland from Mexico City to destinations in Maya Mexico (www.uno.com.mx).

CITIES The term "Aztec and Maya Mexico" covers the largest city in Mexico and many of its most picturesque destinations. Aztec Mexico centers on present-day **Mexico City**, one of the largest urban metropolises in the Americas and one of the largest cities in the world. Greater Mexico City boasts a population of over 21 million people. The Maya empire in Mexico stretches from the Yucatán peninsula to Tabasco, Campeche, and Chiapas. Within these borders lies **Mérida,** the largest city in Yucatán, and one of its most charming. Smaller cities also worth a visit in the state include **Izamal** and **Valladolid**. The capital of Chiapas and its largest city is **Tuxtla Gutiérrez**, but far more beautiful are **San Cristóbal de las Casas**, **Comitán de Domínguez**, and **Chiapa de Corzo.** In Quintana Roo, **Cancún**, **Playa del Carmen**, and **Tulum** are the major tourist hubs.

CLIMATE Mexico is a large country (over 760,000 square miles), and as such, has a varied climate. (Add to that a varied topography with most of the country at an elevation of over 3,000 feet, and you can expect dramatic changes in weather). Generally, there are two main seasons: rainy (May to mid-October) and dry (mid-October to April), with late summer being the wettest time of year. The Gulf Coast often sees wet weather even during the dry season.

Mexico City benefits from fine weather most of the year, with its summer months enjoying

temperatures in the 70s to 80s, and winter months staying cool during the day. During winter nights, you can experience 30-degree weather in and around the Federal District (a.k.a. the D.F.). The coastal lowlands range from temperate in the winter months to quite hot in the summer. From late November to January, the entire Yucatán peninsula also suffers *nortes* (northers), which are northerly winds and showers from the American Midwest. Finally, don't forget about hurricane season in the Yucatán peninsula and Pacific coast from June through October. Even if you're spared the full wrath of these storms, they can bring torrential rains and basically miserable conditions. Road closures, evacuations of beachfront areas, and blackouts are all potential symptoms. In case you find yourself in the path of a hurricane, your best bet is to find a large, well-equipped hotel in which to ride it out.

EMBASSIES A number of countries have embassies in Mexico City. These include:

Canada
55-5724-7900
www.canadainternational.gc.ca/mexico-mexique/index.aspx
Schiller 529, Colonia Bosque de Chapultepec, Mexico City, D.F.

United Kingdom
555-207-2449
http://ukinmexico.fco.gov.uk
Río Lerma 71, Colonia Cuauhtémoc, Mexico City, D.F.

United States
555-080-2000
www.usembassy-mexico.gov
Paseo de la Reforma 305, Colonia Cuauhtémoc, Mexico City, D.F. (Mexico address)

In addition, you can find an American consulate in Mérida (Calle 60 No. 338K between 29 and 31, Colonia Alcala Martin, Mérida, Yucatán 97050, 999-942-5700) and a consular agency in Cancún (Plaza Caracol Two, Second Level, No. 320–323, Boulevard Kukulkán, Km. 8.5, Zona Hotelera, 998-883-0272).

ENGLISH Can you get around Mexico without speaking a single word in Spanish? Maybe, but chances are, you'll be talking with your hands a lot. In the main tourist areas in Mexico City and especially in Cancún and the Riviera Maya, English is widely spoken. However, once you get out of the tourist zones, English becomes far less commonplace, and Spanish is the norm; in rural towns around the peninsula, even Spanish can take a back seat to the Mayan tongue. Learning even the basics of the Spanish language will go a long way toward making your experience in Mexico much more rewarding. The dictionary at the end of this book should help you manage a basic conversation.

EMERGENCIES In case of emergencies, remember these numbers: **066** is the same as 911 in the United States; **060** for reporting crime; **065** for the Red Cross and ambulance service; and **078** or 800-987-8224 for tourist assistance in Mexico City. From the United States or Canada, you can also get safety and security updates by calling 888-407-4747 toll-free or 202-501-4444 from 8–8 Eastern Time, Mon. through Fri. (except U.S. federal holidays).

GEOGRAPHY Mexico takes the shape of a vast cornucopia and has a diverse topography. From arid desert to tropical rainforest, you'll find its geography varies as much as its climate. In general, the northern part of the country is desertlike and arid. Central Mexico, including Mexico City, lies on an elevated plateau thanks to the Sierra Madre ranges, which form the Valley of Mexico; most of the region is at an elevation of more than 5,000 feet. From here, Mexico's borders narrow until only 125 miles separates the Gulf of Mexico from the Pacific Ocean, before the land opens up again into the Yucatán peninsula. From the mountains and forests of Chiapas, the topography gradually changes to the limestone flatlands of northern Campeche, Yucatán, and Quintana Roo. Mexico's other peninsula, Baja California, is separated from much of the mainland by the Sea of Cortés, and presents yet another side of the country. Mexico is bordered by the United States, Belize, and Guatemala; it fronts the Pacific Ocean and the Caribbean Sea on its western coast with the Gulf of Mexico to the east, for a total of over 6,000 miles of coastline.

INAH If you go anywhere near a museum or archaeological site, you'll find the acronym INAH (www.inah.gob.mx) prominently featured. This is the **Instituto Nacional de Antropología e Historia** (National Institute of Anthropology and History), a federal agency responsible for the upkeep, research, protection, and promotion of Mexico's cultural and historic heritage. You'll also find the acronym **CONACULTA**, or **Consejo Nacional Para Las Culturas y las Artes** (National

Council for Culture and Arts, (www.conaculta.gob.mx). This agency is in charge of Mexico's museums and monuments.

PEOPLE Mexicans, like Mexico, have long suffered from an unfair reputation. Let's face it; be the image a poncho-clad, sombrero-wearing slapstick figure or a migrant laborer, we generally paint our neighbors in an unflattering light, and in so doing malign a warm, friendly, and cultured people.

You'll find a great difference in the local people as you move around the country. The city-slick sophistication of the *chilango* (as the citizens of Mexico City are known) is far different from the laid-back mindset of Yucatecos. Each region in Mexico boasts its own cultural contributions and natural resources to the nation, and discovering these delights is among the best parts of a vacation.

A REPRESENTATION OF QUETZALCOATL FROM TEOTIHUACAN, DISPLAYED AT THE MUSEO NACIONAL DE ANTROPOLOGÍA IN MEXICO CITY.

STATES Mexico's official name is the United Mexican States. It's a federal republic comprising 31 states and a federal district similar to Washington, DC. This book covers the Distrito Federal (D.F., or Federal District), home to Mexico City, as well as the states of Campeche, Chiapas, Yucatán, and Quintana Roo.

UNESCO WORLD HERITAGE SITES Mexico has a staggering 27 cultural and 4 natural UNESCO World Heritage Sites. The full list can be found at whc.unesco.org. The ones covered in this book are:

- The archaeological sites of Chichén Itzá and Uxmal in Yucatán
- The ancient capital of Calakmul and the historic town of Campeche in Campeche
- The archaeological site of Palenque in Chiapas
- The historic city center and Xochimilco in Mexico City
- Teotihuacán near Mexico City
- Xochicalco in the state of Morelos
- The Sian Ka'an Biosphere Reserve in Quintana Roo

A TALE OF TWO EMPIRES

FROM HUNTER TO FARMER

Long before there were Aztecs or Maya, Indian tribes roamed Mesoamerica. Evidence of human life in this region dates back 11,000 years, but these early hunters traveled in small bands and covered a wide expanse of territory. Beginning around 7,000 BC, this nomadic existence experienced a cultural leap forward in what is known as the Archaic period. This phase, which lasted until 2000 BC, saw the arrival of settlers who relied on plants for sustenance and developed rudimentary weapons and crafts.

It was during this period that the single most important development occurred for the establishment of the Mexican Indian in the New World: the cultivation of maize, beans, and squash, the ingredients that would form the staple of the Mexican diet. Maize is the foundation of ancient and modern Mexico, the single biggest catalyst to the development of settled life, population growth, and empire building. Some experts say it was the Maya who brought the cultivation of this key crop to Mesoamerica, but this is an unproven theory. The earliest known fossilized remains date back to 4800 BC, and were found in present-day Tabasco. Similar findings in Oaxaca date to 4300 BC, and wild maize remains have been found in the Tehuacán Valley in southeastern Puebla that reach back to 3500 BC.

The prevailing theory is that the early Indians had begun domesticating maize, along with other essential crops, herbs, fruits, and other plants, as far back as 5000 to 7000 BC. Beans, avocado, pumpkin, tomato, yam, and chile pepper . . . these are just a small sample of the ingredients that formed the rich and diverse diet of the pre-Columbian Mexican. This agricultural base led to more sedentary settlements—the first steps toward the great civilizations of Mesoamerica. It was also during this time that the first crude pottery was developed, as well as the practice of grinding maize on milling stones.

The Archaic period was followed by the Preclassic, which introduced more widespread and efficient farming, advanced pottery and an abundance of villages all over Mexico. But here, an important point must be addressed. As we know, Hernán Cortés and the Spanish conquistadors were able to defeat all resistance in the New World, thanks in part to more advanced armor, weaponry, and technology. Why was Europe so far ahead of pre-Columbian Mexico? A main reason was the remarkably long time it took for Mexican Indians to transition from a nomadic lifestyle to a village one. This slow evolution set them back millennia, and proved, ultimately, to be their downfall.

The Preclassic period is generally broken down into three phases: early (1800–1200 BC), middle (1200–400 BC), and late (400 BC–AD 150). This period saw the rise of many early civilizations throughout Mexico. Most of these achieved their birth, zenith, and eclipse during this era. In Chiapas, a primitive culture known as Mokaya, which means "people of the corn" in the Mixe-Zoque languages, emerged. The Mokayas settled in a series of villages; farmed corn, beans, and other plant foods; and mastered a type of crude pottery called Barra. They are believed to be the direct ancestors of the Olmec. In Oaxaca, the Zapotec people established an impressive city-state at Monte Albán. In Jalisco, archaeologists have found shaft tombs and a particular style of architecture known as the Teuchitlan tradition.

In the Valley of Mexico (present-day Mexico City), two cultures arose during the Preclassic era. Little now remains of the village of Tlatilco, but early burial excavations produced a wealth of pottery and unusual figurines. In particular, the burial offerings displayed an artistic style similar to that of the Olmec. Here was also evidence of a type of architecture that was introduced in the late Preclassic era and would become an iconic symbol of ancient Mexico: the temple-pyramid.

The other civilization found in the central highlands of Mexico at this time (and one which can be seen today), was Cuicuilco. Unlike the classic pyramids of other cities, Cuicuilco's temple was circular, topped by a conical structure. Cuicuilco flourished roughly between 700 BC and AD 150, falling squarely within the late Preclassic era; it is possibly the oldest city in the Valley of Mexico.

The Preclassic era gave way to the Classic, which saw the splendor of the Maya and the rise of other impressive civilizations in Teotihuacán, Monte Albán, and in the late Classic, Xochicalco. The Postclassic era brought the warrior civilizations of the Toltec, and culminated in the Aztecs, the last of the great empires of pre-Columbian Mexico.

But the Preclassic era shows us that ancient Mexico was not the land of one or two tribes, but several disparate peoples. As we will see, these diverse cultures shared common characteristics: the development of hieroglyphic writing (the Incan empire, by comparison, had no writing whatsoever); a penchant for astronomy and the use of a 365-day calendar; a common sport played with a rubber ball; the importance of markets and trade; and a complex array of gods and religious rituals. And it all began with the arrival of the Olmec.

Who Were the Maya?

1

THE OLMEC AND THE CRADLE OF MESOAMERICA

All civilization in Mesoamerica stems from the Olmec. While it has been somewhat difficult to trace their origins, all agree that the Olmec dated from the Preclassic period, possibly as far back as 1800 BC. They settled in south-central Mexico, in present-day Veracruz and Tabasco, and their influence and culture spread far and wide, thanks to their artistry and trade.

Predominantly stone-carvers, the Olmec were master artisans who sculpted colossal stone heads, distinctive for their flat faces, thick lips, and rounded helmets. (They are thought to be depictions of rulers.) Much of their art centers on a curious religious depiction of half-human, half-jaguar figurines, typically with cleft heads. One of these "were-jaguars," in infant form, was the Maize God, a chief deity in a large pantheon.

The earliest Olmec center can be found in San Lorenzo. Dating from roughly 1500 BC, it was the largest settlement in Mesoamerica for a period of 300 years, with nothing to rival it in terms of artistic achievement, trade network, or society. The discovery of hieroglyphic writing attributed to the Olmec was made north of San Lorenzo, in El Cascajal. Also near San Lorenzo (10 miles southeast of it, in fact) lies a relatively recent archaeological discovery at El Manatí. This site contained remarkably well-preserved remains of ritual objects, artifacts, and even

AN OLMEC HEAD IN VILLAHERMOSA, TABASCO

Mexico Tourism Board

WHY SO HIGH?

Since humans and gods first communicated with each other, nearly every civilization has attempted to build its religious temples skyward, as if trying to get closer to heaven. Was this the reason the pre-Hispanic civilizations of Mexico constructed such massive temples? It is plausible that these structures were intended to reach closer to their gods, but another theory—one that has been corroborated by the many excavations of bones and other evidence of tombs—hints that these temples were also ceremonial burial mounds. Of course, a much simpler conclusion is that, as symbols of power, there was nothing quite as intimidating as a towering monument to a god. The Spanish would see the truth of that, more than a thousand years after the fall of La Venta.

MAYA TEMPLES MAY BE BUILT SO HIGH DUE TO WHAT'S INSIDE THEM.

rubber balls used for their ritualistic ball game (in which players used their elbows and knees to hit a large ball through large, doughnut-like stone rings on each side of the ball court). Another remarkable find was the discovery of bowls with chocolate residue. We have long known that the Mexican Indian gave the world chocolate; El Manatí proved that the practice of drinking chocolate dated back, at least, to the Olmec.

San Lorenzo began to decline around 1200 BC. It has been theorized that Mesoamerica's first true capital was brought down by either an internal uprising or an invading outside force, but this has not been definitively proven. (We will find this same inconclusive guesswork surrounds the demise of many of Mexico's ancient cities and cultures.) At this time, the Olmec capital shifted to La Venta, in Tabasco, which would become the most prominent center of Olmec civilization until its fall in 400 BC.

A contemporary of La Venta was Tres Zapotes, an important Olmec center and one of crucial significance for our understanding of pre-Hispanic civilization. Tres Zapotes is located roughly 100 miles northwest of La Venta, and dates to the middle Preclassic period. The civilization at Tres Zapotes outlasted that of its sister to the south, and reached its zenith in the late Preclassic period, after 400 BC. It was here that archaeologists found one of the oldest monuments in the Americas bearing a recorded date: a stela containing a date corresponding to the Long Count Calendar.

Olmec influence spread far and wide, thanks to trade, war, conquest, and religious outreach. There is even some evidence, dubious though it may be, that the Olmec civilization itself emerged somewhere other than the Veracruz-Tabasco heartland. While much is still in debate, the general consensus is that the Olmec was the first great civilization in the New World, and that it paved the way those who followed.

Before we turn to the Maya, two other civilizations of the Preclassic era must be mentioned. The Zapotec civilization flourished in Monte Albán, in present-day Oaxaca. A large and advanced society, Monte Albán is known for a few reasons: its Temple of the Danzantes, a mysterious and unusual collection of bas-relief figures, and its ample evidence of writing and the use of the Calendar Round 52-year system (although the Zapotec did not know of the Long Count).

The other culture of note, particularly concerning the Maya, was that of Izapa, in present-day Chiapas. This civilization stems from the early Preclassic and extends into the early Classic period. They are considered to be a chronological and cultural bridge between the Olmec and the Maya, and Izapan art styles, deities, and the use of the Long Count were all found later in the Maya world.

MAYA FORERUNNERS

Up to now, we have been following an all-inclusive timeline of the development of Mesoamerican cultures. From here on, however, we must split

THE 365-DAY CALENDAR, THE 52-YEAR CYCLE, AND THE LONG COUNT

The calendar devised by the ancient Indians is quite a complex means of marking the passage of time. It is based on a 365-day solar year, which we use to this day. However, in line with that calendar is another, 260-day ceremonial year. Both calendars recorded the day but not the year, and a day in one would not coincide with a day in another for a period of 52 years. In other words, the entire cycle would repeat itself every 52 years. This was known as the **Calendar Round**. As the average life span at the time was less than 52 years, it was relatively easy to record the history of events within an individual's life, but the system was obviously flawed for anything beyond this length of time. To address this deficiency, the ancients came up with the Long Count.

The Long Count essentially began counting the passage of time from a fixed date; in this case, it was August 13, 3114 BC. From this point, time is measured by counting off a series of elapsed periods of 144,000 days, 7,200 days, 360 days, 20 days, and finally, one day. Sound confusing? Applying the Long Count to a particular date will show how

our journey to focus first on the Maya, and secondly on the rise of the Aztecs. This is a chronological, geographic, and cultural divide. The Maya preceded the Aztecs by more than a millennium. Both left a lasting legacy, but their empires were markedly different from each other.

The ascent of the Maya, along with the rise of Teotihuacán, marked a great golden age of Mesoamerica, in what historians call the Classic period, which spanned from AD 250–900. This was a time of exponential growth in Mexico, in population, settlements, architecture, and artistic production. Indeed, most of Mexico's most famed ruins stem from this era. But the first evidence of the Maya dates to the Preclassic.

It was during this earlier period (2000 BC–AD 250), that we see a significant rise in village life. Thatched-roof houses were constructed (a style that would last to this day), and early farmers began to develop more advanced societies, building cities and pyramids and fashioning monuments. They also became more adept at cultivating maize, the agricultural and nutritional cornerstone of the Maya civilization.

The advance to village life did not take place evenly across the Maya lands; it is believed that the earliest leaps forward were taken in Guatemala, El Salvador, and—as far as Mexico is concerned—in the

it was used. Take the date found on the Stela at Tres Zapotes: 7.16.6.16.18. The formula for calculating the date would be:

7 x 144,000 days
16 x 7,200 days
6 x 360 days
16 x 20 days
18 x 1 day

Add up the total, and we arrive at 1,125,698 days. Dating from the starting point of August 11, 3114 BC, that gives us a date of September 1, 32 BC.

Why does the Long Count begin on August 11, 3114 BC? That is one of the great mysteries of the system. The other is who invented it. For generations, historians and archaeologists attributed the Long Count Calendar to the Maya. Tres Zapotes, however, showed it to precede the Maya civilization. And finally, we know of at least one other Long Count date that precedes both the Maya empire and the one found at Tres Zapotes: a finding in Chiapas containing a date of December 8, 36 BC, indicates that the origins of the Long Count, as yet, remain unknown.

southernmost state of Chiapas. The hallmarks of the development of this region was the planting of maize and cassava, and the introduction of pottery—in Chiapas, this has come to be known as the Barra phase of pottery. Beginning at around 1800 BC, it is quite probably the oldest in Mesoamerica, and comprises mainly a variety of jars and bowls. The sophisticated decoration on some recovered vessels indicate that they were not mere utilitarian inventions but important in rituals. Another feature of the Barra phase was the production of ceramic figurines, which would be reproduced throughout Mexico in the Preclassic period.

The Barra phase gave way to the Locona phase (1700–1500 BC), which produced advances in pottery, with more stylized pieces and the development of cooking vessels. At this time, a more complex society began to emerge, with communities or villages organized around a central capital. The last phase of the early Preclassic was the Ocós, which saw more sophisticated pottery and the creation of more complex figurines. It is worth noting that there is no evidence of a pottery-using society in the central or northern regions of the Maya world at this stage. Why this is has yet to be properly explained.

The middle Preclassic period was a different story; during this stage, which lasted until roughly 300 BC, the Maya of the highlands in the north and the lowlands began to gather in larger numbers and formed a rudimentary social structure. This is best seen in the Petén region of Guatemala and in Belize. Still, these signs of civilization were but the baby steps of an empire that would come to dominate Mesoamerica and reach unequaled heights in culture, science, and art. The Maya empire, in other words, was only just planting its roots.

The evolution from simple villages to the mighty urban cities that classified the Maya empire is obviously no small feat, and it took place in the late Preclassic period, or roughly from about 400 BC to AD 250. The rise of Maya civilization coincided with the fall of the Olmec in 400 BC; at this time, a rapid advancement of Maya culture took place. In addition to areas inhabited by the Olmec, other sites along the Pacific Coast provided an evolutionary bridge between early village life and advanced society.

In the Maya highlands of the south and along the Pacific Coast, chief among these was the Izapan culture. Izapa was a vast ceremonial center comprised of over 80 earthen mounds located in Chiapas, near Tapachula. It had a sophisticated art style centered on bas-relief carvings, several of which were early precedents of important Maya deities. Other artistic and architectural elements associated with the Classic Maya were found here, including plazas with altars and carved stelae. While its language was different from that of the Maya and it did not use a calendar, there are certainly cultural links between the two cultures.

The Maya lowlands to the north and in the Petén region of present-day Guatemala followed a different route in their leap from village life to city-state. In the late Preclassic, the central and northern region was ruled by the Chikanel culture. Where the Chikanel—competent artists in their own right—truly shined was in their architectural ability. It was the Chikanel who began to build some of the greatest ceremonial centers in the Maya empire, at sites that are well known to us today: Tikal, El Mirador, Nakbe, Uaxactun, and Calakmul (of these, only Calakmul—one of the largest Maya cities ever found—lies in Mexico). El Mirador has been found to be the oldest Maya capital.

The late Preclassic, then, was a deeply formative period for the Maya empire. It is during this phase that characteristic architectural styles such as pyramid-tombs, limestone structures, vaulted arches, stela- and altar-fronted plazas, and frescoes were developed. Decorative pottery is a hallmark of the era. Writing and the use of the Long Count calendar had been established throughout much of the region. The pieces were in place for the full flowering of the Maya civilization.

THE RISE OF MAYA MEXICO

The Classic period, which lasted from AD 250 to 900, represents the full glory of the Maya era. It was during this period that the empire scaled artistic, cultural, and architectural heights unparalleled in the New World and unequaled by most contemporary civilizations. It was a time of large-scale development; extensive trade, and commercial influence; and, contrary to commonplace opinions, of war. We typically reserve the idea of bloodthirsty conquest for the Aztecs and have long considered the socially advanced Maya a peaceful people, but historians have realized that the Maya golden age was one of strife.

The Classic period is divided into two: the early and late periods, with the shift occurring in AD 600. Why the split? There are two principal reasons: the influence of the Izapan culture on the Maya, and the impact of a rising superpower known as Teotihuacán.

THE CITY OF THE GODS

When the Aztecs discovered the ruins of Teotihuacán, they were so awed by it that they believed it to be a city of gods and giants. We know, of course, that the city was the work of man, but who were the Teotihuacanos, and how did a planned urban area of such grandeur crop up in central Mexico in the second century AD? Before we answer that question, let's take a closer look at what made Teotihuacán so special.

The city occupied 8 square miles and was laid out on a grid oriented 15 degrees 25 minutes east of true north. Although no one has been able to adequately explain this positioning, it was clearly an intentional effort by the city's planners. Teotihuacán featured a broad major avenue, with the city laid out in quarters around this road. It was fully urbanized, with a population at its peak comprising as many as 200,000 citizens, and featured three stunning temples that dominated its landscape: the towering Pyramid of the Sun, Pyramid of the Moon, and Temple of Quetzalcóatl, all of which were built during the first three hundred years of the city.

Beyond the temples, the city featured walled residences made up of apartments, not unlike today's gated communities. These one-story compounds must have been quite ritzy in their day: a mix of residences and temples organized around a court. Also similar to today's great cities, Teotihuacán had its ethnic neighborhoods: its western part was occupied by the Zapotec, while the eastern quarter was home to people who had strong ties to the Maya culture. Quite simply, what makes Teotihuacán so amazing is that *there was nothing like it in the New World at the time.* It was without a doubt the largest and most important city of the Classic period.

So, we come back to the question of who made this city of cities. The answer, unfortunately, remains unknown, although many theories have been put forth. While their origins are a mystery, we do know a great deal about the people who lived here. Teotihuacanos were capable artisans. Colorful murals and frescoes, and elaborate sculptures were common in the more elite apartment complexes and religious structures. One of their

Mexico Tourism Board

THE AZTECS CONSIDERED MIGHTY TEOTIHUACÁN A CITY OF THE GODS.

most recognized works is the cylindrical pottery vase resting on a tripod base. They also used obsidian prolifically for weapons and artistic figurines, with as many as 100 obsidian workshops operating at one time in the city. The uniform architecture of the city followed a basic blueprint that relied on the *talud-tablero* style consisting of a base with sloped walls topped by a rectangular panel.

The pantheon of gods at Teotihuacán featured many of the central gods of Mesoamerica; the rain god (a predecessor of the Aztec Tlaloc), the feathered serpent (an early form of Quetzalcóatl), and the gods of the sun, moon, and fire. Two of the more important deities of the city seem to have been Chalchiuhtlicue, the water goddess, and a mysterious goddess whose mouth resembles that of a spider, who may have been the chief deity of Teotihuacán. Along with this pantheon of gods and goddesses came a complex ritual that featured the practice of human sacrifice. The Pyramids of the Sun and Moon both have evidence of this, but they pale in comparison to the souls offered in the dedication of the pyramid of the feathered serpent, the smallest of the three temples but clearly the most elaborate in the city. Excavations have shown that over 200 victims were sacrificed within and around the temple, many of them warriors buried with their hands tied behind their back.

The Teotihuacanos knew a basic form of writing, far inferior to the complex Maya scripture but enough to produce books (although none have survived) and records. The city was an important commercial center for Mesoamerica, and Teotihuacano pottery and artifacts have been found throughout the New World. Trade and tribute were key factors in the prosperity of the city, as its agricultural base was unable to support such a large population; in fact, this shortage may have contributed to its downfall. (As we will see, trade and tribute would also serve as the mainstays of another powerful empire several hundred years after Teotihuacán: the Aztecs.)

Of particular note for this book is the ample recorded evidence of contact between Teotihuacán and the Maya. The Maya, along with most of Mesoamerica, held Teotihuacán in the highest regard, and emulated or incorporated its style and sophistication. The city had such a profound impact on the Maya that it has led historians to bifurcate the Classic into an early and late period.

Teotihuacán fell in the seventh century, at the hands of man. Its palaces were burned to the ground, its temples desecrated, and its elite crushed—the exact cause may have been a combination of factors: internal dissent, political clashes, and/or the erosion of its natural resources. By AD 600, the greatest metropolis of the Classic period had come crumbling down, and although one quarter of its population would continue to live in the area for the next 200 years, Teotihuacán would never rise again.

Numerous other civilizations flourished in the New World during the Classic period, though most of them had some ties either to the Maya or Teotihuacán. In present-day Cholula, a massive pyramid, one of the largest in the world, was in the middle of a multi-phase construction during this era; in the Gulf Coast, many new settlements emerged; and at Monte Albán, the Zapotec prospered in relative isolation. But the preeminence of Teotihuacán was paramount, and its fall was followed shortly by the decline of other power centers such as Monte Albán. In their wake, a new breed of people stepped in, ready to conquer and rule . . . but that is a story for another chapter.

MAYA OF THE CLASSIC PERIOD

The arrival and dominion of Teotihuacán fundamentally changed the course of Maya civilization in the highlands. While great artistic and architectural works were produced, and evidence has been found as to the wealth of the city's elite, many typically Maya elements were lost due to Teotihuacano interference. Most notably, the Long Count calendar and the production of figurines disappeared.

Teotihuacán's presence was also felt in the richly Maya territory of the Petén, with strong indications of military intervention in this region. Tikal was the most powerful of the cities in the Petén, and one of the greatest of all Maya capitals. With its six temple-pyramids—the largest an astounding 229 feet tall—its impressive Great Plaza, and numerous palaces, it was a giant in its time.

North of this great city was Calakmul, in present-day Campeche, one of the largest Maya sites ever discovered. Its roots stretch back to the Preclassic era, but in the Classic it became a true force. In AD 562, Tikal was attacked and sacked by a rival state, possibly with the aid of Calakmul. As the former fell into decline, the latter rose to new heights. It also provides clear evidence that life in the Classic period wasn't the peaceful existence we have long believed it to be.

In Belize, Guatemala, and southeastern Mexico, numerous sites flourished during the Classic era, attesting to the importance of this region to the growth and prosperity of the Maya. For the purposes of this book, we focus, naturally, on the latter, where Yaxchilán, Bonampak, and Palenque rose to prominence. Palenque displays some of the best examples of Maya architecture in existence, and was in its heyday among the most densely populated of all Maya cities.

Not far from Palenque, in central Chiapas, the city of Toniná boasted a fine artistic tradition and considerable military prowess; in AD 711, its king managed to capture the ruler of Palenque, no less a person than the second son of Pakal the Great, Palenque's mightiest king. To the west, in the neighboring state of Tabasco, lies Comalcalco, a Maya city unique in pre-Hispanic Mexico for its use of fired brick in the construction of its buildings.

Of course, Maya development in the Classic period was not limited to the southern lowlands. In the North, in present-day Campeche and Quintana Roo, nestled among the chicle trees (which give us our gum) are scattered a group of sites that present unusual architectural elements. The Río Bec style has a penchant for flamboyance and artifice; here, tall palaces are adorned with tall towers with narrow, ornamental steps and crowned at the top with a doorway that leads to nothing. These temples, believed to imitate temple-pyramids of greater sites such as Tikal, were known as "Flower Mountains," a concept meant to symbolize a heavenly paradise that will be found throughout the Yucatán, including mighty Chichén Itzá. In northern Campeche, the Chenes showed a similar propensity for ornamentation. Although they didn't have the same type of towers, the Chenes elaborated their buildings with sculpture, including entrances to rooms fashioned after a pair of huge jaws.

On the eastern end of the Yucatán peninsula, Cobá once served as a major commercial center for the area. Among the interesting features of this site, which is secluded among dense foliage and wilderness, is a network of paths called *sacbeob,* or white roads. These *sacbeob* connect several structures and extend miles away from Cobá, reaching as far as 60 miles away. (Their whiteness helped travelers along the road at night identify, and avoid, snakes and other nocturnal denizens crossing their path.) It is believed the roads served either a commercial or religious purpose. Cobá is one of the few lowland Classic cities to survive and flourish into the Postclassic era.

THE MAYA WAY OF LIFE

By the Classic period, Maya civilization was at its peak—but what defined Maya civilization? Fortunately, we have detailed accounts of the Maya way of life from the very people who attempted to eradicate those customs and convert them to Catholicism: the Spanish missionaries. Their precious records, coupled with the tireless work of archaeologists and historians, have helped us better understand and appreciate this culture.

THE BUILDING BLOCKS OF EMPIRE

Agriculture was the basis of the Maya empire, with maize being its principal crop. In addition, beans, chile peppers, squashes, and cotton were chief among their crops, the latter being cultivated extensively in the Yucatán for the production and trade of textiles. Elsewhere, cacao trees were planted as a cash crop that produced, literally, cash—the cacao bean was a form of currency in the Maya world, and chocolate was the drink of choice for the elite. Vegetables and fruits were a staple in every home, and the variety at their disposal was enviable: avocado, papaya, custard apple, and other exotic produce were abundant.

The Maya diet also included types of dog (there were several breeds in existence), turkey, deer, peccary, wild fowl, and armadillo, among other meats. Fishing was a mainstay in the Yucatán, but inland, the ingenious Maya would throw drugs into streams and rivers as a means to fish. Maya farmers even raised stingless bees for their honey.

Honey, along with textiles and cacao, helped fuel the Maya economy, but the most important economic resource to the Maya of the Yucatán was salt. The peninsula was the chief producer of salt in the New World, farmed in salt beds lining the coast. Other trade goods included jade, obsidian, and tropical bird feathers (especially those of the quetzal).

GROWING UP MAYA

In the Yucatán, infants became Maya as soon as they were born; that is, they would have their heads compressed between two boards by their mothers, resulting in a much-desired cranial flattening. Following this procedure, the parents would seek a priest's consultation to learn the fate of their child, and the name he or she would have until he or she was baptized. This rite did not take place at a specific age, but after the ritual, an older girl would be considered to be of marriageable age.

Boys lived in communal houses apart from their family. While girls lived under their mother's thumb, boys enjoyed a loose lifestyle, centered on their training but also including gambling, prostitution, and sport, in the form of the ball game. Marriages were arranged and sanctioned according to strict criteria, with most Maya (excepting the very wealthy) practicing monogamy; adultery earned a capital punishment.

Beyond the cranial deformation, beauty had much to do with physical manipulation. Mothers would hang beads over the noses of their children to make them cross-eyed, another mark of beauty. Adults also had their teeth filed into patterns, with some mouths sporting jewelry that, in a strange example of the cyclical nature of fashion, has experienced a resurrection in our time. Maya warriors and single young men painted themselves black; after marriage, men would get tattoos and practice cosmetic sacrifices.

LANGUAGE AND WRITING

One of the hallmarks of the Maya civilization is language. However, while numerous peoples all spoke the Mayan language, several dialects and languages fell under this linguistic family. Before 2000 BC, a single proto-Mayan language existed in Mesoamerica. From this mother tongue, a variety of other languages emerged, varying according to region and ethnicity.

Another important trait of advanced Maya culture was a system of writing. It has taken us much time and effort to decipher this system, and to this day much of it remains unclear. Many of the words that we now understand, we still do not know how to pronounce. We do know that Maya writing is read in double columns, from left to right. The 16th-century Franciscan bishop Diego de Landa has given modern scholars some of the most important chronicles and observations of Maya life and culture. Landa studied the local language and came up with a Mayan "alphabet" comprised of 29 glyphs. Modern studies have shown this was not only inaccurate but incomplete. The signs Landa recorded were syllabic rather than alphabetic, and the Mayan language appears to have been a combination of phonetic and semantic elements. But we have been able to use Landa's work to decipher Mayan writing.

SOCIETY AND GOVERNMENT

Political power stayed in the family, and class distinctions defined Maya society; rank was carefully recorded and governed one's life. Maya nobility made up the political leadership, elite warrior class, affluent farmers and traders, and the clergy. Commoners provided the bulk of the labor force, and at the bottom of the ladder were serfs and slaves. In several areas, the Maya had kings, called *ajawob,* but by the time the Spaniards showed up in the Yucatán, power rested in the hands of local leaders in each city-state called *halach winik,* or real man.

Unlike the Aztecs, Classic era Maya had no single consolidated power center. Instead, they were a cluster of independent states, the influence of each extending only so far. Smaller states were often subject to greater ones, and bonds were cemented through marriage, joint participation at ritual rites, or gifts. The greatest Maya city-states were Tikal and Calakmul, but Palenque, Copán, and Piedras Negras, among others, also exercised considerable power. The increasing rivalry among these sites was surely a factor leading to the great collapse of the Classic period. In the Postclassic era, on the other hand, we will see a consolidation of power, at least in the Yucatán, with the advent of Toltec supremacy.

THE CALENDAR, THE EARTH, AND THE GODS

A popular innovation we automatically associate with the advanced Maya was the Long Count calendar, which was more accurate than the Calendar Round. As noted earlier, the calendar likely originated outside the Maya realm, but it was the Maya who perfected it. Rather than using a 365-day year (called the Haab [Vague Year], because the Maya recognized that a solar year was actually 365 1/4 days long; a chronology we rectify with February 29 every four years), they based their long count on a 360-day cycle called the *tun.* One *tun* was comprised of 18 *winals,* or months of 20 *k'ins,* or days. Twenty *tuns* (a period of 7,200 days) was called a *k'atun*; and 20 *k'atuns,* which marked 144,000 days, was known as a *bak'tun.* If we go back to our previous calendar example of the stela date 7.16.6.16.18 (September 1, 32 BC), we can now interpret this figure as:

7 bak'tuns
16 k'atuns
6 tuns
16 winals
18 k'ins

The Maya also expressed numbers with three symbols: lines, dots, and a symbol resembling a shell used to represent zero. (It is one of the marks of how advanced the Maya were that they independently came up with the concept of zero.) One dot was a "1" and one line equaled "5." Thus, the number 3 would be written as three dots, the number 7 as a line with two dots above it. This enabled the Maya to write down and calculate numbers of infinite size, using a vigesimal notation system that stacked the symbols in vertical columns, ranked from highest to lowest. The lowest tier had a value of 1, the second a value of 20, the third a value of 400, and so on. Sound complicated? Here's how it works:

First (Lowest) Value	1
Second Value	20
Third Value	400
Fourth Value	8,000
Etc.	

Still baffled? Now let's see how our numbers would look on a Maya numerical system:

Maya Number	••• —	•• 𝋠	••• 𝋠 •••
Our Number	8	40	1,203

Examine this numeric system and you'll find that it is intuitive and easy to decipher.

The sophistication of the Long Count calendar and the numerical system under the Maya was a mark of their profound spirituality. Astronomy and the counting of time were inextricably linked to their central belief system. The Maya saw time as cyclical rather than linear and our universe as simply the latest in a long succession of destruction and rebirth. They are celebrated even today for their ability to predict future events, especially eclipses, and of course, the supposèd end of the world in AD 2012.

2012 AND THE MAYA PROPHECIES

Ask any Maya local about 2012 and the end of the world, and you'll get a "those-crazy-gringos" chuckle. Trust me; I asked, and I received. And yet, we continue to give the Maya full credit for predicting the end of the world just a few months from now. Are we wrong? Were they wrong?

According to my guide in the Yucatán, who has researched and explored the Maya world for over 50 years, the "Maya Apocalypse" theory is a media-driven exaggeration. But 2012 is certainly a year of profound change, according to Maya prophecy. According to the *Chilam Balam*—the most important Maya book of prophecy, a collection of nine manuscripts that the Maya of the Yucatán attribute to a priest named Chilam Balam—December 22, 2012, marks the end of a *kat'un, bak'tun* and of a cycle of *bak'tuns.* In other words, this date marks the end of the fourth age of the world, which began on August 12, 3114 BC, and the beginning of a new one. (By the way, the *Chilam Balam* texts also predicted the arrival of the white man, and his catastrophic effect on the Maya world. Just saying.)

December 22, 2012, is important for other reasons. It will be the winter solstice, and shortly before the 12th we will see a conjunction of Venus and the Sun, which only occurs every 104 years, or two Maya 52-year cycles. The prophecy also foretells of a dark rift in the Milky Way.

The Maya believed that 2012 will mark the return of Kukulcán, the serpent-god and cosmic messenger. However, with all that, prophecy clearly speaks of the continuation of the world beyond 2012, and the dawn of the fifth age.

Now, how about us? With regard to human life, I've heard two theories: that the destruction of the world in 2012 includes the destruction of humanity, and that it is simply the turning over of a new cosmic calendar. Without exception, the scholars, experts, and locals I spoke with about this subject during my travels in Maya Mexico believe the latter is the correct interpretation. I, for one, am hoping they're right.

As for terrestrial and celestial matters, it is a daunting task to keep up with Maya deities, whose total number is hard to pin down because many deities had multiple aspects, consorts, and avatars. The Maya believed the Earth was flat, with four corners each representing a color and supported by Chaac, the rain god, one of the most important and revered deities in the Maya pantheon. The Earth is often represented in Classic Maya art as the back of a crocodile resting in a pool. Above, a double-headed serpent represents the sky.

There are two references to a supreme god: one, Hunab K'u, may have

OF RITUALS AND SACRIFICE

When we hear of ritual sacrifice and self-sacrifice, we tend to think of a gruesome spectacle of blood and death. But there are several misconceptions of these practices among the Maya. In fact, human sacrifices may have been a relatively late phenomenon. The Classic Maya seemed perfectly content to sacrifice animals to their gods, whereas the Toltec-influenced Postclassic peoples saw a rise in human sacrifice. These were conducted by the priest and numerous assistants. Four, named Chaac after the rain god, would hold the victim's arms and legs, while a fifth, named Nakom, cut open their chest.

Maya rituals were dictated by the calendar, especially the 260-day count. They were marked with numerous acts of penance, including sexual abstinence, giving up certain foods, and self-mutilation by sticking needles and stingray spines through the ear, cheek, lip, tongue, and penis. The Classic Maya seemed to have a penchant for bloodletting, with a ruler ritually piercing his penis (and his wife, her tongue) during auspicious days defined by the calendar. As in other parts of the world, one's blood was testament to one's nobility. But ritual bloodletting did not involve the sacrifice of pints of blood, just a small, symbolic amount. Stelae show of such ceremonies where the drops of blood were collected on *amate* (bark) paper and burned.

Ritual ceremonies existed for various occasions and reasons, including agricultural bounty, rainfall, and war. Perhaps the most important rite was held to celebrate the New Year, marked by every community and full of good or bad omens. Priests would counter a bad omen through special ceremonies such as fire-walking, in which they would run barefoot over burning coals.

been the result of the teachings of the missionaries. The other was Itzamnaaj, or Itzamna, who brought writing to the Maya and was the patron deity of science and knowledge; he may also have been the Sun god, Kinich Ahau, who in turn became the jaguar-god of the underworld at night. His wife, Chak Chel, was the Moon goddess and also the goddess of weaving, medicine, and childbirth. It is from this couple that all gods were produced. The Maya had deities for war, trade, agriculture, love, tattoo artists, the classes, and a host of other aspects of life. Of the caste gods, Kukulkán, introduced in the Postclassic period, is the most prominent, the god and patron of the ruling class.

The Maya underworld was a realm of many levels, called Xibalba (Place of Fright). The majority of the Maya were destined to reside here after death. One of the more bizarre funerary practices among the elite was apparently the administration of ceremonial enemas; we do not know for certain what liquid was injected during this process, but it is possible that it was *chih,* a beverage made of fermented maguey plants (known today in central Mexico as *pulque*). According to the ancient and modern Maya, Xibalba has numerous entrances in the terrestrial world, through a vast network of caverns and cenotes that dot the limestone karst terrain of the Yucatán peninsula. The Preclassic and Classic Maya often built their holy temples over or around these mouths to the underworld; this is even the case, for example, at Chichén Itzá.

With good reason are the Maya renowned for their astrological prowess. Not only did they chart the sun's progress, but—and far more painstakingly, it seems—also the Moon, which they correlated with the solar calendar. Beyond these immediate celestial bodies, the Maya calculated the trajectory of Venus, which played an important role in warfare. Did the Maya observe other planets? There is evidence to support the theory, particularly for Mars and Jupiter. Maya buildings were planned with the planets in mind, aligned to the position of the stars, and again with particular importance given to Venus (we find this structural alignment at Uxmal and Chichén Itzá).

MAYA ART AND ARCHITECTURE

Classic Maya art was highly sophisticated, displaying a narrative, baroque style in its carved reliefs and paintings. One of the highest expressions of this skill can be found in Palenque, which is why some believe this city stands first among today's Maya ruins. Maya art was primarily two-dimensional, and they were one of the few peoples of the New World to attempt to capture individual personalities through portraiture. While they were master carvers (both stone and wood), their skill in pottery varied by culture, and ranged from simplistic utensils to elaborate artworks. One of the most recognizable elements of Maya art is the brilliant blue pigment used pervasively in the Classic period up to the colonial era. This Maya Blue was discovered in the late Classic era, probably in the Yucatán, and can be seen in a variety of their ceramic works.

The Maya created beautiful works of jade, a highly valued precious stone, but also worked with obsidian, shell, and marble. Sadly, what must have been an astounding wealth of their art is now lost to us; in particular, works made from perishable materials—decorative textiles and books written on bark-paper—have not survived through time, war, and the great cataclysm that spelled the downfall of the Maya empire.

Most iconic to our vision of the Maya civilization is the development of temple-pyramids and palaces. One of the interesting differences between Maya cities and Teotihuacán (as well as the later Aztec capital of Tenochtitlán) was a lack of urban planning. Whereas the latter were organized according to a grid pattern, Maya cities seemed to sprout up and grow without any coordinated blueprint.

A recent school of thought asserts that the Maya carved their history on their very buildings. We know, for example of the existence of a specific type of symbol, known as the "emblem glyph," found on particular sites in over 30 Maya cities, including Palenque, Calakmul, and Tikal. These glyphs were found to be titles of Maya kings and the names of the kingdoms that they ruled. Subsequent research has shown that the majority of reliefs produced in the Classic period were not of deities but human dynasties: rulers and their progeny, and the passage of one ruling clan from another. Other glyphs recorded major events, such as war, rituals, birth, and accession to the throne.

JADE MASKS WERE A MARK OF THE MAYA ELITE.

Campeche Tourism Board

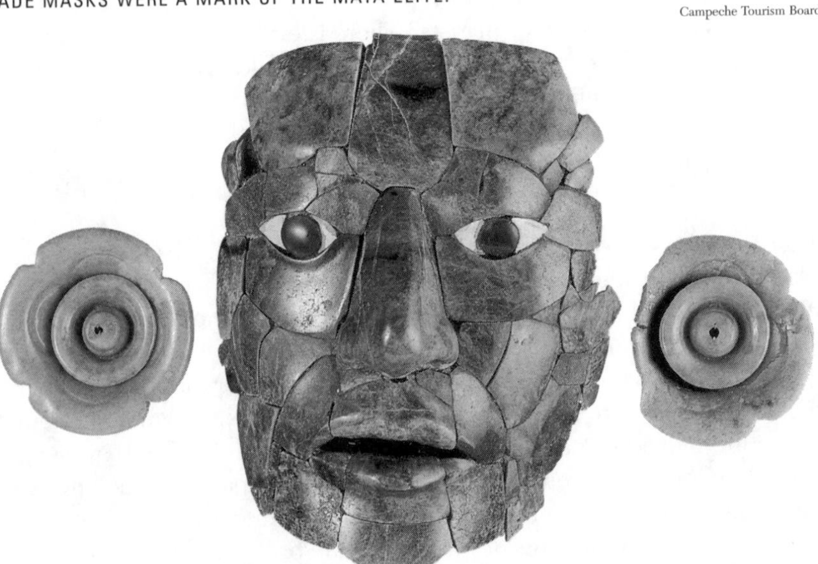

This understanding has helped us map out at least partial ruling histories of some of the most important sites in the Maya empire, which in turn has enabled us to put the rise of their great leaders, and their cultural, archaeological, or military impact, in proper context. It is no small feat, and no small clue to our knowledge of this civilization.

Still, it must be said that we remain woefully uninformed about the extent and prowess of Mayan language, science, religion, and philosophy. Of the myriad books in which they recorded their knowledge, only *four* have survived. Of these, the best is the *Dresden Codex,* a folding-screen book written on bark paper and coated with stucco, which deals primarily with the 260-day calendar. Among the most famous texts to survive through the ages is the *Popul Vuh,* a sacred compilation of the Postclassic Quiché Maya in Guatemala, which recounts the myth of the creation of the world and its living beings. One of the legends from this text was reenacted throughout the Maya world in their ubiquitous ball game.

Of course, we also have a large amount of written data that was transcribed by the Spanish, but it is clear that when we examine our understanding of the Maya, we're looking at an incomplete picture. Thankfully, the advances and breakthroughs of modern epigraphers, archaeologists, and other students of Maya history bring us ever closer to this remarkable people and their incredible legacy.

FALL OF AN EMPIRE

The Terminal Classic era, ranging from roughly AD 800 to 925, was a period of great flux in the Maya world. On the one hand, the Maya civilization of the southern lowlands suffered a monumental collapse, right after it had achieved its pinnacle. However, in the north, the Maya continued to flourish, with the famous Chichén Itzá leading a cultural and political renaissance that produced some of the most remarkable structures in the New World.

We have abundant information about the fall of the Maya empire in the southern area, but we aren't certain of the reasons behind it. Theories include disease, foreign invasion, natural disasters, and internal strife. While we are still somewhat in the dark about one of the greatest social catastrophes in history, here is what we do know: By 830, the death rate in the central area exceeded the birth rate, and construction came to a grinding halt. Three factors played a key role in the doom of the Central Maya.

First, warfare among the fractured Maya took a heavy toll. Toward the end of the eighth century, political alliances began to fall apart, leading to a decline in trade and armed conflict between rival powers. Within a mere half century, once-impressive cities had been reduced to primitive villages, thanks to this destructive wave. Why the surge in violence? The fault, it seems, lies in increased competition among Maya elite, who built lavish structures, engaged in regional conflict, and exploited the land.

This negligent waste only compounded the problems faced by overpopulation. The Central Area Maya numbered in the millions, eventually exceeding their agricultural output. The third factor was beyond the Maya's control: between AD 800 and 1050, the lowlands suffered a massive period of droughts. As peasant farmers saw their crops dwindle, they must have turned with increasing desperation to their rulers, who were charged with calling upon Chaac, the rain god, to bring down the rain.

Chaac's continued refusal to oblige may have led to the kind of internal revolt that some archaeologists believe was the final downfall of Maya society. Supporting this idea is the fact that the Postclassic period is devoid of the iconography, mythology, and other aspects of sophisticated culture that were hallmarks of the Maya elite. Were the suddenly powerless Maya rulers brought down by their subjects? It is a distinct possibility. But even if that were the case, what happened to the population after the overthrow of its leaders? Did the Maya migrate away from their devastated city centers, or did another tragedy wipe them out? We do not know for certain.

While a large portion of the Maya empire was crumbling, other Maya cultures were exploiting the resulting power vacuum. One such example is the Putún Maya of present-day Tabasco, who exerted their influence both in the Maya cities of the Central Area and at far-off non-Maya sites such as Xochicalco and Tula.

But nowhere was the surge in culture and architecture more pronounced than in the Yucatán, home to hundreds of Maya sites. Many of these were contemporaries of the Maya centers of the lowlands; however, it is during the Terminal Classic that they experienced their Golden Age. The heartland for this late renaissance appears to have been the hilly Puuc region, where a highly developed style evolved. The pride of the Puuc

UXMAL IS A FINE SHOWCASE OF THE PUUC ARCHITECTURAL STYLE.

style is Uxmal, the region's largest site, which flourished between AD 850 and 925 and represented the epitome of Maya culture.

Of course, the most famous of Mexico's Maya cities and one of the wonders of the world lies in the Yucatán, west of the Puuc hills: Chichén Itzá. Much of the architecture has Toltec characteristics; however, at Chichén Itzá there are Puuc elements as well.

About 30 miles northeast of Chichén Itzá, Ek' Balam (Black Jaguar) has changed what we know about the Terminal Classic period. A heavily fortified city, it must have been tested often, and its hieroglyphic texts speak of a foreign (possibly from the Central Area) founder by the name of Ek' Balam in AD 770. Ek' Balam prospered until about AD 896, when its fortune changed with the arrival of a new, militaristic force in the region: the Toltec.

The Maya of the Puuc region suffered a similarly enigmatic collapse as that of their kin in the lowlands a century before. Again, the reasons are unclear, but the evidence supports overpopulation and depleted agricultural resources. Whatever the cause, by the end of the 10th century, the once-rich Puuc was abandoned. But there was one great capital that avoided the second collapse of the Maya: Chichén Itzá, under Maya and Toltec dominion, would grow to become the greatest city of its time in the New World, as the Postclassic era eclipsed the Classic.

THE POSTCLASSIC PERIOD

The Postclassic period lasted from the 10th century to the arrival of the conquistadors 500 years later. It was a markedly different era for the Maya, a fall from grace following the monumental collapses of the late Classic era. Looming over this period was a new military order, come from the north and imposing their might, will, and influence throughout the Maya world. They spoke Nahua, which would become the language of the Aztecs, and they were known as the Toltec.

To understand where the Toltec came from, we must remember that the Postclassic period began as a time of turmoil in Mexico, with a rise in militarism and numerous small states warring against each other. These states were often comprised of a melting pot of cultures, including local farmers, foreign hunter-gatherers from the north, and immigrants from other cultures that had collapsed. The most powerful of these hybrid peoples were the Toltec, who established their capital in Tollan (modern-day Tula).

The history of the Toltec presents us with conflicting accounts, but the establishment of the great capital of Tula can be laid at the feet of arguably their greatest ruler, a perhaps mythical figure named Topiltzin. A priest-king who claimed the title of Quetzalcóatl—the feathered serpent–deity who would come to be a major figure in pre-Hispanic

Mexico—Topiltzin was an anomaly in his time, a pacifist who preached against human sacrifice. Unfortunately, many others in Tula paid homage to Tezcatlipoca, patron of warriors, giver and taker of life. (It is this cult that bred the famous warrior classes of the jaguar, the eagle, and the coyote.) Shortly after he founded Tula, Topiltzin was dethroned and, along with his followers, forced to abandon the city at the end of the 10th century AD.

And now, myth and history become intertwined. It is said that Topiltzin undertook a legendary journey, filled with enough trials and divine intervention or persecution to rival anything Odysseus went through, before he reached the Gulf of Mexico. From here, his tale becomes increasingly fantastic; one account has him setting himself on fire and vanishing among a sky full of colored birds, while another tells of him setting sail on a raft made of serpents to a place called Tlapallan (Red Land); in either case, the allusion to the feathered serpent is unmistakable. And that becomes even more telling when you throw in the fact that Maya lore speaks of the arrival, around this time, of a Mexican ruler from the west, whom they named Kukulcán, which means "Feathered Serpent."

In the Maya world, Kukulcán conquered the Maya elite in the Yucatán and proceeded to set up his new capital at Chichén Itzá. The murals in Chichén Itzá's Temple of the Warriors and Temple of the Jaguars chronicled this bloody struggle for power, a somewhat ironic one considering Topiltzin's supposed penchant for peace. By their accounts, Kukulcan's reign was secured through violent conquest culminating in the sacrifice of the vanquished Maya rulers.

Following their victory, the Toltec consolidated their power in the Yucatán and transformed Chichén Itzá into a blend of classic Puuc style and a replica of their beloved Tula. In the process, major cities of the Yucatán, such as Uxmal and Ek' Balam, were likely abandoned, and Maya architecture, art, religion, and culture fused with that of the invading conquerors.

As impressive as Toltec-Maya Chichén Itzá was, it too came to an abrupt end, in AD 1224. And even this synopsis of Toltec-Maya history has come under criticism; for instance, many dates noted during this period are controversial; in addition, some scholars believe the Maya were the ones who exercised their influence over Tula, and not the other way around.

On the heels of the Toltec came another group of foreigners into the Yucatán: The Itza originated in the Petén, and have the ignominious distinction of being universally loathed by the Maya, who called them, among other things, "people without fathers or mothers." Adding insult to injury, the Maya called the Itza's war leader K'ahk'upakal, which means "he who speaks our language brokenly." How he allowed them to get away with that remains a mystery, but he and his motley band settled in Chichén Itzá from AD 1224 to 1244 (before their arrival, the city bore the name Uukil-

Abnal). Their ruler even took the name Kukulkán, after the legendary Toltec leader (further evidence of how the memory of the Toltec lived on even after their fall).

The Itza founded Mayapan in AD 1263 to 1283, and shifted their capital from Chichén Itzá to this new city. Mayapan, a walled city of over 2,000 homes, held between 11,000 and 12,000 inhabitants. Large though it was, it was a distant second to majestic Chichén. Still, through alliance, subjugation, and tribute, the Itza dominated the Yucatán for close to two centuries, before revolt brought their reign to an end.

This doesn't mark the end of the resilient Itza, however. They once again migrated until they settled on an island in the middle of a lake, in the north of present-day Guatemala. Here they founded Tah Itza (which the Spanish later called Tayasal), where—thanks to the dense foliage around them—they were untouched by the Spanish conquest until 1697, almost 180 years after Hernán Cortés landed in Mexico.

The departure of the Itza also signaled the end of hegemony in the Yucatán. In the ensuing power vacuum, sixteen independent states vied for control; war and rivalry became a sign of the times. Of these states, many have been swallowed by time and conquest, but one shining example remains: Tulum, perched on a cliff overlooking the sparkling Caribbean, was a heavily fortified city of 500 to 600 residents. Today, it presents one of the most dramatic landscapes on the Caribbean coast of the Riviera Maya.

In Guatemala, along with Tayasal, numerous independent states existed on the eve of the Spanish conquest. Chief among these were the K'iche' and Kaqchikel, which claimed (dubiously) descent from Tula.

THE SPANISH ARRIVE

In 1517, conquistador Francisco Hernández de Córdoba reached the Yucatán and was promptly killed by Maya warriors. In 1518 and 1519, two additional expeditions were carried out, the latter by Cortés, but the peninsula was spared the wrath of the Spanish, who were much more interested in central Mexico and had their hands full with the Aztecs.

It wasn't until 1528 (seven years after the fall of the Aztec capital), that the conquest of the Yucatán began in earnest, under Francisco de Montejo. But it was a much different kind of battle than the bitter and bloody wars with the Aztecs. The Maya of this era lacked the central leadership of the Aztec capital, Tenochitlán, and fought in guerrilla style, far different from the armies of central Mexico. It took the Spanish 14 years to found a capital in the area, which they christened Mérida, but they faced Maya resistance throughout the 16th century. The last real opposition to the crown was crushed in 1541 by a man whose legacy of cruelty and violence has left tracks all over Mexico: Pedro de Alvarado.

THE (REPEATED) STORY OF THE RESURRECTION

The rapid and comprehensive spread of Catholicism in the New World proved to be one of the most powerful means of establishing Spanish dominion over Mexico. There were many reasons for the success of the new faith. The conquistadors had proven, quite convincingly, that their God was more powerful than the deities worshipped by the Maya; the Virgin Mother proved to be a key figure, a female deity with whom the Maya could easily relate; and the resurrection of Christ, rising from the ground three days after his burial, resonated powerfully in the Maya mindset, because it closely resembled their mythology.

In the *Popul Vuh,* a Maya mythic narrative, the creation myth tells of the twin brothers, Hunahpu and Xbalanque, who defeated their share of monsters, traveled to the underworld, defeated the lord of that realm, and resurrected their father. The legend is very much an agricultural allegory, with the father representing the all-important maize; and it must have been of some spiritual significance to hear tell of another figure dying and then returning from the ground.

It must be said, though, that the Maya never truly gave up. In 1847, and again in 1860, the Yucatec Maya rebelled against "the white man" and almost reclaimed the peninsula. In 1712 and again in 1868, the Tzeltal Maya of Chiapas staged a revolt. More recently, they, along with the Tzotzil Maya, have pestered the government under the banner of the Zapatista National Liberation Army. Also in the 20th century, tribal chiefs in Quintana Roo revolted against Mexico's infamous dictator Porfirio Díaz. In one form or another, the Maya have resisted, and endured, for close to 500 years.

Today, there are more than seven million direct descendants of the Maya. In many parts of Mexico, they continue unconquered, sustaining their tradition and culture. Maya dialects can easily be heard in Chiapas, Campeche, and the Yucatán, as well as the interior of Quintana Roo; and the Mayan language is taught at schools around the country.

The Maya live on. But we have skipped centuries ahead of ourselves in the telling of their history, and must now turn the clock back, to the time of the Aztecs.

2 Who Were the Aztecs?

THE EPICLASSIC PERIOD

THE TOLTEC PREDECESSORS

THE ALLIANCE AND THE TRIUMVIRATE

THE AZTEC WAY OF LIFE

THE SPANISH SIEGE OF TENOCHTITLÁN

Mexico Tourism Board

INTRODUCTION

The chronology of the Aztec empire takes place squarely in central Mexico, far removed from the coastal heartland of the Maya. The Aztecs were the last of the great civilizations of Mesoamerica, and their reign began and ended in the Postclassic period. As we know, they were not the first to settle the Valley of Mexico. The city of Teotihuacán was the mightiest settlement of the Classic period, so grand even in ruin that it would become part of Aztec mythology.

THE EPICLASSIC PERIOD (AD 650–900)

For 250 years after Teotihuacán, numerous tribes fought for power and influence in the void left by Central Mexico's most dynamic urban center. This was also the period of the proliferation of the Maya empire, which expanded even into central Mexico. Of the centers of power established in this part of the New World, a few deserve mention. Cacaxtla, a hilltop post in straddling Puebla and Tlaxcala, is believed to have served as a major stop along the Teotihuacán trade route to the Maya realm.

Far more majestic and impressive is Xochicalco, in present-day Morelos. Xochicalco ("The place of the House of Flowers" in Nahuatl), was a vast walled city-state and urban metropolis that thrived from AD 700 to 900. Its rise to power comes right after the fall of Teotihuacán and before the ascent of Tula. Xochicalco was a religious and economic powerhouse, with access to many of the other important cultures of its day, in Oaxaca, the Gulf Coast, and the Maya empire, but it also borrowed much from Teotihuacán.

Cholula, according to one historian the oldest inhabited city in the Americas, also flourished in the intermediary bridge between the Classic and Postclassic eras. Its most amazing accomplishment, and its most lasting monument, is its great pyramid. Called Tlachihualtépetl (Handmade Hill), this colossal structure reached, at its base, more than 1,300 feet wide per side and over 200 feet high. To put those numbers in perspective, the Cholula pyramid was larger than the Pyramid of the Sun in Teotihuacán as well as that of Cheops in Egypt. In the Epiclassic period, the city was taken over by a people known as the Olmeca-Xicallanca (who also held power in Cacaxtla). The Olmeca-Xicallanca introduced a style of pottery in Cholula that would become among the most treasured items in ancient Mexico.

THE PYRAMID OF THE FEATHERED SERPENT AT XOCHICALCO

In northern Veracruz, another important site was thriving at this time. Like Cholula and Cacaxtla, El Tajín was occupied during the Classic period, and was part of a network of small villages. Toward the end of the period, however, El Tajín began to grow and conquer the surrounding area until, during the Epiclassic era, it became a large settlement, replete with pyramids, ball courts, and palaces for the city's elite. (In particular, the citizens of El Tajín seemed to have placed great importance on the ball game and its associated rituals). With its striking architecture and complex of structures, El Tajín today is one of the finer remnants of Classic and Epiclassic Mexico.

In our review of Mexico's ancient civilizations, we have yet to touch on northwestern Mexico. This is primarily because large-scale settlements in this part of the country did not occur until the Epiclassic period, when the states of Durango, Zacatecas, Alta Vista, and La Quemada were established. By all accounts, life was harsh here, and warfare and ritual sacrifice appeared a predominant way of life. The states of northwestern Mexico served as a conduit for goods and cultural exchange between Mesoamerica and the American tribes to the north, and also provided a rich source of turquoise (mined and processed in Alta Vista), which would become a coveted material for later cultures in Mexico.

Many of the civilizations that ascended during the Epiclassic era also died out by the end of this period, as did much of the Maya empire. As we have seen, the power vacuum was ably filled by the Toltec.

THE TOLTEC PREDECESSORS

We last left the Toltec in the Maya world, but after the departure of Topiltzin, the warrior cult assumed dominion in Tula, and the Toltec would exert their full supremacy over central Mexico. Their capital became a wonder of the age, a vast city of staggering wealth. At its zenith, the city boasted between 30,000 and 40,000 residents, and served as the major religious center of its time.

Its crowning architectural monument was a stepped pyramid, at the foot of which was an ornate colonnaded hall, and which contained at its top a two-room temple. The roof of the outer room was supported by stone statues called Atlanteans—the most distinctive icons of ancient Tula, four of which can still be seen today (even if three out of the four are duplicates). The inner sanctuary of the temple featured a stone altar and an array of reclining figurines known as Chac-Mools, a design we will see again in the great capital of the Aztecs.

The Toltec were proficient artisans who controlled large deposits of obsidian, and had an extensive trade network throughout Mexico, but they were primarily a people ruled by war, conquest, tribute, and sacrifice. There is much evidence for their proclivity for human sacrifice. Two examples are the Chac-Mool sculpture, which was used as a receptacle for human hearts, and the *cuauhxicalli,* or eagle vessel, in which human hearts were kept. In Tula's central plaza, in front of the ball court, there is also a *tzompantli,* which is an altar comprised of rows of skull racks. It is believed the heads placed here belonged to the losers of the ball game.

The Toltec empire flourished for roughly 200 years before a combination of factors brought about its end in the 12th century. Tula itself was subject to a sudden and very violent end, possibly at the hand of the neighboring Chichimeca. At this point, the Toltec dispersed throughout Mexico, transporting their culture and heritage to other tribes. We already know of their influence at Chichén Itzá. The appearance of Quetzalcóatl at this city is most telling, as the feathered serpent (represented at

THE ATLANTES OF TULA

Chichén as a rattlesnake with quetzal—a tropical bird—feathers) was an unknown entity among the Classic Maya.

THE ORIGINS OF THE AZTECS

The Toltec weren't the only civilization to flourish in Postclassic Mexico. After the fall of Monte Albán in Oaxaca, the Zapotec center of power shifted to Mitla, a city of remarkable splendor in its day. Also in this part of Mexico, the Mixtec people established a series of independent states, occupying much of the remaining Zapotec territory. Unlike Tula, both the city of Mitla and the Mixtec would survive to see the arrival of the Spanish. The Mixtec spread their influence and culture throughout most of Oaxaca, and were known as master goldsmiths and workers of turquoise. In the north, in present-day Chihuahua, another settlement was established at Paquimé, which must have served as an important trade link from Mesoamerican Mexico to the Native Americans of the North American southwest.

Meanwhile, in western Mexico, the Postclassic saw the founding of the kingdom of the Tarascan people in Michoacán. The Tarascan appear to be a singularly unique group; they had a unique language, and many of the most popular gods of the time, including Quetzalcóatl and Tlaloc, the rain god, were absent from their pantheon, as were other aspects of life common in nearby civilizations, like the ball court and the Calendar Round system. Although the remains of the Tarascan empire are comparatively sparse today, this was once a powerful settlement, and, it should be noted, they were a group that the Aztecs never managed to conquer.

Which brings us, at last, to the incomparable Aztecs, who rose from modest beginnings to establish an awesome empire that lasted until its fall at the hands of the conquistadors. The Aztecs claimed their origin from an island called Aztlán, which lay in the west or northwest of the country, and from where they get their name. According to Aztec legend, they migrated into central Mexico at around the turn of the 14th century, under the leadership of their chief god, Huitzilopochtli (which means "Hummingbird on the left"), a war god and a sun god. Along the way, the Aztecs adopted a new name—the Mexica—which they kept to the end of their days (even though most of the world remembers them as the Aztecs).

Despite their supposèd divine assistance, it would be a gross exaggeration to say the Aztecs swept through central Mexico uncontested. At this point, they were little more than a band of barbaric nomads who initially survived in a type of prolonged serfdom to one civilized state or another. In this manner they moved across the valley of Mexico until, led by their priest-chief, Tenoch, they settled in a cluster of unoccupied islands in a lake. Again, mythology and lore play a major role here, for the location of their new heartland was supposedly decided by divine foretelling. Aztec prophecy predicted that the new capital would be established at the spot where an eagle would be seen perched on a cactus, devouring a snake. It can only be assumed that Tenoch saw this vision here, for it was here that he founded Tenochtitlán, in AD 1344–45. Immediately north of this capital, the Aztecs established a twin city called Tlatelolco.

It seems that, from the very beginning, the one advantage the Aztecs had was their military prowess. They were among the greatest warriors ancient Mexico would ever see, and they quickly established themselves as mercenaries. In 1367, they joined forces with the large nearby kingdom of Azcapotzalco, which was under the dominion of the powerful Tepanec tribe. Aztec and Tepanec forces conquered numerous other settlements in the valley, and the fledgling Aztec nation began to see an increase in wealth and position.

A critical turning point came in 1426, when the Tepanec decided they no longer wanted anything to do with the upstart island city. In 1427, Itzcoatl (Obsidian Snake) became king in Tenochtitlán. He and his chief advisor, Tlacaelel, led the fight against the larger and more established Tepanec, and utterly destroyed them. But what happened next cemented the Aztec dynasty and changed the history of Mexico.

THE ALLIANCE AND THE TRIUMVIRATE

It was Tlacaelel, more than anyone else, who changed the fortunes of the Aztecs, and he did so by rewriting their history and giving them a new destiny. In essence, he imbued them with the belief that they were the true heirs of the mighty Toltec, and that it was their mission to conquer, capture, and gain sacrifice for Huitzilopochtli. The Aztecs believed that Huitzilopochtli, the sun god and god of war, needed a steady diet of human hearts to fuel his passage across the sky each day; and they systematically set out to provide them.

To help achieve this rather grim goal, Tlacaelel helped organize a "Triple Alliance" with the neighboring states of Texcoco and Tlacopan. Under King Motecuhzoma Ilhuicamina (who reigned from AD 1440 to 1469, and whose name has been translated down through the ages as Moctezuma or Montezuma), the Aztecs and their allies carried out an impressive march across central Mexico. Conquered states would quickly become provinces of the Aztec empire, forced to pay a heavy tribute to the alliance. Each province had a military governor who enforced timely and accurate payment, which would then be divided among the three powers of the triumvirate. The records that survive today tell of a massive haul from these defeated lands.

The greatest expansion came under the reign of Ahuitzotl (1486–1502), the sixth king of the Aztecs, who rampaged across the land reaching up to the border of Guatemala and subduing most of central Mexico in the process. Under his leadership, the Aztecs reached, and then eclipsed, the former glory of their revered ancestors in Tula.

Ahuitzotl was succeeded by Motecuhzoma Xocoyotzin (Moctezuma II), the ill-fated ruler who suffered from the catastrophically bad luck of being in power when the conquistadors arrived, and from the horribly misguided belief that Hernán Cortés was none other than Quetzalcóatl. According to historical accounts, Motecuhzoma received many portents of their

Annual Tribute Paid to Tenochtitlán (Partial List*)	
Item	**Quantity**
Maize	7,000 tons
Beans	4,000 tons
Chia Seed	4,000 tons
Grain Amaranth	4,000 tons
Cotton Cloaks	2,000,000

*Other items included varying quantities of luxury goods, clothing, live animals, and items for military use.

coming demise, dating back as far as ten years before the arrival of the Spanish. Among these harbingers of doom were a comet spotted in 1517, the spontaneous burning of the temple of Huitzilopochtli, repeated apparitions of two-headed men, and, one of the most puzzling, a bird brought to Motecuhzoma that had a mirror sticking out of its head, through which the king saw an approaching force.

Regardless of how he interpreted these signs, the Aztec ruler's erroneous judgment of the conquistadors led him to welcome the enemy into the capital in 1511, and, essentially, to hand them the keys to the last great empire of ancient Mexico. Still, the Aztecs did no go down without a fight. But before we get to that final, bloody, and world-changing conflict, let's examine just what Cortés and his soldiers saw when they entered Tenochtitlán, and how a relatively small band of foreigners conquered the strongest army in ancient Mexico. As we will see, the conquistadors did not fight not alone.

THE AZTEC WAY OF LIFE

The Aztec empire may have been predominantly one of military prowess, but that's not to say that it did not benefit from a rich and complex social order, an impressive architectural heritage, and advanced scientific development. Thanks to the early reinvention orchestrated by Tlacaelel, the Aztecs believed they were the chosen people, and their empire reflected this status. By the late 1400s, Tenochtitlán already had an aqueduct to bring water to the island city, along with an impressive Great Temple complex. By the time Cortés arrived, it was a glorious metropolis, with monumental temples; a large elite class comprised of rulers, priests, and warriors; and the heart of a vast trading empire.

In fact, the Spanish were awestruck by the splendor of this city on the lake, adorned with towers and temples and buildings made of stone. Some described it as an enchanted city, others as a city of dreams, and still others compared it to Venice. Today, one can only imagine the sight that greeted them. Three broad walkways led north, south, and west from the city, connecting Tenochtitlán to the mainland. There were gaps in each for passing canoes, and removable bridges built for defensive purposes.

The comparison to Venice was appropriate. Tenochtitlán was laid out on a grid, intersected by canals through which canoe traffic would pass. The city, in short, was a cluster of floating islands called *chinampas,* an ingenious creation by the natives to provide arable and residential land.

How populous was Tenochtitlán in the 1500s? It is difficult to say for certain, but most estimates fall between 200,000 and 300,000 residents. To put those numbers in perspective, the population of the Aztec capital dwarfed that of London under King Henry VIII, its overseas contemporary. When you factor in the *11 million* or so inhabitants throughout central Mexico who fell under the Aztec aegis, it becomes even more wondrous that a relatively tiny force under Cortés's command conquered this nation.

The most spectacular display of Aztec architecture was the Sacred Precinct, which lay in the center of Tenochtitlán. Huey Teocalli, as the

THE FLOATING ISLANDS OF TENOCHTITLÁN

Most of the land around Lake Texcoco, where the city of Tenochtitlán was founded, was comprised of marshy ground, making for poor farming conditions. To address this shortcoming, the Aztecs constructed artificial islands of gathered vegetation and mud. These were then anchored, providing small fields on which crops could be cultivated.

The creation of the *chinampas* was only half the story of the ingenuity of the Aztecs. The floating plots were perennially susceptible to flooding by the lake, which would drown the islands in saltwater and ruin whatever crop was under cultivation. To remedy this, King Nezahualcoyotl of Texcoco built an extensive dike to protect the city's freshwater supply.

Today, you can enjoy a glimpse of what this system looks like in Xochimilco, which lies south of Mexico City. Naturally, *chinampas* were much more predominant during the zenith of Tenochtitlán, but a visit to the floating gardens of Xochimilco is a must for history buffs, nature lovers, and those who want to experience a small slice of ancient Mexico.

Aztecs called it, was the political, symbolic, and spiritual center of the Aztec universe. This was a walled enclosure of temples and important ritual structures, dominated by the Templo Mayor (Great Temple). Atop this pyramid were two unequal altars to the two most important gods of the Aztec pantheon: the aforementioned Huitzilopochtli, and Tlaloc, the rain god.

Other temples in the Sacred Precinct were devoted to Quetzalcóatl, Tonatiuh (the Sun god), and Tezcatlipoca, among other deities. In front of the Templo Mayor was a *tzompantli,* or skull rack, where the heads of sacrificial victims would be placed in grisly rows. The *tzompantli* in turn lay at the head of the ball court. Next to the Templo Mayor was La Casa de las Águilas (The House of the Eagles), considered one of the most important and aristocratic buildings in the sacred center.

In fact, Fray Bernardino de Sahagún—one of the earliest missionaries to the New World and one of the most important chroniclers of both the Aztec culture and the Spanish conquest—wrote that there were a total of 78 buildings in the Sacred Precinct. And surrounding them on the outside were the palaces of the rulers of the Aztec empire. These were called the *teteuhctin,* and they sat at the top of the social food chain.

Beneath these august figures were the *pipiltin,* or nobles, a mainly hereditary line of lords and wealthy landowners. Another class of noble earned the title of *cuauhpipiltin,* or eagle noble; these were warriors, of any class, who had proven their mettle in battle and so won the designation.

An important feature of Tenochtitlán society were the *calpoltin,* or big houses. A *calpolli* was essentially a cluster of families of varying rank and status but joined by blood or proximity. Each *calpolli* had a mini-hierarchy, beginning with the *calpollec,* or chief, who was elected by the families. The wealthier members of the *calpolli* would provide their poorer kin with land or other assistance, in exchange for services or tribute. Marriages were usually arranged between two families within the same *calpolli,* and were considered more a union of clans over that of man and wife. Working for the *calpoltin* and paying tribute to the nobles in Tenochtitlán were the *macehualtin,* the farmers and labor class that formed the majority of the city's population.

Beneath them were the *mayeque,* serfs who worked the land, and finally, scraping the bottom of the social barrel, the *tlacohtin,* or slaves (literally "bought ones"). A down-on-his-luck person could hock themselves at the market (or be pawned off by their family), but slavery had its rules under Aztec law. Slaves could not be resold without their approval, and could rise above their station if they were productive.

One of the essential features of life in pre-Hispanic Mexican society was the *tianguis,* or market. In Tenochtitlán and, of even more grandeur, in the twin city of Tlatelolco, two immense markets were wonders of their time, easily rivaling the famed marketplaces in Rome and Constantinople. The Tlatelolco market alone attracted over 60,000 vendors and buyers a day, with all manner of products available, from gold to clothing to slaves. Cacao beans, cotton cloaks, and quills filled with gold dust served as currency. (It was at Tlatelolco that the final and decisive battle between the Aztecs and the Spanish was fought, on August 13, 1521.)

The markets bred a merchant class, with a select elite known as *pochteca,* or long-distance merchants, who traveled far to obtain coveted luxury items. The Aztecs even had a band of economic hitmen called *oztomeca,* who spoke the native language of other tribes and infiltrated their markets, purchasing goods and gathering intelligence.

AZTEC GOVERNANCE

The highest office in the Aztec world was that of *huei tlatoani,* or "great speaker," the combined position of commander in chief, principal diplomat, and collector of tribute from the provinces. This august ruler was treated as a god-king by his subjects and even by foreign emissaries. He was carried on a litter borne by noblemen, and if he walked, nobles would carpet his way with cloths so that his feet wouldn't touch the ground. He

GROWING UP AZTEC

Next time your children complain about their lot in life, you might want to tell them about how it was to grow up in the Aztec world. Children were relegated to a strict, gender-specific upbringing: girls would be taught from an early age to be homemakers, learning to weave and make tortillas, while boys would follow typical boyhood activities: fishing, gathering firewood, and being reminded that their mission in life was to feed the Sun and the Earth with the blood and flesh of their enemies.

To their credit, however, the Aztecs did provide universal secondary education for boys and girls, beginning at age 15 and lasting until about age 20. There were two types of schools: the *calmecac¸* where religious teaching took place (attending the *calmecac* was mandatory for anyone with political aspirations), which was then followed by a graduate school of sorts for priests; and the *telpochcalli,* or military school.

had all the pageantry of a king's court, with jesters, lavish banquets, and all manner of luxuries (Motecuhzoma had pleasure palaces, tropical gardens, a royal aviary, royal zoo, and even his own private carnival sideshow).

The second-most-powerful figure had no such privileges but was chiefly responsible for all matters of state. This person held the post of *cihuacoatl,* or female snake. The aforementioned Tlacaelel was *cihuacoatl* to not one but three rulers. The remainder of the Aztec royal house was responsible for enforcing law through two courts, one for nobles and warriors, the other for the masses; maintaining the army's supplies and living conditions; and managing the tribute system that fueled the Aztec economy.

FOOD AND DRINK

Visitors to Mexico are likely to be quite impressed with its gastronomy. Far beyond the tacos and burritos most commonly associated with Mexican food, the cuisine of this country is complex, rich, and healthy—and its tradition dates back to the Aztecs and their predecessors. Trade, tribute, and the *chinampa* system brought a feast to the Aztec table, and few people in the empire went hungry.

The staple of every family's diet was maize, served most commonly as tortillas, steamed as tamales and filled with beans, or in liquid form in hearty drinks called *atolli* (the precursor of *atole*) and *pozolli* (pozole).

Similar to other parts of the world, meat and fish were the province of the wealthy (as was chocolate), and included what can generously be described today as exotic meats: salamander, tadpoles, and a variety of insects (eaten by all classes).

These ingredients were enhanced by a fantastic cornucopia of spices and flavors. The most ubiquitous of these was the chile pepper, which was a main part of the diet. In addition, vanilla, tropical fruits, and native herbs and plants were employed in Aztec kitchens. Amaranth, a grain crop, was widely reserved for ceremonial feasts. And there was the maguey, which holds a special, multipurpose use for ancient and modern Mexicans alike. It is from the sap of this plant that the ancients brewed a fermented alcoholic beverage they called *octli,* which we know better as pulque. Unlike today's customs, inebriation was a crime punishable by death (in extreme cases), unless you were elderly; in that case, you could drink as much as you liked and get away with it.

THIS DIEGO RIVERA MURAL DEPICTS AN AZTEC WARRIOR IN EAGLE ARMOR BATTLING A CONQUISTADOR.

THE AZTECS AT WAR

I'm sure there are at least some who have been reading in anticipation of learning about the Aztecs' vaunted bloodlust. For some reason, the world seems fascinated with the culture of war, sacrifice, and barbarism that surrounds Aztec history and mythology. Many movies concerning pre-Hispanic Indians (Aztec or not) revel in their savage reputation. And the Aztecs, at least, give plenty of credence to this image. War was not just a means to an end for them, but a divine destiny, a way of life, the essential purpose of their state, and their path to glory.

Every healthy male in the Aztec empire carried weapons and could be called on to fight. Similar to other great warrior classes (the Spartans come to mind), there was no greater glory than death on the battlefield. The Aztec warrior ran to meet his fate, armed with a vicious sword-club, spears, and darts thrown from an *atlatl,* or spear-thrower. They sometimes wore quilted tunics and carried round shields for defense. Elite warriors wore fabulous eagle feather and jaguar skin costumes, and high-ranking officers were recognizable to their men (and, unfortunately, to Cortés's men) by additional feathered regalia.

Battle was joined to the sound of shell trumpets played by priests. The Aztecs fought with honor. It was not their goal or desire to overwhelm an opponent on the battlefield. In fact, they would even send weapons to overmatched states to help assure a more even confrontation. Of course, a main reason to go to war was to procure sacrificial victims to keep the gods satiated; just as the Aztec culture was fed by war, so too were their gods. And here is where Hollywood takes a dramatic detour from the pages of history. The depictions we see of bound and beaten captives dragged to a temple and eviscerated while still alive sullies the deep-rooted sense of ritual that accompanied their sacrifice. The most prized captives were enemy fighters, and a special bond would exist between a warrior and his captive, one that stemmed from a universal belief in pre-Hispanic Mexico that death in battle was glorious. So ingrained was this ideal that the following exchange would occur when an Aztec took a victim:

Aztec warrior (of his captive): "Here is my well-beloved son."

Captive (of his captor): "Here is my revered father."

The relationship, thus established, was in a way a ritual preparation for death. Warriors believed they would be transformed in death into hummingbirds and would enter paradise, where the god of the Sun dwelt. (This concept of glory in death on the battlefield was extended to women who died in childbirth; having lost their own personal battle, they were also said to have been granted a space in heaven.)

Before being sacrificed, victims would be bathed. Then, the Aztecs would dispatch their captives in one of five ways.

1. Laying the victim on a stone altar, cutting open his chest with a flint or obsidian knife, taking out his heart, and placing it in a *cuauhxicalli,* or eagle vessel, as an offering to the gods.
2. Decapitation, usually the preferred means to sacrifice women who were passing themselves off as gods.
3. Battle, with the odds heavily weighed against the victim. The captive would be tied to a round stone and forced to fight a better-equipped warrior.
4. Firing arrows or darts at a bound victim.
5. Throwing the victim into a fire (more than once), *followed by* method No. 1.

If you *had* to be a sacrificial victim in the Aztec world, the one to aim for was the embodiment of the powerful god Tezcatlipoca. For this role, the Aztecs would annually select one handsome youth from among their captives. He would live in high style for one year, worshipped as the human incarnation of the god, and was even provided with four comely mistresses. At the end of his "reign," the victim would ascend the temple to be stabbed in the chest with a dagger.

There is plenty of evidence to suggest that some form of cannibalism was practiced upon the bodies of the victims, but this was done for ritual purposes rather than dietary need or desire. Far more unclear is the extent to which these sacrifices were carried out. The popular myth, backed by scholars and even Spanish chronicles, is that sacrifices were carried out on a scale before unseen in the world. I've read of accounts of up to 20,000 people being slaughtered after a single battle, or the killing of 80,000 to consecrate the Great Temple. Without the use of any weapons capable of large-scale destruction, this seems not only logistically implausible but grossly exaggerated. It is far more likely that the Spanish wanted to paint the Aztecs as unparalleled savages . . . an image that has lasted to this day. Still, we can safely assume that thousands of people were sacrificed to the gods each year by the Aztecs.

THE ENIGMATIC QUETZALCÓATL, OR FEATHERED SERPENT, WAS AN IMPORTANT DEITY FOR MANY PRE-COLUMBIAN CULTURES.

RELIGION AND ASTRONOMY

The Aztec religion was an incredibly complex and multilayered belief system, incorporating elements from other Mesoamerican mythologies and founded upon an overall duality that permeated much of Aztec culture. To run through the entire pantheon and every ritual would be impossible; instead, following are the major figures who were responsible for, and who governed, the Aztec world.

The creator of the universe was a bisexual entity called Ometeotl (Dual Divinity). Ometeotl produced four offspring: Tezcatlipoca was the god of war and sorcery, the giver and destroyer of life, and the deity of the royal house; Quetzalcóatl was the lord of life and patron deity of the priests; Huitzilopochtli, the war and sun god; and Xipe Totec, god of spring, agriculture, and rebirth. These gods, along with Tlaloc, the rain god, were the principal deities of the Aztec pantheon.

The Aztecs believed in 12 levels of heaven and nine layers of the underworld. They were also convinced that the world they lived in was a fifth cosmic age (which was created, incidentally, at Teotihuacán); the four previous stages of the world were destroyed, all results of a recurring conflict between Tezcatlipoca and Quetzalcóatl. One or the other of these gods would rule, in succession, over each stage of the world. It was Quetzalcóatl who brought humans into this age, and then, as if that was not enough, he also gave them maize.

The voices of the gods were the priests, among the most powerful people in the Aztec world. Priests were celibate and engaged in a life of complex daily ritual, which included self-mutilation. They wore their hair long and dyed in blood, and were the students of the skies.

Bound up with the cyclical nature of the world and the struggle of the gods was the all-important calendar. The Aztecs followed a 260-day almanac year, broken down into 20 "weeks," each week comprising 13 days. Each week was named after an animal, and came with its own rituals, controlling gods, even its own supernatural bird. The Aztecs also marked a 365-day solar year, comprised of 18 months of 20 days each. This total of 360 days left a 5-day gap between one year and the next, which was considered both unlucky and dangerous. Like the almanac year, solar months also had their special rites.

Astronomy and mythology went hand in hand. According to Aztec legend, when the gods created the fifth age at Teotihuacán, two gods sacrificed themselves to become the Sun and the Moon. (In a humorous aside to this account, the Moon's brightness initially equaled that of the Sun, so the gods decided to diminish its brilliance by throwing a rabbit at it; the rabbit can still be seen today on the moon's face.) In addition to these astral bodies, Venus was of special importance to priests, and the planet's heliacal rising every 584 days was considered a perilous event. It is astounding that every 104 solar years (or two 52 Calendar Round years), the Almanac Year, Solar Year, and the 584-day cycle of Venus would all synchronize.

The end of each 52-year Calendar Round period was an ominous time in the Aztec world, for it heralded the possible destruction of the fifth age. On the last day, all fires in the realm were put out, and priests would scan the skies at midnight, watching for the passage of the Pleiades across the meridian. If this phenomenon occurred, it would signal the continuation of the age, and the event was marked by (naturally) a sacrifice. In this case, a victim would have his chest cut open, into which fire sticks would be placed and a new fire lit. Embers from this sacred flame would be sent throughout the empire. As one can imagine, the new Calendar Round and continuation of the world would also be celebrated with much revelry, feasting, and music.

After death, an Aztec either went to heaven or hell. As mentioned earlier, warriors who died in battle or in sacrifice, along with women who died in childbirth, went to the heaven of the Sun god. Tlaloc, the rain god, also sat in a heaven and accepted those who died in some way related to him. The deepest level of the underworld, on the other hand, was Mictlan Opochcalocan, the Land of the Dead, and it was here where the soul itself became extinct.

ART, ARCHITECTURE, AND LITERATURE

With the slanted focus on Aztec savagery that history presents us, we tend to overlook some of the other factors that made this race the most dominant empire of its time. The Aztecs were among the best stoneworkers in all of ancient Mexico. Much of their art and architecture was religious in nature, with towering statues of deities, intricately carved sculptures of divine beings, and a plethora of magnificent stepped temples.

Like many other Mesoamerican cultures, the Aztecs followed the practice of constructing their temples in successive phases, building over an earlier stage as they expanded and improved the structure. The Templo Mayor in Tenochtitlán was constructed over eight major phases, beginning in 1325 and lasting until the Spanish conquered the city in 1521.

Along with their architectural and artistic prowess, the Aztecs benefited from meticulous chroniclers, eloquent poets, and philosophers. Thankfully, we have an abundance of writings from this time period, and these give us plenty of evidence of the sophistication of Aztec poetry, which was known as *in xóchitl, in cuicatl*, or flowers, songs. There is also ample record of the humility of the Aztecs, a characteristic rarely attributed to them. This was a world of hardship and suffering, and its people abhorred the gluttony and excess that they would find in the strangers who came from beyond their shores.

THE SPANISH SIEGE OF TENOCHTITLÁN

The many accounts of Hernán Cortés rampaging through Mexico with his intrepid conquistadors and demolishing all resistance are highly exaggerated, if not grossly insulting to the Aztecs. For one thing, he had brought only a few hundred soldiers with him from Spain, nowhere near enough to defeat the Aztec hordes. For another, as we have seen, he was invited to Tenochtitlán by Moctezuma, who believed these strange, bearded men who arrived via a "mountain that moved on the water" to be the reincarnation of Quetzalcóatl.

But even Moctezuma's error would not have been enough to assure the destruction of the Aztec empire were it not for the role of other peoples under Aztec dominion. When Cortés landed on the Gulf Coast in 1519, he soon realized that the Indians who lived here paid stiff tribute to Tenochtitlán, and were none too pleased with the status quo. More important than the Gulf Coast tribes were the Tlaxcalans, enemies of the Aztecs who at first resisted the Spanish, but allied with them after Cortés defeated them.

And then there was Malinche, a reviled Pocahontas-like figure in Mexican history and one of the most important people in Cortés's conquest of the New World. Malinche was a beautiful woman of noble birth who came to serve as translator, and later mistress, to Cortés.

Another little-known fact is that the Spanish mandate never called for an invasion. In moving against the Aztecs, Cortés acted on his own, taking advantage of the opportunity to acquire immense wealth and power. It must be said, he did so with little honor. After accepting Moctezuma's invitation, Cortés entered Tenochtitlán and promptly took the ruler captive. That's when things got complicated.

The conquistador learned of another force of Spanish soldiers sent from Cuba to arrest him. Cortés was forced to leave Tenochtitlán to deal with this new threat; when he returned, he found Moctezuma dead and the Aztec capital in rebellion against the Spanish. The conquistadors were routed and forced to flee the island city after suffering such heavy casualties that, upon reaching the mainland, Cortés rested by a great tree and wept for the loss of his people. This moment in Mexican history has come to be known as La Noche Triste (The Sad Night), and the stump of that very tree still stands in Mexico City.

A MURAL OF HERNAN CORTÉS AND LA MALINCHE AT THE ANTIGUO COLEGIO DE SAN ILDEFONSO, MEXICO CITY

Cortés retreated to neighboring Tlaxcala and from there relaunched his invasion. Following a massive battle in which Cortés was victorious, the Spanish and their allies returned to Tenochtitlán in 1521. They built a fleet by the shores of Lake Texcoco and laid siege to the capital. On August 13, 1521, after 75 days of brutal fighting, Cortés defeated the stiff Aztec resistance led by Cuauhtémoc, the last of the Aztec emperors, and took control of the city. What followed was a pitiable moment in the forging of the New World: the Tlaxcalans, bitter enemies of the Aztecs, engaged in wholesale massacre of Tenochtitlán's citizens, a violent bloodbath that is remembered to this day.

There is no doubt that Cortés benefited from superior weaponry and training. The Aztecs had no concept of a cavalry, no counter to cannonfire, and little hope against steel. Unlike the Aztecs, the Spanish also had no problems bringing these advantages into play on the battlefield, eschewing the Aztec principle of a fair fight. Even more influential to the Spanish conquest were not the Spanish at all, but the complementary army of Tlaxcalans that Cortés commanded when he fell upon Tenochtitlán. Tlaxcala would help the Spanish take over the Aztec empire as well as most of Mesoamerica.

And finally, there was that most effective of weapons; disease. The Aztecs had absolutely no defense against smallpox, measles, malaria, and a host of other maladies that were deadly to the native population. Sickness took a massive toll on their numbers, and did much of Cortés's work for him.

Within a mere three years of the fall of Tenochtitlán, the Spanish conquest of Mexico was almost complete. Those who rebelled (and there were many) were crushed. Those who remained were introduced to an all-powerful new God, a new religion in Christianity, and a near-enslavement that decimated the native population. In 1519, just before the Spanish conquest, approximately 11 million people lived in central Mexico; less than a hundred years later, that number had dwindled to about 2.5 million. By 1650, only 1.5 million natives were left in the New World.

The victors christened their land New Spain. They demolished the mighty temples and cities of the Indians and in their place—sometimes directly over a fallen temple—they set up new cities, churches, and cathedrals. And they began a dominion over the country that would last for three centuries, until revolution, war, and bloodshed led to Mexico's independence, empire, and rebirth as a democratic nation.

But the legacy of the Aztecs has survived through the centuries; the image of the Aztec warrior is a revered one, and statues of their great kings can be found all over their former capital. The Aztecs do not exist in modern Mexico the way the Maya do, but their story, their fierce pride, and their traditions remain alive.

Planning Your Trip 3

ENTERING MEXICO

TRAVELER ESSENTIALS AND TIPS

MEXICAN FOOD, MEXICAN DRINK

Mexico Tourism Board

ENTERING MEXICO

You hear a lot about Mexico in the news, and unfortunately, what you hear tends to paint a scary picture. Stories of violence, kidnappings, and the drug wars that have spiked in the country, especially in the border states, have taken their toll on the tourist outlook.

Basically, traveling to certain parts of Mexico these days is not merely inadvisable but practically asking for trouble. Even some of the destinations covered in this book have their reputations: Mexico City gets a bad rap as a dangerous capital stuffed with muggers, kidnappers, and other degenerates. Chiapas has suffered due to the past violence of the Zapatistas (although this has been more of a national concern than an international one); and even in Cancún, you'll hear of the occasional (and usually highly publicized) tourist mishap.

Despite the horror stories, there is good news. Campeche and the Yucatán rank among the safest destinations in the country. And there have been few issues for tourists in Chiapas. But most of all, no matter where you are in Mexico (or any foreign country, for that matter), you need to travel smart; there are ways to safeguard against crime, sickness, and even getting ripped off (although this will be, to some extent, unavoidable). That's what this chapter is all about.

> **USEFUL WEB SITES**
>
> As you can imagine, there's no shortage of online resources to help you get better acquainted with Mexico. www.visitmexico.com is the official tourism Web site for the country. Other resources include www.mexico-travel.com, the wonderfully named www.locogringo.com, and www.mexicoguru.com (author Jane Onstott knows her stuff and has lived in and written about Mexico for many years).

ENTERING MEXICO

All travelers to Mexico are required to present original **photo**

identification and **proof of citizenship**. All U.S. travelers to Mexico are required to present a **valid passport** at the airport and upon reentry to the United States. If you have a foreign passport but are a legal resident in the United States, bring your green card as well. Always treat these documents as your most precious commodities when traveling abroad. Should you lose your passport, contact your country's embassy or consulate immediately.

Citizens (and legal residents) of the United States, Canada, and several other countries around the world do not need a visa to Mexico but are required to have a **Mexican Tourist Permit (FMT)**, which serves the same purpose. Your airline should provide you with this absolutely critical document, but in case you don't get one on board, it is available upon arrival at the airport. The FMT card can be issued for up to 180 days, and will be given a stamped time limit by immigration officials. Often, officials will arbitrarily assign an exit date, so if you are planning to stay a long time (say, more than 60 days), make sure to ask them to stamp the full time limit. Just say, "*Ciento ochenta días por favor*" (180 days, please). Then you'll get the card back. *Do not discard it!* Visitors are required to present the card upon exiting Mexico. Failure to produce it will result in fines and bureaucratic hurdle-jumping that will have you cursing the country before you leave. Just ask my mother.

After immigration, you have to pass through customs. You must have a completed Customs Declaration Form, which is also provided on the flight. Then you punch a button to find out if you have a green light (cleared to proceed) or a red light (have your luggage checked). It is truly arbitrary.

CUSTOMS Customs officials are lenient when it comes to what you can bring into Mexico duty-free. Technically, the list is quite specific: no more than two cameras, five toys, three speedboats (no, really) . . . it goes on. In practice, however, officials are mainly concerned with people trying to bring in items for resale, drugs, firearms, and other taboo items. Tourists traveling by air are allowed to bring in gifts and permitted goods up to a value of $300 (by land, the amount is $50, except for alcohol and tobacco). If you exceed this amount, you have to pay a flat 15 percent tax on the amount exceeding the exemption. You can also bring in a computer with peripherals worth up to $4,000 duty-free, but will be required to hire a customs broker if its value exceeds this amount. If you are carrying in excess of $10,000, you must declare it on the customs form but will not be required to pay tax on it. For the latest customs information, visit www.aduanas.sat.gob.mx or call 1-800-463-6728 toll-free in Mexico.

When leaving Mexico, U.S. citizens who have been in the country for at least 48 hours can take back $800 worth of goods duty-free. (Note that close to 3,000 items, including all Mexican handcrafts, are exempt from

U.S. customs duties.) There is a flat rate of duty on anything above this amount. Lottery tickets, drugs, fireworks, and many meals and fruits are among the items that cannot be brought back into the United States from Mexico. Also on the list are Cuban cigars, which are available in the country (although not all Cubans sold in Mexico are really Cuban). For the full list of what is permissible and duty fees, visit the U.S. Customs and Border Protection Web site at www.cbp.gov or call 1-877-287-8667.

GETTING THERE Of course, you can also reach Mexico by car from the United States, but I would advise against it. For one thing, you'll have to go through the Mexico-U.S. border, which can be a nightmare, especially on the return trip. For another, it's a lengthy drive from the border to the regions covered in this book, and while it's a great way to see the country, it's only advisable for those who have planned a lengthy stay.

By air: Virtually every major American and international carrier flies into Mexico through Benito Juárez International Airport. In addition, a host of regional and national airlines operate there. Following is just a sample of the major carriers serving the airport from U.S. cities. As with any international flight, make sure to arrive at your departure airport at least two hours prior to the flight time.

MEXICAN AIRLINES

Aeroméxico
1-800-237-6639 (U.S.)
555-133-4000 (Mexico City)
1-800-021-4000 toll-free in Mexico
www.aeromexico.com
A member of the Sky Team alliance, Aeroméxico serves more than 40 destinations around Mexico and has direct flights to seven U.S. cities.

Aviacsa
1-866-246-0961 (U.S.)
555-482-8280 (Mexico City)
1-800-AVIACSA toll-free in Mexico
www.aviacsa.com.mx
Primarily a local airline, Aviacsa has one cross-border route to Las Vegas.

Mexicana
1-800-531-7921 (U.S.)
599-848-5998 (Mexico City)
1-800-801-2010 toll-free in Mexico
www.mexicana.com
Mexicana has the most extensive international coverage from Mexico.

U.S. AIRLINES

Alaska Airlines
1-800-252-7522 (U.S.)
www.alaskaair.com

American Airlines
1-800-433-7300 (U.S)
555-209-1400 (Mexico City)
1-800-904-6000 toll-free in Mexico
www.aa.com

Continental Airlines
1-800-523-3273 (U.S.)
555-283-5500 (Mexico City)
1-800-900-5000 toll-free in Mexico
www.continental.com

Delta Air Lines
1-800-221-1212 (U.S.)
555-279-0909 (Mexico City)
1-800-123-4710 toll-free in Mexico
www.delta.com

Northwest Airlines/KLM
1-800-225-2525 (U.S.)
555-279-5390 (Mexico City)
1-800-907-4700 toll-free in Mexico
www.nwa.com

United Airlines
1-800-864-8331 (U.S.)
555-627-0222 (Mexico City)
1-800-003-0777 toll-free in Mexico
www.ual.com

US Airways
1-800-428-4322 (U.S.)
www.airways.com

INTERNATIONAL AIRLINES

Air Canada
1-888-247-2262 (U.S. and Canada)
555-208-1883 (Mexico)
www.aircanada.com

Air France
1-800-992-3932 (U.S.)
555-627-6060 (Mexico)
www.airfrance.com.mx

British Airways
1-800-247-9297 (U.S.)
1-866-835-4133 toll-free in Mexico
www.britishairways.com

Iberia
1-800-772-4642 (U.S.)
551-101-1515 (Mexico)
www.iberia.com

Japan Air Lines
1-800-525-3663 (U.S.)
555-242-0150 (Mexico)
www.jal.com

Lufthansa
1-800-399-5838 (U.S.)
555-230-0000 (Mexico)
www.lufthansa.com

Qantas
1-800-227-4500 (U.S.)
1-800-892-9761 toll-free in Mexico
www.qantas.com.au

Taca
1-800-400-TACA (U.S.)
555-553-3366 (Mexico City)
1-800-400-8222 toll-free in Mexico
www.taca.com

BY LAND: Again, I urge tourists not to travel by car to the regions covered in this book unless they are coming for a long stay and plan to tour the country extensively. Why am I so adamant? Let's start with the paperwork. At the border checkpoint, travelers are required to present the original and two copies of the following documents:

- Valid proof of citizenship (passport or birth certificate)
- The Mexican Tourist Permit (FMT)

- A valid vehicle registration certificate or a document, such as the vehicle's title, which certifies legal ownership by the driver
- A leasing contract, if the vehicle is leased or rented, in the name of the renter. If the vehicle belongs to a company, you must have documentation that certifies your employment with that company.
- A valid driver's license
- An international credit card in the name of the driver of the vehicle

Drivers also need a temporary car importation permit. To acquire this, you have to bring all these documents to the customs office at the border. Go through the Declarations Lane and look for the MODULO DE CONTROL VEHICULAR sign. Your life will be a lot easier if you have a credit card, which you can use to post the required "return guarantee" bond. Otherwise, you'll have to leave a guarantee deposit based on the model year of the vehicle. In Texas, California, and Illinois, drivers can arrange for the certificate and payments in advance from the Mexican consulate. **Note: The owner of the car or a relative must be in it at all times while it's being driven in Mexico.** Drivers must also get their vehicle insured in Mexico, as liability insurance is mandatory and U.S. coverage is invalid. U.S. companies that provide insurance in Mexico are located at the border.

Then there's the driving time, which can vary from 12 to 48 hours from the border. From the city of Juárez, for example, Mexico City is roughly 23 hours away. From Los Angeles to Cancún, it's easily over 40 hours.

Finally, rentals are readily available once you get here, and bus travel around Mexico is excellent.

MEXICO'S BUS SYSTEM IS CLEAN, EFFICIENT, EXTENSIVE, AND ECONOMICAL

Israel Kumul

TRAVELER ESSENTIALS AND TIPS

There are many preconceived notions about traveling to Mexico, from near-death horror stories of consuming the local food, to getting ripped off everywhere you go, to kidnappings and worse. Unfortunately, these stories often have more than a grain of truth to them. At the same time, a bit of common sense will enable you to avoid many of the pitfalls that snare the less savvy tourist.

SAFETY Safety is a major concern for most Americans traveling to Mexico. A healthy paranoia about visiting this country, and especially its capital, reached new heights during Mexico's swine flu epidemic. But the basic fact is that millions of U.S. citizens visit Mexico every year without incident, and the regions that comprise Maya Mexico are generally considered among the safest parts of the country. For every horror story, there are many more tales of wonderful vacations.

A September 2010 travel warning issued by the Department of State cautioned U.S. travelers specifically against traveling to the border cities, where a vicious drug war has raged since 2006, when Presidente Felipe Calderón vowed to crack down on the cartels. The report cautioned against travel to Monterrey, Tamaulipas, parts of Chihuahua, Sinaloa, Durango, and Coahuila. No specific reference was made to the areas covered in this book, and these cities are far from Mexico City and the Yucatán peninsula.

Tourists should always exercise caution in any foreign country. In Mexico City, the most frequent incidents are mugging, armed robbery, and kidnapping. A common practice for the latter involves taxis, especially green-and-white Volkswagen Beetles (although have been almost completely phased out in favor of newer models). The way the scam works is as follows: A taxi picks up an unsuspecting passenger and follows a predetermined route. At a prearranged intersection, armed men jump in the cab and mug or kidnap the victim. For this reason, it cannot be stressed enough that tourists should rely on radio taxis when they are in Mexico City.

As soon as you check into your hotel, it's a good idea to lock your extra cash, valuables, and passport in your room safe (if you have one). A few other precautions to follow while in Mexico:

- When driving, use main roads whenever possible; when driving longer distances, especially at night, use toll roads.
- If possible, carry a cell phone with international coverage. If you don't have one of these, buy a phone card, which are widely available.
- Remember three numbers:
    - 060 for reporting crime
    - 065 for the Red Cross and ambulance service
    - 078 for tourist assistance
- In the city, try to stay in well-lit areas at night, and keep to secure neighborhoods.
- Always keep the phone number and address of your hotel handy; many hotels have keycards with this information printed on them.
- Before you go, check the latest U.S. State Department travel advisories to Mexico at www.travel.state.gov.

MONEY MATTERS The currency of Mexico is the peso. It is indicated by the $ symbol and the code MXN. As of this printing, $1 USD was the equivalent of about $12 MXN. While there are some businesses that will take payment in dollars, expect to pay in pesos everywhere you go.

You can change money at banks or *casas de cambio* (money-changing booths). In the cities, these are usually a short walk away; in rural areas, they're more spread out. If the line at the bank is long, *casas de cambio* are almost always quick and they're open later. Cash in Spanish is known as *efectivo.* When it comes to your *efectivo,* a useful tip is to horde your change. Buses, taxis, and taquerias all crave or require it, and you'll need plenty for tips.

Credit cards are widely accepted in most tourist areas and major cities, MasterCard and Visa more than American Express. A few exceptions are Isla Holbox and the more rural parts of Campeche and Chiapas. Cards are called *tarjetas de crédito.* Some establishments will add a small surcharge (3 to 6 percent) to your bill if you're paying by card. You can use ATMs, and some banks also issue cash advances on credit card accounts.

Determining a budget is a tough thing to do in Mexico. Depending on

EVEN SITES AS IMPRESSIVE AND IMPORTANT AS PALENQUE CHARGE ONLY A NOMINAL ENTRY FEE.

where you are, your expenses may range from minimal to exorbitant. The good news is, the archaeological sites are all cheap, and you can tailor your vacation to just about any budget you set, even in the ritzy Riviera Maya. If that means a steady diet of street food, there are worse fates.

A 10 to 15 percent tip is customary and expected at restaurants and hotels, and at the end of tours, but not at taco stands, inexpensive eateries, or taxis. Still, a tip is always appreciated. A 15 percent Value Added Tax, known as *impuesto al valor agregado* (IVA) is added to all goods and services purchased in Mexico. Hotels add an additional 2 percent lodging tax.

Mexico also has a Tax Back tax refund service. When you shop at affiliated Tax Back stores (look for the Tax Back logo), ask for an official invoice. (Your purchases must be greater than $1,200 pesos and up to $3,000 pesos if paid in cash, no limit if paid by credit card.) At the airport, present your invoices along with your passport, a copy of your immigration form (make a copy before you go to the airport), your boarding pass, and the bank account number or credit card number where you want the refund to be deposited. For more information, visit www.taxback.com.mx.

MEXICAN FOOD, MEXICAN DRINK

Mexican food has been as misrepresented as the land it comes from. The cuisine of this county far exceeds tacos, burritos, and enchiladas, and even those don't look anything like what we're used to in the United States. Mexico's culinary roots span millennia and incorporate ingredients, recipes, and techniques from the Aztecs, the Maya, the Spanish, the French, and the United States (when McDonald's first opened in Mexico City, there was a line around the block to get in).

Cuisine in Mexico also varies with each region. For example, Mexico City cuisine uses plenty of *flor de calabaza* (squash blossom), *nopales* (the fleshy pads of the cactus), and *cuitlacoche* (a trufflelike fungus found on corn). The Yucatán has its own traditions, such as roast suckling pig cooked in an achiote-based sauce. Campeche is known for its seafood. Of course, the nation's most essential foods and ingredients—including tortillas, tamales, cocoa, corn, and chile—are basic staples of the country, and come from its indigenous peoples.

The Spanish brought other essentials, including beef, pork, rice, garlic, and oil. Their influence, along with later contributions by other cultures (including African, Asian, and other European nations), greatly expanded Mexican gastronomy. This diverse legacy has produced a broad range of cuisine, from strips of meat slapped together between a tortilla to refined dishes that use techniques and flavors subtle enough to please the most discriminating gourmand.

Sampling all of these flavors and delicacies is one of the joys of traveling to Mexico, but to really enjoy the experience, be a bit adventurous. Some of the delicacies available to you will range from eyebrow-raising to run-for-the-door. Then there's the language. Even if you know Spanish, you'll be dumbfounded by many items on the menu, either because they are in Nahuatl or Maya (if you can figure out what goes into *poc chuc* from your Spanish class, I'll be extremely impressed).

A VENDOR IN MÉRIDA SELLS HABANERO CHILES.

As for what to drink, alcohol goes back to the pre-Columbian tribes, but they went about things a little differently. The Aztecs only allowed the priest class and the elderly to drink; every one else faced capital punishment for their alcoholic binges. Modern Mexicans have more variety and more lenient rules. The locals love their *cerveza,* or beer, which is available just about everywhere. Then there's a smorgasbord of local liquor, starting with the world-famous tequila, which has been around for over 400 years, and of which there are over 700 varieties. Tequila is made from the blue agave plant. The spirit is generally found in two categories: 100% blue agave and *mixto* (mixed). Within these categories, there are finer distinctions:

Tequila blanco: (White tequila) The purest form of the blue agave, clear and not aged

Tequila joven abocado: A gold-colored, young, and relatively inexpensive variety

Tequila reposado: A popular golden variety aged between two and 11 months

TEQUILA LEADS THE WAY FOR MEXICO'S FAVORITE LIBATIONS.

Tequila añejo: A refined, rich, and smooth spirit that must be aged for at least one year

Tequila extra añejo: A classification given to tequilas aged more than three years, with a darker hue than regular añejo

After tequila comes a parade of Mexican liquors. Mescal is a cousin of tequila, a strong liquor made from different types of maguey plants. Pulque, the fermented sap of the agave plant, has a nutty flavor; the best place to find one, both for variety and local ambience, is at a *pulquería.* Pasita is a liqueur made from raisins. The Yucatán produces an anise-based liqueur called Xtabentún. And *aguardiente,* which is typically made from sugar cane, begins at around 75 proof. It's not called "firewater" for nothing. There are also several other regional brews.

Finally, a host of other liquors are popular here: brandy, Kahlúa, Cointreau, wine (specified as *vino de uva,* or grape wine), and a variety of mixed drinks and cocktails. The most famous of these is the margarita.

Also take your gastronomic tour of Mexico in gradual steps. Heading from the airport directly to the nearest taco stand isn't the wisest move on your first trip. Here are a few tips to help keep you healthy as you dine your way through Mexico:

- The easiest and most important is to never drink tap water. Many hotels and restaurants serve purified water, but to play it safe, always order bottled water.
- Try to avoid spices and raw vegetables until you're completely acclimated.
- Practically every restaurant in Mexico has fresh limes on the table; make liberal use of them.

Even with these precautions, your body will need time to adjust to its new environment, and that includes adjusting to new foods; but even if Montezuma wags his finger in your direction and you feel a little unsettled, it's a good idea to persevere. Mexican food is worth the initial trouble!

"MONTEZUMA'S REVENGE"

"Montezuma's Revenge" is the popular term among foreigners for the potent and unpleasant effects of consuming unhygienic food or drinking unclean water. The Mexicans call it *turista.* The symptoms include nausea, diarrhea, stomach cramps, and fever. If your condition is severe, visit a doctor.

Can you avoid it? Yes and no. Some tourists, especially those traveling abroad for the first time, will have an adverse reaction to foods that are so foreign to them. It's impossible to predict exactly how your stomach will respond, but follow the tips outlined above and you might keep Montezuma's vengeful spirit away.

✱ Special Events and Holidays

There are literally thousands of festivals, parades, and parties in the country each year; these are among the biggest and the most beloved.

January 1: **Año Nuevo** (New Year's Day), a national holiday, a day when many a hangover is nursed back to health.

January 6: **Día de Los Reyes** (Three Kings Day), traditionally the gift-giving day in Mexico, rather than December 25.

February 2: **Día de Candelaria** (Candlemas), a nationwide celebration marking the end of winter and honoring the rebirth and fertility of the land.

February 5: **Día de la Constitución** (Constitution Day), a national holiday commemorating the ratification of the Mexican constitution in 1917.

February: **Carnaval**; the date varies—takes place in the weekend before Lent

February 24: **Flag Day—**A nationwide holiday when public figures outdo one another in their efforts to proclaim their patriotism.

March 21: **Benito Juárez's Birthday**, a national holiday to honor one of Mexico's most revered leaders.

March/April: **Semana Santa** (Holy Week), the most popular religious celebration in Mexico, marked by pilgrimages, huge masses, and parades.

May 1: **Día del Trabajo** (Labor Day), a national holiday

May 5: **Cinco de Mayo**, celebrated around the United States (and Cancún) as a time to get drunk. Most people don't know that the holiday marks a historic battle between French and Mexican troops in Puebla.

May 10: **Día de la Madre** (Mother's Day). Moms are venerated in Mexico.

September 1: **Presidential "State of the Nation,"** a great time to be in Mexico City's Zócalo to hear the president wax poetic . . . or passionate . . . or loquacious.

September 15–16: **Independence Day**. Celebrated in every nook and cranny of Mexico, these two days honor the end of Spanish rule in Mexico. In Mexico City's Zócalo, the president gives El Grito (The Cry), echoing Miguel Hidalgo's cry for independence in 1810.

November 1–2: **Días de los Muertos** (Days of the Dead), my favorite holiday in Mexico. The first is All Saints' Day, while the second is the official Day of the Dead. Skeleton costumes abound, parades are held, and people throw open their homes to strangers bearing offerings for the dead.

November 20: **Día de la Revolución** (Revolution Day), another national holiday where politicians take center stage and launch patriotic speeches.

December 12: **Feast of the Virgin of Guadalupe** and also **Flag Day**. One of the most important religious holidays in the country, December 12 brings an annual horde of people to La Virgen's shrine in Mexico City.

AN EASTER PARADE IN MEXICO CITY

Mexico Tourism Board

December 16: Christmas season begins, stretching from December 16 to January 6, and including parades, processions, and parties:

- Beginning on December 16, there are nine days of **posadas**—candlelight processions that travel to a community's nativity scene montage or a neighbor's home, reenacting Joseph and Mary's search for lodging.
- On **Nochebuena** (Christmas Eve), a midnight mass called Misa del Gallo (Rooster's Mass) is held, with masses continuing throughout Christmas Day.
- December 28 is the **Día de los Inocentes** (Day of the Innocents), Mexico's April Fool's Day.
- January 6 is **Día de los Reyes** (Three Kings Day), the most important day of the season, when gifts are traditionally exchanged and families eat a special cake called *rosca de reyes* (kings' wreath), a large doughnut-shaped fruitcake into which is baked a small figure of a baby. The person who gets the slice with the baby has the responsibility of throwing a party on (or before) **Candelaria** (Candlemas). This is the last bash of the season.

December 31: **New Year's Eve**, a night of revelry and partying, to close the chapter on the old and welcome the new. In Mexico, it's called Nochevieja (Old Night).

Chiapas 4

CHIAPAS

Mountain, valley, jungle, river, waterfall—these are my primary associations and most vivid images of Chiapas, which quickly became my favorite state in Mexico for its spectacular geography, awe-inspiring archaeological sites, and quaint colonial cities.

This is a large state whose riches are spread far apart; as such, distances must be factored in when planning your trip. Also, I strongly recommend renting a car: While the drive can get a bit hair-raising on the winding curves through the mountains, the freedom of seeing what Chiapas has to offer at your own pace beats the reliance on numerous tours. Either way, yours will be a nomadic experience, as you hop from quaint colonial city to mighty Maya capital, modern era to ancient glory, through the mountains and over the rivers.

THE LAND AND ITS PEOPLE

Chiapas is the southernmost state in Mexico, and closer to neighboring Guatemala than it is to Mexico City. In fact, Chiapanecos will tell you they are "Mexican by decision, not obligation." During the colonial era, this territory was administered by the Captaincy General of Guatemala. But in 1824, the state chose to annex itself to the fledgling United States of Mexico.

This is a beautiful land with a tropical climate and some of the most breathtaking landscapes in all of Mexico, a back-to-nature charm, and an undeniable sense of Mexican mysticism. Chiapas is also an interesting mix of cultures and a very Maya melting pot. The state is home to the Choles, the remnants of the mighty people who built Palenque and Yaxchilán; the Tzeltales and Tzotziles, who live in the highlands in the north and east; Tojolabales, who inhabit the Comitan plains; the Mames, who live in the mountains of the Sierra Madre; the reclusive Lacandón, who make the jungles around Bonampak their home; and the Zoques, who reside in the

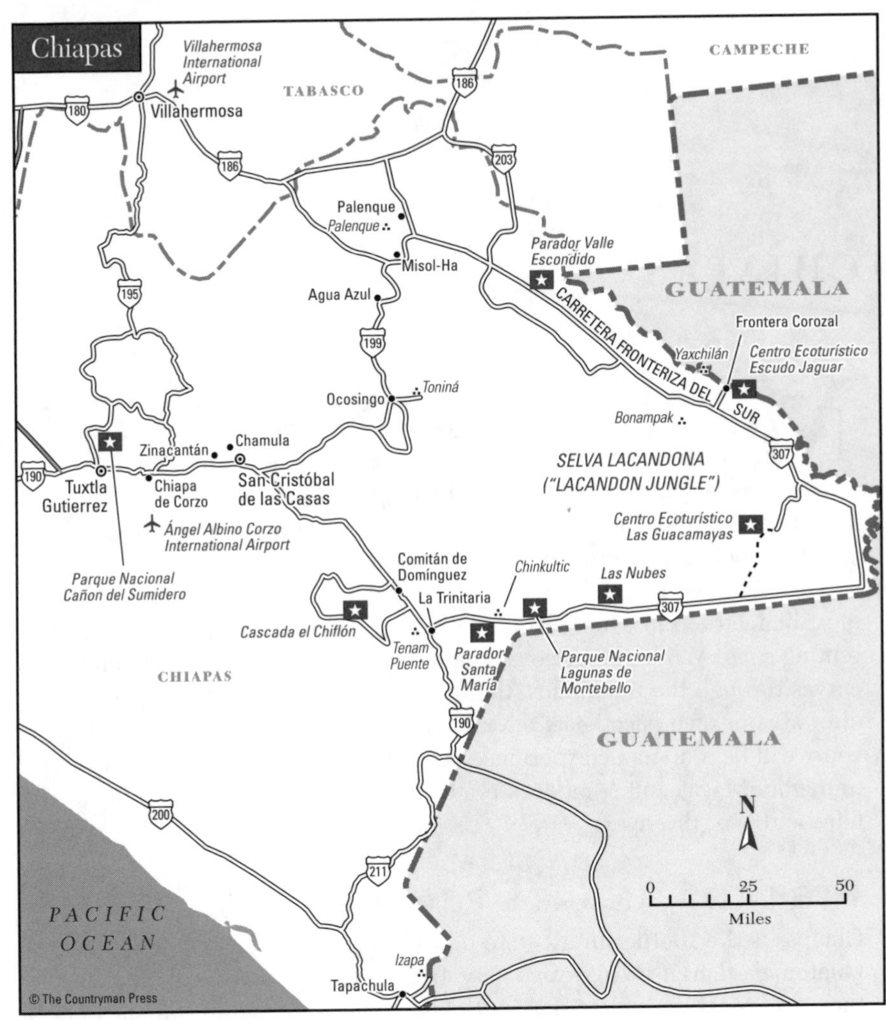

northwest. These disparate descendants give us insight into Chiapas's ancient status in the Maya world.

They also represent a strong and proud indigenous community with a history of disenfranchisement, resistance, and strained relations with the federal government. In 1868, the Tzotzil Maya led a native rebellion that had to be put down by the Mexican army. More recently, the Ejército Zapatista de Liberación Nacional (Zapatista National Liberation Army, or EZLN), more commonly known as the Zapatistas, launched an armed rebellion against the federal government on January 1, 1994, to combat what they felt were economic policies (NAFTA included) that crippled the indigenous population. Led by the masked and infamous Subcomandante

THE GEOGRAPHY OF CHIAPAS IS ONE OF JUNGLES, RIVERS, WATERFALLS, AND MOUNTAINS.

Marcos, the Zapatistas made headlines around the world for their bold and often violent clashes with the Mexican army. Across Chiapas, you'll find graffiti proclaiming support of the EZLN. The good news is that the Zapatistas have become more political party than guerrilla group, but their presence in Chiapas remains strong.

That said, I wouldn't hesitate to encourage you to explore this part of Mexico. While you're at it, you'll have the chance to enjoy Chiapas's astounding natural wonders and colonial charm.

Tuxtla Gutiérrez has been the state capital since 1893, but far more appealing to tourists are the beautiful cities of **San Cristóbal de las Casas** and **Chiapa de Corzo**. However, given how spread out the archaeological sites of Chiapas are, my recommendation in this state is to drive around, staying at various places along the way.

GETTING THERE AND GETTING AROUND *By air:* Chiapas is served by two main airports: **Ángel Albino Corzo International Airport**, also known as **Tuxtla Gutiérrez**, which is the largest airport in the state; and **Carlos Rovirosa Pérez International Airport**, also known as

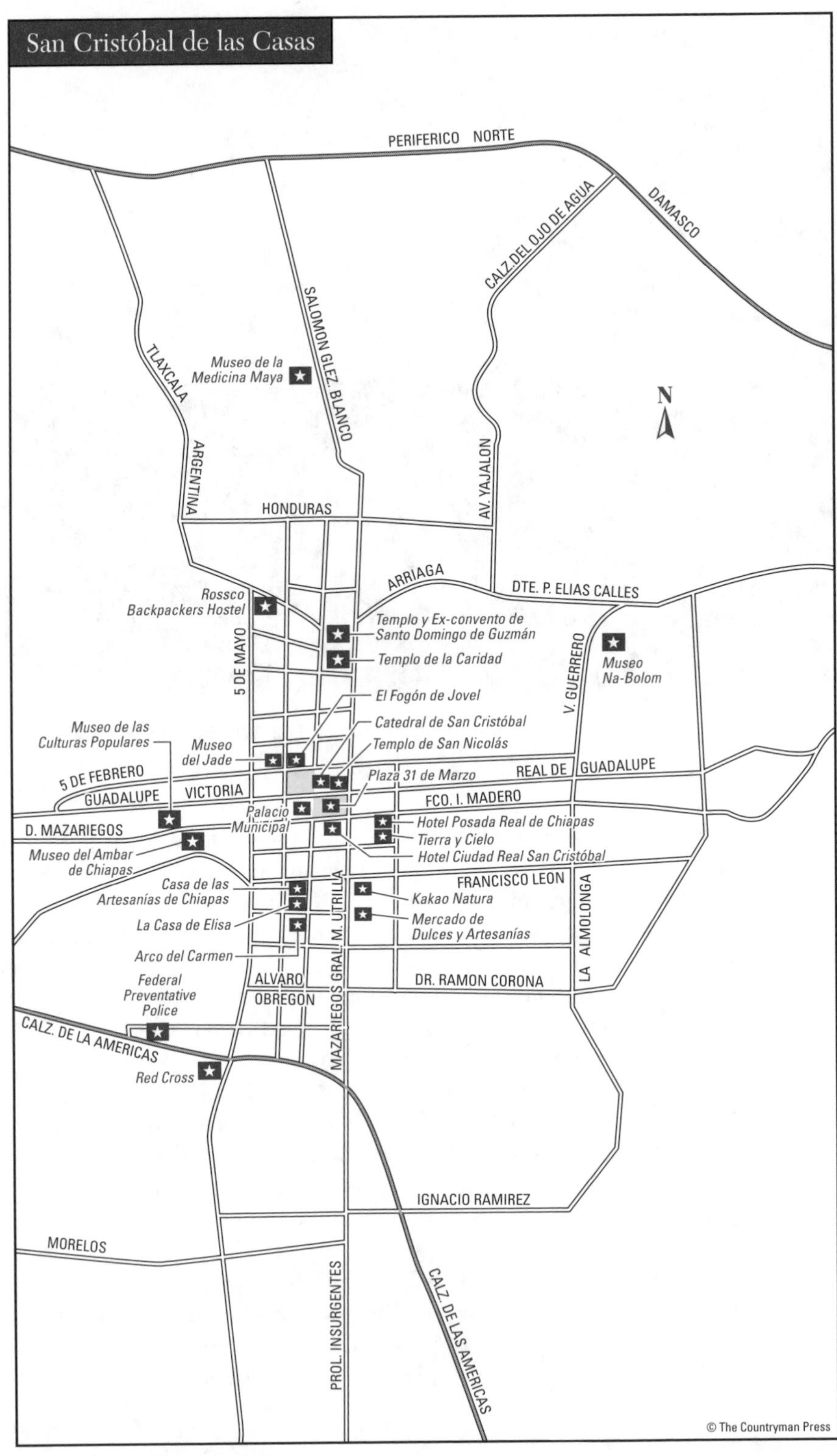
San Cristóbal de las Casas
PERIFERICO NORTE
DAMASCO
CALZ.DEL OJO DE AGUA
SALOMON GLEZ. BLANCO
TLAXCALA
Museo de la Medicina Maya
N
ARGENTINA
AV. YAJALON
HONDURAS
ARRIAGA
DTE. P. ELIAS CALLES
Rossco Backpackers Hostel
Templo y Ex-convento de Santo Domingo de Guzmán
Templo de la Caridad
5 DE MAYO
V. GUERRERO
Museo Na-Bolom
El Fogón de Jovel
Catedral de San Cristóbal
Museo de las Culturas Populares
Museo del Jade
Templo de San Nicolás
5 DE FEBRERO
Plaza 31 de Marzo
REAL DE GUADALUPE
GUADALUPE
VICTORIA
FCO. I. MADERO
Palacio Municipal
D. MAZARIEGOS
Hotel Posada Real de Chiapas
Tierra y Cielo
Museo del Ambar de Chiapas
Hotel Ciudad Real San Cristóbal
FRANCISCO LEON
Casa de las Artesanías de Chiapas
Kakao Natura
La Casa de Elisa
Mercado de Dulces y Artesanías
LA ALMOLONGA
Arco del Carmen
MAZARIEGOS GRAL. M. UTRILLA
Federal Preventative Police
ALVARO OBREGON
DR. RAMON CORONA
CALZ. DE LA AMERICAS
Red Cross
IGNACIO RAMIREZ
MORELOS
PROL. INSURGENTES
CALZ. DE LAS AMERICAS
© The Countryman Press

Villahermosa International Airport, in the neighboring state of Tabasco, which lies closer to Palenque. For the purposes of this book, I recommend flying into Villahermosa. From Mexico City, Aeroméxico and Mexicana have frequent flights to the city; Continental Airlines also has direct flights to the airport from Houston.

By car: Renting a car gives you the freedom to explore Chiapas and is particularly useful if you plan to travel on to Campeche and Yucatán. Although the main roads are in decent shape, travelers must bear in mind a few basic facts:

- Distances are great, as much as five or six hours between destinations.
- Roads winding around the mountains can be treacherous, especially if they succumb to a sudden and ferocious downpour.
- The ubiquitous infernal speedbumps will slow you down and generally irritate you.
- You'll occasionally run into military checkpoints, with soldiers sometimes stopping cars for inspection; if this happens, don't panic and don't worry; they aren't looking for tourists, and will likely perform a review of your vehicle and wave you on.

✷ Archaeological Sites

Sites in Chiapas are open daily 8–5 and charge a nominal fee.

Palenque

GETTING THERE By car, you can reach the city of Palenque via Highway 199 from Tuxtla Gutíerrez or Highway 114 from Villahermosa. Once you reach town, drive east on Juarez and take the fork in the road to Palenque ruins. You can also take a taxi from the ADO bus station and the town plaza, or grab a *colectivo* with destination "Ruinas" across the street from the bus station.

I'm giving Palenque its own space atop the ladder of Chiapas's archaeological sites, due to its tremendous importance to archaeologists, its significance as an ancient capital, and its undeniable beauty. In the entire Maya world, there is nothing quite like Palenque.

The ancient city lies nestled against a backdrop of lush verdant hills, its stark white buildings standing out dramatically against the green canvas. Palenque was occupied as far back as 100 BC, but grew during the early Classic period and reached its zenith during the late Classic. The city once ruled over present-day Chiapas and Tabasco, had more than a thousand buildings, and featured a distinct architectural style that showcased the refined skill of its builders and artists. Most representative of this style were the roofs; tall, pierced cresting; elaborate stucco reliefs; and false façades.

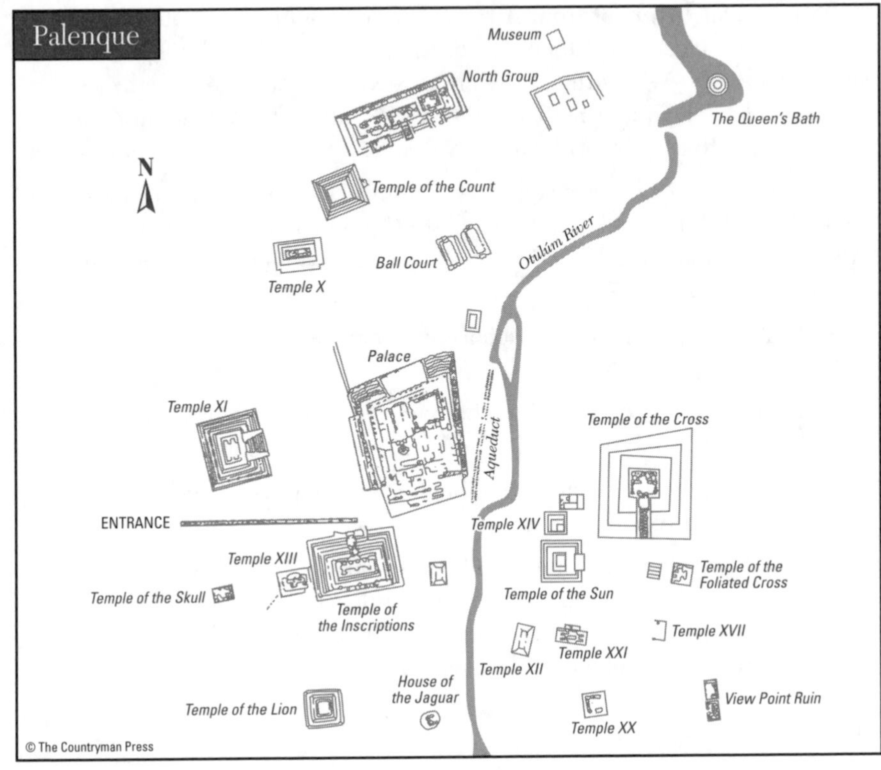

There's an undeniable aura around Palenque, and even though only a fraction of its ancient urban sprawl has been uncovered, these few remnants give you an idea of how awe-inspiring the city must have been.

Your first stop, once you pass the crowd of vendors, tour guides, and other hawkers, is the **Templo de la Calavera** (Temple of the Skull), named for the skull-shaped stucco relief (believed to be a rabbit skull) that can be seen on a portico. Adjacent to this is **Temple XIII**, which connects the Temple of the Skull to the **Temple of the Inscriptions**.

Fronting the great square, this is one of the most important buildings in all Mesoamerica. I say this because, as breathtaking as Palenque is from the outside, its true treasure lay in the Temple of the Inscriptions. It was here that Mexican archaeologist Alberto Ruiz, in 1952, made one of the most groundbreaking discoveries in Maya history: the fabulous, monolithic funerary crypt of Palenque's greatest ruler, K'inich Janahb' Pakal, better known as Pakal the Great. This august ruler was buried in a massive tomb along with a priceless collection of jade, including a now-famous jade mask.

Along with Palenque, crypts found under temples at Tikal and Calakmul gives ample credence to the belief that Maya temple-pyramids doubled as funerary monuments; this has been corroborated by finds throughout the Maya empire. But nowhere else in Mesoamerica has a tomb as rich and detailed as Pakal's been found, making this temple, his final resting place, a priceless treasure of the Maya world.

The Temple of the Inscriptions was built in 692, after the sarcophagus and crypt had been built. It is named for the 620 glyphs carved on the portico and inside the structure (this section is closed to the public).

Perpendicular to the Temple of the Inscriptions, the **Palace** is Palenque's most iconic building. An immense and intricate complex, the Palace features an unusual four-story square-shaped tower—a unique structure in the Maya world—that may have served as a watchtower, although many believe it was used as an observatory. The windows of this tower are all perfectly aligned, evidence of the skill of its architects.

The Palace's importance to the city is evident; around it are corridors, residential spaces and numerous patios, places where the city's elite lived and governed. Note in particular the Oval Panel depicting the ascension of the ruler Pakal to the throne, presided over by his mother, Sac K'uk'.

THE TEMPLE OF THE INSCRIPTIONS

THE TEMPLE OF THE SUN

Beyond the Palace and Temple of Inscriptions, a winding path leads to a remarkable cluster of three temple-pyramids known as the Temples of the Cross Group. These buildings were erected following Pakal's death by his son, Chan Bahlum II (Serpent Jaguar). Built around an open plaza, the three structures of this group are the **Temple of the Sun**, **Temple of the Cross**, and **Temple of the Foliated Cross**. The Temple of the Sun, the smallest of the three, is one of the most completely preserved buildings in Palenque. Designed to represent the Underworld (where the Sun went after each day), the temple is identified by a relief of the Sun ascending to the throne. The cross in the Maya world represents the Earth, the midpoint between heaven and the Underworld. The Temple of the Cross is the largest of the three buildings, a towering structure that offers panoramic views of the city. At the summit is a shrine flanked by two reliefs: a god smoking tobacco, and Chan Bahlum.

Tucked into the hill, the Temple of the Foliated Cross (representing leaves of corn, key to life) holds an impressive tablet that depicts Chan Bahlum's enthronement, with his father in attendance. During the summer solstice, the temple's inner sanctuary is dramatically lit by the sun.

Beyond this cluster lies the North Group of buildings, which includes a modest ball court and the **Temple of the Count**, so named for the French count Jean-Frédéric Waldek, who moved in for two years when he was working on the site.

From here, walk down, past a second residential complex, to the foot of the city, which leads to the **Museo del Sitio** (Site Museum). Don't miss a trip to this excellent facility, which includes numerous artifacts (check out the marvelous display of incense burners) and a meticulous re-creation and interpretation of Pakal's tomb.

Bonampak

GETTING THERE Bonampak lies about 92 miles from Palenque, and will take you about three hours by car. Stay on Highway 199 and follow signs for the ruins. There is also third-class bus service from Palenque, but the service is spotty.

Nestled in the heart of the Lacandón jungle, the largest area of high forest in Mexico, Bonampak was a ceremonial center whose importance stretched from the early to the late Classic era. An ally and satellite of nearby Yaxchilán, Bonampak reached its zenith during the rule of Chaan Muan II, its last governor, who reigned from 776 to 792 (another lord, Jaguar-Knotted Eye, also features prominently).

The city is another of the many sites in this region that lie mostly undiscovered, with little beyond the buildings around the main plaza open to visitors. Its architectural wealth lies in its brilliant, vibrant and detailed murals, which have been wonderfully preserved through the centuries, as well as its stelae.

CHAAN MUAN II DEPICTED ON STELA 1

Before you ascend the acropolis, notice the large **Stela 1** in the plaza, which was commissioned by Chaan Muan II and depicts him in glorious fashion, clutching his ceremonial staff and standing over the Monster of the Earth. This stela also features the all-important emblem glyph of the city, underscoring Palenque's importance, and the date AD 781, five years into the realm of Chaan Muan II. **Stelae 2** and **3** are located on the Acropolis. The former is very elaborate and shows Chaan Muan II performing a self-sacrifice ritual, using a stingray spine, accompanied by his wife and mother. The latter stela shows the ruler with a captive (captives are always depicted with a hand on the captor's shoulder).

THE ARCHAEOLOGICAL SITE OF BONAMPAK

Bonampak means "Painted Walls," and the frescoes inside the **Temple of the Paintings** (Building 1) are truly spectacular. The temple is divided into three chambers, each depicting a different scene of a pictoral story starring Chaan Muan II. In the first, the heir to the throne is presented by his family in a grand celebration complete with a procession of musicians; note, as you enter, the musicians spreading out from the doorway to your left and right. This is designed to make visitors feel like part of the festivities as soon as they enter. The second chamber chronicles a great battle that took place in 792. Chaan Muan II, attired with a jaguar-skin headdress, emerges victorious, and the chamber is filled

THE OUTSTANDING MURALS MAKE BONAMPAK A WONDER OF THE MAYA WORLD.

with prisoners who are depicted being captured, sacrificed, and executed. Again, the room is designed to make the visitor feel part of the battle, this time flanked by two warriors. The last chamber shows the postwar celebration with musicians and plenty of revelry (this time, you're surrounded by dancers). Chaan Muan II can be seen performing a ritual self-sacrifice.

I can't write about Bonampak without mentioning the people who claim to be the direct descendants of its founders: the Lacandón Maya. Dressed in long white tunics, Lacandón guides are on hand to take you around the site, or, for a steeper price, on a longer tour of Bonampak and a jungle walk where you'll find other vestiges of ancient Maya sites. Also, at the entrance of the site is a series of dioramas representing Lacandón life and the fabulous natural richness of their environment.

Chinkultik

GETTING THERE Chinkultik is located about 28 miles east of Comitán, east of Highway 190 along the Carretera de la Trinitaria.

A small, rarely visited site, Chinkultik (whose name means "terraced well") is located close to the city of Comitán. A contemporary of Bonampak, Chinkultik was also a ceremonial center. Most noteworthy here is the Acropolis, which hugs the hillside and gives you sweeping views of the impressive surrounding countryside. The temple at the top overlooks a sheer drop to a large blue *cenote*, or sinkhole. Bones found in the well lend credence to the theory that virgin maidens were thrown from the temple into the water. On the way to the Acropolis, you'll pass a sunken plaza surrounded by stone stairways and half-hidden pyramids. A side path to the left of the rough stairs leading to the Acropolis takes you to one of three ball courts (the only one open to the public) and a second plaza.

Tenam Puente

GETTING THERE Tenam Puente lies just over 6 miles south of Comitán, off Highway 190.

Another site that doesn't get the traffic it deserves, Tenam Puente impresses both in size and significance. Its name is derived from the Nahua word for "fort" and an old estate named "The Bridge." The first archaeologists on the scene were Frans Blom and Oliver La Farge, in 1925. They discovered a city occupying 1.24 square miles that served as a residential, civic, and ceremonial center. Tenam Puente reached its apogee during the late Classic period (AD 600–900), and appeared to have been a major commercial capital.

TENAM PUENTE WAS A LARGE RELIGIOUS, CEREMONIAL, AND CIVIC CENTER

The most important temples and buildings are grouped together in the Acropolis. I love how the forest has been allowed to grow among and around the ruins, including the middle of one of the three ball courts; while this is an inaccurate depiction of the city during its zenith, it makes for a pleasant and scenic change.

Within the Acropolis, **Buildings 11**, **7**, and **17** stand out. Building 11 features distinct archaeological styles, including the *talud-tablero* slope-and-panel combination common in Central Mexico, placing its construction in the Postclassic period. The importance of Building 7 can be measured by the human burials and offerings discovered here. Building 17 has a large rectangular base and the ruins of a temple. At the foot of the structure, a tomb was discovered containing a sculpture of a decapitated prisoner.

Tenam Puente has long been abandoned, but it continues to hold spiritual significance for nearby communities. Each year on May 3, the Day of the Holy Cross, ritual ceremonies are performed here by residents of nearby Francisco Sarabia. In August, ritual prayers are offered to honor the Virgin of the Heart of Mary.

Toniná

GETTING THERE Toniná lies just outside the town of Ocosingo, which lies between Palenque and San Cristóbal on Highway 199. Once you reach the town, follow the signs for the ruins, which lie east of Ocosingo.

Toniná ranks among my favorite sites in Chiapas for its unique construction, dominating façade, spectacular murals, and, above all, for the bells and whistles that allowed its rulers to pull off a bit of magic for their subjects.

Looking at the mighty Acropolis rising above the treetops, you would naturally suspect it was built on a mountain. In actuality, recent studies by archaeologist Dr. Carlos Pallan Gayol have discovered that the Acropolis at Toniná *is* the mountain. The entire structure is man-made, comprising

THE CRESTED ROOF OF ONE OF THE TEMPLES ON TONINÁ'S MASSIVE ACROPOLIS

seven platforms and artificial terraces, and reaching 246 feet (75 meters) high. That's 5 meters higher than the Temple of the Sun at Teotihuacán, making the Acropolis at Toniná one of the grandest structures in Mesoamerica.

Impressive as it is for its size, equally astounding is the way it was built. The Acropolis is a veritable warren of temples (13 to be exact, the same number as the levels of the heavens), palaces, residential complexes, sanitary facilities, sacred sanctuaries, and other buildings, all incorporated into one monolithic building. The right side of the structure was dedicated to the nobility; the left, to warriors and workers. It even had a dike system designed to supply water year-round.

The last Maya date at Toniná is AD 909, considered the last inscribed date of the Classic Maya period. The city dates from 100 BC but flourished from AD 250 to 800, making it a contemporary of Palenque, Tikal, Bonampak, and Teotihuacán. Of these, Toniná was also one of the last to be abandoned.

Your first stop at the site is the large **Ball Court**, which lies intentionally half-overgrown with grass. (There are two schools of thought when it comes to archaeology in Mexico: those who believe in total restoration, such as at Chichén Itzá, and those who favor partial restoration, which looks imperfect but is, perhaps, a more authentic effort at preservation; Toniná is an example of the latter.) The site has a second, smaller ball court believed to be a practice court.

Next on your tour will be the **Altar of Sacrifices**; Toniná favored decapitation of its victims, and it is important to note that prisoners who were sacrificed died with honor; the sacrifice gave value to their lives. As you climb the Acropolis's platforms, you'll come upon various important structures. The third platform is home to the **Palace of the Underworld**, which in its time was covered in red paint and stucco. You can see windows in the shape a cross here, a representation of the four cardinal points.

On the fourth platform lies the **Temple of Frets (Grecas) and War**, easily spotted for the giant mural representing the four cardinal points. On the eastern side of the temple, under a thatched roof, you'll find the remains of an elaborate throne decorated in stucco. And here is where one of Toniná's coolest secrets reveals itself. Note to the right of the throne a passageway leading into the Acropolis. The governors used these secret tunnels ingeniously; sitting on the throne before their subjects, they would vanish and "reappear" upon a different platform without the watching masses in the plaza ever knowing how they got there. This bit of trickery was a powerful tool used to convince the population of the governor's power and divinity.

Continue heading east and you'll arrive at a residential complex built for the city's elite (ask your guide to show you the lavatory in one of the open chambers). Following a few spectacular stucco finds at the site, plans are now underway to build a museum of stucco near this complex. Also nestled within this space is a huge jaguar mural, still only partially uncovered.

The fifth platform contains the impressive **Mural of the Four Suns**, or Mural of the Four Eras, which was built between 790 and 840. A kind of three-dimensional codex, the mural gives us a cornucopia of symbolism and legend. Note especially the three upside-down descending suns (the fourth lies in the museum), a serpent emerging from a skull, and the wonderful depiction of the god of death clutching a severed human head by the hair.

Keep climbing and you'll come to three grates covering holes in the ground where royal tombs were discovered, the last in December 2009. On the sixth platform, you'll come upon the **Altar of the Monster of the Earth**, a cave that supposedly leads to the underworld. Check out the spherical black rock inside, meant to represent the sun swallowed whole by the monster every night. Ironically, the highest level at Toniná is reserved not for the nobility, but for prisoners. (This way, they wouldn't have anywhere to escape.) On the sides of the building are reliefs of prisoners, including one with a recent haircut indicating an imminent sacrifice.

Before you leave, make two last visits. The first is the kiosk near the exit, where you can buy a slice of fresh macadamia cake (macadamia is grown here); the second is the small but excellent **Site Museum**, where you'll find numerous artifacts, sculptures, and a terrific model of the city. (You'll also find skulls showing cranial deformation to look more like grains of corn, a practice quite in vogue among the Maya.)

Yaxchilán

GETTING THERE Yaxchilán is almost 110 miles from Palenque and is best accessed by boat. To get here, take Highway 199 south from Palenque, and turn left on the Carretera Fronteriza del Sur. The site is about four hours away by car. Take the Frontera Corozal to the edge of the river, where you can hire a boat to the site.

Located on the banks of the sacred Usumacinta River (the longest river in Central America) and accessible only by boat, unless you're a truly adventurous person, Yaxchilán is a special place. For one, the languid, hourlong boat ride here from the **Centro Ecoturístico Escudo Jaguar** takes you far from modern amenities and plonks you in the middle of a broad river with pristine scenery all around you.

The magnificence of Yaxchilán begins with its jungle environment. In one afternoon, I saw a tarantula scuttling away from me and a family of howler monkeys in the trees above, and these sightings made my visit even more memorable. The city amazes as much as the jungle: *Yaxchilán* means "Green Stones," an appropriate name for the green moss that covers many of the structures in the city. Records show evidence of life at this site in AD 250, but the city flourished from AD 350 to 810. It was a powerful capital that presided over Bonampak and counted among its main rivals Tikal and Palenque, two superpowers of their time.

When you walk into Yaxchilán, you might be surprised at the narrow, rather uninspired entrance to the site. This was not the main entrance to the city. In its heyday, visitors arrived to Yaxchilán by boat and walked up a broad slope directly to the main plaza. Modern visitors come through **Building 19**, a man-made labyrinth complete with bats. This building served a defensive purpose, confusing would-be attackers and ensuring any attack on the city by land would force invading forces to enter Yaxchilán in single file.

From Building 19 you'll emerge onto the Great Plaza, one of three complexes in the city that comprise more than 120 structures. Among the interesting buildings here are **Building 17**, a *temazcal*; and **Buildings 12** and **22**, which show examples of the detailed lintels that must have once covered the structures and chronicled the history of the ruling dynasties. The city is known for its marvelous sculptures, found on lintels, stelae, bas-relief carvings, and murals. With over 110 inscribed sculptures, we are lucky enough to have a solid understanding of the dynastic chronology of the city, and its economic, political, and social sophistication.

Stela 1 shows Bird Jaguar IV, one of the city's greatest rulers. **Stela 2** lies on its side, unfortunately broken during an attempted move to Mexico City. **Building 20** features a near-perfectly preserved and restored group of lintels depicting Bird Jaguar IV and the sacred art of self-sacrifice. At the southwest end of the plaza, a cluster of buildings (**21**, **73**, and **89**) feature another series of lintels, again depicting Bird Jaguar IV undergoing ceremonial self-sacrifice, with one of his wives in attendance.

The soaring Grand Acropolis comprises the second section of the site. Climb up to the summit to get to **Building 33**, 133 feet above the Great Plaza. Built by Bird Jaguar IV, it's the finest and best preserved of Yaxchilán's ruins. Building 33 gives us further examples of the sculptural and architectural splendor of the city, with its hieroglyphic stairway depicting the ball game, carved lintels, and the crest, which gives the structure both symmetry and ornamentation. Inside is a sculpture of a decapitated Bird Jaguar IV. According to Lacandón legend, when the head of the ruler returns to its place atop his body, the world will face a cataclysm wrought by celestial jaguars.

BUILDING 40 AT YAXCHILÁN

Walk around the building to begin your descent, and you'll soon come to a fork in the road. Take the longer route and hike across a narrow jungle trail to reach **Buildings 39**, **40**, and **41**, which were part of the Great Acropolis. Of these, Building 40 is very well preserved and includes traces of mural paintings. Finally, the Small Acropolis contains two buildings, **42** and **44**, with elaborate inscriptions, which may have been reserved for the city's elite.

✱ Lodging

The small city of Palenque has little to recommend it beyond the archaeological site, but it does boast a variety of lodging and dining options. Located on the outskirts of the town about 10 minutes from the ruins, **Hotel Ciudad Real Palenque** is a welcome refuge, with 66 spacious guest rooms, a large open-air pool, full-service restaurant, and rustic décor. A more opulent option closer to Palenque is **Villa Mercedes**. Check in at the chic lobby under a tall *palapa* roof, and walk or ride (in a golf cart) to one of the thatch-roofed bungalows, furnished with wrought-iron beds, flat-screen TVs, and large windows with views of the surrounding jungle. The hotel also has a lobby restaurant and bar, two swimming pools, a spa with a fantastically decorated *temazcal,* and conference and meeting space.

Nestled in the jungle, **Hotel Chan-Kah** is among the closest to Palenque, and offers 73 rustic suites spread out in casitas along the 50-acre property. Four pools, lush grounds with observation terraces, and meeting facilities complete the resort village. Perhaps my favorite destination in Palenque is the boutique **Hotel Quinta Chanabnal.** Just a few miles from the ruins, the hotel was built by Mayanist Rafael Tunesi, who has done an incredible job combining ancient Maya splendor with modern luxury and amenities. My favorite features in the seven richly decorated suites are the murals that depict, in Maya glyphs, Tunesi's own journey to Chiapas and the creation of the hotel. (The small lagoon pool and *temazcal* aren't bad, either.)

RUSTIC DIGS AT CENTRO ECOTURÍSTICO LAS GUACAMAYAS

Chiapas is full of rustic country inns and *centros ecoturísticos,* or eco-touristic centers. Between Palenque and Bonampak lies **Parador Valle Escondido**, a hidden retreat known for its delicious food. A few cabins across the road from the restaurant offer a very comfortable stay, in a kind of Flintstones-meets-the-modern-era way (think rough-hewn stone walls, bamboo shower heads, and hammocks). One of the few ways to get to Yaxchilán is by hiring a boat at the **Centro Ecoturístico Escudo Jaguar** (its name means "Jaguar Shield"), which also has cheap, Spartan cabins and a decent restaurant.

A similar setup, in varying degrees of rusticity, can be found at the **Centro Ecoturístico Causas Verdes Las Nubes**, (bare cabins near a breathtaking waterfall and hiking trail); **Centro Ecoturístico Cadena de Cascadas El Chiflón** (attractive cabins along the river near a spectacular series of waterfalls); and the **Centro Ecoturístico Las Guacamayas**, among the nicest and most complete of the bunch. Named after the resident *guacamayas* (scarlet macaws), the center was built by an indigenous Chinanteca com-

PARADOR SANTA MARÍA OFFERS A SERENE AND PICTURESQUE GETAWAY.

munity of Oaxacan origins. These handsome wood cabins enjoy a verdant setting along the banks of the river. Morning boat trips can be arranged to secluded spots for swimming, and the restaurant is quite good. Finally, the **Centro Ecoturístico Chinkultic** is a brand-new facility with well-appointed duplex suites near the archaeological site.

One of my favorite stops in Chiapas is the lovely **Parador Santa María**, located between Chinkultic and the Lagos de Montebello. A restored hacienda, each of the eight rooms at the parador is decorated according to a unique theme, and feature beautiful antique furnishings. The hotel's restaurant is excellent, the grounds are serene, and the small chapel holds an impressive museum of religious art dating from the 16th to the 19th centuries.

As the main tourist city in Chiapas, San Cristóbal has numerous hotels and inns. Among these, **Hotel Posada Real de Chiapas** is the only hotel dedicated to women artisans and textiles of the region. The rooms are cozy, the restaurant occupies a beautiful space in the courtyard, the piano lounge is an inviting late-night hangout, and the hotel is centrally located near Plaza 31 de Marzo. **Tierra y Cielo** offers the winning combination of spacious accommodations in a neoclassical house and one of the best restaurants in the city.

La Casa de Elisa is a small, cute boutique property that includes a spa and one of the few pools among the city's hotels. **Hotel Ciudad Real San Cristóbal**, sister of the Palenque property, is located right on the main square, with rooms decorated in colonial style set in a neoclassical mansion. Finally, a fine budget option is **Rossco Backpackers Hostel**, which offers women's and mixed dorms with hammocks, bonfires, a kitchen, and free continental breakfast at bargain rates.

✷ Dining

Although you can certainly eat well in Chiapas, it doesn't have the gourmet reputation of the Yucatán, Mexico City, and other parts of the country. I found menus across Chiapas to be rather uniform, especially at the *centros turísticos*—hearty, tasty fare that won't blow you away but certainly makes for a satisfying meal.

In Palenque, you'll be hard-pressed to find bigger portions of good food than at **Las Tinajas** (named after the hanging clay jars found around the restaurant). Order a mammoth goblet of fresh juice and try the *pollo al estilo Tinajas,* a ridiculous amount of chicken served in a tomato and white wine sauce with carrots, onions, cilantro, and capers. If you're in Palenque over the weekend, don't miss the Sunday buffet at **La Selva**, which offers a variety of continental and local dishes. And **Café Restaurante Don Mucho** is popular for its location right next to the archaeological site, its pizzas and pastas, and its dinner shows. **Parador Valle Escondido** is almost a rite of passage in the morning, where tour buses on the way to Bonampak will make routine pit stops for their freshly prepared and filling breakfasts. Lunch and early dinner is also served here in rough-hewn tables tucked into the jungle.

A HEARTY BREAKFAST AT PARADOR VALLE ESCONDIDO IS A GREAT WAY TO START YOUR DAY.

I found a refreshing, gourmet change from the norm at **Parador Santa María**, which served a fantastic house salad (made with ingredients grown on the premises) and tequila-fired shrimp. At the Lagunas de Montebello, you'll find numerous stalls selling a fresh-made local snack called *chin kuualj.* These are delicious dough patties stuffed with beans and topped with white cheese. Also try the *flor de calabaza* (squash blossom) quesadillas and chocolate (not in bar form but the original stuff).

In Comitán, check out **La Techumbre**, located right on the main plaza, which has a bilingual menu and serves tasty *comales* (flour tortillas covered with tomato sauce, ham, chorizo, bacon, mushroom, and melted cheese) and tacos stuffed with beef tips and *nopales.* Across the plaza at **Café Quiptic**, you can snack on *antojitos* and sandwiches. In Chiapa de Corzo, **Restaurante Jardines de Chiapas** serves up regional fare buffet style, including local specialties like *tasajo,* which is sun-dried beef served with a pumpkin seed sauce.

My favorite restaurant in San Cristóbal was **Tierra y Cielo**, where I tried two local specialties: *agua de chía,* a lemony drink filled with chía seeds, and *sopa de pan,* a hearty and dense soup filled with ingredients that should never be put on the same dish but somehow work: soaked bread, egg, raisins, peas, zucchini, carrots, and sweet plantains. **El Fogón de Jovel** is a bit too touristy for me, with a multilingual staff dressed in folkoric outfits serving regional dishes.

Two good sources for cheap, quick meals is the **Mercado de Dulces y Artesanías**, which specializes in pastries, candied fruits, and sweets (don't mind the swarm of bees, they're just after the candy), along with *ponche,* a hot tea filled with fruit (served with or without alcohol), but also has a cluster of casual eateries; and **Emiliano's Moustache**, which has a gringo-friendly name but appeals to locals just as much for its tacos and *comida corrida* (set menu). Whatever you do, don't leave San Cristobal without visiting **Kakao Natura**, which specializes in some of the best hot chocolate you'll ever try. For something with a kick, try the chocolate mixed with seven chiles.

✷ Don't Miss

Take away every Maya pyramid and Chiapas would still be a magical destination thanks to its spectacular natural beauty (particularly its waterfalls and lagoons), colonial cities, and indigenous communities.

About an hour away from Palenque, the wide, shallow falls of **Agua Azul** are among the most swimmable cascades in Chiapas,

THE *SOPA DE PAN* AT TIERRA Y CIELO IS A MUST-TRY LOCAL SPECIALTY

and draw happy crowds looking for a refreshing dip on a hot day. The falls are formed by blue water flowing over travertine deposits that look like still-life white-water cascades. It's a welcome respite from the Chiapas jungle.

Centro Ecoturístico Cadena de Cascadas el Chiflón. You could easily spend a few days here, escaping from the rest of the world and enjoying a chain of five waterfalls that seem to get more spectacular the higher up you go. Just 10 years old, the center is well managed by a local community, and includes a small museum that gives you detailed information about the natural environment. Walk along the wide walkway and you'll come to the first falls, El Suspiro (The Sigh), followed by Ala de Ángel (Angel's Wing). Here you'll see the first of two Tyrolean zip lines, this one intended for kids. The climb gets a bit steeper from here, but the path is lined with signs to let you know how far you have left to go and pit stops that serve snacks and drinks.

However tough you find the walk, don't give up, because the third waterfall, Vela de Novia (Bride's Veil) is truly breathtaking. A huge fall almost 400 feet in length, it dominates the landscape and is among my favorite views in all of Chiapas. There is no swimming at these falls (there are plenty of spots along the trail where you can take a dip), but I highly recommend trying out the zip line here, which takes you across a chasm to the other side of the falls and back. Beyond this waterfall are the final two, Arcoíris (Rainbow) and Quinceañera (Fifteenth Birthday), but none equal the majesty of Bride's Veil.

The center includes a restaurant, 10 cabins, and a cluster of stalls selling primarily clothing and accessories for swimming and the outdoors.

Centro Ecoturístico Causas Verdes Las Nubes. Named for the clouds, or *nubes,* of mist formed by the waterfall, Las Nubes offers a serene, verdant oasis. You're likely to find more butterflies than people here on some days, and you get to swim in the shadow of the powerful falls. The center offers guided nature walks up a hill for lovely views and the chance to spot the local flora and fauna. During the winter months, the center also runs a Tyrolean zip line and a restaurant.

Centro Ecoturístico Las Guacamayas. The beauty of Las Guacamayas extends beyond its rustic accommodations, lush greenery, and nature trails. You have the chance to see, at close range, a variety of fauna here, from the macaws to tapirs to (much rarer) jaguars. I had the wonderful fortune of running across a family of howler monkeys on the way to breakfast. To enjoy the center to its fullest, hire a boat to take you deep into waterways and tributaries of the Lacantún River, where you can hear monkeys howl, spot crocodiles lazing

THE SPECTACULAR VELA DE NOVIA WATERFALL AT CASCADAS EL CHIFLÓN

on the banks, and marvel at the massive, centuries-old ceiba trees along the banks. You'll have a few chances to jump in for an early-morning swim at Edenic spots selected by your captain.

Chiapas Regional Museum. Tuxtla Gutiérrez, the state capital, is dedicated more to business travel than tourism, but it has a few worthy destinations, including the Chiapas Regional Museum, which houses one of the country's most impressive archaeological exhibits. Divided into five stages, the collection takes you from the prehistoric era to the Preclassic, Classic, and Postclassic periods. A second exhibit takes over from when the colonial epoch begins and runs to the present day.

HOWLER MONKEYS CAN OFTEN BE HEARD AND SEEN IN THE JUNGLES OF CHIAPAS.

Comitán de Domínguez

This quaint colonial town gets overlooked, thanks to the popularity of San Cristóbal, but it's a picturesque stop close to Chinkultik, El Chiflón, and the Lagunas de Montebello. Comitán gets its name from the Aztecs, who arrived in this region in 1486 and gave this site the ignominious title "Where the fevers abounded." The city was conquered in 1528 by Pedro de Portocarrero.

Enter Comitán from the south, and the first thing you'll see is a sculpture of two intertwined hands representing the friendship between Mexico and Guatemala. From here, drive along the Boulevard de la Federación, which is interspersed with monuments representing each state in Mexico, to Calle Central Licenciado Benito Juárez. Turn right and drive to the *zócalo*, or main plaza.

This attractive square is itself a showcase for art, thanks to the symposium of urban sculpture; artists from all over the world come here in October, and many of their works have been donated to the city and reside in the *zócalo*. Dominating one end of the square is the bright yellow **Iglesia**

de Santo Domingo, which dates from 1556 and stands as the last Dominican church built in Chiapas. Next to it stands a former convent, now the **Centro Cultural Rosario Castellanos** and the all-Spanish **Museo Arqueológico de Comitán**. The former has a library and a mural that depicts the history of the city, starting with a local legend about a puma that led the town's first settlers to water. The most impressive exhibit in the latter is the reproduction of a burial ceremony found in the cave of the Andasolos.

On the north side of the plaza is the pink-colored **Presidencia Municipal** (City Hall), which houses a dramatic mural that depicts the history of the region from pre-Columbian times to colonization to the drafting of the 1857 constitution. Note the warriors in the lower right corner, battling the conquistadors and, in the distance, falling off a mountain. These are said to be Chiapanecos, ferocious fighters who, rather than surrender to the Spanish, threw themselves into the Canyón del Sumidero.

Two blocks east of the *zócalo,* the rust and gold rococo **Templo de San Caralampio** has an unusual legend. Remember the name of the city and its reference to abundant fevers? The story goes that a soldier named Caralampio found an image of a saint in a nearby

A BOAT TRIP FROM LAS GUACAMAYAS TAKES YOU TO IDYLLIC SPOTS ALONG THE LACANTÚN RIVER.

ranch, in an area where the fevers (cholera and smallpox) did not reach the locals. The saint was transferred to the church, and it is now the site of an annual event each February called the **Romería de San Caralampio**, a religious procession where revelers, masked figures, and a marching band take to the street with the saint carried out in a flower-covered float.

THE PRESIDENCIA MUNICIPAL AT COMITÁN DE DOMINGUEZ

The church is located in the **Barrio de la Pila**, the oldest neighborhood in the city and the site of the city's first water source. According to legend, settlers came to these parts in search for water and came upon a puma drinking from a pond.

Lagos de Montebello. The Lakes of Montebello National Park is located about 10 miles south of Comitán. Travel east off Highway 190 just north of La Trinitaria, and you'll come to Chinkultic after 19 miles. The park is just a few miles beyond.

Chiapas offers one natural wonder after another, and the dazzling Lakes of Montebello certainly qualify. The first national park in Chiapas, its lakes are in fact a chain of ancient *cenotes* surrounded by forests. With deep waters of variegated blue mirroring the green canopy and open sky, the lakes are nothing short of stunning.

I spent my time in four lakes, each different, each special. **Laguna Cinco Lagos** connects five lakes; you can rent rafts here and visit a natural cavern as well as a beach. **Laguna Montebello** is a broad expanse of water framed by low green hills. Facilities include boat rentals and horseback riding. **Laguna Pojoj** was my favorite by far, both for its dazzling blues and the crude rafts you can rent to take you to the island in the center of the lake, which has a small orchid garden, a natural diving ledge, and breathtaking

LAGUNA POJOJ IS MY FAVORITE SPOT IN MONTEBELLO.

surroundings. **Laguna Tziscao**, the largest of the lakes, is also the closest to Guatemala, and you'll find Guatemalan arts, crafts, clothing, and other and items for sale here (including clove-flavored gum and crude chocolate).

Cascada Misol-Ha. Another of Chiapas's beautiful waterfalls, Misol-Ha lies just over 12 miles from Palenque, an easy side trip from the city. Guided tours take you to the top of the falls, where you can swim in calm natural pools and even fish with the guide's approval. The eco-touristic center also offers a visit to a tilapia nursery and a trek down a small *gruta*, or cave.

Parque Nacional Cañón del Sumidero. With its steep faces spanning a depth of over 3,000 feet at points, the Sumidero Canyon is among the most impressive in the world, and a boat ride through it on the broad Grijalva River is an experience. The canyon has been designated a national park and ecological reserve. Keep an eye out for the massive crocodiles found (and protected) here. Boat rides can be arranged at Chiapa de Corzo, easily accessible from San Cristóbal or Tuxtla Gutiérrez. **Amikúu** conducts boat rides and other excursions in the park.

San Cristóbal de las Casas

San Cristóbal draws students, tourists, and a hodgepodge of travelers from around the country and around the world. You almost can't help but enjoy this city, with its period architecture, soaring cathedral, and pedestrian promenades lined with shops and restaurants. There's plenty to see and do when you come to the city of the *coletos*, as the local residents are called.

Tuxtla Gutiérrez may be the capital of Chiapas today, but San Cristóbal was the provincial capital during the colonial era, receiving its coat of arms from Holy Roman Emperor Carlos V in 1538. Over the centuries, the indigenous communities that sprouted around the city gradually became incorporated into San Cristóbal, resulting in an inevitable cultural and ethnic melting pot. In fact, the city is named after its patron saint, Saint Christopher, and Bartolomé de Las Casas, a Spanish priest who fought for native rights and became the first bishop of Chiapas.

The heart of the city is the main square, known as the **Plaza 31 de Marzo**, which historically was a civic center and market, as well as a water source for the town. This attractive plaza is especially beautiful at night, when live bands perform in the turn-of-the-century bandstand and fairy lights are sprinkled over the surrounding shrubs and trees. Some of the city's most beautiful buildings can also be found here.

Start with the colorful **Catedral de San Cristóbal**. Originally the Templo de La Asunción, it graduated to cathedral status in 1528, when the province of Chiapas became a diocese. Construction of the present building began in the 17th century, and over the next 200 years or more, a variety of artists and architects lent their aesthetic style to the building. The result is an elaborate mélange of design and construction. The baroque and neoclassic façade, divided into three levels, showcases this diversity.

The plaster pattern across the middle level is believed to represent a huipil, a traditional Maya tunic. The bright colors of the cathedral—red, yellow, white, and black—represent the colors of the cardinal points. Above the main door stands the *Virgen de la Asunción.* Flanking the choir window are two double-headed eagles, and above it stands a relief of Saint James. In an unusual nod to nature, the water spouts of the cathedral were at one point all decorated to look like crocodile mouths.

Inside the cathedral, check out the Reyes Altarpiece, elaborate wooden pulpit, and paintings by colonial-era artists. Finally, note the large Atrial Cross in front of the cathedral in the Plaza de la Paz (renamed in 1994 to commemorate the agreement between the Zapatistas and the government that essentially changed the relationship from one of armed conflict to one of political discourse).

Adjacent to the cathedral, the **Iglesia de San Nicolás**, dates from 1613 and served as the church reserved for the native community. Today it houses a museum of religious art. The handsome neoclassic **Palacio Municipal** occupies one entire side of the plaza. Continuing around the plaza, the Plateresque-style **Casa de las Sirenas** (House of the Mermaids) is the best remaining example of the residential opulence of the colonial elite. It is believed to have belonged to Andrés de la Tovilla, compadre of Comitán conquerer Pedro de Portocarrero.

THE CATEDRAL DE SAN CRISTÓBAL

THE IGLESIA DE SAN NICOLÁS WAS THE CHURCH OF THE INDIGENOUS COMMUNITY DURING THE COLONIAL ERA.

Stretching away from the cathedral and the Palacio Municipal is the *andador turístico,* a pedestrian-only walkway lined with shops, restaurants, bars, and nightclubs. While the removal of auto traffic here has resulted in a lot of congestion in and around the city center, the promenade certainly adds to the city's charm, and joins two of the city's most well known landmarks.

The **Arco del Carmen**, a picturesque bell tower of Moorish design built in 1680, is a unique structure in Mexico. Built as part of a convent, it served the dual purpose of a bell tower and passageway for the nuns who lived within its walls, giving them a way to cross from one part of the convent to the other without breaking their vows. On the other end of the *andador* stands the fabulously decorated **Templo de Santo Domingo**, which showcases baroque art and elaboration at its finest. The present-day church, dating from the 17th century, was built over a more primitive church built in 1547. The façade of the church is extremely detailed and quite impressive. Above the choir window you'll find a statue of Santo Domingo flanked by double-headed eagles (emblem of the Habsburg family), in turn flanked by Solomonic columns. Also note the face in the arch above the doorway, from whose mouth issues an elaborate floral pattern; this represents the Franciscan faith spreading through the spoken word. Inside, the pulpit, carved from a single piece of wood and decorated with gold leaf, is especially lovely, as are the baroque altarpieces.

On the way to Santo Domingo, you'll pass the **Templo de la Caridad**, built in 1739. The church is beloved for the *Virgen de la Caridad,* a painting of the Virgin of Guadalupe; Legend has it that she came forth and fought with the people of the town, defending San Cristóbal against a superior force during the revolution. Behind Santo Domingo is the Mercado Público José Castillo Tiélemans, located on Avenida Insurgentes.

San Cristóbal has a variety of interesting museums that will appeal to anyone interested in Maya culture:

Mesoamerican Museum of Jade. Jade was the most valuable stone for the pre-Columbian Indians, and this museum houses jade pieces from numerous cultures spanning different regions and eras, from the Olmec to the Aztecs. One of the most magnificent jade works unearthed in this continent is Pakal's mausoleum in Palenque. You'll find a replica of it here. Not surprisingly, the museum is attached to a well-stocked jewelry store.

Museo del Ambar. Known as *pauch* by the Tzotzil, amber is the fossilized resin of trees. Chiapas has the third-biggest bed of amber in the world, and this museum, housed in the former convent of La Merced, houses some 300 pieces of amber. In particular, check out the marimba made entirely out of the substance.

Museo de las Culturas Populares. In addition to its permanent collection, which chronicles the arts, crafts, rituals, industry, and social life of the state's diverse indigenous cultures, the museum hosts frequent art exhibits, such as arts-and-crafts workshops and photography galleries. The museum is located two blocks behind the municipal palace.

THE ARCO DEL CARMEN IS AN ICONIC MONUMENT IN SAN CRISTÓBAL.

Museo Na Bolom. The name means "House of the Jaguar," and it was once the home of pioneering archaeologist Frans Blom and his wife, photographer Gertrude Duby. The museum has exhibits dedicated to the Lacandón culture, archaeological findings around the city, and traditional textiles.

Museum of Maya Medicine. Located on the outskirts of the city, this interesting museum covers Tzotzil and Tzeltal healing practices; you can even arrange for a healing ceremony in a *temazcal* with a resident traditional healer.

Shopping in San Cristóbal is also an enjoyable experience, thanks to its markets and promenades, handicrafts, and jewelry. There are numerous arts-and-crafts markets at several spots around the city, including in front of the Iglesia de Santo Domingo and in front of the cathedral. For shopping, check out:

Casa de las Artesanías de Chiapas. Located on the *andador turístico,* this shop is a good, central resource for textiles, pottery, wood-carving, and other arts and crafts of the region.

Iconos Mayas. I couldn't leave without one of their beautiful wood-carved Maya masks, but the store is more known for its custom-made bracelets and necklaces made with your birthdate written in Maya glyphs. You also get a full explanation of what your birthdate means (in Maya).

Jades & Joyas. Jade was widely coveted by the Maya, and this store honors its importance to the ancients. In addition to its collection of jade jewelry, you'll find pieces made with other semiprecious stones.

Kiki Suárez, La Galería del Corazón Abierto. The name means "Gallery of the Open Heart," but it's more than a display of the works of German-born artist and photographer Kiki Suárez. In addition to her paintings, which celebrate her love for the colors of Mexico, you'll find art, jewelry, and clothes inspired by indigenous people but embellished with modern touches. Also on display is a collection of amber jewelry, including the rare red amber.

Quintosol. One of the most complete stores in the city, Quintosol has a large variety of amber and semiprecious stone jewelry, along with a separate room full of high-quality arts and crafts from around the country.

Tierra de Ambar. As the name implies, "Amber Earth" focuses on amber jewelry, and designer Philippe Chatillon puts together unique and beautiful pieces at this small boutique.

San Juan Chamula

An indigenous community located just outside San Cristóbal de las Casas, San Juan Chamula is home to one of the most unusual churches in all of Mexico, and a blending of Catholic and indigenous faith quite different from the norm.

The town is comprised of three neighborhoods: San Pedro, San Sebastián, and San Juan. In San Sebastián, you'll find the empty shell of a 17th-century church that was once used as a fort. The town was one of the main battlegrounds of the Caste War in 1869. In front of the church is a graveyard with three types of crosses: black, white, and green-blue. Each neighborhood has a cemetery like this, and the colors correspond to the age of the deceased: white for children, green-blue for adults, and black for the elderly.

San Juan Chamula practices a strict, albeit unique, brand of Catholicism. So much so that, if you're not Catholic, you can't live here. You also cannot take photos inside the **Iglesia de San Juan** in the main plaza, under penalty of potential arrest. (Also, make sure to remove your hat before entering.) You can, however, take pictures of the white, green, and blue exterior, as well as the men and women in traditional dress (black wool skirts and black pelt ponchos) around town.

But the main reason to visit San Juan Chamula is to witness what takes place inside the church. Strewn with pine needles and filled with incense, flowers, and the smoky warmth of hundreds of candles, the interior itself is quite unusual. When you walk inside, you're likely to find clusters of people gathered around a man who is either chanting, speaking, or praying. This man is a traditional healer, and the people around him are a family who has come seeking his help to cure a sick or afflicted loved one. A live chicken, glass of Coke, and *poch* (a local, fermented cane liquor) complete the necessities. (The pine needles, candles, *poch,* and incense represent the four elements.) The *hilol,* or healer begins the ceremony by throwing the liquor over the candles. (Incidentally, if a person is born with six fingers, this is taken as an absolute sign that he or she will be a healer.) As part of the ceremony, the chicken is sacrificed by having its neck snapped. It is then buried in the home of the afflicted, if the person's illness is severe, or cooked and shared by the family. The entire family also drinks *poch,* and the Coca-Cola is used to expel evil (the carbonation is the key ingredient here).

The ceremony is fascinating to behold, and the church is equally memorable. Over 50 saints are represented within its walls, and each has an assigned majordomo in town, a person of importance who is responsible for throwing a patron saint festival in honor of his saint. You'll also find a row of bells on the floor of the church. Legend has it that the bells were brought here to be cured; in fact, one bell with a fracture in it was at one point supposedly completely broken. Another story says that the bells come from the ruined Church of San Sebastián. Their

THE IGLESIA DE SAN JUAN IS AMONG THE UNIQUE CHURCHES IN MEXICO.

duty was to protect the church, and as it was destroyed, they obviously failed; hence they stay on the floor, as an ongoing punishment.

The only Catholic sacrament that takes place at the church is baptism; there are no confessions or Mass. It's a truly special, and unique, place, and one that should be on your shortlist of places to visit in Chiapas. To maximize the experience, come during the **Fiesta de San Juan**, when fireworks are set off in the main plaza.

Zinacantán

Another indigenous community just a few miles from San Cristóbal de las Casas, Zinacantán is a Tzotzil community of textile weavers. You can take a guided tour to this area (tour operators such as **Viajes Pakal** run tours), or come here on your own via rental car or *combi* (public van) from San Cristóbal. If you do so, simply go to the town's church, the **Iglesia San Lorenzo**, where friendly neighborhood girls stand ready to escort you to their home. You'll be welcomed as a guest to watch the women at work weaving elaborate designs using an old-fashioned, traditional technique. You'll also be invited to sample fresh tortillas made on a *comal* and drizzled with cheese, beans, pumpkin seed and tomato sauce, along with homemade coffee or *poch*.

There's no charge for the food, and you don't have to buy any of the textiles on sale, but at the very least, a tip is expected, and the women of the house are happy to

THE TRADITIONAL ART OF TEXTILE WEAVING IN ZINACANTÁN

talk to their guests. I went to the house of Magdalena, a plain adobe structure. Two cousins sat on the floor, their legs bent under them, with one end of a loom around their waist, the other around a wood post (the thread originating from the navel symbolizes an umbilical cord.) The patterns, which can be quite complex, are done by rote and generally combine two techniques: brocade and embroidery. Feel free to browse the finished pieces, especially the intricate bride's dress (sometimes made with feathers) and groom's outfit, which can take weeks to make. August is a good time to visit Zinacantán, when the town holds its colorful *fiesta de pueblo*, or town fair.

Zoológico Miguél de Álvarez del Toro (ZooMAT). Tuxtla's fantastic zoo occupies close to 250 acres. It's a unique park in that it houses only animals native to Chiapas, including macaws, jaguars, tapirs, and the rare and precious quetzal—a bird of supreme importance to the Maya and the Aztecs. Also check out the Casa Nocturna, ingeniously designed so that the nocturnal animals within think night is day, and are therefore far more active than in other zoos.

A WEEKEND IN CHIAPAS

A weekend in Chiapas is just enough time to see its most impressive archaeological sites; unfortunately, given its size, it also prohibits your visiting some of its best geographic wonders.

I recommend flying into Villahermosa airport, renting a car, and driving down Highway 186 to the city of Palenque (roughly three hours from the airport). Ideally you want to arrive early enough to visit the archaeological site, which can take anywhere from three hours to the whole day. Afterward, return to the town center (there's a small display of folkloric costumes at one end of the *zócalo*) and have dinner at a local restaurant such as **Las Tinajas** before checking into a hotel to fit your budget and taste. On your second day, get an early start and drive to **Parador Valle Escondido** to enjoy a hearty breakfast. You'll need it, because your day is a full one: continue on to **Bonampak**, and from here visit **Yaxchilán**. You can grab lunch at the **Centro Ecoturístico Escudo Jaguar** before or after your trip to the site.

On your last day, enjoy the beautiful falls of **Misol Ha**, and maybe even **Agua Clara** before heading back to Villahermosa. If you're leaving the next day, continue on Route 199 past Misol Ha (skipping Agua Clara) to **Toniná.**

SIDE TRIP TO COMALCALCO

I've done the state of Tabasco a disservice in this guide by not devoting more space to its archaeological treasures. This is due mostly to the fact that Tabasco's best sites are not Maya but Olmec. However, those planning an extended stay in Chiapas may want to spend a night in Villahermosa and devote the next day to a trip to Comalcalco. (Take the 1 ½-hour bus ride from the ADO station at Villahermosa to get to the city of Comalcalco, and hop in a taxi for the short ride to the site, which is open daily 8–5.)

Comalcalco is remarkable for a singular reason: it is the lone Maya site in Mexico to feature buildings made of kiln-fired brick and mortar made from oyster shells. Even more interesting, many of these bricks bear inscriptions and glyphs, the meaning of which remains unclear. Why is this the only site in Maya Mexico to feature brick structures? Theories abound, including one that proposes a link with ancient Rome.

The city may originally have been of Olmec lineage, but the Chontal Maya made it their home from roughly AD 250 to 750. The principal structures at Comalcalco are Temple 1, the Great Acropolis, and the Palace. Also, visit the small site museum at the entrance for more information about the city's ancient inhabitants.

THE UNUSUAL BRICK-AND-MORTAR STRUCTURES AT COMALCALCO

Mexico Tourism Board

EXTENDED STAY

Chiapas is ideal for the visitor who has time on his or her hands and can take a road trip through the state. I would still recommend starting in Villahermosa and driving to Palenque. Visit Bonampak and Yaxchilán on Day 2. From here, continue east on the **Carretera Fronteriza** and you'll see a right turn leading to **Las Guacamayas** just outside Chajul. Stop here for the night (remember, this is rustic, so don't expect marble tubs and flat-screen TVS; in fact, there are no TVs).

In the morning, grab your swimsuit and take a boat ride along the Lacantún River, followed by a rich breakfast at the eco-touristic center's restaurant. When you leave Las Guacamayas, head south until you return to the Carretera Fronteriza. Turn right and head west (you're essentially looping around the jungle). If you want a refreshing stop at a beautiful waterfall, look for the signs from the main road to **Las Nubes**. Otherwise, continue on to the breathtaking **Lagos de Montebello**; you might be tempted to spend the night here, especially if you want to enjoy more than one of the lakes; if so, the simple but clean **Hotel Lagos de Montebello** will serve you well. If a day-trip is all you need, skip the hotel and drive on to **Chinkultic**. You have two options for lodging here: the more-than-adequate **Centro Ecoturístico Chinkultic** or, a bit farther on the highway, the cozy **Parador Santa María**. Visit the archaeological site the next morning.

After Chinkultic, continue west along the Carretera Fronteriza until you come to Highway 190. Turn right toward **Comitán**, and Route 190 will take you to **Tenam Puente**. Enjoy the site and then head to **El Chiflón**, which is so spectacular that I recommend renting one of their cabins for a night or two. From El Chiflón, you're a short drive away from **Comitán**, another pleasant stop. Then continue north along 190 to **San Cristóbal de las Casas**. Factoring in the neighboring communities of **San Juan Chamula** and **Zinacantán**, plan for at least three days here. If you want to include the **Cañon del Sumidero** and attractions at **Tuxtla Gutiérrez**, you might want to stay a day or two more.

From San Cristóbal (or San Cris, as it's called), make your way back to Palenque via Route 199. This will allow you to stop by **Toniná** and the waterfalls of **Agua Azul** and **Misol Ha**. Spend one last night in Palenque before heading back to Villahermosa.

IF YOU HAVE THE TIME, DON'T MISS A VISIT TO THE WATERFALL AT LAS NUBES.

✷ Local Knowledge

Chiapas has two very useful online resources: the English-language Travel Chiapas (www.travelchiapas.com) and the Spanish-language Tour Chiapas (www.tourchiapas.com). If you want more in-depth knowledge of the state, the book *The State of Chiapas* is an excellent, all-inclusive guide. Keep in mind the distances in this state. Combine them with the speed-bumps and winding roads, and it will take longer than you think to reach your destinations. Fortunately, road travel has improved greatly in Chiapas, but it's still slow going through much of the area. Here are a few approximate distances:

Palenque to Bonampak—97 miles

Palenque to Yaxchilán—120 miles

Palenque to San Cristóbal de las Casas—126 miles

Comitán to San Cristóbal de las Casas—54 miles

Comitán to Bonampak—223 miles

San Cristóbal to Tapachula—205 miles

LOCAL TIPS As a more rustic part of Mexico, Chiapas has its charm but also its limitations. For example, timing can be a tricky issue, because when daylight saving time kicks in, some folks don't bother changing their clocks or adjusting to the new time.

The weather will fluctuate as you travel around the state. Palenque and its surrounding area is generally hot and humid, but you'll want a sweater at night (and early morning) in San Cristóbal. Also don't forget about the rainy reason, which stretches from June to September and can comprise anything from brief showers to daylong downpours.

Most people speak Spanish, although you're also likely to find smaller communities where people speak their local, Maya dialect. English is spoken in major tourist areas, but don't rely on the locals' grasp of the language.

Don't forget the following when you're traveling to Chiapas:

- Sunblock
- Hat
- Water (You can't get water or food at most archaeological sites, so come prepared.)
- Cash! Many places in Chiapas, including small hotels and ecotouristic centers, restaurants, and shops, don't accept credit cards. Make sure to have cash on hand, as banks and ATMs outside the cities aren't that easy to find.
- When visiting the archaeological sites, bring the most powerful, industrial-strength bug repellant you can find.
- Bathing suit and towel, especially if you're going to such places as the Lagos de Montebello.
- An English-Spanish dictionary, if you don't speak Spanish.

As mentioned before, I recommend driving around Chiapas, which gives you the freedom to visit some of its more remote treasures. You can also travel by bus; interstate travel is reliable and efficient, especially the ADO line (www.ado.com.mx), which covers major points such as Palenque and San Cristóbal. The best way to find out the bus routes to smaller stops is to check in at the local bus station and inquire within. You can also book one of numerous tours to the major archaeological sites, both by bus and by air in small planes (given the distances, this is sometimes a good option for those with limited time; you also get the added bonus of spectacular aerial views of the topography of the area). Local and national outfits include:

Amikúu Offers boat tours through the Cañon del Sumidero.

Best Day Travel Covers all of Mexico, including a variety of day tours to Palenque, the Montebello lakes, San Juan Chamula and Zinacantán, and other destinations from San Cristóbal de las Casas.

Chiapas Tours and Travel Comitán-based, outfit offers a variety of tours and services, including airfare, car rental, language schools, scuba diving, camping, and other excursions.

Eco Chiapas Multiday tours focusing on adventure and nature, including rafting.

Lacandona Tours Offers a range of multiday driving tours; run by a family-owned business based in Tuxtla Gutiérrez.

Tours Por Chiapas With 10 years' experience and based in San Cristóbal, offers a variety of tours via plane.

Viajes Pakal A San Cristóbal–based tour operator and destination management company; covers Chiapas and also extends its tours to Guatemala and the Yucatán.

✷ Special Events

January 15: The **Festival of the Lord of Esquipulas**, or "Black Christ" of Esquipulas, is celebrated around Latin America, as well as in Chiapa de Corzo and small towns around the state, with parades and food.

January 8–23: Chiapa de Corzo honors its *mestizo* roots with a citywide festival known as **La Fiesta Grande de Chiapa**. It's one of the biggest traditional celebrations in Mexico, culminating with a meal shared by the entire community and the colorful "Parade of the Parachicos," featuring floats and masked dancers. The town also simulates a naval battle with fireworks on the Grijalva Rivero on January 21.

February 9–22: Among the most important events in Comitán, the **Feria de San Caralampio** is marked with flowers and children dressed in devil masks parading through the street toward the Templo de San Caralampio.

July 16–25: The **Fiesta de San Cristóbal** culminates in a procession of colorfully adorned cars toward the Iglesia de San Cristóbal.

October 11-18: The year 2009 inaugurated the first **Festival Internacional de las Culturas** (International Festival of the Cultures), in San Cristóbal, which featured arts-and-crafts expositions, music, poetry, and song, plus a variety workshops. The event brought 200 local and international artists to the city.

First 15 days of December: The **Feria de Chiapas** of Tuxtla Gutiérrez is among the most important in the state, and features bullfighting, equestrian events, and other sporting competitions, along with arts-and-crafts stalls and agricultural workshops.

✷ Contacts

Amikúu 961-600-6708/6712, Boulevard Belisario Dominguez, No. 302, Local 3 29030. www.amikuu.com. $$$$.

Best Day Travel 800-593-6259 (within the U.S.), 01-800-BEST-DAY (within Mexico), 998-287-3699. Numerous locations. www.bestday.com. $$$–$$$$.

Café Quiptic Avenida Rosario Castellanos Sur S/N, Colonia Centro, Comitán, Chiapas 30000. Open daily 7:30–midnight. $.

Café Restaurante Don Mucho 916-341-8209/103-2711, Carretera Palenque-Ruinas Km. 4.5, Palenque, Chiapas 29960. www.elpanchan.com. Open daily 7–11. $$.

La Casa de Elisa 967-674-0880, Miguel Hidalgo No. 11, Andador Eclesiástico, Colonia Centro Histórico, San Cristóbal de las Casas, Chiapas 29200. www.hotelescoloniales.com/casadeelisa. $–$$.

Casa de las Artesanías de Chiapas 967-678-1180, Calle Niños Héroes S/N and Avenida Hidalgo, San Cristóbal de las Casas, Chiapas 29200. Open Mon.–Sat. 10–9, Sun 10–3. $–$$$$.

Cascada Misol-Ha 555-151-3377, Carretera 199 Catazaja-Rancho Nuevo Km. 46.5, Ejido San Miguel, Municipio Salto de Agua, Chiapas. www.misol-ha.com. $–$$.

Catedral de San Cristóbal Avenida 20 de Noviembre at Real de Guadalupe, San Cristóbal de las Casas, Chiapas 29200. Open daily 7–6. Free.

Centro Ecoturísto Cadena de Cascadas El Chiflón 963-596-9709, S.C. de R.L. de C.V. Tzimol, Chiapas. www.chiflon.com.mx. Open Mon.–Fri. 9–6, weekends 8–6. $–$$$.

Centro Ecoturístico Causas Verdes Las Nubes 963-100-9732/963-565-4720, Ejido Las Nubes, located about 7 miles off the Carretera Fronteriza, Municipio de Maravilla, Tenejapa, Chiapas. Open daily 8–5:30. $, guided tours $$$.

Centro Ecoturístico Chinkultic 963-102-1172, Desviación Km. 35, Carretera de la Trinitaria, Colonia

Manuel Hidalgo, Chiapas. Restaurant open daily 8–6. $.

Centro Ecoturístico Escudo Jaguar 502-5353-5637, Frontera Corozal, Ocosingo, Chiapas. www.escudojaguarhotel.com. Restaurant open daily 7–8. $, boat trip to Yaxchilán $$$.

Centro Ecoturístico Las Guacamayas 555-151-1869, Ejido Reforma Agraria, Municipio Marqués de Comillas, Chiapas. $–$$.

Centro Cultural Rosario Castellanos and Museo Arqueológico de Comitán 963-632-5760, 1ª Calle Sur Oriente and Avenida Rosario Castellanos. Open Tue.–Sun. 9–6. Free.

Chiapas Regional Museum 961-613-4439/4479/4554, Calzada de los Hombres Ilustres S/N, Tuxtla Gutiérrez, Chiapas, 29000. www.inah.gob.mx. Open Tue.–Sun. 9–6. $.

Chiapas Tours and Travel 963-101-4105, Avenida Central Belisario Dominguez No. 38, Local 4, Barrio de San José, Comitán de Domínguez, Chiapas 30000. www.chiapastoursandtravel.com. $$$$.

Eco Chiapas 800-397-5072 (within Mexico), 967-631-7498, 1º de Marzo No. 30, San Cristóbal de las Casas, Chiapas 29200. http://ecochiapas.com. $$$$.

Emiliano's Moustache 967-678-7246, Avenida Crescencio Rosas No. 7, Colonia Centro Histórico, San Cristóbal de las Casas, Chiapas 29200. Open daily 8–1. $.

El Fogón de Jovel 967-678-1153/2550, Avenida 16 de Septiembre No. 11, Colonia Centro Histórico, San Cristóbal de las Casas, Chiapas 29200. Open daily 1–10:30. www.fogondejovel.com. $$.

Hotel Chan-Kah 916-345-1100/1134, 800-714-3247 (within Mexico), Carretera Palenque-Ruinas Km. 3, Palenque, Chiapas 29960. www.chan-kah.com.mx. $$–$$$.

Hotel Ciudad Real Palenque 916-345-1315, Carretera Pakal-Na Km. 1.5, Palenque, Chiapas 29960. www.ciudadreal.com.mx. $–$$.

Hotel Ciudad Real San Cristóbal 967-678-4400, Plaza 31 de Marzo No. 10, Colonia Centro, San Cristobal de las Casas, Chiapas 29200. www.ciudadreal.com.mx. $–$$.

Hotel Quinta Chanabnal 916-345-5320, Carretera Palenque-Ruinas Km. 2.2, Palenque, Chiapas 29960. www.quintachanabnal.com. $$$.

Hotel Posada Real de Chiapas 800-701-3611 (within Mexico), 967-678-0626, Francisco I. Madero No. 19, Colonia Centro Histórico, San Cristóbal de las Casas, Chiapas 29200. www.hpreal.com.mx. $$–$$$.

Iconos Mayas 976-116-0599, Colonia Centro Histórico, San Cristóbal de las Casas, Chiapas 29200. Open daily 10–10. $$–$$$$.

Iglesia de San Juan Main Plaza at San Juan Chamula, Chiapas 29320. Open daily 8–1 and 4–7. $.

Iglesia de San Nicolás Real de Guadalupe at Avenida General Utrilla, San Cristóbal de las Casas, Chiapas 29200. Open daily 10–7. Free.

Iglesia de Santo Domingo Avenida Rosario Castellanos at Calle Central Oriente. Open daily 10–7. Free.

Jades & Joyas 967-631-4324, Andador Turístico 20 de Noviembre No. 21, Colonia Centro Histórico, San Cristóbal de las Casas, Chiapas 29200. $–$$$$.

Kakao Natura 967-116-0954, Pedro Moreno No. 2-A, Colonia Centro Histórico, San Cristóbal de las Casas, Chiapas 29200. Open Mon.–Sat. 8 AM–10 PM, Sun. 4–10. $–$$.

Kiki Suárez Hidalgo 3ª, Colonia Centro Histórico, San Cristóbal de las Casas, Chiapas 29200. Open daily 9 AM–10 PM. www.kikitheartist.com. $–$$$$.

Lacandona Tours 961-671-8394, Avenida 6ª Sur Poniente No. 1276, Colonia La Lomita, Tuxtla Gutiérrez, Chiapas 29060. www.lacantours.com. $$$$.

Mercado de Dulces y Artesanías Avenida Insurgentes at Calle Hermanos Domínguez. Open daily 7 AM–10 PM. $–$$.

Mesoamerican Museum of Jade 967-678-1121, Avenida 16 de Septiembre No. 16, Colonia Centro Histórico, San Cristóbal de las Casas, Chiapas 29200. www.eljade.com. Open Mon.–Sat. noon–8, Sun. noon–6. $.

Museo del Ambar 967-678-9716, Diego de Mazariegos S/N, Parque de La Merced. Colonia La Merced, San Cristóbal de las Casas, Chiapas, 29240. www.museodelambar.com.mx. Open daily 9–6. $.

Museo de las Culturas Populares Calle Diego de Mazariegos No. 37, Esq. 12 de Octubre, Colonia Centro Histórico, San Cristóbal de las Casas, Chiapas 29200. Open daily 9–6. $.

Museo Na Bolom 967-678-1418, Avenida Vicente Guerrero No. 33, Colonia Centro Histórico, San Cristóbal de las Casas, Chiapas 29200. Open daily 10–7. www.nabolom.org. $.

Museum of Maya Medicine 967-678-5438, Avenida Salomón González Blanco No. 10, Colonia Morelos, San Cristóbal de Las Casas, Chiapas 29230. www.medicinamaya.org. Open Mon.–Fri. 10–6, weekends 10–5. $.

Palacio Municipal West Side of the Parque Central, Colonia Centro Histórico, San Cristóbal de las Casas, Chiapas 29200.

Parador Santa María 963-632-5116, Carretera Trinitaria-Lagos de Montebello Km. 22, Municipio de la Trinitaria, Comitán, Chiapas. www.paradorsantamaria.com.mx. $$–$$$.

Parador Valle Escondido 916-100-0399/391-917-3636, Carretera Fronteriza del Sur Km. 61, Selva

Lacandona, Palenque, Chiapas. Open daily 7–6. $.

Presidencia Municipal 963-632-0244, North Side of the Zócalo, Comitán, Chiapas 30000. Open Monday to Friday 9–8. Free.

Quintosol 967-678-1358, Casa del Congreso, Real de Guadalupe No. 5, Colonia Centro Histórico, San Cristóbal de las Casas, Chiapas 29200. Open daily 9–9. $–$$$$.

Restaurante Jardines de Chiapas 961-616-0198/0070, Avenida Francisco I. Madero No. 395, Chiapa de Corzo, Chiapas 29160. www.restaurantesjardines.com.mx. Open daily 9–7:30. $–$$.

Rossco Backpackers Hostel 967-674-0525, Real de Mexicanos No. 16, Colonia Centro Histórico, San Cristóbal de las Casas, Chiapas 29200. www.hostelinsan cristobal.com. $.

La Selva 916-345-0363, Carretera Palenque-Ruinas Km. 0.5, Colonia Nandiume, Palenque, Chiapas 29960. www.laselvarestaurante .com.mx. Open 11:30–11:30. $$.

La Techumbre 963-110-6836, Portal Pte. Centro Histórico, Comitán, Chiapas 30000. Open daily 7–midnight. $–$$.

Templo de la Caridad Avenida General Utrilla and Comitán, San Cristóbal de las Casas, Chiapas 29200. Open Mon.–Sat. 10–2 and 5–8. Free.

Templo de Santo Domingo Avenida 20 de Noviembre and Nicaragua, San Cristóbal de las Casas, Chiapas 29200. Open daily 10–2 and 5–8. Free.

Tierra de Ambar 967-678-0139, Real de Guadalupe 16 y 28ª, Colonia Centro Histórico, San Cristóbal de las Casas, Chiapas 29200. Open daily 9–9. $$–$$$$.

Tierra y Cielo 967-678-1053, Avenida Benito Juárez No.1, Colonia Centro Histórico, San Cristóbal de Las Casas, Chiapas 29200. www.tierraycielo.com.mx. Open daily 7 AM–11 PM. $$–$$$.

Las Tinajas 916-345-4970, Avenida 20 de Noviembre, Esq. Abasolo, Palenque, Chiapas 29960. Open 7–11 daily. $–$$.

Tours Por Chiapas 800-832-8321, 967-678-5581, Bugambilias No. 5, Colonia Bismark, San Cristóbal de las Casas, Chiapas 29267. http://www.toursporchiapas.mx. $$$$.

Viajes Pakal 967-678-2818/6522, Cuauhtémoc No. 6A, Colonia Centro, San Cristóbal de las Casas, Chiapas 29200. http: //viajes.pakal.com.mx. $$$$.

Villa Mercedes 916-345-5231/2, Carretera Palenque-Ruinas Km. 2.9, Palenque, Chiapas 29960. www.hotelesvillamercedes.com. $$–$$$.

Zoológico Miguél de Álvarez del Toro (ZooMAT) 961-614-4700, Boulevard Samuel León Brinois N/N, Private Reserve of El Zapotal, Tuxtla Gutiérrez, Chiapas. Open Tue.–Sun. 9–5:30. $.

Campeche 5

Campeche Tourism Board

CAMPECHE

Given all that it offers, it's a wonder Campeche doesn't get more international tourism. Then again, the mere fact that it's overlooked is part of its charm. Part of the Yucatán peninsula and yet distinct from the adjacent state of Yucatán, Campeche is also bordered by Tabasco, Chiapas, Guatemala, Belize, and Quintana Roo. This is a fascinating place to explore, with a diverse geography, an archaeological treasure trove, and a tremendous variety of things to do and see.

GETTING THERE AND GETTING AROUND *By air:* There are three main ways to get to Campeche by air. **Ingeniero Alberto Acuña Ongay International Airport**, or **Campeche International Airport**, is located about 4 miles southeast of the city. Mexicana and Aeromexico flies from Mexico City to this small airport. **Ciudad del Carmen International Airport** is another option, but it's smaller (although it does have daily direct flights to Houston, Texas), and lies about 130 miles from the capital city of Campeche. A better option would be to fly into **Mérida International Airport**, about 100 miles north. There are frequent shuttles to the capital city of San Francisco de Campeche from either airport.

By bus: Bus travel to the city is efficient and cheap, with ADO offering transport from numerous cities to Campeche. From Mérida, buses run almost every hour and take two hours to reach the capital. Buses from Ciudad del Carmen take about an hour longer. If you want to travel by bus from Mexico City, treat yourself to first class; the 17-hour trip can feel a lot longer. From Palenque, Chiapas, ADO runs frequent trips (a manageable five hours). From San Cristóbal de las Casas in Chiapas, the journey is twice as long.

By car: Driving here from Mérida is a short and easy journey south along Highway 261. Conversely, if you're traveling down from Palenque, plan on a longer journey, and a full day's travel from San Cristóbal.

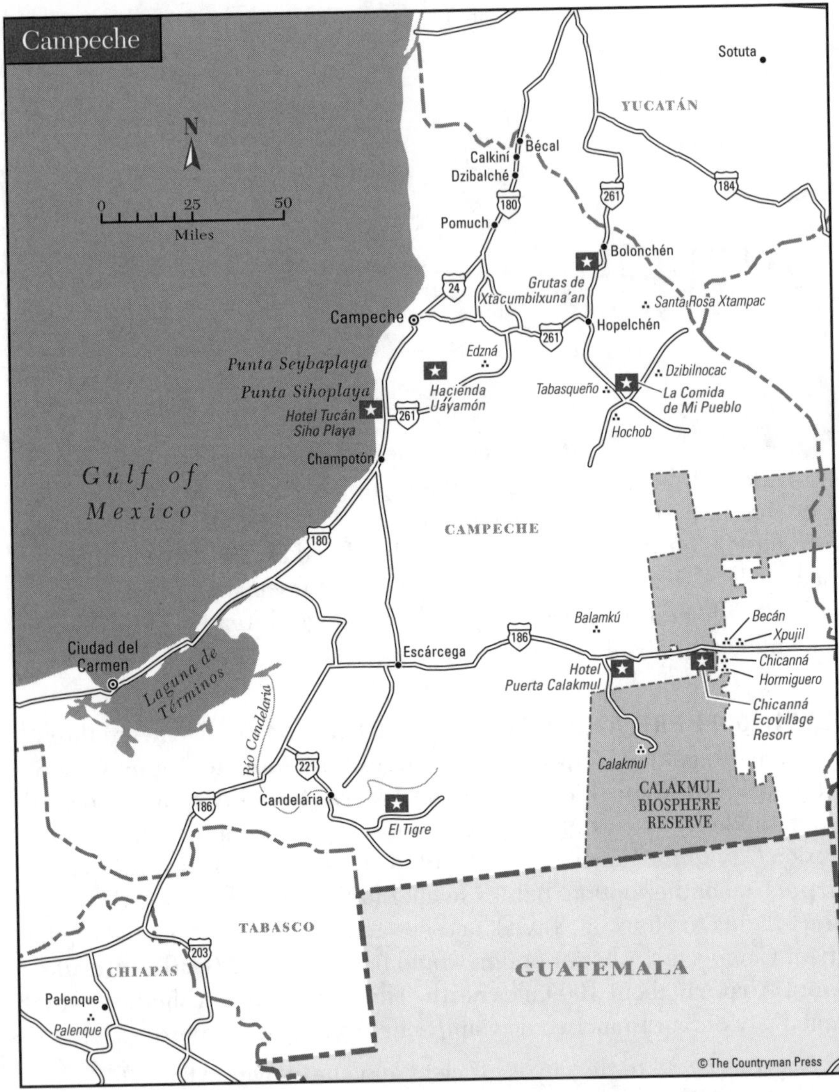

To tour the archaeological sites in Campeche, you'll either be taking tour buses, a long and sometimes complicated combination of bus and taxi, or going by car (which I recommend). The roads are generally good, but some sites, like Tabasqueño, are easier to reach by jeep. Car rentals are easy to find in the city center, main hotels, and airport.

However, while you're exploring the city of Campeche, a car is completely unnecessary. This beautiful colonial town is best enjoyed on foot, and taxis are a plentiful and cheap means of getting around. The city's buses are nothing fancy and often crowded, but they'll also get you just about anywhere and cost next to nothing.

FROM AH KIN PECH TO CAMPECHE

The history of Campeche, and particularly its capital city of San Francisco de Campeche, starts with its ancient indigenous roots. This area was once part of the heartland of a vast and prosperous Maya empire, with mighty capitals like Calakmul, Balamkú, and Edzná dominating the region (however, the indigenous history of this land stretches back before the Maya, to as early as 3,000 BC).

As we know, the Maya civilization underwent a sharp decline in the eighth and ninth centuries. By the time the Spanish showed up in the 1500s, the indigenous population had dwindled, but still managed to resist the conquistadors. In fact, the Spanish lost their first battle here, in the town of Champotón, in 1517. Francisco de Montejo tried to conquer this territory in 1527; it took him until 1540 to finally take the important Maya port of Ah Kin Pech, which he christened San Francisco de Campeche (he would go on to establish Mérida two years later).

CAMPECHE WAS A WALLED FORTRESS CITY BUILT TO REPEL PIRATE ATTACKS AND NATIVE REBELLION.

Campeche Tourism Board

Initially, the city of Campeche was the only port on the peninsula, making it a vital asset to the conquistadors. The Spaniards continued to encounter stiff resistence from the natives, despite the best efforts of the Franciscans to convert them to Catholicism. The discovery of a natural red dye produced from trees led to an economic boom, but also to a spate of pirate attacks during much of the 17th century. To protect themselves, the citizens of Campeche built fortresses and a 26-foot-high wall around their city, punctuated by four large gates. Campeche became a fortified city.

After the War of Independence, the entire Yucatán peninsula, including modern-day Campeche and Quintana Roo, was annexed as a state of the Mexican empire, and Campeche became one of five seats of government of the Yucatán.

Its early years were turbulent and marked by uprisings and declarations of an independent Yucatecan republic. The peninsula permanently joined Mexico in 1848, but unrest continued in the region. In 1857, civil war led to Campeche's separation from the rest of the Yucatán, forming a new state with a new capital city of Campeche. The state of Campeche was recognized by the Mexican congress in 1862.

Campeche's struggles did not end with statehood. In 1902, it was forced by Porfirio Díaz to surrender part of its territory to help create the province of Quintana Roo, which became a state in 1972. But Campeche's fortunes really changed in the 1970s, when the discovery of oil off its coast transformed its economic fortunes and converted the city of Ciudad del Carmen into practically a satellite of the oil industry. Oil remains the chief source of revenue for Campeche today, and accounts for over half of the country's oil; tourism ranks a distant second, and centers on Campeche's most fascinating, if not wealthiest, resource: its ancient Maya cities.

As with Chiapas and Yucatán, I cannot hope to write about every archaeological site in Campeche; 2,200 of them are registered, and unknown thousands more have not been documented. Instead, I've chosen to review those I believe are among the most interesting and influential of their era.

✷ Archaeological Sites

Most archaeological sites in Campeche are open from 8 to 5 (El Tigre is open until 4) and charge a nominal fee. Note: Calakmul charges a separate fee to enter the biosphere reserve leading to the site.

Calakmul

GETTING THERE From Campeche, head south along Carretera 261 until you reach Carretera 186. Turn left and pass the town of Escárcega. Near the town of Conhuás, you'll come to the entrance of the reserve; pay the toll and drive to the site, another 37 miles from here.

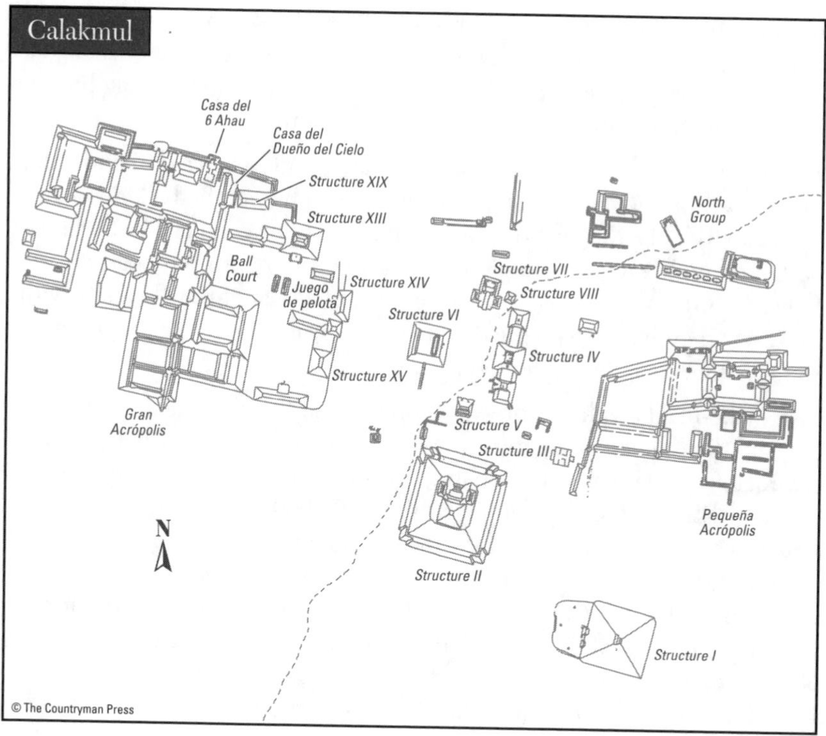

"Calakmul" means "The City of Two Adjacent Pyramids" in Maya, but this was a name given in the 1930s. Its original name was Ox Te' Tuun ("Three Stones"). This city's size, importance, and history propel it to an exclusive class of civilization rivaled by few others in the Maya world.

A UNESCO World Heritage Site, the ancient city is located within the Calakmul Biosphere Reserve, Mexico's largest nature preserve. While this makes for a lengthy entrance to the site (approximately an hour from the gate), it also protects the majority of the 400 endangered species found in this region. I happened to encounter a spider monkey on my way to Calakmul (who kept throwing things at me because my guide and I were too loud), but also found here are jaguars, tapirs, and 235 bird species. To put it in perspective, the reserve is a bit larger in size than the state of Delaware.

To put something else in perspective, consider that Calakmul is believed to be among the largest of all Maya cities. Its chronology runs from roughly 900 BC to AD 900, although there was life here until the time of the conquest. Calakmul reached its apex during the 6th and 7th centuries, when it housed a population of around 50,000. By AD 650, 70 percent of Maya territory fell under its dominion. In 1932, pioneering archaeologist Sylvanus Morley opined that Calakmul was a second-rate city, big but not particularly important. Today, we know differently.

To understand Calakmul's place in the Maya world, we have to understand the concept of the *emblem glyph*. Emblem glyphs signified a kind of royal dynastic title, like the coat of arms, of the most powerful cities. And one particular emblem glyph, depicting a snake head, pops up repeatedly in Maya records. Archaeologists have found stelae that chronicle a city with a snake-head emblem glyph sacking and destroying mighty Palenque in AD 599. That city is believed to be Calakmul.

The snake-head glyph is more widespread (and listed on more hieroglyphic texts) than the glyph of any other Maya city. It most likely belongs to the Kaan royal line, which probably dates back to the Prelassic-era powerhouse of El Mirador, in Guatemala. With 200,000 people and 10,000 structures, El Mirador was bigger than Calakmul, and it is likely that the latter fell under its dominion. After it fell, between AD 150 and 250, Calakmul and Tikal, bitter rivals, continued its hegemony, with the former serving as the seat of the Kaan dynasty. Another sign of Calakmul's power: Nine jade masks—a treasure found only at the most important Maya centers—have been discovered at the city. Researchers have also uncovered close to 7,000 structures and 120 stelae at Calakmul (more than any other site), but only a fraction of this number is open to the public today.

To get to the city, you first have to walk about 20 minutes along a trail through the jungle (where I had my spider monkey encounter). Calakmul's nucleus is built around two massive pyramids that rise majestically above the forest canopy to offer breathtaking views that reach to Guatemala and even, with a pair of binoculars, to El Mirador. The tallest of these, **Estructura II**, originally measured 656 feet square by 200 feet in height, making it one of the largest structures in the Maya world. A tomb found at this pyramid is believed to belong to Yukom Yich'ak K'ak' (Jaguar Paw), who ascended to the throne in 686 and was one of the city's greatest rulers. **Estructura I** appears to be the larger of the two pyramids, but benefits from being built on a hillock. In actuality, it measures 160 feet in height.

The **Gran Acrópolis** was designed as an urban space divided into areas for the elite and the rest of the population. Here you'll find **Estructura IX**, the only ball court uncovered at Calakmul. West of the acropolis lies a large residential area made up of palaces facing 14 patios and plazas. **Estructura VIII** was most likely used for astronomical observations, while **Estructura V**, with its remarkable ten stelae, may have served as a memorial. At the smaller acropolis of **Chik Naab**, north of the Great Plaza, a painted mural shows it was used as a residential area.

Campeche Tourism Board

ESTRUCTURA II IS CALAKMUL'S LARGEST BUILDING AND ONE OF THE LARGEST STRUCTURES IN THE MAYA WORLD.

One of Calakmul's more technologically advanced features is its network of waterways. Because of the lack of surface water, the city developed an impressive hydraulic system comprised of cisterns, canals, and reservoirs, one of which is the largest example in the Maya world.

And finally, with most of the stelae at Calakmul in poor shape (limestone does not hold up well to time and weather), **Stela 51** is easily the best preserved at the site. The Stela shows ruler Yuknoom Took' K'awiil and dates to AD 731.

I cannot mention Yuknoom Took' K'awiil without giving due to the most prominent of Calakmul's rulers, Yuknoom Ch'en. A contemporary of Pakal the Great in rival Palenque, Yuknoom Ch'en governed from AD 636 to 686. During his reign, Calakmul made war on Tikal a remarkable four times, in 657 and 659, and again in 677 and 679. The city also battled Palenque twice in 657 and 659 (dispelling the myth of the Classic-period Maya as primarily a peaceful civilization). Calakmul was victorious in all of these battles. (To give Tikal its place in the sun, the city took its vengeance on Calakmul in 695, attacking the city and killing Yuknom Ch'en's son, Yuknoom Yich'ak K'ak'.)

Balamkú

GETTING THERE Balamkú is located almost 2 miles northeast of the community of Nuevo Conhuás, which is located on Km. 95 of Carretera Federal 186.

A recent discovery (it was first reported in 1990 by archaeologist Florentino García Cruz), Balamkú is a small site with a major treasure: one of the largest stucco friezes ever found in Maya lands. Its name, which means "Temple of the Jaguar," comes from one of the stucco jaguars on the frieze. The site is typical of the Petén style; the Río Bec style, by comparison, featured much less stucco work.

Although the site has been occupied since 300 BC, its zenith seems to have occurred from AD 300 to 600, and its spectacular friese dates from AD 400. As yet, only the central and south groups have been explored. The masterpiece of stucco found in the temple in the central group measures close to 55 feet long by almost 6 feet high. It illustrates the opposite sides of the underworld, as well as dynastic and solar cycles. The frieze originally depicted four kings, or governors, of which only two remain. They are shown both in the act of dying (descending into the Monster of the Earth's fanged mouth) and being born, rising from the jaws of an amphibian. Amphibians, as creatures who live in both land and water, symbolize this duality: land being earth, and water traditionally serving as the entrance to the underworld (as in *cenotes*). The friese also shows two jaguars tied up, symbolizing both war and sacrifice.

A word on stucco: My guide informed me that, to create just a single square meter (3.28 square feet) of stucco decoration, the Maya needed to burn 25 trees in wood ovens. The vast use of stucco used to beautify their cities thus points to the truly immense effort that went into their ornamentation.

Becán

GETTING THERE From Campeche, head south along Carretera 261 until you reach Carretera 186. Turn left and pass the town of Escárcega. You'll also pass turnoffs to Balamkú and Calakmul before you arrive at Becán. The distance from Campeche City is about 186 miles.

Becán has a long history. Settled as far back as 600 BC, it became a regional capital several centuries later. The site experienced its apogee from AD 600 to 900, marked by the construction of several major buildings in the Río Bec style.

Because of its strategic location at the midpoint of the Gulf and the Caribbean, Becán served as a major trading center. One might think it was its vital commercial value that led to the creation of Becán's most distinguishing and unusual feature: a broad moat that encircles the heart of the

Campeche Tourism Board

BALAMKÚ'S IMPRESSIVE FRESCO DEPICTS NUMEROUS THEMES CENTRAL TO MAYAN CULTURE AND BELIEFS.

city. In fact, it is believed the ditch served as a drainage system to avoid flooding. Measuring over 50 feet wide and 8 feet deep, it's a unique construction. The ditch had seven entrances into the city center, and it is through one of these that you enter the site today. Numerous structures—primarily residential and agricultural in nature—have been found around the moat, but the largest and most important buildings lie within.

The major structures at Becán combine two architectural styles: Chenes and Río Bec. Begin your tour at the monumental Plaza A, which contains Structures I through IV. **Structure I** shows the remains of twin towers measuring almost 50 feet high, a characteristic element of the Río Bec style. Construction on this temple began in AD 300, but continued up to AD 1000. A temple atop the pyramid was accessed by a secret stairway and features a door in the shape of the mouth of the monster of the Earth. **Structure II** is a residential building that in its heyday bore great elaboration and ornamentation. In the central hall of this building, archaeologists uncovered two elaborately decorated tombs which were never occupied. The long **Structure III** was a later addition to the plaza and dates to the terminal Classic period, while **Structure IV** gives us more Río Bec elements with its rounded corners and ornamental staircases.

The next cluster of buildings comprise Structures VIII to X. **Structure VIII** resembles Structure I with its twin towers, and features a broad

Campeche Tourism Board

BECÁN COMBINES THE ARCHITECTURAL STYLES OF THE CHEN AND THE RÍO BEC.

stairway leading to an entrance framed by the ruins of a mask of the Monster of the Earth. Beneath the base of this pyramid, archaeologists discovered ten large chambers that may have been reserved for ritual purposes and sacrifices. **Structure IX** is the tallest pyramid at Becán, measuring close to 140 feet in height. It was built over at least three phases dating back to the Preclassic era. **Structure X** was another large residential building with elaborate ornamentation that still retains vestiges of its elaborate roof comb. Behind Structure X is Becán's main ball court.

Chicanná

GETTING THERE Chicanná is located 180 miles southeast of Campeche, just west of Becán, and follows the same route from Campeche (Carretera 261 to Carretera 186).

Chicanná, which means "The House of the Mouth of the Serpent," is a site that shows us a dramatic mix of Río Bec and Chenes architecture. This small site flourished in the late Classic period, from AD 550 to 700, and fell under the dominion of Becán.

CHICANNÁ'S ANTHROPOMORPHIC FAÇADE JUSTLY GIVES IT ITS NAME, "THE HOUSE OF THE MOUTH OF THE SERPENT."
Campeche Tourism Board

The most outstanding edifice here is **Structure II**, a squat, one-story building with a spectacular, intricately detailed façade of a giant mouth with jaws wide open, which serves as its main entrance (you can see the "bottom teeth" and mandible on the floor in front of the doorway). The zoomorphic mask, believed to represent the Monster of the Earth, is typical of the Chenes style and is flanked by *witz* masks. In contrast, **Structure I** on the west side of the plaza represents the Río Bec style, with its rounded corners, twin towers, decorative staircases, and comb roof. The other structure of note is **Structure XX**, located about 100 feet northeast of the main plaza, which gives us another example of the giant mouth façade and *witz* masks.

Dzibilnocac

GETTING THERE Take Carretera Federal 261 from Campeche to Hopelchén, which lies 56 miles away from the capital, and from here continue along the road to Dzibalchén, about 25 miles east. Once you get here, head northeast along the road for just over 12 miles to Iturbide, which is adjacent to the site.

Although Dzibilnocac was a large city with numerous structures, it's been reclaimed by the jungle, and only a single building is open to visitors today. Lying squarely in Chenes territory, the city boasts distinctly Río Bec elements, while its size points to regional hegemony in this area.

Edificio A-1 measures 230 feet long by almost 100 feet wide by 42 feet high. Over its long base, three Río Bec–style towers were built, along with rooms with vaulted ceilings. Only the eastern tower still stands, atop which sits a highly decorated temple accessed only by a decorative, nonfunctional staircase. At the sides of the temple's base you can see the lower jaws of the Monster of the Earth flanked by *witz* masks.

Edzná

GETTING THERE Edzná is the closest archaeological site from Campeche city, located just 37 miles southeast off Highway 180.

While I fully acknowledge Calakmul's dominance, Edzná is my favorite archaeological site in Campeche for its unparalleled splendor. Southernmost of the Puuc sites, Edzná was inhabited as early as 400 BC and abandoned as late as the 15th century. Protected by Calakmul, the city at its height was also a regional capital. The name "Edzná" translates to "House of the Itza," although the city also bore the monikers "House of the Gestures," thanks to its stucco relieves, and "House of the Echo" for its incredible acoustics (we'll get to that in a minute).

The importance of Edzná was underscored when archaeologist Ivan Šprajc discovered a nearby complex in 2002. Named the **Altar de los Reyes** (Altar of the Kings), the complex included an altar on which was inscribed 13 emblem glyphs, denoting 13 sacred lands. Of these, only five proved legible: Calakmul, Palenque, Tikal, Motul de San José, and Edzná. One of the main reasons for its prominence was its complex system of canals and reservoirs. The Itza knew about hydraulics; their water control system may have served multiple purposes in addition to giving the capital water year-round. It also helped to be an ally of Calakmul, which, through Edzná, extended its influence in the peninsula. (In AD 730, Edzná fought and defeated the large city of Cobá.)

Of the 200 buildings found here, 19 are open to the public. The most striking group is the **Gran Acrópolis**, which has eight temples crowned by the magnificent **Edificio de los Cinco Pisos** (Building of the Five

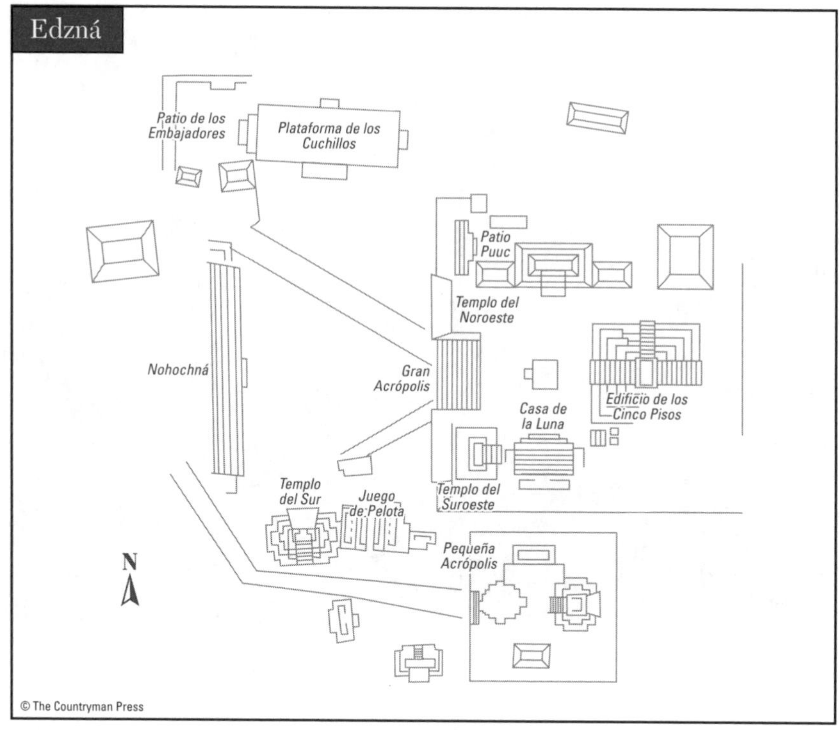

Floors). On the way, stop by the palapa, which houses some of the 30 stelae found at the site, depicting the ball game and some of Edzná's governors (including its most powerful ruler, Kal Chaahk, on **Stela 22**, and a *kalomte'*, or female governor, on **Stela 20**).

One of the newer buildings opened is **Building 518**, notable for its monolithic Petén construction (predating the days of the city's apogee). Continue past this structure to **Nohochná** (Big House). This uncommon elongated structure spans the length of one side of the main plaza. Four halls atop the building once served as a customs house, convention center, auditorium, and administrative offices.

The function of this deliberately large structure was both simple and effective: Edzná welcomed merchants and traders from all over the Mesoamerican empire. One of its canals connected to the Champotón River, giving traders easy access to the city. The Big House restricted access to the main square for commoners, and also funneled visitors through an entrance in the center of the building (kings and dignitaries entered through a different path). To truly appreciate this city, follow in their ancient footsteps: Instead of entering the main plaza with the Big House on your right, loop around and climb to the top of Nohochná, and walk through the niche to get your first glimpse of the city center.

Campeche Tourism Board

THE EDIFICIO DE LOS CINCO PISOS IS EDZNÁ'S CROWN JEWEL.

As you emerge on the other side to the magnificent main plaza, sit down with the Gran Acrópolis in front of you and clap your hands to test its wonderful acoustics. There's another piece of magic at play here. From May 1 to 3 (the time of farming) and August 7 to 8 (the time of harvest), the last room in the Big House, dedicated to the god of maize, is illuminated by the sun. The Nohochná is also the best place to catch the **Sound & Light Show** at Edzná on Friday and Saturday nights.

STICK AROUND FOR EDZNÁ'S BEAUTIFUL LIGHT AND SOUND SHOW.

Campeche Tourism Board

Descend the Big House and walk to the right of the plaza, to the ball court and the **Templo de Mascarones** (Temple of Masks). Built between AD 200 and 400, the temple shows two stucco masks of Kinich Ahaw, the Sun god, in two phases: sunrise and sunset.

The temple is part of the Small Acropolis, the oldest group of buildings at the site. From here, continue to the marvelous Gran Acrópolis, which was built and remodeled throughout several centuries. As you enter the plaza, you'll pass by a low, square opening in the wall, which provided access to a *temazcal*; before entering the sacred core of Edzná, visitors were required to ritually cleanse themselves. The low opening simulated exiting from a womb.

Here's a tip to experience the incredible acoustics at the acropolis. When you enter the plaza, clap your hands; you'll hear a normal echo. Then, walk toward the **Templo de la Luna**, clapping your hands as you go; the sound of the echo changes. When you reach the temple, clap repeatedly; the echo supposedly resembles the call of the quetzal.

The Building of the Five Floors, with its handsome roof comb and central double-staircase of 65 steps, measures just over 100 feet and is the site's most striking structure. The temple features six different architectural styles, evidence of four remodeling phases as well as outside influence in the city. Note the glyphs at the base of the staircase and, on the north side, a concave talud construction and stucco relief typical of the Petén style.

As you leave the acropolis, walk north to the **Templo del Norte**, another structure that was remodeled at least four times over the course of its life and features a blend of Puuc, Chenes, and Chontal architecture. The temple faces a Puuc patio characterized by the precise cut of its stones.

Hochob

GETTING THERE Follow the route from Campeche to Dzibalchén, taking Carretera Federal 261 to Hopelchén, and continue along the road to Dzibalchén. Keep heading southeast past Dzibalchén for another 15 miles to reach Hochob.

Another small site deep in Chenes territory, Hochob, which translates to "Place Where the Corn Was Harvested," is one of the best-preserved examples of its architectural style. The site is similar to Chicanná in that its main attraction is a fantastic zoomorphic mask of the Monster of the Earth framing a doorway.

There are three buildings at Hochob, along with a *chultún,* or cistern, that the Maya used to safeguard their water supply. **Structure I**, or **The Palace**, boasts an elaborate mouth of the serpent monster; in fact, you'll find five of them in the intricate and beautifully preserved façade. **Structure II** is residential, but here again you can see an entrance fashioned to look like the mouth (and, in this case, outstretched tongue on the floor) of the Monster of the Earth. Inside are traces of bedchambers of some sophistication, with stone beds and even holes in the wall where curtains were once hung. **Structure III**, with its high, crested roof, returns us to the Río Bec style.

Campeche Tourism Board

HOCHOB GIVES US ANOTHER MAGNIFICENT ANTHROPOMORPHIC MASK AS A TEMPLE OPENING.

Santa Rosa Xtampak

GETTING THERE From Campeche, head east on Highway 261 to Hopelchén. North of the town you'll find a turnoff onto a rough road that will slow you down unless you have a four-wheel drive. The site is another 28 miles along this road.

The out-of-the-way Santa Rosa Xtampak is worth the visit for its two most important buildings: the **Palacio** (Palace) and **Edificio Boca de Serpientes** (Serpent Mouth Building). The site's curious name comes from the Santa Rosa Hacienda that used to be here, and the Mayan *xtampak,* which means "old walls." It traces its origins to 800 BC, and lasted until about AD 1200.

The three-level palace, built in AD 790 and dedicated to K'awiil, is an intriguing and highly complex construction. It has 11 staircases and a total of 45 rooms. Among its most distinguishing features are two internal stairways that connect the building's three levels. The exterior stairs on the sides are narrow and ornamental.

The other building features a doorway with an elaborate façade in the form of a serpent's mouth. An interesting sidenote: The locals call this the

Maternity Building because of the resemblance of its façade to a woman in the position of giving birth, legs spread open (the "fangs" of the serpent) and womb open (the doorway). The building's most interesting feature is found on the other side, where you'll see the descending body and head of a second serpent. Archaeologists believe this building represented a supernatural being.

Two other buildings can be seen here: The **Cerro de Las Estrellas** (Hill of the Starts) is almost hidden by the forest, but rises almost 100 feet in height and was built in one constructive phase. The **Cuartel** (Barracks) has a façade on the right side of the building with a criss-cross pattern representing the royal mat upon which a king or governor would sit. This indicates a residence of a royal.

With structures of this refinement and obvious importance, some archaeologists theorize that this city was once a great capital of the Chenes empire. Xtampak had its own emblem glyph, giving credence to this viewpoint. (Given that there are around 500 Chenes sites in this region, that's quite a statement.) Because the site is still being explored, you might find archaeological work in progress while you're here.

Tabasqueño

GETTING THERE The small site of Tabasqueño is located 80 miles southeast of Campeche. Take Highway 261 to Hopelchén and continue toward Dzibalchén. Tabasqueño is less than 4 miles from this site, and less than a mile off the main road on a rough, potholed trail.

Another marvelous example of Chenes architecture, Tabasqueño's star attraction is the **Palacio-Templo** (Temple-Palace), built between AD 650 and 850. You can't help but be drawn almost magnetically to the outstanding zoomorphic façade atop a low base, which represents, again, Itzamná. The upper incisors of its jaw form a T shape, representing Ik, god of the Sun. On each corner, note the "waterfall" of *witz* masks.

A short walk from the temple-palace is an unusual structure: **La Torre** (The Tower). A ramp leads up to a square column, rising a mere 16 feet in height, which was used for astrological observations, particularly to register the solstices and equinoxes. Next to the Tower is **Structure 3**, a small building with two cylindrical altars, one at its base and the other before the inner enclave at the top.

El Tigre

GETTING THERE El Tigre is located 186 miles south of Campeche City, but it's a full day's journey to get here. Take Highway 261 to Escárcega. From here, follow the road to Candelaria, where you can either hire a boat to bring you to the site, or take the Escárcega-Villahermosa Highway to Nuevo Coahuila Village, turning on the detour to Monclova at Km. 13.5 to reach the site.

Remote and pristine, El Tigre is best reserved for travelers who have the time and interest to see as much as possible. Of course, El Tigre (The Tiger) is not its original name; the city was called Itzamkanac. Its location on the banks of the Río Candelaria made El Tigre, first settled in the Preclassic era, an important port and trade post between the Petén region and the coast. Its most important structures were built from 200 BC to AD 200. During the height of the Classic period, El Tigre did not have much relevance, but it flourished in the late Classic, and in the Postclassic period was considered one of the great Chontal capitals of the Acalan region (over 180 sites have been discovered here). An aerial view of the site shows not only its vast construction but also the ingeniously designed network of canals built to channel the river inland to agricultural plots.

El Tigre also pops up in Aztec history; it was in this area where Cuauhtémoc, ruler of the Aztecs from 1520 to 21, was executed by Hernán Cortés after his capture and torture.

In the ceremonial center of El Tigre lies its largest building, **Structure 4**, a massive quadrangular temple with a base of 650 feet long by 650 feet wide. **Structure 1** is almost as impressive, with a temple atop an elongated base reaching 75 feet in height. In front of the temple are four platforms. At Platform 1C you'll find two molded stucco masks of human faces. A third stucco mask is more zoomorphic, taking a hybrid iguana-crocodile form. On the southeast corner of this building lies the **Palacio**, which shows strong Río Bec architectural influence.

✱ Lodging

Campeche City is a wonderful place at which to stay. While it's only close to one prominent ruin, a rental car will get you around without too many difficulties. However, there are plenty of options for those who want to stay close to the major archaeological zones.

Within Campeche City, you generally have a choice of smaller, colonial-style boutique hotels in the historic city center and larger, more modern waterfront properties. Among the former, one of the most outstanding and luxurious is **Hacienda Puerta Campeche**, a beautifully restored 17th-century colonial building that was once known as Casa Guerrero, a general goods store specializing in items from Europe. Your stay here begins with a welcome cold towel and beverage. The 15 spacious suites and massive bathrooms are richly decorated with antique pieces and modern comforts. The hotel's most outstanding feature is its spectacular pool, which is cleverly built around the exposed walls of the original building.

CASA DON GUSTAVO'S PERIOD FURNITURE AND OLD-WORLD STYLE MAKE IT MY FAVORITE HOTEL IN CAMPECHE.

A personal favorite is **Casa Don Gustavo**, which recreates 18th-century aristocratic Campechano living. Everything has an old-world charm here; the reception is intimate and personal; the 10 suites are furnished with carefully chosen period furniture (the original tiled floors are a wonderful extra touch), and truly impart a sense of bygone luxury. The hotel has numerous niches worth exploring, including an open-air terrace pool and a rooftop Jacuzzi with views of the cathedral.

For value for money, consider **Hotel Castelmar**, centrally located, rustic, and pleasant. Built in 1800, the building still has its original mosaics and a pleasant courtyard where meals are served, along with a decent pool. Rooms might be on the bare side but are well maintained, and some even come with a balcony.

Two budget options in the city center (with breakfast included in the rate) are **Hostal San Carlos**, located a few blocks away from the heart of the city with rooms for under $10, and **Hostal del Pirata** (Pirate Hostel), which has clean rooms, a full kitchen, bike rentals, and a rooftop terrace with wonderful city views.

Hotel Plaza Colonial is an excellent midrange option. The attractive building has 41 colorful guest rooms, a small pool, free wireless Internet, and the benefit of its prime location two blocks from the main plaza.

Along the boardwalk facing the water, three properties offer modern, comfortable accommodations. The **Ocean View Hotel** is a charming destination with warm and friendly service. Rooms are on the small side (unless you pay a bit extra for the executive floor, which gets you a larger space and free breakfast), and the amenities are all up to the standard of a four-star hotel. The courtyard pool, surrounded by leafy vegetation, offers a welcome refuge on a hot day, and the hotel has a small spa.

With 164 rooms, the **Best Western Hotel del Mar** is one of the larger properties in the city. The accommodations run from standard rooms to master suites, and the hotel includes a pool, gym, and a solid restaurant named Lafitte's. All in all, it's a reliable choice.

Finally, the green-and-white **Holiday Inn Campeche** offers

CLOSE TO THE HISTORIC CENTER, THE HOLIDAY INN KEEPS THINGS MODERN AND COMFORTABLE.

plenty of value. The spacious, well-equipped guest rooms have a separate sofa area, coffeemaker, and a 32-inch flat-screen TV. The on-site pool, meeting center, and business center lets the hotel cater equally to leisure and business travel.

If you prefer hotels near the archaeological sites, you have options. **Hotel Puerta Calakmul** is easily the closest hotel to Calakmul, and its 15 cabins provide a true jungle retreat. If you don't mind thatched roofs and mosquito netting, ceiling fans over air-conditioning (not that you usually need an A/C here), and rustic wooden furnishing, you'll be rewarded by a hotel nestled in the biosphere reserve, with a terrific restaurant and plenty of privacy.

Hacienda Uayamon, located between Campeche and Edzná, is built over the shell of a former hacienda that once produced corn, sugar, and henequen (a variety of agave used to make rope and twine). The rooms are luxurious, far outstripping their former use as residences for the hacienda's staff, and the colonial villa and the suites offer hacienda-style living at its best.

A budget-friendly option near the Río Bec region is **Chicanna Ecovillage Resort.** A cluster of two-story, thatched-roof buildings, the resort has bright, clean rooms with private bathrooms, ceiling fans, and solar-powered hot water. Each room has a large terrace facing the surrounding foliage.

Finally, if the beach trumps both the colonial city and the archaeological zones, the **Hotel Tucán Siho Playa**, a former henequen factory, is right on the beach, with large, comfortable rooms and balconies overlooking the ocean.

✷ Dining

Campeche is known for its seafood, and there are several local specialties that should be savored while you're here.

My first brush with *pan de cazón* came courtesy of **El Bastión de Campeche**, which offers a standard but tasty recipe, along with other typical fare, including a wide variety of ceviches, fish, and shrimp dishes. The restaurant is well located in the colonial city center and attracts a local crowd. Nearby, **Marganzo** offers an upgraded experience. Waitresses dressed in colorful folkoric outfits present a menu that includes all the usual suspects as well as a page of more creative *cocina del autor, or* author's cuisine. Start your meal with the refreshing and original beet carpaccio, and follow up with their *camarones al coco,* which are plump and delicious. The best restaurant for elegant fine dining and superb seafood is **La Pigua**, although it's one of the priciest options in town.

PAN DE CAZÓN AT EL BASTIÓN DE CAMPECHE

Lafitte's offers local kitsch and a varied menu of international and local dishes. Named for the famous pirate (they like their pirates here) and even staffed with pirate-costumed waiters, this large restaurant in the lobby of the Best Western has a bit of everything, from salads and pastas to regional specialties. Judging by the *suprema de esmedregal Capitan Lafitte,* a fillet of cobia in an herb sauce accompanied by a very European medley of steamed veggies, the restaurant doesn't disappoint.

One place that every Campechano I know raves about is **Los Portales de San Francisco**, a casual hangout that serves up delicious *panuchos, sincronizadas* (tortillas stuffed with beans and topped with shredded turkey and pickled onion), and *merienda campechana,* along with fresh juices at an open-air setting in a historic plaza. Just as popular are the *cocteleros,* seafood-heavy kiosks that line the boardwalk along the water. On weekends, these become active hangouts for

CAMPECHANO COOKING

Pan de cazón: Campeche's signature dish, this savory entrée comprises three layers of tortilla stuffed with chopped *cazón* (baby hammerhead shark meat) and refried beans. The stack is drenched in tomato sauce and finished off with slices of avocado. You can also sample *tacos de cazón* or Xcatic chiles stuffed with *cazón.*

Camarones al coco: The Campechano version of coconut shrimp is large, succulent Gulf shrimp, breaded in shredded coconut and corn crumbs, deep fried and served in a coconut shell with a side of applesauce (yup, I said applesauce).

Cangrejo moro: You know them as stone crabs, which the locals call "the king of crustaceans"; they're available in the summer months and best served chilled.

Dulce de papaya verde: A popular and saccharine local dessert, this is green papaya cooked in lime water and glazed with sugar and honey syrup.

Merienda campechana: This dish, which dates back to colonial times, is comprised of small cakes of cornmeal, chicken, pork, and beans.

Pámpano en escabeche: Pompano cooked in a pickled *escabeche* sauce comprised of oil, onions, garlic, chiles, paprika, herbs, and sour orange juice.

YOU CAN'T GO WRONG WITH THE *PANUCHOS* AT LA COMIDA DE MI PUEBLO.

Campechanos. Another popular hangout is **Chocol 'Ha**, a casual eatery that serves up fresh sandwiches, crepes, and a mean hot chocolate, among other drinks.

After a half-day's exploration at Calakmul, I was more than ready for lunch at **Puerta Calakmul**, and was rewarded with al dente spaghetti with chile guajillo, white wine, and shrimp (ask for the shrimp; the plate typically doesn't include it), followed by the deliciously sweet and spicy *pechuga*

Pámpano en salsa verde: Pompano cooked in a sauce made with chiles, cilantro, lime, onion, and green bell peppers.

Pulpo: In season from August to December, octopus (*pulpo*) is a favorite food that can be enjoyed in a variety of dishes, from fresh ceviche to *pulpo en escabeche.*

MY FAVORITE CAMPECHE FOOD IS *CAMARONES AL COCO* WITH APPLESAUCE.

de pollo Calakmul, made with local honey, onion, and a touch of habanero chile.

Around Dzibalchén, a local woman uses her driveway as a small restaurant called **La Comida de Mi Pueblo** (The Food of My Town). It is indeed, with a limited menu of daily dishes. Her specialty is *panuchos*; and the *café de olla,* or pot-cooked coffee, is delicious as well.

Arrecifes Restaurant at the Tucan-Siho Playa makes for a nice stop even if you aren't staying at the restored hacienda. Located steps from the beach, you can dine on fresh seafood entrées such as octopus in a spicy garlic sauce and a shrimp steak à l'orange. For something a bit more elegant, drop in at **Hacienda Uayamon** for fine regional dining in an incomparable setting.

✷ Don't Miss

As much as I'm awed by Campeche's archaeological offerings,

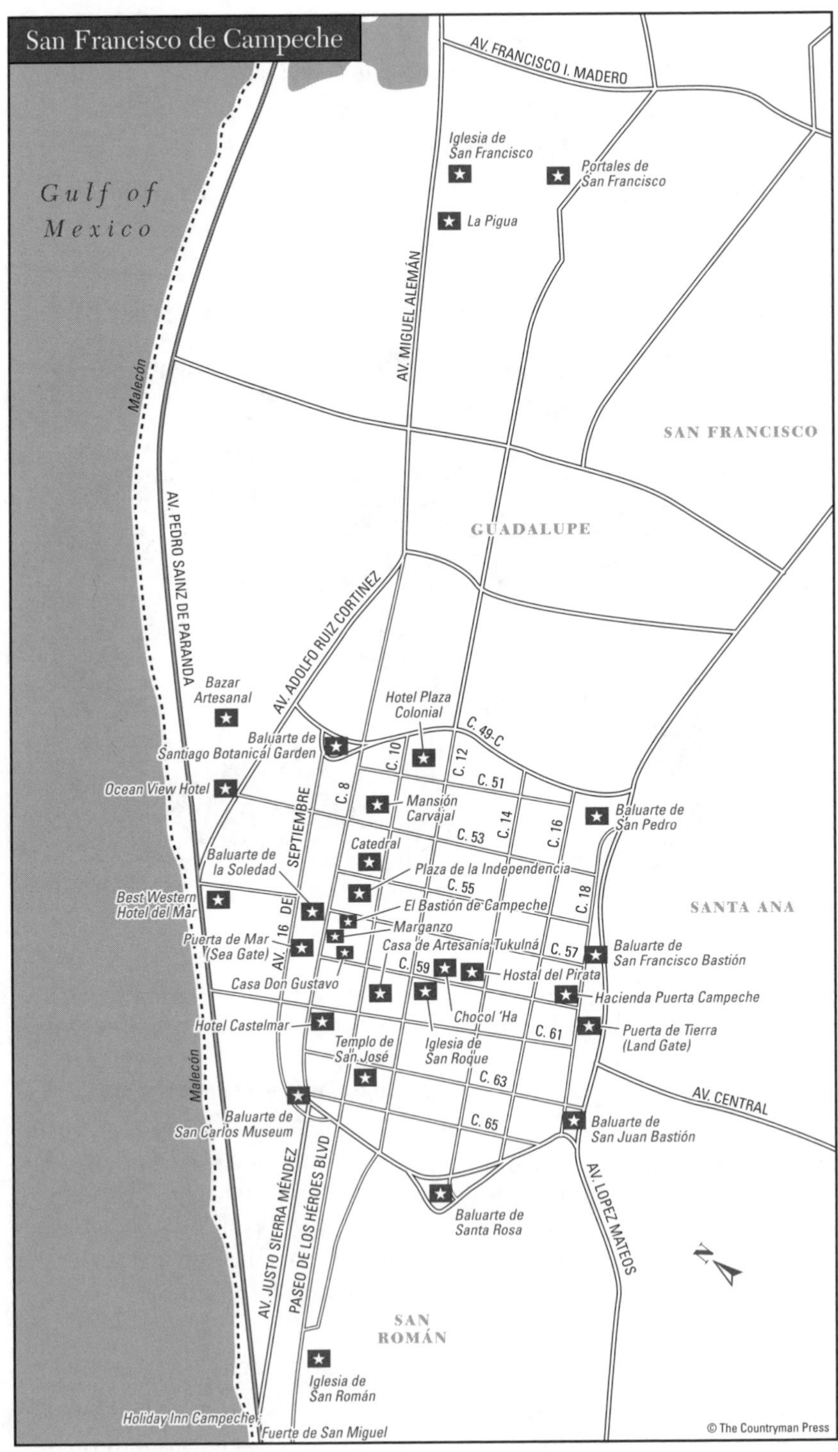

San Francisco de Campeche
Gulf of Mexico
AV. FRANCISCO I. MADERO
Iglesia de San Francisco
Portales de San Francisco
La Pigua
AV. MIGUEL ALEMÁN
Malecón
SAN FRANCISCO
AV. PEDRO SAINZ DE PARANDA
GUADALUPE
AV. ADOLFO RUIZ CORTINEZ
Bazar Artesanal
Hotel Plaza Colonial
C. 49-C
Baluarte de Santiago Botanical Garden
C. 10
C. 12
C. 51
C. 8
Ocean View Hotel
Mansión Carvajal
Baluarte de San Pedro
SEPTIEMBRE
C. 53
C. 14
C. 16
Catedral
Baluarte de la Soledad
Plaza de la Independencia
C. 55
Best Western Hotel del Mar
El Bastión de Campeche
C. 18
SANTA ANA
AV. 16 DE
Marganzo
Puerta de Mar (Sea Gate)
Casa de Artesanía Tukulná
C. 57
Baluarte de San Francisco Bastión
C. 59
Hostal del Pirata
Casa Don Gustavo
Hacienda Puerta Campeche
Chocol 'Ha
Hotel Castelmar
C. 61
Puerta de Tierra (Land Gate)
Templo de San José
Iglesia de San Roque
C. 63
AV. CENTRAL
Baluarte de San Carlos Museum
C. 65
Baluarte de San Juan Bastión
Malecón
AV. LOPEZ MATEOS
Baluarte de Santa Rosa
AV. JUSTO SIERRA MÉNDEZ
PASEO DE LOS HÉROES BLVD
N
SAN ROMÁN
Iglesia de San Román
Holiday Inn Campeche
Fuerte de San Miguel
© The Countryman Press

I'm also enchanted by the city of San Francisco de Campeche. Beyond the colonial capital, Campeche offers beaches and boating, ecotourism, and a few fascinating indigenous communities.

San Francisco de Campeche
The colonial city, with its museums, forts, boardwalk, and colorful architecture, is among Campeche's treasures, a UNESCO World Heritage Site, and a place that demands exploration. This is a completely safe and friendly city that rarely fails to impress visitors. Calle 59 is the city's most touristic thoroughfare, home to boutiques, hotels, restaurants, and linking the Puerta de Tierra and Puerta de Mar, two of Campeche's original access points into the walled city. But any tour of this lovely capital has to start in its main plaza.

Plaza de la Independencia. Built in 1540-41, this broad, picturesque plaza, also known as the Zócalo, is the heart of the historic center. The leafy square gets especially busy on weekends, when the roads are closed to cars and bands play in the central bandstand. Bordered on all sides by beautiful colonial architecture, it also boasts the beautiful **Catedral de Campeche**, dedicated to the Virgen de la Purísima Concepción. Begun in 1650, the cathedral was finally completed in 1850, when its second tower, known as La Campechana, was added. From the plaza you can also grab the touristic trolley, or Tranvía, which runs a circuit of Campeche's major points of interest.

Puerta de Tierra and Puerta de Mar. The Land Gate and Sea Gate are two of the four ancient entrances into the old city. The latter takes you from the city center to the malecón, or boardwalk, and was rebuilt after being destroyed in the 19th century. The sea used to come straight to this gate, giving it its name.

Puerta de Tierra is the more interesting destination for its small museum, a tribute to the city's pirate past and Campeche's early leaders. A 1732 French cannon stands silent sentinel in the passageway. But the true fun here is the **Espectáculo de Luz y Sonido** (Light and Sound Show),

THE CATEDRAL DE LA VIRGEN DE LA PURÍSIMA CONCEPCIÓN AT NIGHT

THE CATEDRAL DE LA VIRGEN DE LA PURÍSIMA CONCEPCIÓN IN CAMPECHE

THESE GUYS OFFER AN ENTERTAINING TRIP BACK THROUGH TIME.

a fun pirate reenactment, cannon, and light spectacle. From here, walking tours travel around the walled city during the day, with multilingual guides on hand to relate the city's colorful history.

Fuerte de San Miguel. Located outside the city walls, the San Miguel fort is a taxi ride away. The old Spanish fortification—one of six that guarded Campeche against attack—was designed in 1779 and completed in 1801. It's an excellent example of a colonial fort, with a curved walkway (to prevent cannon fire's getting through) leading to a drawbridge over a dry moat, barracks, and beautiful views from the balustrade.

The fort is also the city's Maya Museum, with an impressive collection of artifacts, ceramics,

THE FUERTE DE SAN MIGUEL FORT AND MAYA MUSEUM

A BURIAL EXHIBIT AT FUERTE DE SAN MIGUEL

sculpture, and jade masks from sites around Campeche.

Baluarte Museums. Many of the city's old fortifications (*baluarte* means "bastion") have been converted into small museums. **Baluarte de la Soledad**, located next to the Plaza de la Independencia, has a permanent exhibit of stelae found throughout Campeche. Baluarte San Carlos is now the City Museum; it houses a detailed model of old Campeche and chronicles the city's early history. Baluarte de Santa Rosa contains a small regional art gallery, and Baluarte de Santiago is now the city's botanical garden (Jardín Botanico Xmuch'haltun), focusing on local flora.

CHURCHES IN CAMPECHE

Like most colonial Spanish cities, Campeche has its share of churches. **Iglesia de San Roque**, built in 1565, was originally called Iglesia de San Francisco in honor of Saint Francis. Inside, take a look at the Solomonic altars, with Saint Francis featured prominently, along with Saint John and Saint Anthony of Padua. (The two figures holding up the altar are a distinctly Maya touch.) The name San Roque comes from a French nobleman who forsook his life of decadence to help the sick.

Iglesia de San Román is rather austere looking and typical of the Franciscans. It has only a single bell tower and—its crown jewel—an ebony figure of Jesus, called "Black Christ," which was brought here from Italy in 1575. Legend has it that two ships were asked to transport the statue; the one that accepted the job reached

IGLESIA DE SAN ROMÁN

THE "BLACK CHRIST" AT THE IGLESIA DE SAN ROMÁN

Campeche safely, while the one that refused was lost at sea.

The last temple built by the Jesuits in the New World was the **Ex-Templo de San José**, and the beautiful baroque façade and Talavera-tiled interior do justice to their final church. The tower on the right hand served as Campeche's first lighthouse, and dates to 1864. And finally, if you want to tread the hallowed ground where the first Mass in the New World was held, hop in a taxi and head to the Barrio de Guadalupe and the **Iglesia de San Francisco**, which isn't the grandest of Campeche's churches but certainly the oldest. Check out the baptismal font where one of Cortés's own grandsons was baptized.

Malecón. The boardwalk is a winding path interspersed with monuments and fountains that stretches across more than 2 miles of the waterfront. By day it's a pleasant place to stroll or jog; if it's too hot, you'll be better served by waiting until the Sun goes down before heading out, when neon lighting adds a touch of man-made beauty to the strip. On the weekend, however, this place transforms, especially near the kiosks that serve fresh seafood and form the heart of a party atmosphere.

Mansión Carvajal. This mansion in the heart of the city center is striking not only for its opulence but for its strong Moorish accents. Owned by Fernando de Carvajal Estrada, once one of the wealthiest landowners in Campeche, the mansion recalls the splendor of the colonial aristocracy of the Yucatán. The mansion now hosts government offices, but you can still walk in and see the most opulent of Campeche's old structures.

Pirate Ship Lorencillo. A day or night cruise aboard a wooden replica of an 18th-century buccaneer's ship, the Lorencillo provides a unique, if slightly cheesy, way to see the city at night. Snacks and drinks are served on board, and the calm waters make for a relaxing excursion at sea.

SHOPPING FOR ARTS & CRAFTS IN THE CITY

Campeche's best handicrafts include hammocks, Panama hats, ceramics, and clothing. Here's where to find them.

Bazar Artesanal. If haggling's not your thing, you'll appreciate the state-run Folk Art Bazaar located by the boardwalk. You'll find a bit of everything Campechano here, and one area even has live arts-and-crafts demonstrations.

Casa de Artesanía Tukulná. Centrally located off Calle 59, this store specializes in jewelry, handicrafts made out of bull horns, hammocks from the town of

DAY OR NIGHT, THE MALECÓN IS A SCENIC DESTINATION.

Campeche Tourism Board

Calkiní, ceramics from Tepakán, and Panama hats from Bécal.

Taller Maya. Located across the street from the Puerta de Tierra, Taller Maya is a cooperative of Maya women who specialize in indigenous arts and crafts such as silver filigree work, henequen hammocks, traditional clothing, bags, and jewelry made with dried seeds.

BEACHES If you're looking for idyllic beaches in the city of Campeche, you'll be disappointed, but venture out and you'll be rewarded with isolated paradises where the Cancún crowds don't flock, and where nature still holds sway over man-made construction.

Playa Bonita is the closest beach to the capital, just 4 miles south of Campeche along highway 180. Both the beach and the ambience here are tranquil. A bit farther on (18 miles southwest along the coast) lies **Playa Seyba**, a white-sand beach with azure waters and

PLAYA SIHO

Campeche Tourism Board

a devoted local following, thanks to its pristine natural setting and a cottage industry of seafood eateries. **Playa Siho**, 6 miles from Seyba, is another white-sand beach, and is famed for a rather infamous rumor: Apparently the privateer and buccaneer Henry Morgan (whom you might know from Captain Morgan rum), is believed to have lived here for a time.

Punta Xen, 16 miles from Champotón, is a small, quiet fishing town with a large beach framed by palm trees. This is also one of 11 areas in the state earmarked for the conservation of hawksbill turtles. Across the road from the beach are a string of decent local eateries. **Playa Sabancuy**, 80 miles southwest of Campeche, is known as a family beach for its super-calm, shallow waters.

Finally, while I recommend making Campeche City your home base, Ciudad del Carmen is known for lovely beaches, and among the best are **Playa del Norte, Playa Caracol**, and **Playa Bahamitas**.

Bécal

Bécal (53 miles north of Campeche City) is a community known for a singular skill: Panama hats, or *jipis* (pronounced "heepees"). The hats are made from the fiber of the dwarf palm and are woven in homemade caves that seal in the extreme humidity required to work the delicate, silken material. Because artisans build these caves in their homes, visitors to Bécal are welcome to visit their residences (ask around once you get here and you'll be pointed in the right direction).

ARTISANS AT BÉCAL

Campeche Tourism Board

Most of the families are involved in the trade, which is a laborious and skilled cottage industry. Hats come in a variety of styles (cowboy, Panama, and Cuban, among others), and the finest, called *sombrero de cuatro partidos*, or four-strand hat, can take up to a month to make. Don't expect bargain prices, but do expect outstanding quality. One highly recommended and decorated master artisan in town is Don Eulegio Chi Tzel, who lives at Calle 27 No. 234.

ECOTOURISM AND FISHING

From tarpon and big game fishing to jungle kayak tours, Campeche takes full advantage of its natural resources. Baby tarpon, or *sábalo,* is particularly abundant here year-round in the Petén nature reserve, although the best fishing months are May to December.

Balam Ka'ax (Tiger's Jungle) is located in the rustic and back-to-nature region of Candelaria, which makes it ideal for fishing, camping, bird-watching, waterskiing,

A WEEKEND IN CAMPECHE

Because Campeche is so spread out, a weekend won't give you the chance to see all of its ruins, but you can see its two most prominent ones, and leave room for some time in the city. Devote the day of your arrival to San Francisco de Campeche. I suggest the following walking tour:

1. Enter Campeche from the **Puerta de Tierra** and turn left to get to the **Plaza de la Independencia** and a visit to the iconic **Cathedral**.
2. Keep going left and you'll come to **Mansión Carvajal**. When you get to Calle 51, you can either turn left and walk down to the **Baluarte de Santiago** and its botanical garden, or, for a quicker tour, turn right and head down Calle 51 to the **Iglesia de San Juan** and the **Baluarte de San Pedro**.
3. Turn right along Calle 18 and pass the **Baluarte de San Francisco** to get to **Puerta de Tierra**. If they have a walking tour, you might want to sign up. Another option is to walk through the gate, turn left, and walk to the **Bazar Artesanal**.
4. When you get back to Puerta de Tierra, walk down Calle 59, enjoying its many attractions, including the **Iglesia de San Roque**, arts-and-crafts shops, and the **Puerta de Mar**.

kayaking, and boat rides. The group also conducts tours to nearby **El Tigre**.

Campeche Tarpon. A Campeche-based company that sticks to what it knows best, which is tarpon fly-fishing.

Campeche Tours. Offers kayak trips in the Petén biosphere, sport and fly-fishing, boat tours through mangrove swamps, and bird-watching excursions.

Sabaleando. Captain Victor Rodríguez runs fly-fishing tours from Campeche, Champotón, and Palizada in the south. In addition, he offers archaeological tours, kayak tours, snorkeling, rappelling, cross-country cycling, and photographic safaris.

Tarpon Town. This company puts together tarpon fly-fishing excursion and lodging packages in Campeche City, including airport transfer to the hotel and pickup the next morning to hit the seagrass flats and mangrove creeks.

5. Stop for lunch at **Marganzo** and then check out the **Baluarte de la Soledad** and its museum.
6. From here you'll need to take a taxi to the **Fuerte de San Miguel** and its Maya museum. You might ask your driver to take you via the **Iglesia San Román** so you can visit the "Black Christ."
7. Return to the city center and explore at your leisure. When you're ready to eat, you can choose between **La Pigua**, if you want an elegant dinner, or hop in a cab and head to **Los Portales de San Francisco**. Ask your driver to take you by the **Iglesia de San Francisco** along the way.

Reserve Day Two for **Calakmul**. You can take a tour, but I recommend renting a car for this day and the next. You can easily spend all day at this site, or you can combine it with visits to **Balamkú, Becán, Chicanná**, and, if time allows, **Xpujil.** Ideally, visit Balamkú first, and then proceed to Calakmul. After, enjoy a hearty lunch at **Puerta Calakmul** and continue on to the other sites.

On Day Three, head out to **Edzná**, and also check out nearby **Tabasqueño, Hochob, Dzibalchén**, and **Santa Rosa Xtampak**. If you have time, you can even try to visit **Dzibilnocac** and **Nohcacab**, part of this group. Enjoy a gourmet dinner at **Hacienda Uayamon** after.

EXTENDED STAY

You can extend the three-day itinerary above to include overnight stays at Puerta Calakmul and Hacienda Uayamon, giving you more time in each site. After, treat yourself to one, or more, of Campeche's beaches. Keep the rental car and head south along Highway 261, beach-hopping as you go, with a stop at a seafood eatery at **Punta Xen** or **Arrecifes Restaurant** at **Hotel Tucán Siho Playa**. You might even want to spend a night or two here. And if you love fishing, enjoy Campeche's teeming waters.

Visiting Campeche's indigenous communities is a must-do. Start with a road trip to **Pomuch** and **Bécal**. You can combine these in a day with the Grutas de Xtacumbilxuna'an. Another day can be enjoyed on the Candelaria River and the **El Tigre** archaeological site. A tour with **Balam Ka'ax** can cover both.

Union Estatal de Silvicultores y Empresarios Forestales de Campeche. Okay, that's a mouthful, but this group is committed to conserving the environment and ecotourism. Their tours (for Spanish speakers only) include rappelling, horseback riding, scuba diving, mountain biking, and camping.

Yax-Ha Ecoturismo Campeche. A park just outside Campeche city, where you can enjoy a variety of activities, including camping, horseback riding, and paintball (they call it *Gotcha* in Mexico).

GRUTAS DE XTACUMBILXUNA'AN. In 1845, in the small town of Bolonchén, two archaeologists—John Stephens and Frederick Catherwood—arrived at the entrance to the Maya Underworld. At least, that's what the locals told them when they brought them to the **Grutas** (Caves) **of Xtacumbilxuna'an** (Hidden Woman). Today, you can descend deep into this natural cave, down 205 steps where fantastic stalagmite and stalactite formations tease the imagination (including human forms that inspire Maya legends about the "hidden woman" and the warrior she loved).

Pomuch

The town of Pomuch is known for two homegrown traditions: its delicious bread, and the ancient ritual of honoring its dead. Located 30 miles northeast of Campeche, Pomuch is beloved for its heavenly homemade loaves of bread, which you can get stuffed with ham, cheese, and jalapeño, and which are available at stores, stalls and bakeries all over town.

Each year, at the end of October (the eve of the Day of the Dead

Festival throughout Mexico), people come to Pomuch for a very different reason: to witness how this community honors its dead. Following Maya customs, the locals respectfully exhume their dead after three years; the skeletons are taken apart and their bones cleaned by their surviving loved ones in the cemetery. The women of the community embroider cloths with the names of their deceased family members and the dates of their death, and place them beneath the cleaned bones. Fresh Pomuch bread is offered to the dead.

✷ Local Knowledge

Campeche has a very thorough and useful English-language online resource for visitors in www.campeche.ca. In the city you'll find numerous tourist information booths, which supply maps and other useful information. They can be found at:

Baluarte de San Pedro Calle 51 and Circuito Baluartes (open 9–1 and 5–9).

Centro Cultural "Casa No. 6," Calle 57, between Avenidas 8 and 10 (open 9–9).

Plaza Moch-Cuouh Avenida Ruiz Cortines S/N (open 8–4 and 6–9).

It's good to have an idea of distances in this state, especially if you're renting a car.

San Francisco de Campeche to:

- Calakmul—190 miles
- Edzná—38 miles
- Santa Rosa Xtampak—80 miles
- Mérida, Yucatán—122 miles
- Palenque, Chiapas—226 miles

Campeche's main hospital is **Hospital Manuel Campos**, located at Avenida Central (981-816-0957, 816-0920). You'll also find the **Red Cross** at Avenida Las Palmas S/N (981-815-2411/2376) and a clinic, **Clínica Campeche** at Avenida Central No. 72 (981-816-5612).

✷ Special Events

Campeche's biggest annual events include:

February 2: **Fiesta de la Candelaria**, celebrated on February 2 in Hool, Champotón, and Candelaria, features folkloric dances, fireworks, rides, and religious processions.

February, leading to Lent: Campeche celebrates **Carnival** in grand style, with parades, processions, live music, and rituals. The festivities begin with Quema del Mal Humor (Burning of Ill Humor) to ensure a happy festival. There are coronations, of "child kings," King and Queen of Carnival, and Queen of the Television.

July 15–30: Ciudad del Carmen comes alive with **Fiesta del Virgen del Carmen**, a festival dedicated to the Virgin. Religious processions, amusement park rides, and dances mark the festivities.

September 14–30: The religious procession **Feria de San Román** is marked with the removal of the "Black Christ" from its place within the Iglesia de San Román. The sacred statue is paraded through the streets, accompanied by processions and revelers.

October 1–11: **Fundación de Campeche and Feria de San Francisco**, the annual homage to the patron saint of Campeche City, takes place.

✱ Contact

Arrecifes Restaurant at the Hotel Tucán Siho Playa 982-823-1200, Carretera Campeche-Champotón Km. 35, Champotón, Campeche 24460. www.tucansiho playa.com. Open daily 7 AM–10 PM. $$.

Balam Ka'ax 981-108-1572, 987-112-7758, 982-103-1565, 1 Avenida de Julio No. 16, between Calles 11 and 13, Candelaria, Campeche 24300. www.ecoturismobalamkaax .com. $$$–$$$$.

Baluarte de la Soledad Calle 57 and Calle 8, next to Plaza de la Independencia, Colonia Centro Histórico, Campeche, Campeche 24000. Open Tue.–Sat. 9 AM–8 PM, Sun. 9 AM–1 PM. $.

Baluarte de Santa Rosa Calles 14 and Circuito Baluartes Sur, Colonia Centro Histórico, Campeche, Campeche 24000. Open Tue.–Sun. 10 AM–3 PM and 6–9. $.

Baluarte de Santiago Avenida 16 de Septiembre and Calle 49, Colonia Centro Histórico, Campeche, Campeche 24000. Open Mon.–Fri. 9 AM–8 PM, weekends 9 AM–1 PM. Free.

Baluarte San Carlos Circuito Baluartes and Avenida Justo Sierra, Colonia Centro Histórico, Campeche, Campeche 24000. Open daily 8–8. $.

El Bastión de Campeche 981-816-2128, Calle 57 2-A, Colonia Centro Histórico, Campeche, Campeche 24000. www.elbastion .com.mx. Open daily 6:30 AM–midnight. $–$$.

Bazar Artesanal 981-127-1036, Avenida San Pedro Sainz de Baranda, Centro Comercial Ah Kim Pech Locales 201–223, Colonia Centro Histórico, Campeche, Campeche 24000. Open daily 10–8. $–$$$$.

Best Western Hotel del Mar 981-811-9191/92, 800-560-8612, Avenida Ruiz Cortines No. 51, Campeche, Campeche, 24000. www.delmarhotel.com.mx. $–$$.

Campeche Tarpon 981-120-4708, 888-777-5060 (within the U.S.), Calle 57 No. 6, between Calles 8 and 10, Colonia Centro Histórico, Campeche, Campeche 24000. www.campechetarpon.com. $$$$.

Campeche Tours 981-816-5452, 981-152-3251, Avenida 16 de Septiembre and Calle 59, Colonia Centro Histórico, Campeche, Campeche 24000. www.campeche tours.com. $$$–$$$$.

Casa de Artesanía Tukulná 981-816-9098, Calle 10 No. 333, between Calles 59 and 61, Colonia Centro Histórico, Campeche,

Campeche 24000. Open Mon.–Sat. 9–8, Sun. 10–2. $–$$$$.

Casa Don Gustavo 981-811-2350, Calle 59 No. 4, Colonia Centro Histórico, Campeche, Campeche 24000. http://casadon gustavo.com. $$$.

Catedral de Campeche On the Plaza de la Independencia on Calle 55, between Calles 8 and 10, Colonia Centro, Campeche, Campeche, 24000. Open daily 6–9. Free.

Chicanna Ecovillage Resort 981-811-9192, Carretera Escárcega-Chetumal Km. 144 S/N, Xpujil, Campeche. www.chicannaecovil lageresort.com. $–$$.

Chocol 'Ha 981-811-7843, Calle 59 No. 30, between Calles 12 and 14, Colonia Centro Histórico, Campeche, Campeche 24000. Open Mon.–Sat. 6 PM–11 PM. $–$$.

La Comida de Mi Pueblo 996-434-4017, Calle 28 S/N, Colonia Centro, Dzibalchén, Hopelchén, Campeche 24611. Open daily 7 AM–9 PM.

Ex-Templo de San José Calle 10 and corner of Calle 65, Colonia Centro, Campeche, Campeche, 24000. Free.

Fuerte de San Miguel and Maya Museum Ruta Escénica S/N, Campeche, Campeche. Open Tue.–Sat. 9–8 PM, Sun. 8 AM–noon. $.

Grutas de Xtacumbilxuna'an Located in the town of Bolonchén, about 74 miles northeast of Campeche. From the city, take Highway 261 and drive past Hopelchén. You'll see a turnoff leading to Bolonchén and the caves. Open daily 9–5. $, guided tours $$, only with five or more people.

Hacienda Puerta Campeche 981-816-7508, 800-325-3589 (within the U.S.), 800-545-7802 (within Mexico), Calle 59 No. 71, Colonia Centro Histórico Campeche, Campeche 24000. www.luxury collection.com/campeche. $$$$.

Hacienda Uayamon 981-813-0530, Km. 20 Carretera, Uayamon-China-Edzná, Uayamon, Campeche 24530. www.luxury collection.com/uayamon. $$$$.

Holiday Inn Campeche 981-1273700, 877-859-5095, Avenida Resurgimiento S/N, Campeche, Campeche 24040. www.holiday inn.com/campeche. $–$$.

Hostal San Carlos 981-816-5158, Calle 10 No. 255, Barrio Guadalupe, San Francisco de Campeche, Campeche 24000. $.

Hostal del Pirata 981-811-1757, Calle 59 No. 47, Colonia Centro Histórico Campeche, Campeche 24000. www.piratehostel.com .mx. $.

Hotel Castelmar 981-811-1204/05, 800-010-1515 (within Mexico), Calle 61 No. 2, Colonia Centro Histórico Campeche, Campeche 24000. www.castel marhotel.com. $–$$.

Hotel Plaza Colonial 981-811-9930, Calle 10, No.15, Colonia

Centro Histórico, San Francisco de Campeche, Campeche 24000. www.hotelplazacolonial.com. $–$$.

Hotel Puerta Calakmul 998-892-2624, Km. 98, Carretera Chetumal-Escárcega, Municipio Calakmul, Campeche. www.puertacalakmul.mx. Restaurant open daily 7 AM–9 PM. $$.

Hotel Tucán Siho Playa 982-823-1200, Carretera Campeche-Champotón Km. 35, Champotón, Campeche 24460. www.tucansiho playa.com. $$.

Iglesia de San Francisco Avenida Miguel Alemán with Mariano Escobedo, Colonia San Francisco, Campeche City, Campeche, 24000. Open daily 8–noon and 5–7. Free.

Iglesia de San Román Calles 10 and Bravo, San Román, Colonia Centro, Campeche, Campeche, 24000. Open daily 7–1 and 3–7. Free.

Iglesia de San Roque Calles 12 and 59, Colonia Centro, Campeche, Campeche, 24000. Open daily 8–noon and 5–7. Free.

Lafitte's 981-811-9191, at the Best Western Hotel del Mar, Avenida Ruiz Cortínes No. 51, Campeche, Campeche, 24000. www.delmarhotel.com.mx. Open Tue.–Thu. 1–midnight, weekends until 4, Mon. 6 PM–midnight $$.

Marganzo 981-811-3898/3899, Calle 8 No. 267, Colonia Centro Histórico, Campeche, Campeche 24000. Open daily 7–10:45. $$.

Mansión Carvajal 981-816-7644, Calle 10 No. 584, between Calles 51 and 53, Colonia Centro, Campeche, Campeche, 24000. Open weekdays 9–3. Free.

Ocean View Hotel 866-539-0036, Avenida Pedro Sainz de Baranda con Joaquin, Malecón de la Ciudad, Campeche, 24010. www.oceanview.com. $$.

La Pigua 981-816-4636, Malecón Miguel Alemán No. 179A Centro, Colonia Centro Histórico, Campeche, Campeche 24000. www.la pigua.com.mx. Open daily 1–5:30 and 7:30–11. $$$.

Pirate Ship Lorencillo 981-816-1990/108-2857, leaves nightly from the Unidad de Lerma Pier (API Port No. 5). Tours leave at noon and 6 PM. $$$.

Los Portales de San Francisco Portales de San Francisco No. 86, Colonia Centro Histórico, Campeche, Campeche 24000. Open daily 6:30 PM–12:30. $.

Puerta Calakmul 998-892-2624, entrance to the Calakmul Biosphere, Escarcega-Chetumal Highway Km. 98, Campeche 24645. www.puertacalakmul.com.mx. Restaurant open daily 7 AM–9 PM. $$.

Puerta de Tierra Calle 59 at Circuito Baluartes, Colonia Centro Histórico, Campeche, Campeche 24000. Open daily 9–9. Free, light and sound show Thu.–Sun. at 8. $. Walking tours Mon.–Fri. 9–5, Sat. and Sun. 9–4. $.

Sabaleando 981-120-4248, puma4001@sabaleando.com.mx. www.sabaleando.com.mx. $$$$.

Taller Maya 981-811-5703, Calle 59, between 16 and 18, Colonia Centro Histórico, Campeche, Campeche 24000. Open Mon.–Sat. noon–8. $–$$$$.

Tarpon Town 981-133-2135, Calle 57 No. 35, between Calles 14 and 16, Colonia Centro Histórico, Campeche, Campeche 24000. www.tarpontown.com. $$$$.

Union Estatal de Silvicultores y Empresarios Forestales de Campeche 981-816-2272, Calle Adolfo Ruiz Cortines S/N, Centro Comercial Ah Kim Pech, Local 302, Colonia Centro Histórico, Campeche, Campeche 24000. www.silvicultorescampeche.org.mx. $$$–$$$$.

Yax-Ha Ecoturismo Campeche 981-819-3470, 981-815-1284, Km. 7, Carretera Chiná-Edzná, Campeche. www.yaxha.com.mx. $$$–$$$$.

The Yucatán: Treasures of the Maya World

6

MÉRIDA

COLONIAL CITIES

INTRODUCTION

For centuries, the Yucatán peninsula formed the heart of the Maya world. In these broad, flat lowlands the Maya erected some of their greatest cities and extended their power and influence to unprecedented heights. Today, the peninsula is home to the greatest concentration of Maya people in Mexico. Originally one state, the Yucatán peninsula is now divided into three: the Yucatán, Campeche, and Quintana Roo.

If you've never heard of these places, chances are you've heard of some of the destinations within their borders. Chichén Itzá, Cancún, Playa del Carmen, Uxmal . . . these are among the most visited sites in Mexico, and give you some idea of the importance of this region. And even they merely scratch the surface of what the Yucatán has to offer.

Like so much of Mexico, this area has a rich, multilayered history that intertwines the fate of the native Indian and the colonial Spanish, the traditions of the ancient and the advances of the modern. In the case of the Yucatán, we also find a historically crucial mixing of disparate indigenous peoples throughout Mexico, including the Toltec predecessors of the Aztecs.

The Yucatán is globally cherished for the incredible surge in culture and architecture of the Maya civilization in the Classic and late Classic period. During a span of roughly 800 years, hundreds of Maya sites settled in the peninsula, and particularly in the modern-day state of Yucatán. The state is also home to rustic Maya villages where the old ways are very much a part of daily life, as well as coastal fishing villages and beachfront communities, and colonial cities of quaint beauty and elegance.

A HISTORY APART

The Yucatán is literally and figuratively apart from the rest of Mexico, and it owes its unique place in modern Mexico to its geography. Long considered too far away and too difficult to reach from the rest of the country, the peninsula enjoyed a relatively long period of isolation. Even during

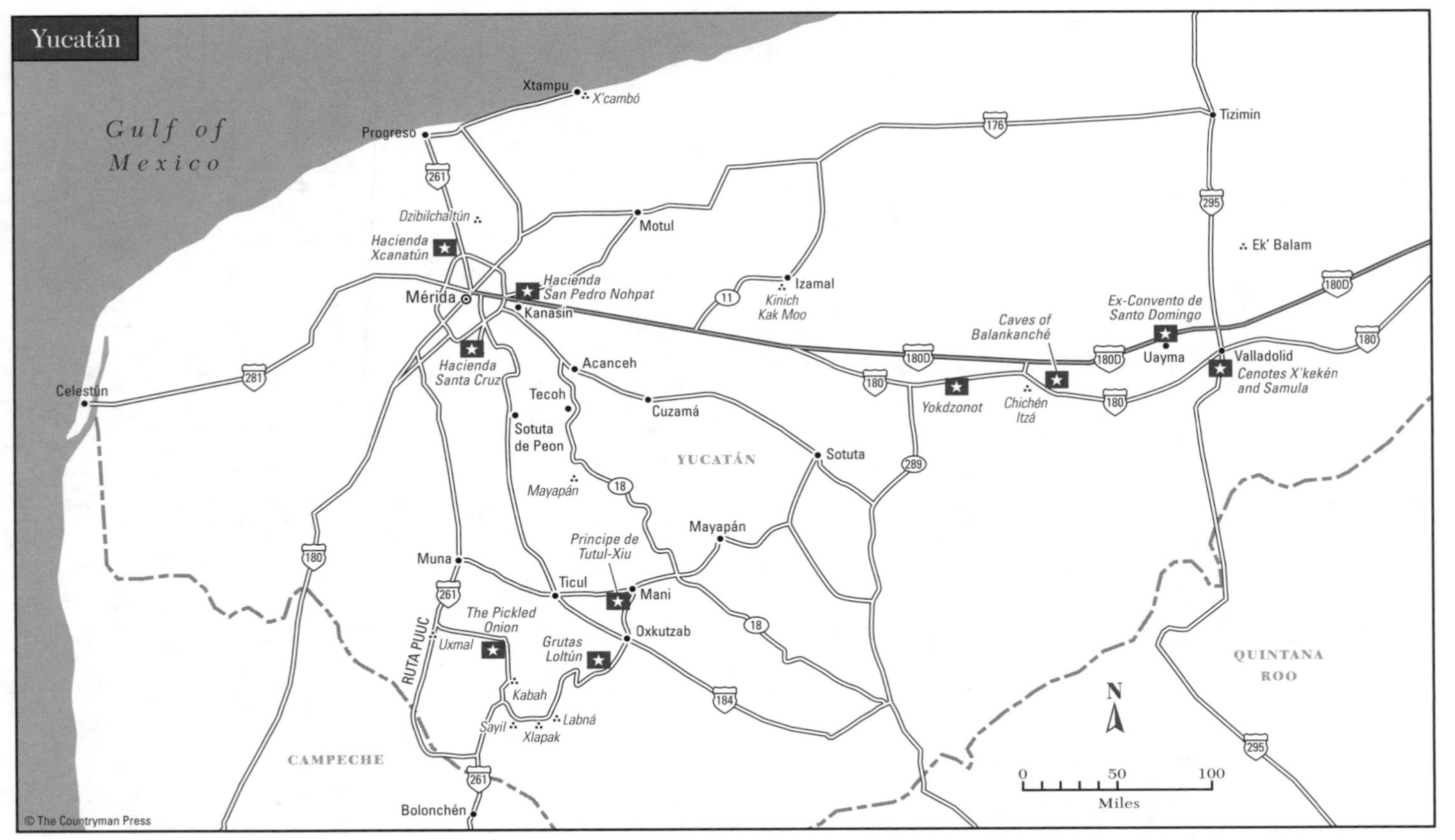
Yucatán
Gulf of Mexico
Xtampu
X'cambó
Progreso
Tizimin
Dzibilchaltún
Hacienda Xcanatún
Motul
Ek' Balam
Mérida
Hacienda San Pedro Nohpat
Kanasin
Izamal
Kinich Kak Moo
Ex-Convento de Santo Domingo
Caves of Balankanché
Uayma
Valladolid
Cenotes X'kekén and Samula
Celestún
Hacienda Santa Cruz
Acanceh
Tecoh
Cuzamá
Yokdzonot
Chichén Itzá
Sotuta de Peon
Sotuta
YUCATÁN
Mayapán
Mayapán
Principe de Tutul-Xiu
Muna
Ticul
Mani
The Pickled Onion
Oxkutzab
RUTA PUUC
Uxmal
Grutas Loltún
Kabah
Labná
Sayil
Xlapak
QUINTANA ROO
CAMPECHE
Bolonchén
N
0
50
100
Miles
176
261
295
180D
11
180
281
289
18
184
© The Countryman Press

conquest, it was left alone for a good decade or so before Francisco de Montejo established the cities of Campeche and Mérida.

The first Spanish expedition to the peninsula occurred in 1517, when conquistador Francisco Hernández de Córdoba arrived and asked some of the indigenous people where he was. To Córdoba, their response (which went along the lines of "What language are you speaking?") sounded like Yucatán. Two years later, Hernán Cortés stopped by on his way to Veracruz. Neither Spaniard was interested in conquest at the time; they took the Yucatán for an island disconnected from their main prize of Mexico.

The conquest of the peninsula took 18 years and involved four figures of notable fame in Mexico: Gaspar Pacheco, a man remembered for his cruelty toward the Indians; Diego de Landa, the first bishop of Yucatán and one of the most polarizing figures in Maya history for his role in both the destruction and preservation of its culture; Nachi Cocom, the *halach uinik* (Maya leader) of the Sotuta region; and Gonzalo de Guerrero, whose remarkable tale has all the makings of a *Braveheart*–meets–*Dances with Wolves* Hollywood blockbuster.

Gonzalo de Guerrero came upon the Yucatán by accident when his ship foundered off the coast of the peninsula in 1511. Of his shipmates, only one other survived: a priest named Gerónimo de Aguilar. Captured and enslaved, they were separated from each other, and each followed a very different path. When Cortés arrived on the scene in 1519, he heard rumors of two white men living with the natives and decided to rescue them; the priest, Aguilar, jumped at the chance, and soon became a valuable interpreter for the conquistadors.

UXMAL IS THE GRANDEST OF THE PUUC SITES IN THE MAYA EMPIRE.

But Guerrero, now tattooed, married, and living a respectable life as a full-fledged Maya warrior, balked. Instead, he took up arms against the Spanish, defending his new home until his death (no one knows with certainty where or when he was killed). Besides his role as a defender of the Maya people, Guerrero is remembered as the father of the mestizo (mixed

Spanish and Indian) race, and was, indeed the first Spaniard to sire mestizo children.

As soon as the conquest came to an end, the Spanish governors faced two immediate problems: how to subjugate the indigenous population, and how to reward the conquistadors who fought for the crown. (It helped that, within the first five years of the conquest, the indigenous population of the Yucatán decreased by 80 percent, largely due to disease.)

To address the former, the Spanish turned to the church, and specifically, to one of the most controversial figures of the conquest: Diego de Landa. Landa arrived in the Yucatán in 1549, one of the first Franciscan monks to reach the peninsula. His was an important charge: to convert the Maya of the region to the Roman Catholic faith. Landa made the city of Izamal his headquarters, where he built the massive Convent of San Antonio de Padua. The monk went about his work with, shall we say, excessive zeal. He is both vilified and respected for two particular episodes that have changed our understanding of the Maya forever.

DIEGO DE LANDA MAY BE HATED BY MANY, BUT HE'S GOT A STATUE IN HIS HOME CITY OF IZAMAL.

In 1562, Landa orchestrated an act that Maya people and historians bemoan to this day. In the town of Maní, he interrupted a native ceremony and ordered the burning of thousands of Maya idols and, far more important, precious Maya codices (books of knowledge written on deerskin), calling them works of the devil. In this one brutal swipe, which Landa called an *acto de fé* (act of faith), the world lost an invaluable store of Maya lore, knowledge, and literature. Such was the ripple effect of this decision that Landa had to return to Spain to defend himself for his actions; however, he could not have been too severely punished; he returned in 1573 as a bishop and continued his work among the Maya.

During his time in Spain, Landa recorded his observations and studies among the Maya in his seminal work, *Relación de Las Cosas de Yucatán* (Relation of

Things in the Yucatán). In these pages, he made extensive notes on the Maya religion, language, culture, and writing system. For centuries, this work became the basis for practically every scholar's interpretation of the Maya way of life. While it cannot be called redemption (in fact, Landa's conclusions were eventually proven to be erroneous), scholars do acknowledge the substantial contribution Landa has made to helping bridge the wide gap in our understanding of this ancient culture.

The other issue of rewarding loyal and influential subjects of the conquest was resolved by a system known as *encomienda,* under which important families were assigned a population of Indians, from whom they could demand a tribute in the form of money, work, or a portion of their agricultural production. Under *encomienda,* the land ostensibly remained with

HENEQUEN RULED THE FORTUNE OF THE YUCATÁN FOR OVER A CENTURY.

the Indians, but when they inevitably couldn't pay their dues, the *encomenderos* took possession of their property and became landowners, with the natives turning to a form of indentured servitude. The new Spanish lords built sprawling haciendas around the peninsula, and quite literally sowed the seeds of an agricultural economy.

From the 16th to the 19th century, this economy evolved in five stages. Initially, the primary product was corn. This was followed by tobacco, cotton, sugar, and finally (and most lucratively), henequen. This tough agave plant became known as *oro verde*, or green gold, and was coveted for its fiber, which was exported around the world and used as rope, particularly in shipping. Following a technological innovation in 1852 that enabled the plant to be quickly machine-stripped (a similar overnight transformation to Eli Whitney's cotton gin), henequen production soared, and the Yucatán's *hacendados* counted among the richest nobles in the world. They lived in luxury, either in beautiful mansions in Mérida or abroad in Europe.

An obvious side effect of this wealth was the growing disparity between the indigenous people who worked the land and the *hacendados*. The people of the Yucatán under Spanish rule fell under a caste system, which predictably began at the top with native Spanish officials and ended with the natives. In 1847, tensions broke out into what became known as the Caste War. Although the war was at its bloodiest in the initial years, the conflict continued for over 60 years, lasting until the Mexican Revolution in 1910 ushered in agrarian reforms. It claimed over 300,000 lives and remains one of the most violent episodes in the history of the peninsula.

The 20th century brought the end of the henequen era. Long an exclusive product, the plant was exported and manufactured in other nations (notably Brazil), and the introduction of nylon and synthetic fibers greatly reduced its demand. Amazingly, the Yucatán today *imports* henequen to meet the local demand.

YUCATÁN AND YUCATECOS

For a long time after the conquest, while the geography eventually got clarified, the perception of the Yucatán as a far-flung and inaccessible area continued even in subsequent centuries. However, the peninsula formed ties to Europe, notably France, and the Caribbean through its ports. This dynamic spawned a very Yucatecan sense of nationalism that continues to this day, along with a unique culinary heritage that combines European flavors with Maya traditions and local ingredients that cannot be found anywhere else in the country

Yucatecans are generally a mild-mannered, laid-back, and convivial lot. They're sometimes viewed as country bumpkins by *chilangos* (the moniker of Mexico City residents), although that doesn't stop droves of Mexico

City residents from migrating to this city each year. I find them to be a warm, proud, and friendly people.

Given its vast number of destinations, spread-out distances, and broad, flat makeup, Yucatán is best explored by car. The roads are generally well kept (a sad footnote here; I know of at least some roads that were built with stones from nearby ruins), safe, and well labeled. Mérida, the beautiful cultural and commercial capital of Yucatán, makes for a perfect starting point from which to explore the state's many wonders.

MÉRIDA

By all accounts, this is one of the most pleasant cities in Mexico. A number of factors contribute to this assessment. For one, Mérida has been ranked the safest city in Mexico, and enough late nights walking the streets in complete security affirms the claim. Second, this city celebrates its strong European influence. From broad, tree-lined boulevards to neo-classic *quintas,* or mansions, Mérida is a living tribute to the splendor of the colonial New World and the riches that the land bestowed upon its citizens.

The city is a melting pot of cultures but retains its strong Spanish and Maya identity. And finally, with its lovely Historic Center, frequent events and celebrations, and vibrant social life, there is always something to do in Mérida . . . even if that something is getting out of Mérida to visit an archaeological wonder a short drive away.

GETTING THERE AND GETTING AROUND *By air:* **Mérida International Airport** is about 8 miles from the city center. Aeroméxico and Mexicana are the most frequent flyers to the airport, and most flights from the United States come to Mérida through Mexico City or Cancún. Other airlines flying into the city include Continental and Aviacsa.
By bus: There are five bus stations in the city, with service to cities around the country.

Terminal CAME has first-class service to/from Cancún, Campeche, Ciudad del Carmen, Veracruz, Minatitlán, E. Zapata, Palenque, Puebla, Mexico City, Valladolid, Ocosingo, Tuxtla Gutiérrez, Playa del Carmen, Chichén Itzá, San Cristóbal de las Casas, Tulum, and Cordoba.

Terminal CAME, 2nd Class has service to/from Chiquilá, Calkini, Campeche, Ciudad del Carmen, Champotón, Escárcega, Villahermosa, Umán, Halacho, Pomuch, Izamal, Valladolid, Tizimín, Cobá, Tulum, Muna, Ticul, Oxkutzcab, Tekax, Peto, Carrillo Puerto, Cancún, Becal, Playa de Catazaha, Hecelchakan, Chichén Itzá, Playa del Carmen,

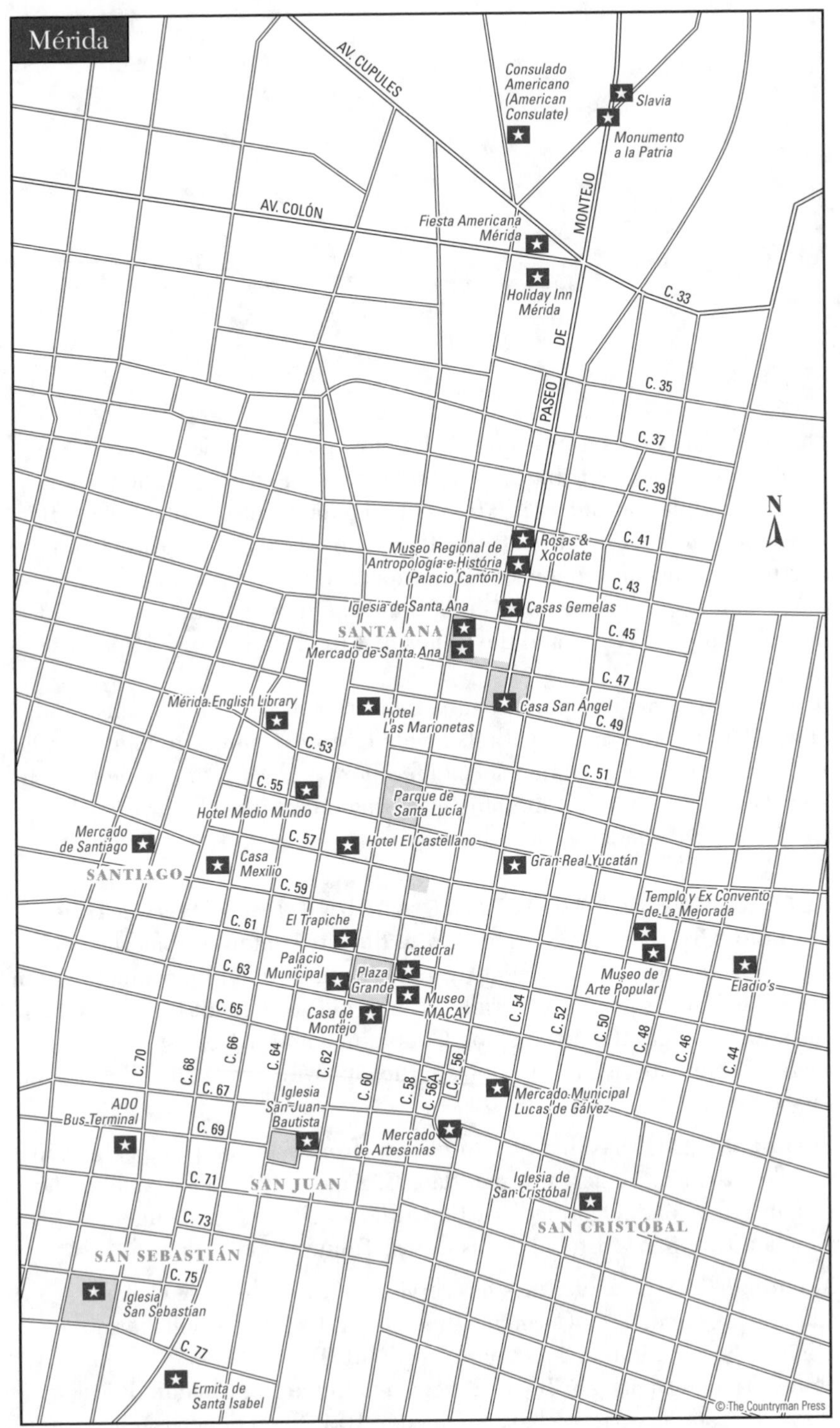
Mérida
AV. CUPULES
Consulado Americano (American Consulate)
Slavia
Monumento a la Patria
AV. COLÓN
Fiesta Americana Mérida
MONTEJO
Holiday Inn Mérida
C. 33
DE
PASEO
C. 35
C. 37
C. 39
N
Rosas & Xocolate
C. 41
Museo Regional de Antropología e História (Palacio Cantón)
C. 43
Iglesia de Santa Ana
Casas Gemelas
SANTA ANA
C. 45
Mercado de Santa Ana
C. 47
Mérida English Library
Hotel Las Marionetas
Casa San Ángel
C. 49
C. 53
C. 51
C. 55
Parque de Santa Lucía
Hotel Medio Mundo
Mercado de Santiago
C. 57
Hotel El Castellano
Gran Real Yucatán
Casa Mexilio
SANTIAGO
C. 59
Templo y Ex Convento de La Mejorada
C. 61
El Trapiche
Catedral
Palacio Municipal
Plaza Grande
C. 63
Museo de Arte Popular
Eladio's
Museo MACAY
C. 65
Casa de Montejo
C. 54
C. 52
C. 50
C. 48
C. 46
C. 44
C. 70
C. 68
C. 66
C. 64
C. 62
C. 60
C. 58
C. 56A
C. 56
C. 67
Mercado Municipal Lucas de Gálvez
ADO Bus Terminal
Iglesia San Juan Bautista
C. 69
Mercado de Artesanías
C. 71
SAN JUAN
Iglesia de San Cristóbal
C. 73
SAN CRISTÓBAL
SAN SEBASTIÁN
C. 75
Iglesia San Sebastian
C. 77
Ermita de Santa Isabel
© The Countryman Press

QUIET AND QUAINT, MÉRIDA IS RANKED AMONG THE SAFEST CITIES IN MEXICO.

Palenque, Ocosingo, San Cristóbal, Tuxtla Gutierrez, Acayucan, Puebla, and Mexico City.

Terminal de Autobuses has service to/from Celestún, Cancún, Izamal, Seye, Sotuta, Hoctun, Yaxcaba, San Cristóbal, Acanceh, Cantamayec, Cuzama, Chapab, Cholul, Chumayel, Eknakan, Homun, Mayapán, Tepich, Teabo, Ticul, Mana, Maní, Huhi, Tekit, Oxkutzcab, Baca, Calotmul, Canshacab, Chicxulub Puerto, Colonia Yucatán, Conkal, Buctzotz, Dzemul, El Cuyo, Dzidzantún, Las Colorados, Rio Lagartos, Telchac, Chiquilá, and Holbox.

Progreso has service to/from Progreso.

ADO Ticket Bus has express service to Cancún.

By taxi: Taxis are relatively cheap and easy to find.

By other means: There's a decent intercity bus service with stops all over the city, along with combis, or minivans run by collectives, which are a safe, if crowded, means of transportation. On the more touristy side, you can hop on a Turibus (www.turibus.com.mx), the bright red single-deck or double-decker buses that cover many of the city's points of interest, or hail a calesa, or horse-drawn carriage, in the Plaza Grande. A romantic hour-long tour will take you through the city center and along Paseo Montejo.

NEOCLASSICAL EUROPEAN ARCHITECTURE IS A HALLMARK OF MÉRIDA'S BEAUTY.

A BRIEF HISTORY

Mérida was founded on January 6, 1542, by Francisco de Montejo. At the time, the city held a large Maya population and bore the name T'Ho. The Spanish conquered the land and followed standard operating procedure in razing its temples and using the stones to construct the new city. Mérida was the second city established following the conquest; it took Montejo three tries, beginning in 1527, to accomplish the task.

The city became the regional seat of the Spanish government. In 1561, work began on the imposing **Catedral de San Ildefonso**, the oldest cathedral in the Americas. Montejo set up house in the same plaza in 1542, and it still stands as the oldest private building in Mérida. A walled city until the 19th century, Mérida became an architectural showcase of the colonial era, with major buildings and churches built around leafy plazas. The city's *centro histórico*, or historic center, still ranks among the largest in the Americas.

Following the henequen boom, the wealthy nobles of the Yucatán began to fashion Mérida after the splendor of European capitals. In the late 19th century, they built the grand Paseo de Montejo Boulevard as a Champs-Élysées of the city, and lined it with neoclassical mansions. Its colonial beauty and grandeur earned Mérida the moniker "Paris of the West." And while many of its buildings now stand in various stages of dilapidation, its cleanliness (which has spawned another nickname, "The White City"), colorful architecture, and romantic charm make it a city to explore and embrace.

MÉRIDA'S NEIGHBORHOODS

Mérida's heart is its charming city center, which revolves around the **Plaza Grande**, or *zócalo*. A walk around this quaint area will take you past many of the city's landmarks, as well as restaurants, shops, and points of interest. Here you'll find the city's iconic cathedral; the original house of Montejo, **Casa de Montejo**, of which little remains except the striking façade (the building is now a bank branch) on the south side of the plaza; and the **Museo de Arte Contemporáneo de Yucatán** (Museum of Contemporary Art).

Beyond the main plaza, the historic downtown spreads out into various neighborhoods, called *colonias* or *barrios*. East of the city center, **Barrio Santiago** is known for its 17th-century church, dedicated to the Spanish apostle Santiago; its park, which hosts free big band concerts each Tuesday evenings; and vibrant market. Below this area and southeast of the city center lies **Barrio San Juan**, also named after a church, the 16th-century **Iglesia de San Juan Bautista**. One of the oldest *colonias* in the city and an indigenous neighborhood during the colonial era, it is also known for its distinctive yellow-painted arch, one of the last original gateways that once delineated Mérida's city border and began the road to Campeche.

Adjacent to San Juan to the west is **Barrio San Cristóbal**, a neighborhood founded by Montejo in the 1540s. You can find another of Mérida's ancient arches here, as well as the lovely and popular **Iglesia de San Cristóbal**, the last church to be built by the Spanish in the Yucatán. Completed in December 1796, the church is dedicated to the Virgin of Guadalupe, making it an immensely popular destination on December 12, when Mexico's patron saint is honored around the country. East of the city center, the **Templo y Ex-Convento de la Mejorada** was the home of the military barracks during the colonial era. The neighborhood is also the site of Arco de los Dragones (Arch of the Dragons), named after the *colonia*'s military presence. Today, La Mejorada boasts a few museums, some great local restaurants, and a park where you can find a monument to the Niños Heroes, or the child heroes from the Mexican War of Independence.

South of the city center and consequently bearing the local moniker "Some" is **Barrio San Sebastian**, a once-rough part of town known for its free-swinging spirit. Today it is just as calm and peaceful as the rest of the city, and its **Santa Isabel Hermitage**, food market and numerous festivals (notably the **Feria de San Sebastian** during the first two weeks of August) make it worth visiting. On the opposite side, the **Barrio de**

THE MONUMENTO A LA PATRIA ON PASEO DE MONTEJO

Santa Ana dates from the 1500s and was once the city's northernmost neighborhood. Today it is the starting point of the sprawling Paseo de Montejo, and also features the small and pretty **Iglesia de Santa Ana**, a food and handcrafts market, some of the city's largest hotels, and several art galleries and museums.

You're probably detecting a pattern in the above descriptions: church, plaza, park, and market. Colonial life in Mexico revolved around these community staples, and continues to do so in Mérida (and much of Mexico).

These neighborhoods make up the vast majority of the Mérida that tourists will want to experience. Beyond, the Paseo de Montejo continues past the **Monumento a la Patria** into residential areas, where you can find wonderful dining and nightlife destinations. Of course, you'll also want to get well out of Mérida to discover the Yucatán's true treasure: the ruins of the Maya heartland.

✷ Archaeological Sites

The Yucatán's Maya sites represent a diverse network of cities from different eras and different stages of civilization. They include mighty capitals, trade centers, subterranean caves, and *cenotes* (sinkholes), which held supreme importance in Maya spiritual beliefs and customs. Of course, the peninsula is chock-full of sites, both on the map and off, which are not featured in this book. The places listed below stand out for their remarkable architecture, historical importance, and preserved beauty.

Most archaeological sites in the Yucatán are open daily from 8–5 and have only modest admission charges (Chichén Itzá charges a bit more than the rest).

Chichén Itzá

GETTING THERE From Mérida, take the Periferico (the beltway that loops around the city) to Highway 180 (toward Cancún). Take the toll road and get off at the Chichén Itzá exit. ADO also has daily service to the site.

I'm again going to ignore alphabetical considerations and put the unparalleled Chichén Itzá first on this list. To understand this ancient Maya metropolis, we must consider the era in which it was built. From AD 700 to 900, Mesoamerica underwent a period of great upheaval and transformation, as people migrated, cultures mingled, and alliances formed and fell apart. In the Yucatán peninsula, this change is mostly attributed to the influence and infusion of the militaristic Toltec culture, and to two figures in particular: the mythical, magical feathered serpent deity, Quetzalcóatl, and his priest, Ce Ácatl Topiltzin. Legend has it that Quetzalcóatl and his priest (often considered the same figure) left the city of Tula, arrived in

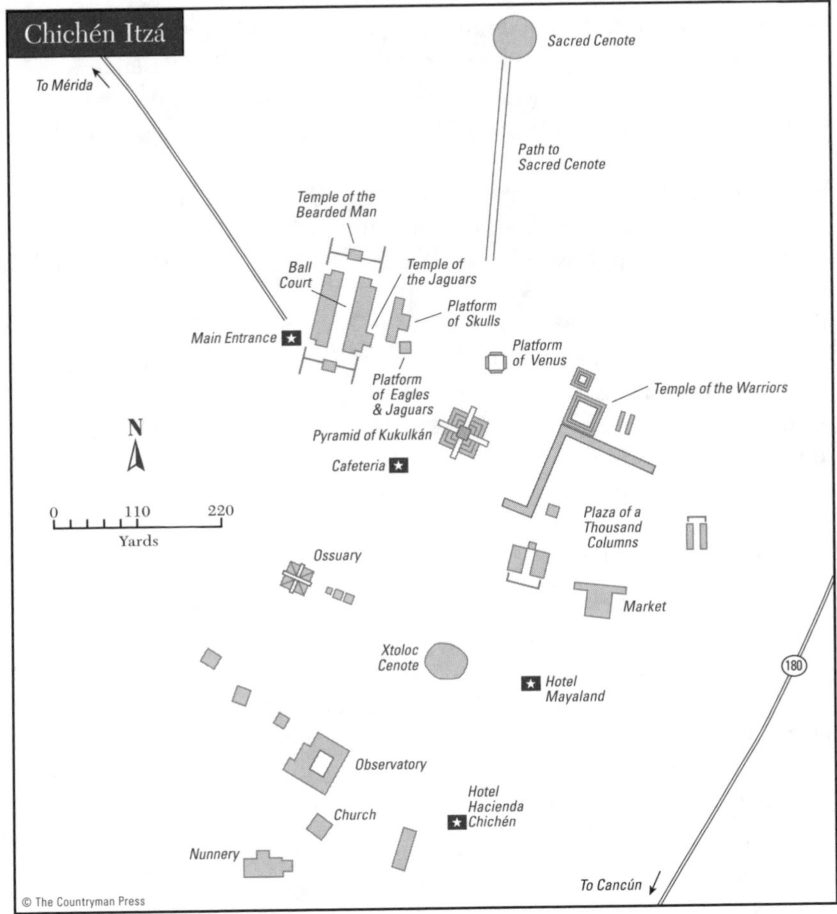

the Maya heartland and renamed himself Kukulcán. The cult of Kukulcán would spread throughout the region, but he was particularly linked to the Itzá, a group believed to be Putún or Chontal Maya.

The Itzá settled in Chichén in the ninth century, building their city by the mouth of an enormous *cenote* ("Chichén Itzá" means "Mouth of the Well of the Itzá"), and this proved vital to their growth and importance. The Itzá claimed (and promoted the idea) that Chaac himself, one of the principal deities in Maya theology, lived in the well. This legend catapulted the city's fame and importance, drawing pilgrimages from around the Maya world and greatly enhancing its wealth and power.

The city would become one of the greatest centers in Maya history, a cosmopolitan, multicultural capital encompassing, at its zenith, 600 buildings of stone and occupying over 15 square miles. With the influx of Toltec culture came a blending of architectural styles, known today as Mexicanized Maya, which can be appreciated in the city's most iconic structures: the Kukulcán Castle, Temple of the Warriors, and ball court. The Toltec also brought with them a surge of militarization. Naturally, this growth led to friction with the city's contemporaries. During their consolidation of power, the Itzá formed strategic alliances with neighboring powerhouses Mayapán, Uxmal, and Izamal (a coalition known as the League of Mayapán), which established Chichén as the center of a trade, spiritual, and political empire.

As the city grew, however, conflicts arose; according to Maya history, Mayapán conquered the city in AD 1185 (although recent studies have proposed the theory that the city collapsed around 1000 BC). While controversy surrounds the dates of Chichén Itzá's decline, one fact remains clear: Even long after its demise, the city remained an important pilgrimage sight.

Visiting Chichén Itzá today, you'll find a vast city full of buildings; a broad *sacbe* leading to the sacred *cenote*; and, quite unfortunately, a sea of vendors hocking all manner of souvenirs and handicrafts to passersby. This commercialization of the site (the only such case in the region) can dilute the experience but shouldn't deter you from exploring one of the Earth's ancient wonders.

Castillo de Kukulcán. The designation of Chichén Itzá as one of the wonders of the world is actually erroneous: it is the magnificent Kukulcán Castle that has earned this status. The nine-tiered pyramid stands 82 feet high by almost 200 feet wide. As my guide informed me, this exact spot is the *only place on Earth* where this structure could have been built. Quite simply, it is perfectly oriented, built for its exact angle and meridian. The castle is replete with symbolism and, more important, functions as a precise tribute to the Maya calendar. Each face of the pyramid features 91 steps, for a total of 364. Add the top platform, and you get 365 days, the number of calendar days in a year. There are also 91 days between the equinox and the solstice.

It gets more amazing. Each face of the pyramid is bifurcated by a staircase. On each side of this staircase you'll find nine platforms, which, added together, make 18—the number of months in the Maya calendar. Look further; each platform features imbedded panels, in sets of three, except the uppermost platform, which has 2. Add these up, and each face has 52 panels, representing the 52-year cycle when the two calendars synchronize. And finally, each side of the temple has five adornments. Multiply by the four sides and you total 20: the number of days in a Maya month. In short, *the entire Castillo de Kukulcán is a 3-D calendar.*

The pyramid is perhaps most famous for the play of sun and shadow that takes place each equinox. Along the west side of the north face of the

THE CASTILLO DE KUKULCÁN IS A MASTERPIECE OF MAYA ARCHITECTURE.

pyramid, at the rising and setting of the sun, you can witness a shadow descending the face of the pyramid in very snakelike undulations until it joins with the head of the snake resting at the foot of the pyramid. It's an awe-inspiring sight, but only one reason why this building is special.

We know of at least one building underneath the present pyramid, the latter built atop and completely covering its predecessor (think the architectural equivalent of Russian dolls). Inside is a throne room where archaeologists discovered a red-painted, jade-encrusted jaguar throne and a reclining Chac-Mool.

Chichén Itzá's **Juego de Pelota (Great Ball Court)** is unlike any other you'll see in the Maya world. The biggest and most impressive in all Mesoamerica, it is also one of 14 in the city (a huge number). The court is noted for its near-perfect acoustics and its detailed carvings. One of these is a disk-shaped figure of a talking skull, symbolic of the decapitated team captain whose duty it was to talk to the gods on behalf of his people. Another carving shows the decapitated body of a player with fountains of blood pouring from the neck in serpent form. Players competed in the ball game by hitting a large ball (with elbows and knees, no less) through large doughnutlike stone rings on each side of the court. Note also the prominent Temple of the Jaguars on the east wall, and the separate North Temple at the far end of the court. This is the Temple of the Bearded Man, so-called for its relief of a bearded head.

Tzompantli, Eagle and Jaguar Platforms. Among the strongest indicators of Toltec influence at Chichén are the *tzompantli,* or skull rack,

THE GREAT BALL COURT AT CHICHÉN ITZÁ IS THE GRANDEST IN ALL MESOAMERICA.

traditionally used to display the human skulls of sacrificial victims and warriors (note the rows of skulls carved along the side), and small platform dedicated to the elite Eagle and Jaguar warrior classes, which depict eagles and jaguars holding human hearts in their clutches.

A DECAPITATED BODY OF A PLAYER IS DEPICTED WITH BLOOD POURING FROM HIS NECK IN THE FORM OF SERPENTS.

Temple of the Warriors. The building with the square columns—another signature Toltec style—is the Temple of the Warriors. Note the Chac-Mool atop the structure, depictions of jaguars, eagles, and feathered serpent heads; these disparate elements indicate a Mexicanized Maya building typical of Postclassic Chichén. The temple is a part of the group of 1,000 columns, carved with warriors, around a patio. This was the *tianguis*, or marketplace, of the city.

Sacred Cenote. Follow a *sacbe* north of the castle past a small platform dedicated to Venus and you'll soon come to a massive sinkhole, the *cenote sagrado* where Chaac was rumored to live. You can still see the platform from which offers to appease the gods and ask their favor were thrown into the well. Incidentally, while we automatically associate these gifts with human sacrifice, the practice didn't really come into vogue until the Postclassic period in the region. From 1904 to 1969, archaeologists repeatedly explored the *cenote*'s depths, and although they found human remains (notably skulls of small children in 1969), ritual sacrifices appear to have been few in number.

The **Ossuary,** located to the south of the Castillo, is not really an ossuary, but a place of worship. Built over a limestone cavern, it's a smaller replica of Castillo Kukulcán, and the central building of a miniature duplicate of the city; note the smaller copies of the Temples of the Warrior, Eagle, and Jaguar, as well as a replica market and a *sacbe* leading to the Xtoloc Cenote.

El Caracol (The Snail), is an iconic observatory at Chichén, modified over centuries and unmistakable for its cylindrical tower. The "door" you see is actually a window that was used to track celestial movements. Inside the tower are three concentric circles, with the innermost containing a spiral staircase, giving the building its name. It is believed that the building's three windows were used to track Venus as well as the approach of the equinoxes and summer solstice; in fact, my guide informed me that the observatory corroborated the "descending serpent" shadow at the Castillo before the pyramid was even built.

One of the oldest structures in the city is **Chichánchob** (Small Holes), so named for its roof comb, and is notable for its smooth, simple façade, and three *witz* masks.

Edificio de las Monjas. This large nunnery is representative of the Puuc style, and was probably home to Chichén nobility. The building is believed to be contemporary to the interior edifice of the Castillo. In a rather unfortunate historical anecdote, the French archaeologist Augustus Le Plongeon—by all accounts an eccentric character—decided to prove his theory that the exterior building of the nunnery was built over an earlier structure by blowing up a part of it to reveal its inner building.

THE OBSERVATORY AT CHICHÉN ITZÁ

The nunnery is part of a larger complex that includes the Iglesia ("Church," a fine example of the conquistadors' penchant for assigning the wrong name to a place), a beautifully ornate annex, and a ball court. If you head southwest from here (follow the signs), you'll come to a part of the city known as *Viejo Chichén (*Old Chichén), which has yet to be explored fully.

Researchers estimate that not even 10 percent of the great city has been opened to us, which gives us a better appreciation of how magnificent Chichén Itzá must have been in its day.

Acanceh

GETTING THERE From Mérida, take the Periferico (the beltway that loops around the city) to Route 18 (toward Kanasín), which

CHICHÉN ITZÁ'S LIGHT AND SOUND SHOW

For a view of the ancient city at night, sign up for the nocturnal light and sound show, offered every night. The show is in Spanish, but headsets translating it into multiple languages can be purchased at the ticket booth. It's a colorful production, a bit on the cheesy side in the telling of the history of the city and the Maya, but worth it for the chance to see Chichén's main buildings spectacularly illuminated, and the beautiful finale of a multicolored descending snake.

will take you to the town of Acanceh, and to its main plaza, where the site is located.

One of the lesser-visited sites in the Yucatán, Acanceh has a few things going for it. For one, the admittedly worn-down pyramid, squeezed into the main plaza of the city, holds vestiges of the pre-Classic period (5th–6th century AD); for another, this site features impressive original stucco work. Once a series of eight large stucco masks depicting solar deities, you can still see the details and original paint on the remaining ones. The site is located on the Plaza of Three Cultures (representing ancient, colonial and modern Yucatán), which also includes a colonial church dedicated to the Virgin of the Nativity.

Balankanché

GETTING THERE Balankanché is located 3.7 miles east of Chichén Itzá along Highway 180.

The caves of Balankanché were discovered by local guide Humberto Gómez (who happened to be my guide during my research in the Yucatán) in 1959. Located just a few miles from Chichén Itzá, the caves had clear ceremonial importance. In the central chamber, around a huge stalagmite surrounded by a forest of stalactites, Gómez found a variety of offerings to the god Tlaloc, unseen by man for centuries until his arrival.

Dzibilchaltún

GETTING THERE Take the Mérida-Progreso Highway north for just under 7 miles and you'll see signs for Dzibilchaltún. Turn right and continue 1.8 miles to the site.

One of the most ancient Maya cities in the Yucatán, Dzibilchaltún may have been inhabited from as early as 500 BC. The name translates to "the Place Where There Is Writing on the Stones," a reference to the numerous stelae discovered at the site, notable for their combination of illustration and hieroglyphs. Among these, stela 19, which identifies the city's original name as Chantiho, gets particular attention. The city originally covered a concentric area of over 11 square miles and, with an estimated population of 40,000, ranked among Mesoamerica's largest ancient cities. Sadly, the site suffered from deliberate vandalism, when many of its stones were used to pave the nearby road, but that doesn't take away from its present charm. The ruins you see today are spread out in clusters, and offer a very diverse experience.

The most spectacular complex at Dzibilchaltún is the Grupo Siete Muñecas ("Seven Dolls Group," named for a set of six female and one male figurines found here). At the end of a broad *sacbe* stands the Temple of the Seven Dolls, site of a remarkable astrological-archaeological phenomenon. On each equinox, the descending sun will first sit directly atop the temple, then shine squarely through the portals, creating a dazzling effect that only confirms the incredible precision of the Maya.

Across the *sacbe* in the large central plaza lie the remnants of a Franciscan church, which the Spanish built to cement their dominance of the new religious order. Nearby is another of Dzibilchaltún's worthwhile stops, its *cenote*. Bring your bathing suit and enjoy a dip, especially after a hot day of archaeological exploration. Finally, the site also has an informative museum, ecological park, restaurant, and small arts-and-crafts shop.

DZIBILCHALTÚN'S TEMPLE OF THE SEVEN DOLLS

Ek' Balam

GETTING THERE From Mérida, take the Periferico to Highway 180. Take the toll road and drive toward Valladolid. When you get near the city, you'll come to an exit for Route 295. Turn left and drive north toward Tizimin. You'll see signs for Ek' Balam on your right. The site is located 114 miles east of Mérida.

Ek' Balam (Black Jaguar), is a remarkable site even in this region of astounding Maya ruins, and one of the most important recent finds in the Maya world (long ignored, the site began to be properly explored in the late 1980s). The walled city, which is believed to have been once part of an empire called Talol, retains archaeological features of most Maya cultures, which have led some to speculate that this was once a great commercial meeting point. At one point, perhaps fearing the threat of attack from Chichén, the governors of Ek' Balam built a double wall around its perimeter. It must have worked, because there is no sign that the city was attacked.

The site has several well-preserved structures, including a lovely Maya arch and a circular pyramid believed to be a residential complex. But the single most astonishing feature of Ek' Balam can be found at the immense pyramid known as the Acropolis, one of the largest structures uncovered in the peninsula. In 2000, researchers hit an archaeological jackpot when they uncovered the tomb of Ukit Kan Lek Tok, a governor of great importance who was buried in a "White Room." The chamber features extraordinary sculptures of winged warriors, and its entrance is ornamented with stucco in a spectacular façade of a huge, white, fanged mouth. It is believed to represent the mouth of a monster from the Underworld. The fascinating construction is unique to Ek' Balam. After visiting it, climb to the top of the pyramid for breathtaking views.

Kinich Kak Moo

GETTING THERE Located just off the main plaza of Izamal, Kinich Kak Moo is located about 40 miles east of Mérida. To get here, take the Periferico to Highway 180. Once you get to the town of Hoctun, you'll see an exit heading left to Izamal (Route 11). The site is located on Calle 27 between Calles 28 and 26B.

This pyramid may lack the finery of others in the region, but at over 650 feet long by 590 feet wide, it's the largest pyramid in the Yucatán, and one of the most important structures in ancient Mesoamerica. A temple dedicated to the Maya Sun god (who descended in the shape of a fiery macaw to accept daily offerings) and built over a cave, Kinich Kak Moo was a sacred ceremonial capital. Located in the city of Izamal, you could almost miss it despite its size, or rather, mistake it for a hill. The climb to the top will reward you with numerous large iguana sightings and lovely views.

The massive stones used in the construction, particularly of the staircase on its southern side, were designed for gods rather than men.

Mayapán

GETTING THERE Take the Periferico to Highway 180 toward Cancún. Shortly after Teya, take the exit for Route 18 on your right (toward Tecoh). Follow this road until you see signs for Mayapán on your left.

The last great Maya capital, Mayapán, which means "Banner of the Maya," gets lost in the shuffle of more well-known destinations, but its importance and size (over 4,000 structures have been uncovered) cannot be understated. A walled city, Mayapán was home to 12,000 to 13,000 people. The city rose in prominence during the Postclassic period, when Mayapán's ruling Cocom tribe formed a triple alliance with the Xiu tribe of Uxmal and the Itza of Chichén, joining the three strongest Maya capitals of the age. (Scholars disagree on the dates of this pact, with many believing that Mayapán flourished after the other cities.)

In around AD 1200, the rulers of Chichén broke the alliance, leading to war between the two cities. Then, in 1441, Uxmal attacked Mayapán and sacrificed its entire royal family save for one son. This attack and

MAYAPÁN'S ARCHITECTURE CLOSELY RESEMBLES THAT OF CHICHÉN ITZÁ.

subsequent acts of violence spawned a deep and lasting bitterness between the tribes. A century later, Tutul-Xiu, the *cacique* of the Xiu, traveled to the conquistadors' capital of Mérida and laid down his arms in exchange for a united effort to defeat Nachi Cocom, leader of the hated Cocom tribe.

Against this historical backdrop, the impressive ruins of Mayapán take on a greater significance. The city duplicates buildings found at Chichén, including a smaller Castillo de Kukulcán, built near a large *cenote,* and a circular observatory. Mayapán is known for its stucco sculptures, murals, and frescoes, traces of which can still be seen in their original color in the Temple of the Painted Niches, Room of Frescoes, and Room of Kings. Also impressive is the detailed work found in the Room of the Chaac Masks.

ONE WALL OF KABAH'S CODZ POOP IS COVERED WITH *WITZ* MASKS.

The Ruta Puuc

GETTING THERE Take the Periferico to Highway 180 toward the airport. When you reach Uman, take the exit for Route 261 heading south, which leads directly to Uxmal and the Ruta Puuc.

The Ruta Puuc (Puuc Route) is a 25-mile stretch of road that winds its way past some of the most important examples of the Maya Puuc cultural heritage. *Puuc* is Mayan for "hills," and these small hills are certainly a contrast to the broad, flat peninsula. But in archaeological terms, the Puuc style is defined by its complex ornamentation, geometric proportions, and exquisite façades.

A satellite of mighty Uxmal, **Kabah** is connected to the city by a 9-mile long *sacbe* that begins at a stone arch. The name translates to "hand that sculpts," a worthy name given the exceptional architectural quality found here. Two buildings in particular stand out here. The Codz Poop (which means "rolled mat," a reference to the curving nose of the god Chaac) Temple of Masks is a square-shaped structure with an impressive façade of over 250 carved masks. Note also the statues on the other side of the building; originally a set of four, they are believed to be representations of a ruling dynasty because of their similar characteristics.

The other notable structure at Kabah is the governmental palace, which, like the temple of the masks, was constructed in two phases. For the second phase, the engineers decided to fill the first floor of the palace with rocks to bolster the structure. It was a fitting expansion for what was, during the 9th and 10th centuries, the second-largest city in the north of the Yucatán.

The magnificent Great Palace alone makes **Sayil** a jewel in the Puuc crown. The immense three-story building featured over 90 bedrooms and could have housed as many as 350 people. The palace is an amalgamation of different styles and workmanship, with the most distinctive feature being its second-story columns. Beyond the palace, other ruins can be found scattered around the brush, including a pyramidal temple (El Mirador), an almost destroyed temple noted for the hieroglyphs around its doors, and a sculpture of Yum Keep, god of fertility or the phallus.

The ruins of **Labná** are mainly comprised of two main sections connected by a sacbe: a governmental complex and a scientific sector. The former includes the broad palace, a result of no less than 12 construction phases, and the building of the columns, most likely a residence of the elite. But it is in the other group of buildings where Labná truly shines. Here you'll find the elegant Mirador, its roof comb distinctive of early Puuc

THE GREAT PALACE AT SAYIL

LABNÁ PRESENTS A FINE EXAMPLE OF TWO DISTINCTIVE ARCHITECTURAL ELEMENTS: THE ROOF COMB AND THE MAYA ARCH.

architecture, and—easily the most striking structure at the city—the Arch of Labná, a paragon of Maya architecture.

Grutas de Loltún. The *grutas*, or caves, of Loltún don't qualify as an archaeological site, but they were certainly of great importance to the ancient Maya and are found along the Puuc Route. The word "Loltún" comes from the Mayan words "*lol*" for flower and "*tun*" for stone, but they also happen to be the sounds made when you hit the two hollow columns in the central chamber; this was a sacred ceremonial site, and many offerings and Maya instruments were discovered here. At one point, the room also served as a home to around 800 people. In addition to the sacred chamber, the caverns' vast cavities and formations include many natural wonders and man-made vestiges. In particular, keep an eye out for the black handprints found in one room, the Grand Canyon gallery, and the magnificent Gallery 3, which, thanks to its collapsed ceiling, has the effect of an enchanted underground garden.

Oxkintok. (Note: to get here, stay on Route 180 and exit at the town of Kopomá): Evidence shows inhabitants at Oxkintok dating to the late Preclassic period, which would give the city seniority over many of its counterparts. The site is best known for a structure called the *tzat tun tzat,* or labyrinth, a small building with a maze of vaulted tunnels inside that is believed to represent a voyage to the Underworld. Also note the carved columns, which represent nobles, warriors, and gods.

The Greece to Chichén Itzá's Rome, **Uxmal** was in many ways its equal. The site has a history of habitation dating back to 500 BC, long before a city of stone was built. During its evolution, Uxmal went through three major stages, with the third beginning after AD 900. Hence its name, which means "That Which Was Built Three Times." Uxmal is perhaps the most authentic example of the Puuc style (although it later adopted Postclassic elements such as depictions of Quetzalcóatl), and remains today a city-state of imposing and impressive beauty.

There are many buildings worth exploring at Uxmal. Because of its size and its importance, I recommend separating the rest of the Ruta Puuc from Uxmal so you can devote enough time to enjoy the city during the day and catch its light and sound show at night, which wins my vote for the best nocturnal spectacle in the Yucatán's ruins.

Topping the list at the site, literally and figuratively, is the unique and awe-inspiring Pyramid of the Soothsayer, the first structure you see after entering Uxmal. Distinctive for its elliptical shape—the result of various

THE PYRAMID OF THE SOOTHSAYER AT UXMAL

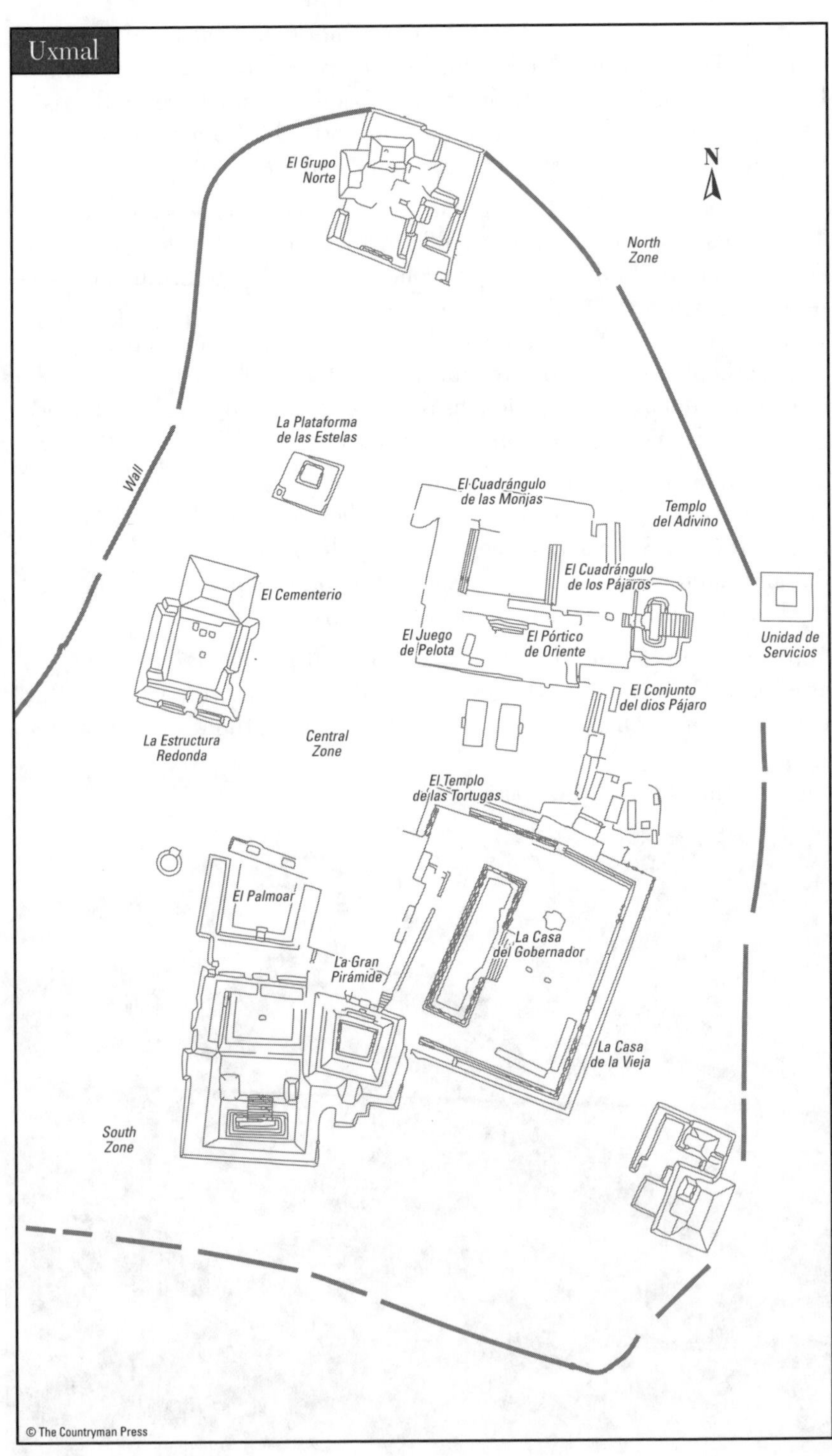
Uxmal
N
El Grupo Norte
North Zone
La Plataforma de las Estelas
Wall
El Cuadrángulo de las Monjas
Templo del Adivino
El Cuadrángulo de los Pájaros
El Cementerio
El Juego de Pelota
El Pórtico de Oriente
Unidad de Servicios
El Conjunto del dios Pájaro
La Estructura Redonda
Central Zone
El Templo de las Tortugas
El Palmoar
La Casa del Gobernador
La Gran Pirámide
La Casa de la Vieja
South Zone
© The Countryman Press

stages of construction—the pyramid, which measures about 115 feet, also bears the ironic name of Pyramid of the Dwarf. Legend has it that it was built by the son of a witch who was born from an egg. Beyond the pyramid, the city of Uxmal opens up before you. Among the most important structures here is the large, open Quadrangle of the Nuns, a complex of four palaces around a patio. The buildings provide a tapestry of decorative motifs including colonnades, witz masks, and entwined serpents. The quadrangle also makes for the perfect spot from which to watch the Sound and Light Show at night.

The stately Governor's Palace at Uxmal is praised by archaeologists for its precise workmanship and architectural detail. Note especially three transversal vaults that separate the elaborately sculpted façade into three sections. Facing the palace is the original Throne of the Jaguar, depicting a two-headed creature joined at the middle. Located southwest of the palace are the Great Pyramid, the aptly named pigeon-house cluster, and the ball court. Astoundingly, the buildings you see today represent not even 10 percent of Uxmal.

And finally, the only free stop along the Ruta Puuc, **Xlapak** is a small site with only one building—the Palace—worth visiting for its detailed façade and, in particular, its *witz* masks.

X'cambó

GETTING THERE This one's a bit tricky because you'll need to follow the signs for Xtampu, not X'cambó. Take Highway 261 to its end and turn right toward Progreso. Continue past the town to arrive at Xtampu/ X'cambó.

This small site is the remains of a city that served an important role as a producer and exporter of salt. Before you get to the site you'll cross salt flats where you can still see the nails used to hem in the water. You might wonder why, its being essentially a port city, the Maya built X'cambó inland from the shore. The answer speaks to their acumen and understanding of their environment. The Maya did not want to destroy the mangroves along the coast and ruin the surrounding ecology, and they wanted protection from hurricanes. Ironically, centuries later, many owners of pricey beachfront vacation homes face flooding and exposure to these very problems because they did not follow Maya wisdom.

More recently, the site gained recognition due to the X'cambó Virgin, who is said to have appeared here over 50 years ago and led a lost man to safety. A small chapel built among the ruins commemorates the sighting, and brings an annual pilgrimage each May for a festival in her honor.

ONE OF THREE ARROW-SHAPED ARCHES AT UXMAL

It's not often you get to travel to a legendary place in the company of a living legend. But I was very lucky; I had the pleasure and good fortune of visiting this region with Humberto Gómez, a guide who locals simply refer to as *leyenda,* or legend. Gómez has been a guide for decades, and was in fact the man credited with the discovery of the Balankanché Caves. He's still quite spry, incredibly knowledgeable about the Maya world and the Yucatán, and genial, pleasant company. A vast amount of the insights found in this chapter come from my days spent with Humberto traveling the Yucatán and listening to him relate its history. Gómez is available for private tours, and I highly recommend him. He can be reached at 999-970-1020 or joseh_258@hotmail.com.

HUMBERTO GÓMEZ IS A TERRIFIC GUIDE, LOCAL LEGEND, AND THE MAN WHO DISCOVERED THE CAVES OF BALANKANCHE.

COLONIAL CITIES

Mexico's pre-Hispanic ruins, whether Aztec, Maya, or other, go hand in hand with its colonial cities. Yucatán offers three shining examples: Mérida, Izamal, and Valladolid.

Izamal

The charming white and yellow city of Izamal, also known as the "City of Three Cultures," is a microcosm of the peninsula: an all-important spiritual center for the Maya, a bastion of the Roman Catholic Church, and present-day, laid-back quotidian life. The city's name comes from Itzamna, a creator deity and who lived in the sky. The Maya believed Itzamna was buried in the temple city of Izamal, and it became a site of holy pilgrimage that continued even after the decline of the city.

Following the conquest, the city's spiritual focus caught the attention of Diego de Landa, who arrived in the city in 1549 at the age of 25 and decided it would be the perfect place to build a church. He commissioned the construction of the **Convento de San Antonio de Padua** (Saint Anthony's Convent), extraordinary both for its proportions (the convent's atrium is second in size only to the Vatican) and its legends. In 1562, the church was finished, and Landa found a family willing to contribute a Virgin statue for it—*La Virgen de la Inmaculada Concepción* (Virgin of the Immaculate Conception)—on the condition that a twin Virgin be made for their home. Izamal's Virgin soon began to speak miracles. Her fame grew to the point that people from neighboring towns came to borrow her. Eventually, a special chamber was built behind the altar of the convent where the Virgin "slept."

In 1829, a fire burned the convent's statue to the ground, and the people of Izamal begged the family who originally gifted the Virgin for her twin. They complied, and the new Virgin soon continued to speak miracles. In fact, she still does, and is now the patron saint of the Yucatán. In 1993, Pope John Paul II visited the city, bringing with him a crown from the

DIEGO DE LANDA'S MASSIVE CONVENTO DE SAN ANTONIO DE PADUA

Vatican for the Virgin (a statue and small museum commemorate the pope's visit).

Now more than 450 years old, the Virgin can still be seen today at services; when she is ready to retire to her sleeping chamber, a mechanism automatically turns her around and rolls her away. Make sure to visit her room (from 7 to 2 and 4 to 7), where you'll find well-worn places to kneel and pray before her, as well as a litany of wishes scribbled on notes, gifts, and offerings.

Beyond its cultural treasures, Izamal is a city of picturesque beauty. The buildings, awash in yellow and white, add plenty of charm to the city, and the Plaza de la Constitución, with its 19th-century city hall, marketplace and fleet of *calezas,* or horse-drawn carriages, is a beautiful reminder of its colonial grandeur.

Valladolid

Valladolid's location on the road from Cancún to Chichén Itzá is both a curse and a blessing. Many tour buses pass through the town, giving visitors a glimpse of the quaint colonial gem of a city, or an hour or two to

THE HEAVY VIRGIN AND THE BITTER ARCHAEOLOGIST

An 18th-century legend tells of a time when the citizens of Valladolid asked to borrow the Virgin. As they began to carry her toward their city, her bearers noticed that she kept getting heavier, until her weight increased so much that they couldn't take another step forward. However, when they turned back to return her to Izamal, they found she had returned to her normal weight. Izamal's residents believed the Virgin refused to go because she knew the Valladolicenses would not return her home. The people of Izamal built an Arch of Resistance at the spot where the Virgin would go no farther (you can find it north of the convent).

A much more contemporary story concerns the statue of Friar Diego de Landa, located behind the church. A disgruntled Mexican archaeologist (and obvious Maya enthusiast) used to spit on the friar's likeness every day as he passed it on his way to work.

wander around. But only a small percentage of these tourists return for a longer sojourn. A pity, as Valladolid is an authentic, unpretentious city with much to offer.

Not least among these assets is Valladolid's close proximity to the archaeological sites of Ek' Balam (15 miles), Chichén Itzá (25 miles), and Cobá (37 miles). Closer to town, you can visit some of the peninsula's most picturesque *cenotes,* enjoy the quiet, leafy beauty of the **Plaza Principal**, which is bordered by the whitewashed, baroque **Catedral de San Servacio** and **Palacio Municipal** (Municipal Palace), and stroll along its streets admiring the colorful colonial architecture. Also worth a visit is the austere and imposing Ex-Convent of San Bernardino de Siena, which was founded in 1552.

TOON AND MEXIGO TOURS INTRODUCE YOU TO MAYA COMMUNITIES AROUND VALLADOLID.

But my favorite reason to come to this city is **MexiGo Tours.** Owners Vivyana Hernández Molina and Toon Vande Vyvere will show you a side of the Yucatán that few other people have access to; through their tours, you can bike through the surrounding area or ride with them to visit Maya communities in nearby villages, swim in spectacular *cenotes,* and check out seldom-seen, out-of-the-way landmarks such as the Church of the Three Crosses. Of all the tour guides I have had in Mexico, Toon and Vivyana were among the most memorable for their enthusiasm, knowledge, and love of their city and its heritage.

✷ Lodging

The variety of lodging options in the Yucatán run the gamut from Maya huts with little more than a hammock to five-star luxury hotels. Geographically, you also have choices, from the three main cities to the bigger Maya sites.

Mérida

Mérida is home to a wonderful assortment of boutique hotels, inns, and guesthouses, many of them historic landmarks that enhance the quaint colonial landscape. Topping the list for sheer style and luxury is the wonderfully named **Rosas & Xocolate**, an ultra-exclusive boutique hotel located on Paseo de Montejo. Each of the hotel's 17 rooms are different, each flawless in their contemporary opulence, chic design, and

ROSAS & XOCOLATE IS EASILY ONE OF MÉRIDA'S MOST STYLISH BOUTIQUE HOTELS.

state-of-the-art amenities. With an absolutely must-visit chocolate store, top-class restaurant, elegant tequila bar, a brand-new spa and even an upper-deck lounge, the hotel is the epitome of modern style clothed in colonial charm.

If you really want to immerse yourself in the colonial comforts of the city, check out **Casa San Ángel**. The former home of Graciano Ricalde (the mathematician who calculated the precise trajectory of Haley's Comet in 1910, debunking the theory that the comet was going to destroy the Earth), the hotel has been meticulously restored by its current owners. Each of the beautiful 15 rooms have a unique look and rich antique furnishings, but all share a colonial theme, ample space, and a sense of living history. The leafy courtyard is an oasis after a long day, and the hotel's gift shop has products of excellent quality.

Budget-minded travelers can also find excellent boutique hotels. **Hotel Medio Mundo** falls nicely into this category. The distinctive blue and white property is well worth the price, especially for rooms without air-conditioning, which are a bit cheaper (honestly, most nights you don't need it). The 12 brightly painted rooms may lack the finery of other hotels, but have a rustic charm and are all spacious, with large bathrooms (bring your own shampoo and conditioner). Additional touches include a small pool and bar (the welcome hibiscus drink on arrival is a nice touch), free Wi-Fi access, and free breakfast of fresh mixed bread, fruit, and fresh fruit juices.

Among the most unique boutique properties in the city, **Casa Mexilio** is an M. C. Escher–like property with 10 rooms tucked away among its winding stairs, hidden recesses, and open-air corridors. The hotel is an organized chaos of leafy gardens, antiques, and memorabilia, and a stay here is akin to a step back in time. The fantastic gourmet breakfast (which comes with a highly tongue-in-cheek note from the hotel owner) and grottolike small pool are pleasant amenities.

If a friendly staff and owner are important to you, check into **Hotel Marionetas**. Owner Daniel is an absolute delight, a person I felt very fortunate to

HOTEL MARIONETAS IS ONE MY FAVORITE PLACES TO STAY IN MÉRIDA.

have met during my travels. The small hotel is hidden in a quiet corner of the city, and provides a true get-away-from-it-all ambience. It's the kind of place where a dip in the pool followed by a snooze in the hammock in your room can take up a languid, pleasant afternoon. The rooms aren't fancy, but they're comfortable, and Daniel and the wonderful staff will make you feel at home.

Hotel El Castellano will appeal to travelers on a budget who prefer larger hotels. All rooms have air-conditioning (not always the case in Mérida), cable TV, tiled floors, minibar, Wi-Fi access, ironing board, and desk. Add the large pool, gym, free parking (another plus in this city), and decent in-house restaurant with a terrific buffet breakfast, and the hotel offers great value for the money. Plus, you're just a few blocks from the *zócalo.* The **Holiday Inn Mérida**, located just off Paseo de Montejo, is a step up in price, amenities, and luxury. The red and yellow four-story hotel, one of the larger ones in the city, occupies a colonial building and has retained its architectural touches. Most notable of these is the lovely courtyard. Rooms are comfortable, and the upgrade to the junior suite and its four-poster bed is worth serious consideration.

Hotel Gran Real Yucatán is a stately hotel and a tale of two buildings. The beautiful lobby, courtyard, and main public space comprise a converted baroque-style French mansion that dates back to the 19th century. The 73 guest rooms occupy a more modern building and have a more contemporary style. All rooms have a private balcony, air-conditioning, and LCD TVs, among other amenities. The hotel's pool is a pleasant place to unwind, especially if you've opted for a poolside massage. And its restaurant, located in the courtyard, serves excellent local fare.

The largest hotel in the city, and in many locals' opinions the best, is the neoclassic **Fiesta Americana Mérida**, which appropriately straddles the old city and its newer environs. The only property with a tennis court in Mérida, the Fiesta Americana has well-appointed rooms decorated in contemporary Mexican style, along with a pool, gym, and spa; a huge and pleasant atrium lobby; and a branch of one of the most respected Yucatecan restaurants in Mexico: **Los Almendros**. If you're looking for space to spread out, excellent service, and a more traditional upscale hotel experience (President Bush stayed here), this property will do nicely. And if you can swing it, the fifth-floor Club Level includes separate check-in/check-out, complimentary breakfast, and snacks throughout the day. Finally, kids will enjoy the Fiesta Kids Disney-themed club and activity center.

HACIENDAS AROUND MÉRIDA There are plenty of haciendas around the Yucatán, but only a few have been converted into boutique hotels. These historic estates, rescued and restored with meticulous care, make for a wonderful alternative to a typical hotel stay.

Hacienda San Pedro Nohpat is unique in at least two ways: It's among the most affordable haciendas in the area, and it's the closest to Mérida. Over 400 years old, the hacienda retains an air of authenticity and a lived-in feel more akin to a house than a hotel. The rooms, each with their own décor, add to the rustic, homey ambience, as do the owners, who bought the property ten years ago and continue to live on-site. Guests have free rein of the house, kitchen (food available on an honor bar system), grounds, and the living rooms. Part of the hacienda's charm is the many pets who call it home (I woke up to birdsong), from the Amazon parrots to the adorable burros (small donkeys). Throw in the complimentary full breakfast, and this hacienda is well worth the money.

If I had found **Hacienda Santa Cruz** on the Internet as the current owners did, I'd probably be just as tempted to pack up my things and move in. That's exactly what they did, taking a dilapidated ruin and converting it into a charming boutique hotel. Santa Cruz has 10 rooms (including three suites and a casita for families) spread across 15 landscaped acres. The hacienda carefully preserves its history, both as a Franciscan monastery in the 17th century and as a henequen farm 200 years later. Note the exposed brick façades, the smokestack, and the converted chapel room, among other nods to the past. With its beautiful rooms, inviting pool, French-Creole dining, and the benefit of owners who live on the premises, the hacienda provides a cozy, pleasant escape.

Easily the most prestigious property on this list is **Hacienda Xcanatún**, a singularly beautiful and elegant estate that will make you feel like a henequen *hacenda-*

HACIENDA SANTA CRUZ

do of old. The hacienda's huge rooms are luxuriously furnished in grand colonial style, with the master suite sporting an in-room Jacuzzi tub. The grounds are built for long strolls and relaxation, and the hotel's spa and restaurant are among the best in Mérida. If you want the best of the hacienda experience and have a large enough wallet, look no further than this marvelous retreat.

Izamal

Two hotels come to mind in Izamal: the new and lovely **Hacienda Sacnicte** (White Flower), on the outskirts of the city, and **Macan Ché Bed & Breakfast.** The former is an artistic property far more contemporary in décor than the typical hacienda. The rooms, named after flowers and plants, are unique and dramatic in their furnishings and style, particularly the two-floor Ginger Suite. Depending on availability, I'd recommend touring the property and checking out a few before choosing the one that suits you. The hotel's restaurant is predominantly Italian (like owner Nadia), another departure from the norm. With a mere six rooms, the hacienda will feel like your personal luxury hideaway. In comparison, Macan Ché lacks the finery of Sacnicte, but makes up for it with excellent service, delicious breakfast, affordability, and location. The B&B also has private cottages tucked into its gardens, decorated in unique themes such as Maya, Colonial, and Safari.

Valladolid

Casa Hamaca is a small hotel a decent walk from the *zócalo,* or main plaza. The rooms are each designed according to a Maya or nature theme. Owner Denis Larsen is a kind and helpful host, and the amazing breakfast alone (cooked by a terrific local chef) merits an overnight stay. The property has a small pool, but far more interesting is the palapa where you can book a depilation, bodywork, or a traditional shamanic cleansing.

With 110 rooms, the **Ecotel Quinta Regia** is the biggest hotel in the city, a short taxi ride or moderate walk from the city center. The rooms are basic but offer room to spread out, tiled floors, and distinctly Mexican décor. The hotel offers plenty of amenities, including a pool, a solid local restaurant call El Mexicano, tennis courts, a palapa bar, and wi-fi access. The lovely **El Mesón del Marqués** has 90 rooms decorated in quaint style and set in a restored colonial building. The pool, courtyard, and terrace with gorgeous views of the cathedral make this a wonderful destination.

Near the Ruins

The Yucatán has numerous properties close to its largest archaeological sites. Chief among these is **Hacienda Chichén**, a boutique green hotel that has hosted archaeologists since the 1940s and, as a result, has witnessed the evolution of Chichén Itzá. The 26 rooms (note: no TVs) in the restored hacienda are spread out in cabins around the main house, home to an excellent restaurant, pool, and pleasant garden. Guests can also visit the original 16th-century chapel, organic garden, and landscaped grounds on the premises, and book a traditional Maya treatment at the Yaxkin Spa, voted one of the world's 10 best eco spas by Condé Nast Traveler. Located a short walk from the ancient city, Hacienda Chichén is in a class of its own, and the service, from the refreshing pineapple and *chaya* welcome drink to the ever-helpful concierge, is outstanding. Finally, ask about the hacienda's ongoing philanthropic work in the local Maya community. They'll be happy to show you what they're doing.

Even closer to Chichén Itzá, **Mayaland** was the first hotel built at the site. It offers 55 decent, comfortable rooms and five spacious suites in a three-story main house and a cluster of bungalows set in landscaped, leafy grounds.

You'll also find a few lodging options near Uxmal and the Puuc Route. A wonderfully authentic experience is **The Pickled Onion**, which is nothing more than two individual Maya-style huts built (by Maya workers) behind Valerie Pickles's rustic and delicious restaurant. The huts are equipped with a bed and hammock (believe me, the hammock is the way to go), and basic bathroom. Don't even think about TV and A/C; it's just not that kind of place. Outside the hut, the restaurant and a rather beautiful pool awaits. The Pickled Onion is definitely not for everyone, but if you want truly indigenous digs, I highly recommend it. You can't walk to Uxmal from here, but it's a short drive away. Far closer to Uxmal is **Misión Uxmal**, a more modern hotel with rooms that aren't as memorable but offer a pleasant night's sleep, nice pool, and wonderful views.

✷ Dining

Yucatecan cuisine is quite different from other parts of Mexico, and includes a few specialties that are revered around the country. However, you'll find after a few days of exploring the local dining scene, the menus start to look awfully similar. The usual suspects can be found at every typical eatery, with little to differentiate them among restaurants. Fortunately, Mérida in particular has seen a rise in fusion restaurants and haute cuisine that offers a change for the palate.

In Mérida

By and large, I found the best Yucatecan food outside Mérida's historic city center. One no-frills exception was **El Trapiche**, just off the Plaza Grande on Calle 62, which serves cheap and tasty local fare like *queso fundido* (a smoky melted cheese served with tortillas), *pollo pibil* (marinated chicken thigh) with rice and

YUCATECAN CUISINE

Critical to Yucatecan cuisine are two native ingredients: *chaya* (a leafy plant similar to spinach) and lime. Other common ingredients include chiles (Yucatecans like their food spicy, and habanero chiles are never far from the table), achiote (annatto seeds), sour orange, pumpkin seeds, and red onion. Yucatecans cook with pheasant, turkey, deer, pig, and fish from the coast. Throw in tortillas and beans, and you have a hearty, protein-heavy diet that is delicious but takes getting used to. Here are a few classic Yucatecan dishes which are worth sampling while you're here:

Cochinita pibil: Hands down, the most famous and well-loved Yucatecan dish in Mexico, this is slow-roasted pork marinated in achiote, sour orange juice, peppercorns, garlic, cumin, and salt, and wrapped in banana leaves before baking. Traditionally, a whole roast suckling pig is cooked underground. The annatto seed gives the dish its trademark reddish hue, but it only looks spicy. If you don't eat pork, *pollo pibil* (chicken) is also widely available.

Huevos motuleños: A hearty breakfast dish consisting of tortilla covered with refried beans and a fried egg, drowned in tomato sauce, peas and topped with chopped ham and shredded cheese.

Múkbil pollo: An extremely filling dish, this is a large pie made from tamale dough and stuffed with beans and chicken.

Panuchos & salbutes: Small corn tortillas fried and filled with either shredded chicken or turkey, and garnished with lettuce and onion. The difference between *panuchos* and *salbutes* is the refried beans inside the *panucho.*

Papadzules: Tortillas filled with hard-boiled egg and pumpkin seed sauce, and topped with tomato sauce and habanero chile.

Pavo en relleno negro: The wild turkey is native to the Yucatán and was a frequent victim of the Maya diet. In this dish, the cooked turkey sits in a black, almost oily bath made from burnt chiles de árbol. The soup flavors the meat, making for a watery stew that looks more intimidating than it tastes.

Poc chuc: A simple but immensely popular dish, *poc chuc* consists of slices of pork (most common, although it can also be found with chicken or beef) marinated in sour orange juice, grilled, and served with a *chiltomate* sauce, pickled onions, and tomatoes.

Sopa de lima: One of the view light meals to be found, the tangy lime soup includes shredded chicken, fried tortilla strips, and lime juice.

If you're a beer drinker, make sure to wash down at least one meal with a *michelada,* which is beer with lime, coarse salt, Worcestershire sauce, soy sauce, Tabasco sauce, black pepper, and Maggi seasoning. If that sounds a bit too exotic for you, opt for the *chelada,* which is beer simply with lime and salt.

POC CHUC IS A CULINARY STAPLE OF THE YUCATÁN.

beans, and a variety of delicious fresh juices.

Of course, once you migrate out of the city center, Mérida has its share of fine restaurants. For grassroots Yucatecan food, you shouldn't miss a visit to the **Mercado de Santa Ana**, where you'll find rows of *loncherias,* rustic stalls serving basic breakfast and lunch staples. You can sample a great variety of foods at budget rates (it's always a good idea to ask the price of dishes in a market before committing to them). I gorged on *panuchos* and *relleno negro* on my last visit.

With five locations in the city, **Eladio's** is a local dining institution, a favorite gathering spot for families and large groups, and a place that believes in feeding its clients. It's a great spot where you can mingle with the locals, watch festive live shows, and be quite literally plied with *botanas* (appetizers or small plates) with your drink order. In particular, look out for the *brazo de reyna* (a roulade made with boiled egg, *chaya,* pumpkin, and tomato sauce), *longaniza asada* (roast pork sausage with grilled onions and spicy tomato sauce), and egg tacos. The menu is fortunately bilingual.

A WAITER AT ELADIO'S SHOWS OFF A BOTANA.

A bit farther out in the Kanasín neighborhood, and far more rustic, is **La Susana Internacional**, the self-dubbed "capital of the *panucho.*" A Yucatecan favorite for close to 50 years, it's off the tourist map but well worth the trip for heaps of solid local food. The sign in the main dining room says it all: FRIENDS WHO VISIT US, ABSTAIN FROM ORDERING TOO MUCH, BECAUSE HERE YOU EAT WELL. Surrounded by kitschy folkloric décor, you can feast on a terrific *sopa de lima, poc chuc, cochinita,* and, of course, *panuchos.* Also make sure to order the fresh fruit juice to help wash it down.

The perhaps overblown standard-bearer of dressed-up traditional Yucatecan cuisine is **Los Almendros**, which has grown from its beginnings on Calle 60 in front of the Mejorada Park to locations around Mexico. You'll find all the usual dishes here, including *cochinita pibil, poc chuc, salbutes,* and *papadzules,* helpfully pictured on the menu. While the original address offers an unbeatable setting, I recommend the branch at the Fiesta Americana, which has a magnificent mural featuring a strange assortment of local and international figures (Frida Kahlo next to Gandhi? Okay . . .) as well as an excellent chef.

Paseo de Montejo is full of restaurants, but you need to know where to go to have a good meal. **Rosas & Xocolate** offers sophisticated cuisine and an ever-changing menu in a wonderful setting. **Local 3** is one of my favorites for its bistrolike ambience, high-end comfort food philosophy, and simple yet well executed dishes. And **Slavia** combines an exotic lounge atmosphere with creative fusion cuisine and a ridiculous martini menu.

The best fine dining I enjoyed in the city was at **Néctar Food & Wine**, which is located in the city's Zona Norte (Northern Zone), a taxi ride away from any hotel in the city. Award-winning chef Roberto Solis is a bold and gifted cook leading the vanguard of new Yucatecan cuisine. In a bright, contemporary-chic setting (love the Wonder Woman poster) with an open kitchen, the chef whips up a local and global mix of dishes like *tártara de venado* (venison tartar), accentuated with an emulsion of cilantro, quail egg, olive oil, and radish; *carnitas* (small tacos made with shredded pork) of tuna, avocado, and cilantro; and crawfish served with avocado ravioli, onion foam, and a touch of habanero chile.

Finally, I'd be remiss if I didn't mention at least one of Mérida's many Lebanese restaurants, which are authentic and numerous thanks to the city's Lebanese pop-

LOCAL 3 IS A CASUAL HANGOUT WITH GOOD FOOD AND A RELAXED AMBIENCE.

ulation. **Gurú** is a fine ambassador; located in the north of the city, the restaurant is best visited during its weekend buffet, which gives you an all-you-can-eat passport to *kibbes* (a kind of kebab made with bulgur and ground lamb), *sambusic* (fried pastries filled with ground beef and onion), and other dishes from the Levant. Gurú also offers live shows every Saturday night and weekend karaoke nights.

Beyond Mérida

One reason to rent a car is the opportunity to sample local restaurants around the Yucatán. In the town of Maní, near the convent where Diego de Landa committed his atrocious "Act of Faith," the **Principe de Tutul-Xiu** restaurant receives justifiable reverence for its *poc chuc*. You can order from a selection of Yucatecan specialties, but if you've made it out here, you might as well stick to the pork or chicken version of the classic dish that made this place famous. Another decent, if less famous, choice lies in Acanceh. The **Parador Turístico Acanceh** won't blow you away with its cuisine, but under its monumental conical thatch roof you'll find tasty *poc chuc, pavo en pipian* (turkey in pumpkin seed sauce), *relleno negro,* and other local dishes served with handmade tortillas.

Near Uxmal, I became an instant fan of **The Pickled Onion**, a rustic, out-of-the-ordinary eatery. Providing a departure from all the *poc chucs* and *rellenos negros,* owner Valerie Pickles started me off with fresh papaya juice, followed by a delicious cold avocado soup. My entrée was a succulent chicken marinated in sour orange and cooked with capers, raisins, olives, tomatoes, and onions, and peppers. The dish came with a *camote* (sweet potato) puree and a very British assortment of cauliflower, carrot, and beans.

Close to Mayapán, **Restaurante Na Lu'um**, about 30 minutes from Mérida, offers excellent traditional cuisine. Specialties include *pollo pibil, pavo en escabeche* (turkey in a vinegar-based seasoning), and *filete de res maya* (a house recipe of grilled fillet in a *recado* sauce).

In the town of Celestún (covered later in this chapter), **La Palapa** offers up fantastic seafood right on the water. The bilingual menu includes *jaiba en mayonesa* (lump blue crab meat and mayonnaise

THE CRABMEAT PATTY AT LA PALAPA IS ONE OF ITS BEST DISHES.

patties), a variety of ceviches, and crunchy coconut shrimp.

And finally, if you want a special night out, book a table at Hacienda Xcanatun's award-winning **Casa de Piedra** for dinner. The restaurant, set in the lovely main building of the hacienda, serves an outstanding fusion of French and Yucatecan cuisine, with such dishes as roasted beet and orange salad, *madrigal a los tres chiles* (a kind of cobia served in a three-chile sauce), and Pacific and Atlantic oysters.

In Izamal, head straight to the **Mercado Municipal** near the Plaza de la Constitución to dine on succulent *tacos de dzik de venado* (shredded venison tacos with cilantro, radish and sour orange seasoning, with avocado dressing on the side). And in Valladolid, **El Oasis** has little in the way of décor but makes up for it with a fantastic and extensive juice menu, a menu of specials like *poc chuc* made with *longaniza asada* and *pollo feliz* (happy chicken), and terrific breakfast meals.

✷ Don't Miss

Even with its many wondrous Maya cities, Yucatán is more than its archaeological bounty. Its naturally porous geography, colonial-era convents and many cultural, entertainment, and tourist attractions in its main cities can keep you happily busy between ruins.

CENOTES The Yucatán was originally underwater, and its limestone foundation is as porous as a sponge; time and water erosion have allowed for the proliferation of *cenotes,* or sinkholes. The word comes from the Mayan *dzonot,* which the conquistadors translated into *cenote.* These are natural freshwater pools that come in three basic varieties: open, partially submerged, and fully submerged. For the Maya, *cenotes* were sacred spiritual places, gateways to the Underworld. There are literally thousands of them around the peninsula, ranging from often crowded natural swimming pools that charge admission, to free, unsupervised, bat-ridden wonders.

In the small town of **Cuzamá,** a local indigenous cooperative runs a tour of three beautiful *cenotes*—Chelentún (Stone Rainbow), Chansinic'che (Red Ant Tree), and Bolonchoojol (Nine Rat Hole)—linked together by a rickety old railway track. Half the fun is taking the mule-pulled carts to each one.

The closest accessible cenote to Chichén Itzá, **Ik Kil** is a large, round, open pool at the bottom of a staircase surrounded by vegetation and waterfalls. The "Sacred Blue Cenote" is huge (almost 200 feet wide by about 130 feet deep), but I find the man-made enhancements (restaurant and palapas) takes away from the unspoiled beauty and magic of other cenotes.

Kankirixche. This picturesque cenote lives up to its name (Tree with Yellow Fruit) thanks to the alamo tree roots that hang down to the water level. Beautifully lit by natural light, the cavern has crystal-clear water and is a favorite for divers and snorkelers. The caverns here are among the largest in the Yucatán.

Tzabnah. A truly rustic excursion, you'll have to keep an eye out in the town of Tecoh for this guided tour of a deep an underground cavern, which leads to no less than 13 cenotes along a 1.2-mile route that is often pitch black (your guide wears a miner's helmet, so don't lose him!).

Located right next to Ek' Balam, **X'canché** is a large, well-run facility that includes biking, walking tours, restaurant, hammocks, arts-and-crafts shops, rappel and zip line, and, of course, a beautiful open-air natural pool.

X'kekén and Samula. Ask me to pick my favorite cenotes in Mexico, and I'll lead you to these two beautiful spots. Located in Dzitnup, a few miles southeast of Valladolid, these cenotes are located across the street from each other. The former is a magical underground grotto, where you can swim in crystal blue water lit by well-placed floodlights, and explore the surrounding natural limestone formations, many of which resemble animals (a popular

COMPLETELY SUBMERGED, CENOTE X'KEKÉN IS AN UNDERGROUND TREASURE.

SAMULA RANKS AMONG THE MOST BEAUTIFUL CENOTES IN THE REGION.

activity here is jumping off the "elephant" into the water). The latter is a stunning natural pool deep in the ground with a hole in the middle allowing sunlight and a curtain of hanging vines and roots. The entrance to Samula is surrounded by local vendors and includes changing rooms and restrooms.

Yokdzonot. A beautiful *cenote* just minutes from Chichén Itzá, this is a full-service park where you can rent life jackets, stay at a nearby eco-hotel, bike ride, and rappel in addition to swimming in a lovely natural setting.

Zaci. Smack in the town of Valladolid, this may not be the most charming *cenote*, but it's easy to access, huge (150 feet wide by 260 feet deep), and a cool place to go swimming on a hot day.

CELESTÚN. An ecotourism wonderland, Celestún is an estuary on the western coast of the Yucatán, 60 miles from Mérida. The area has been declared a Biosphere Reserve, and is prized for its mangrove forests and over 230 mammal species, including ocelots, spider monkeys, jaguars, and sea turtles; but the star attractions are the large numbers of flamingos that live here, which can be seen on boat, bike and canoe tours. Tours also visit the Tampeten petrified forest and *ojo de agua* (eye of water) natural spring for a swim. If you want to spend the night here, check into the inviting and affordable Hotel Manglares, especially if they have one of their beachfront cabanas available.

Manglares de Dzinitún. A 2½-hour journey into a mangrove forest by bicycle and canoe, this tour offers a chance to see the natural ecosystem of Celestún in the least invasive way.

THE FLAMINGOS AT CELESTÚN ARE JUST ONE REASON TO SPEND THE DAY HERE.

Unidad Turística Celestún. At this central visitor and tourist center, you have access to locker rooms, a snack shop, and a ticket booth where you can book a 2½- or 1½-hour boat tour (the smaller one skips the petrified forest) to the flamingo reserve and *ojo de agua*.

CONVENTS The various convents spread out throughout the Yucatán stand witness to the Catholic Church's power and influence over the peninsula during and after the conquest. There is a Convent Route through the region, but I've highlighted the ones below for their historic importance and picturesque appearance.

Convento de San Antonio de Padua. The jewel of Izamal, the monumental convent built by Diego de Landa is the chief reason to visit this lovely colonial city.

Convento de Maní. The somewhat run-down, orange-colored Convent of Maní has an infamous name thanks to Diego de Landa's disastrous "Act of Faith" carried out here in 1562.

Convento de San Bernardino de Siena. In Valladolid, this massive convent, built in 1552, marked the arrival of the Franciscan order in the city.

Ex-Convento de Santo Domingo. In the small town of Uayma stands perhaps the most visually striking convent in the Yucatán. Built by the Franciscan order in 1646, the church was burned to the ground during the Caste War. Restoration of the church in 2003 revealed the marvelous stucco rosettes and starbursts that make the convent so distinctive.

MÉRIDA'S CULTURAL HOTSPOTS It goes without saying that Mérida's city center merits exploration. In particular, don't miss these destinations.

Catedral de San Ildefonso. Located on the east side of the Plaza Grande, this massive

THE 16TH-CENTURY CATEDRAL DE SAN ILDEFONSO IS ONE OF THE OLDEST CHURCHES IN MEXICO.

REMOTE AND RESPLENDENT, THE EX-CONVENTO DE SANTO DOMINGO IS THE MOST PICTURESQUE OF THE YUCATÁN'S CONVENTS.

cathedral was built by indigenous laborers using stones from the Maya temple upon which it now sits. Inside, check out the painting of Tutul-Xiu, *cacique* of Maní, paying his respects to Francisco de Montejo; the Cristo de la Unidad, a tall crucifix behind the altar, symbolizing the reconciliation between the Spanish and Maya; and the small chapel to the left of the altar, which houses a replica of Mérida's most famous religious artifact, a statue called *Cristo de las Ampollas* (Christ of the Blisters). The original was lost during the Mexican Revolution.

Mérida English Library. The city's only English-language library is a gathering place for locals and expats to share books, mingle, and participate in a variety of events. Chief among these is their weekly House and Garden walking tours, which gives visitors unique glimpses into the city's restored buildings.

Museo de Arte Popular de Yucatán. Representing some of the best folk art from around the peninsula and around the nation, the museum of popular art is equally impressive for its collection as its location in a turn-of-the-century mansion known as Casa Molina.

Museum of Anthropology and History. Also known as the Museo Palacio Cantón for its stunning setting in a beautiful neoclassic mansion, this is the definitive destination for those who want to learn about the Maya. The museum has gathered artifacts from around the peninsula; especially impressive are the jade artifacts found in the Cenote Sagrado at Chichén Itzá.

Museum of Contemporary Art of Yucatán (MACAY). The museum, located next to the cathedral, is an ironic neighbor to the 16th-century structure. MACAY features a permanent collection and revolving exhibits from around the world, and is the largest and most complete source of contemporary art in the region.

Palacio de Gobierno. On the north side of the Plaza Grande, the bright green Governor's Palace, built in 1892, houses 27 murals that depict some of the central figures and conflicts in the history of the Yucatán.

MÉRIDA'S WEEKLONG EVENTS Mérida has a cultural activity (almost always free) going on around town literally every day, from big band concerts to folkloric dances. The grandest outdoor event of the week is **Mérida en Domingo** (Mérida on Sunday), which takes over the Plaza Grande from 7 AM to 2 PM. Food stalls, arts-and-crafts shops, and a family ambience pervades the day. The city also closes many of its roads, giving them full access to pedestrians.

Monumento a la Patria. If nothing else, visit this landmark on the Paseo de Montejo for the photo op. Begun in 1945 by sculptor Rómulo Rozo, the monument

FOLKLORIC DANCES, SUCH AS THE NOCHE MEXICANA ON SATURDAY NIGHTS, TAKE PLACE THROUGHOUT THE WEEK AROUND MÉRIDA.

combines symbols of Yucatán's past, including the coat of arms of the city of Mérida, a Chac-Mool figure, and a variety of animal figurines. The sculpture of the eagle devouring a snake is a symbol of Mexico.

The Paseo de Montejo at Night. Mérida's nightlife is best experienced along the Paseo de Montejo, which is home to chic lounges, bars, and nightclubs. Among the best are **Mandala**, a South Beach–style rooftop terrace bathed in white, featuring a live DJ and a good cocktail menu led by the fruity Martini Mandala; the aforementioned **Slavia**, with its eastern and Indian-themed décor and intimate, sultry vibe; and **La Musa**, where you'll find great rock bands and a lively bar atmosphere.

SOUVENIR SHOPPING IN MÉRIDA Mexico's arts and crafts vary from region to region, and the Yucatán has its specialties. In particular, the peninsula is renowned for its hammocks; you'll find vendors all around the city, and particularly along the Paseo de Montejo, where I bought mine from an indigenous producer after a round or two of good-natured haggling. Other places to find hammocks include the family-run **Hamacas El Aguacate** and **Artesanías el Xiric**.

Another popular product sold in the region is the comfortable guayabera. These mens' shirts, loose-fitting with two or four front pockets, can be bought at **Ravgo** and **Guayaberas Jack**, which sell high-quality merchandise. Finally, two fine arts-and-crafts shops worth a look while you're in town are **Artesanaria**, and the **Casa de las Artesanías**, both of which offer high-quality products.

A trip to the **Mercado Municipal de Artesanías Lucas de Galves** is a must for shoppers who love the bustle and haggling of a typical Mexican marketplace. You can find a wide variety of products for sale here, including one very odd, and typically Yucatecan, souvenir: the *makech,* a live, bejeweled beetle that you hang from a chain and pin to your clothing.

SOTUTA DE PEÓN. This living museum is a fantastic all-around experience, a hacienda and functioning henequen factory that takes you on a firsthand tour of production of the henequen plant and hacienda life. The Peón family once owned dozens of haciendas in the Yucatán, and lived in a style typical to the grand colonial era. Jorge, our wonderful guide, spoke several languages on the tour with admirable fluency, proved intelligent and knowledgeable about much more than Sotuta de Peón, and showed us all the machinations and innovations behind henequen production. We then jumped onto a mule-pulled train, visited an old Maya who had worked the henequen fields for decades (and taught us a few words in Mayan, as well as how to lie in a hammock), and ended our journey at a breathtaking *cenote* (life jackets available). The tour includes hotel pickup if needed.

✷ Local Knowledge

My favorite online resource for the Yucatán is **Yucatán Today** (http://yucatantoday.com), which is a comprehensive listing of everything related to travel and tourism to the area. You can even download free maps. The official portal of the Yucatán Tourism Board is www.mayayucatan.com, and is also quite detailed. One of the best local informational sites is **Yucatán Living** (www.yucatanliving.com), a

A VENDOR ON PASEO DE MONTEJO CONVINCES ME TO BUY ONE OF HIS HANDMADE HAMMOCKS.

THE MULE-CART RIDE IS PART OF THE FUN AT SOTUTA DE PEÓN.

project by self-styled "working gringos" Ellen and James Fields. It's a good place to go to discover more about life in the region and what's happening in town. A listing of off-the-beaten-path bars, restaurants, hotels, and other listings can be found at **Ubícate en Mérida** (www.ubicateenmerida.com). Finally, the **Mérida English Library** is also a great place to hang out with local expats and get their take on what's going on.

It's good to know distances in and around the Yucatán. Although the roads are generally in good shape,

THE BASICS

Area code: 999

Climate: The city is usually hot, which can make for sweltering walks in the city. There's a rainy season from July to October, and a cool season (it never really gets cold) from November to February.

Tourist Police: This squad patrols Mérida's historic city center, and can be reached at 999-942-0060.

American Consulate: 999-942-5700, Calle 60 No. 338K, between Calles 29 and 31, Colonia Alcala Martin, Mérida, Yucatán 97050.

Hospitals: Two very good hospitals in the city are the Clínica de Mérida (999-942-1800) and The Centro Médico de las Américas (999-926-2111).

the ubiquitous speed bumps, checkpoints (don't worry about these; the last thing they are trying to do is disturb the tourists), and general traffic can slow you down. This table should help:

Mérida	Chichén Itzá 75 miles	Celestún 56 miles	Izamal 52 miles	Valladolid 99 miles	Uxmal 48 miles
Chichén Itzá	Mérida 75 miles	Celestún 132 miles	Izamal 43 miles	Valladolid 25 miles	Uxmal 100 miles
Valladolid	Mérida 99 miles	Chichén Itzá 25 miles	Izamal 69 miles	Celestún 158 miles	Uxmal 148 miles

A WEEKEND IN THE YUCATÁN

My first question to those spending a weekend in the Yucatán is, "Can you stay a bit longer?" There's so much to see and do here that one weekend is hardly enough to cover it all. Over a weekend, your time in the region will be spent in Mérida, with side trips to the ruins.

Landing on Friday, your first day should be spent enjoying the **colonial city center**, with visits to the cathedral, governor's palace, and, if you have time, the wonderful museum of history and anthropology on **Paseo de Montejo**. The latter option makes sense, as you can stay on Montejo, enjoy dinner at a fun eatery like Slavia or Local 3, and hang out late into the night.

Much as I would love to send you along the Puuc Route on Day 2, if you've never seen **Chichén Itzá**, you can't miss it. The city will take most of your day (a guide is expensive, but recommended), but you'll have time to visit the nearby **Cenote Yokdzonot**, so bring your bathing suit. At 7, you can return to catch the **light show** at Chichén. On Sunday, **Mérida en Domingo** offers a terrific way to enjoy the city when it lets its hair down. But you can also work in another site to contrast against Chichén Itzá, and I'd recommend its mighty contemporary, **Uxmal**. Better yet, hang around Sunday night for dinner at the Pickled Onion and the Uxmal light show.

EXTENDED STAY

Over a longer period, you can canvass the Yucatán at your leisure. A recommended seven-day itinerary would involve a rental car at the airport and be comprised as follows:

Days 1 & 2: Arrive in Mérida, enjoy the city's **colonial center** and its shopping, museums, dining and nightlife.

Day 3: Head out to **Uxmal**, the **Ruta Puuc**, and the **Pickled Onion**. If you fancy a night in true Maya fashion, book yourself into one of the Pickled Onion's Maya huts after dinner. Another option is a stay at the **Hacienda Santa Cruz**, which lies on the road back from Uxmal toward Mérida.

Day 4: You have a choice of visiting **Celestún**, which anyone who loves the outdoors will want to see; taking a tour of **Sotuta de Peón**, for a unique look into the henequen history of the peninsula; or a visit to **Dzibilchaltún** and the beautiful colonial city of Izamal.

Day 5: Devote the day to **Chichén Itzá** and a *cenote* or two. If you can swing it financially and want to live like a *hacendado,* check into **Hacienda Xcanatún** or **Hacienda Chichén**. Enjoy dinner at the hacienda, and reserve a treatment at their excellent spas.

Days 6–7: Head to **Valladolid** and **Ek' Balam**. Spend a night here, and the next day hit the road with **MexiGo Tours**, who will take you to the Maya heartland, beautiful *cenote*s, and off-the-beaten-path gems.

XCANATÚN IS HACIENDA LIVING AT ITS MOST REFINED.

✷ Contacts

ADO Ticket Bus 999-925-0910, Calle 60 with Colón, Mérida, Yucatán 97000.

Los Almendros 999-942-1111, at the Fiesta Americana Mérida, Paseo Montejo 451, Colonia Centro, Mérida, Yucatán, 97000. www.losalmendros.com.mx. Open daily 11:30–11:30. $$–$$$. (Another location is at the Parque de la Mejorada.)

Artesanaria 999-252-3736, Calle 60 No. 480 and Calle 55, Colonia Centro, Mérida, Yucatán, 97000. Open daily 11–10:30. $–$$$$.

Artesanías el Xiric 999-924-9906, Calle 57-A Nos. 15 and 16, Pasaje Congreso, Colonia Centro, Mérida, Yucatán, 97000. Open daily 8–8. $–$$$$.

Casa de las Artesanías 999-928-6676, Calle 63 No. 513, Colonia Centro, Mérida, Yucatán, 97000. Open Mon.–Fri. 10–9, Sat. 10–11, Sun. 10–2. $–$$$$.

Casa Hamaca 985-856-5287, Parque San Juan, Calle 49 No. 202 x 40, Valladolid, Yucatán 97780. www.casahamaca.com. $.

Casa Mexilio 888-819-0024 (within the U.S.), 999-928-2505, Calle 68 No. 495, between Calles 57 and 59, Mérida, Yucatán 97000. www.casamexilio.com. $–$$.

Casa San Ángel 999-928-1800/0800, Montejo No. 1 in El Remate, Mérida, Yucatán 97000. www.casasanangel.com.mx. $$–$$$.

Catedral de San Ildefonso Calle 61 on the east side of Plaza Grande, Colonia Centro, Mérida, Yucatán 97000. Open daily 6–noon and 4–7. Free.

Catedral de San Servacio Plaza Principal at Calle 41, between Calles 42 and 40, Valladolid, Yucatán 97784. Open daily 7–1 and 4–8. Free.

Cenote Ik Kil Eco-archeological Park Ik Kil along Highway 180, Pisté, Yucatán. http://cenote-ik-kil.com. Open daily 8–6. $.

Cenote Kankirixche Highway 281 at the town of Mukuiche, Yucatán. Open daily 8–6. Free.

Cenote Tzabnah 999-995-6676, Calle 25 No. 113 between Calles 32 and 34, Tecoh, Yucatán. Open daily 9–5.

Cenote X'canché 985-107-4774, 985-100-9915, Km. 1.5, Ek' Balam Archaeological Zone, Ejido Hunuku, Municipio de Temozón, Yucatán. Open daily 9–5. $$.

Cenote X'kekén and Samula Located in the town of Dzitnup, along Highway 180, 4.3 miles south of Valladolid. Open daily 8–5. $.

Cenote Yokdzonot 985-100-0026, Calle 20 No. 111, between Calles 25 and 27, Community of Yokdzonot, Yucatán. www.cenoteyokdzonot.com. Open daily 9–5. $$.

Cenote Zaci Calle 36 between Calles 37 and 39, Valladolid, Yucatán 97780. Open daily 7–5. $.

Convento de Maní Plaza Principal, Maní, Yucatán. At last visit, the interior was closed for restoration.

Convento de San Antonio de Padua Calle 31 facing Plaza Zamná and Plaza de la Constitución, Izamal, Yucatán 97540. Open daily 8–9:30. Free.

Convento de San Bernardino de Siena 985-856-2160, Calle 41-A, Valladolid, Yucatán 97780. Open Tue.–Sat. 8–noon and 5–7, Sun. until noon. Free.

Ex-Convento de Santo Domingo Plaza Principal, Uayma, Yucatán. Open Mon.–Sat. 8–noon and 4–7, Sun. until noon. Free.

Cuzamá Cenotes 999-992-8133, Carretera Cuzamá-Chunkanán Km. 2.1, Cuzamá, Yucatán. Open daily 8–5. $$.

Ecotel Quinta Regia 985-856-3472/73/76/79, Calle 40 No. 160-A x 27, Colonia Santa Lucia, Valladolid, Yucatán 97780. www.ecotelquintaregia.com.mx. $$–$$$.

Eladio's 999-925-0720, 999-927-2126, 999-922-5855, 999-984-0057, Five locations around town: Calle 28 No. 171 and 7 Garcia Gineres, Sucursal Pensiones; Calle 59 No. 425 and 44, Sucursal Centro; Calle 21 and Crucero de Itzimná, Colonia Itzimna; Calle 4 No. 119 a and 19b, Colonia Chuminopolis; Calle 80 and Avenida Itzaes, Colonia Obrera, Mérida, Yucatán 97000. Open daily 11–9. $–$$.

Fiesta Americana Mérida 999-942-1111, Paseo Montejo 451, Colonia Centro, Mérida, Yucatán, 97000. www.fiestaamericana.com. $$$.

Guayaberas Jack 999-928-6002, 999-928-5999, Calle 59 No. 507-A between Calles 60 and 62, Colonia Centro Mérida, Yucatán 97000. www.guayaberasjack.com.mx. Open Mon.–Sat. 10–8, Sun 10–2. $$–$$$$.

Gurú 999-252-8400, Calle 20 S/N, Colonia México Norte, Mérida, Yucatán 97000. Open 1–1 daily. $$–$$$.

Hacienda Chichén 985-851-0045, 999-920-8407, 877-631-4005 (within the U.S., Carretera 180 Mérida Puerto Juárez, Km. 120 Zona Arqueológica Chichén Itzá, Yucatán. www.haciendachichen.com. $$$.

Hacienda Sacnicte 999-278-3299, Calle 24 x 31 (two miles off Calle 31), Izamal, Yucatán 97540. www.haciendasacnicte.com. $$$.

Hacienda San Pedro Nohpat 999-988-0542, Carretera Cancún 180 Km. 8, Colonia San Pedro Nohpat, Yucatán. www.haciendaholidays.com. $–$$.

Hacienda Santa Cruz 999-254-0541, Calle 86 Sur, Santa Cruz Palomeque, Mérida, Yucatán 97135. www.haciendasantacruz.com. $$–$$$.

Hacienda Xcanatún 999-930-2140. Calle 20 S/N, between Calles 19 and 19-A, Comisaria Xcanatún, Mérida, Yucatán 97302. www.xcanatun.com. $$$$.

Hamacas El Aguacate 999-928-6429, Calle 58 No. 604 and

Calle 73, Colonia Centro Mérida, Yucatán 97000. www.hamacaselaguacate.com.mx. Open Mon.–Fri. 8:30–7:30, Sat. 8–5. $$–$$$$.

Holiday Inn Mérida 877-859-5095, Avenida Colon No. 498, Paseo de Montejo, Mérida, Yucatán 97000. www.Holidayinn.com. $$–$$$.

Hotel El Castellano Calle 57 No. 513, between Calles 62 and 64, Colonia Centro, Mérida, Yucatán 97000. www.elcastellano.com. $–$$.

Hotel Gran Real Yucatán 999-924-8268/928-6081, Calle 56 No. 474 at Calle 55, Colonia Centro, Mérida, Yucatán 97000. www.granrealyucatan.com. $$.

Hotel Manglares 988-916-2156, Calle 12 No. 63, Celestún, Yucatán 97367. www.hotelmanglares.com.mx. $–$$.

Hotel Marionetas 999-928-3377/923-2790, Calle 49 No. 516, between Calles 62 and 64, Colonia Centro, Mérida, Yucatán 97000. www.hotelmarionetas.com. $–$$.

Hotel Medio Mundo 999-924-5472, Calle 55 No. 533, at Calles 64 and 66, Colonia Centro, Mérida, Yucatán 97000. www.hotelmediomundo.com. $.

Iglesia de San Juan Bautista Calle 62 No. 822, Mérida, Yucatán 97000. Open daily 7–noon and 4–8. Free.

Iglesia de Santa Ana Calle 60, between Calles 45 and 47, Mérida, Yucatán 97000. Open daily 7–1 and 4–8. Free.

Local 3 999-927-9196, Avenida Prolongación Montejo No. 454-B, Plaza Arboleada Local 3, Colonia Itzimná, Mérida, Yucatán 97000. Open Mon.–Sat. 1–midnight, Sun. 1–5. $$–$$$.

Macan Ché Bed & Breakfast 988-954-02-87, Calle 22 No. 305, between Calles 33 and 35, Izamal, Yucatán 97540. www.macanche.com. $–$$.

Mandala 999-286-7445, Calle 34 No. 386, between Calles 37 and 39, Colonia Emiliano Zapata, Mérida, Yucatán 97000. www.mandalaloungebar.com.mx. Open 7 PM–4 AM daily. $$.

Manglares de Dzinitún 999-232-5915/988-967-8023, Calle 2b S/N x 15, Colonia Felipe Carrillo Puerto, Celestún, Yucatán 97320. $$$.

Mayaland 800-235-4079 (within the U.S.), 998-887-2495, Zona Arqueológica, Chichén Itzá, Yucatán 97751. www.mayaland.com. $$–$$$.

Mercado de Santa Ana Between Calles 47 and 60 in Barrio Santa Ana, Mérida, Yucatán 97000. Hours vary by stall. $–$$.

Mercado Municipal de Artesanías Lucas de Galves Calle 56 by Calle 57, Colonia Centro, Mérida, Yucatán 97000. Hours vary by stall, generally open 8–6 daily. $–$$$$.

Mercado Municipal Calle 31-A facing the Plaza de la Constitución, Izamal, Yucatán 97540. Hours vary but some stalls stay open Mon.–Sat. 6–8. $.

Mérida English Library 999-924-8401, Calle 53 No. 524, between Calles 66 and 68, Colonia Centro, Mérida, Yucatán 97000. www.meridaenglishlibrary.com. Open Mon.–Fri. 9–1, Sat. 10–1. Also open Mon. 6:30–9 and Thu. 4–7. Free.

Mérida International Airport 999-946-1530, Carretera Mérida a Uman Km. 14.5, Mérida, Yucatán 97000. www.asur.com.mx.

El Mesón del Marqués 985-856-2073, Calle 39 No. 203, between Calles 40 and 42, Colonia Centro, Valladolid, Yucatán 97780. www.mesondelmarques.com. $–$$.

MexiGo Tours 985-856-0777, Calle 43 No. 204-B, between Calles 40 and 42, Valladolid, Yucatán 97780. www.mexigotours.com. $$–$$$.

Misión Uxmal 997-976-2022, 800-900-3800 (within Mexico), Carretera Mérida-Campeche Km.78 S/N, Uxmal, Yucatán 97840. www.hotelesmision.com. $–$$.

La Musa 999-948-3838, Prolongación Paseo Montejo No. 349 and 5, Fraccionamiento Campestre, Mérida, Yucatán 97000. Open daily 5 PM–3 AM. $.

Museo de Arte Contemporáneo de Yucatán 999-928-3258/36, Calle 60 between Calles 61 and 63, Colonia Centro, Mérida, Yucatán 97000. www.macay.org. Open Wed.–Mon. 10–6. $.

Museo de Arte Popular de Yucatán 999-928-5263. Calle 50A and 57 No. 487, Colonia Centro, Mérida, Yucatán 97000. Open Tue.–Sat. 9:30–6:30, Sun. 9–2. $, free on Sun.

Museum of Anthropology and History 999-923-0557, Paseo de Montejo and Calle 43, Colonia Centro, Mérida, Yucatán 97000. Open Tue.–Sun. 8–5. $.

Néctar Food & Wine 999-938-0838, Avenida 1 No. 412 between Calles 6A and 8, Colonia Diaz Ordaz, Mérida, Yucatán 97000. www.nectarmerida.com. Open daily 7:30 PM–2 AM. $$$.

El Oasis 985-856-4827, 985-856-5768, Calle 36 No. 221 between Calles 45 and 47, Colonia San Juan, Valladolid, Yucatán 97780. Open daily 7 AM–5. $.

Palacio de Gobierno Calles 60 and 61, north side of the Plaza Grande, Mérida, Yucatán 97000. Open daily 8–10. Free.

Palacio Municipal Calle 40 between Calles 39 and 41, Valladolid, Colonia Centro, Yucatán 97780. Open Mon.–Fri. 8–9, weekends 9–9. Free.

La Palapa 988-916-2063, Calle 12 No. 105, Colonia Centro, Celestún, Yucatán 97320. Open daily 9–6. $–$$.

Parador Turístico Acanceh 999-178-5548, Carretera Mérida-Peto Km. 20, Acanceh, Yucatán. Open daily 11–7. $–$$.

The Pickled Onion 997-111-7922, Located in Santa Elena on Highway 261, Santa Elena, Yucatán. http://thepickledonionyucatan.com. $.

Principe de Tutul-Xiu 997-929-7721, Calle 123 No. 216 between Calles 46A and 46B, Colonia Serapio Rendón, Maní, Yucatán. Open daily 11–7. $–$$.

Progreso Bus Terminal 999-928 3965, Calle 62 No. 524, between Calles 65 and 67, Mérida, Yucatán 97000.

Ravgo 999-923-0444, Calle 62 No. 632 by Calle 79, Colonia Centro, Mérida, Yucatán 97000. www.guayaberasravgo.com. Open Mon.–Fri. 8–6, Sat. 8–2. $$–$$$$.

Restaurante Na Lu'um 999-195-6294, Carretera Mérida-Chetumal Km. 22, Tecoh, Yucatán 97820. www.naluumtm.com. Open daily 8–8. $–$$.

Rosas & Xocolate 999-924-2992, Paseo de Montejo 480 x 41, Colonia Centro, Mérida, Yucatán 97000. www.rosasandxocolate.com. $$$$.

Santa Isabel Hermitage Calles 66 and 77, Colonia Centro, Mérida, Yucatán 97000. Open daily 7–1 and 4–8. Free.

Slavia 999-926-6587, Paseo de Montejo facing the Monumento de la Patria, Colonia Centro, Mérida, Yucatán 97000. www.slavia.com.mx. Open daily 7 PM–2 AM. $$–$$$.

Sotuta de Peón 999-941-8639, Municipio de Tecoh, Calle 39 No. 286 by Calles 32 and 34, Ampliación Dzodzil Norte, Mérida, Yucatán 97115. www.haciendatour.com. Tours daily at 10 and 1. $$$.

La Susana Internacional 999-988-0100, Calle 21 No. 89-A, between Calles 16 and 18, Kanasín, Yucatán. Open 5 PM–12:30. $.

Templo y Ex-Convento de la Mejorada Calle 59 between Calles 48 and 50, Mérida, Yucatán 97000. Open daily 7–noon and 4–8. Free.

Terminal CAME 999-924-8391/923-4440, Calle 70 No. 555, between Calles 69 and 71, Mérida, Yucatán 97000.

Terminal CAME, 2nd Class 999-923-2287, 923-4440, Calle 69 No. 544, between Calles 68 and 70, Mérida, Yucatán 97000.

Terminal de Autobuses 999-924-7868, Calle 50 No. 531, between Calles 65 and 67, Mérida, Yucatán 97000.

El Trapiche 999-928-1231, Calle 62 No. 491, between Calles 59 and 61, Colonia Centro, Mérida, Yucatán 97000. Open daily 8:30–11:30. $.

Unidad Turística Celestún Calle 2b S/N Km. 1.2, Colonia Felipe Carrillo Puerto, Celestún, Yucatán 97320. $$$.

Cancún and the Riviera Maya: Ruins Along the Coast

7

FROM CANCÚN TO
PUERTO CARRILLO

INTRODUCTION

The Riviera Maya is the catchy name given to a stretch of Mexico's sun-drenched Caribbean coast. While this region pales in the richness and variety of its archaeological treasures to the Yucatán, Chiapas, and Campeche, there remains plenty to see and do here in Mexico's most visited destination.

Located in Quintana Roo, Mexico's newest state, this stretch of Caribbean Coast comprises over 230 miles, from the Riviera Maya in the north to the Costa Maya in the south. Bisecting the two regions is the Sian Ka'an Biosphere Reserve. But Cancún and the Riviera Maya offer more than their vast bounty of archaeological, cultural, natural, and hedonistic attractions. Both destinations are also popular gateways to the Maya world of the Yucatán.

GETTING THERE AND GETTING AROUND *By air:* **Cancún International Airport** is the primary entry into Cancún and the Riviera Maya. The airport services flights from well over 50 regional and international carriers, including most U.S. airlines. The airport is large and well equipped. Most major car rental agencies have branches here, and there are numerous options for getting to Cancún and the Riviera Maya. From the airport Web site (www.cancun-airport.com) you can calculate the fare to your destination via bus, shuttle, taxi, and limo service.

By bus: If you're arriving by bus, Cancún's **ADO** bus terminal (www.ado.com.mx) in downtown—at the intersection of Avenidas Tulum and Uxmal—will be your entry into the city. Playa del Carmen has two bus stations. The Riviera Station on the corner of Avenida 5and Avenida Juarez services buses to and from Cancún, Tulum, and various stops along the Riviera; it's also steps away from the ferry to Cozumel. The ADO station on Avenida 20 between Calles 12 and 14 services buses from more distant points in Mexico.

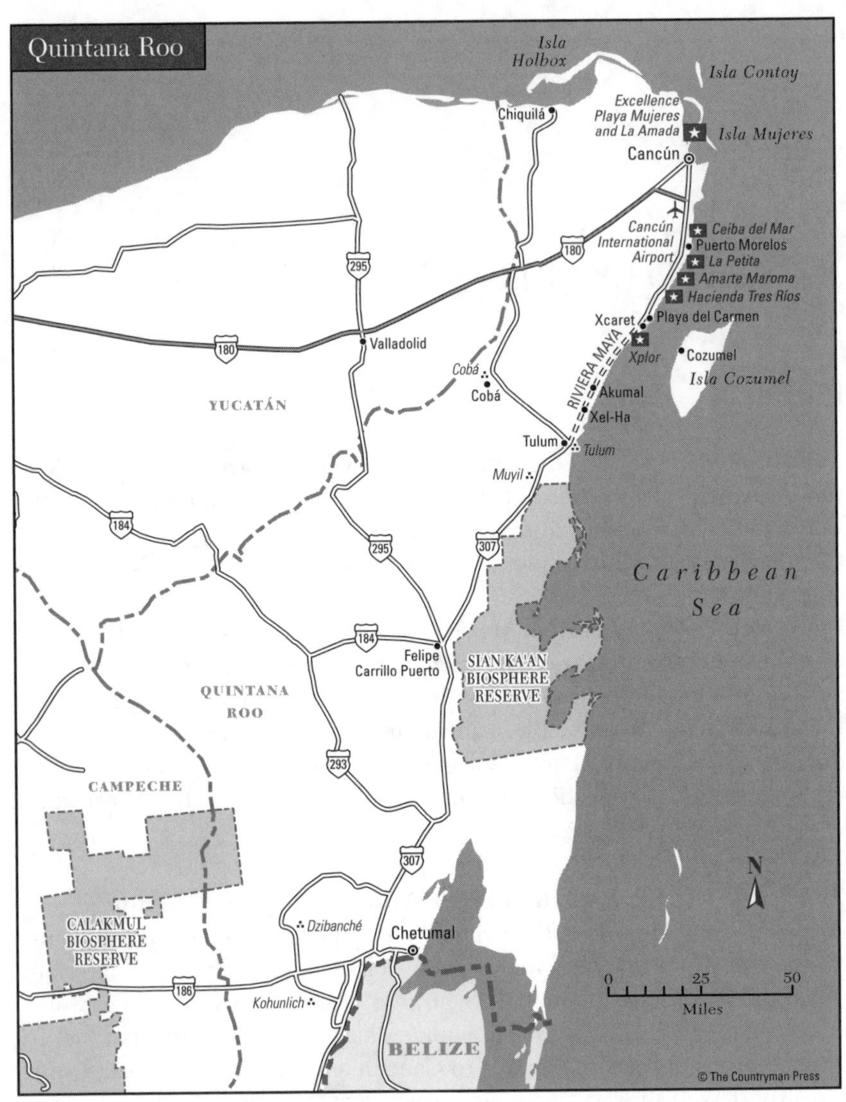

Quintana Roo
Isla Holbox
Isla Contoy
Chiquilá
Excellence Playa Mujeres and La Amada
Isla Mujeres
Cancún
Cancún International Airport
Ceiba del Mar
Puerto Morelos
La Petita
Amarte Maroma
Hacienda Tres Ríos
Xcaret
Playa del Carmen
Xplor
Cozumel
Isla Cozumel
Riviera Maya
Akumal
Xel-Ha
Tulum
Tulum
Muyil
Cobá
Cobá
Valladolid
Yucatán
180
180
295
295
184
184
307
307
293
186
Caribbean Sea
Felipe Carrillo Puerto
Sian Ka'an Biosphere Reserve
Quintana Roo
Campeche
Calakmul Biosphere Reserve
Dzibanché
Chetumal
Kohunlich
Belize
N
0
25
50
Miles
© The Countryman Press

FROM CANCÚN TO PUERTO CARRILLO

The Riviera Maya encompasses a chain of towns and cities along the coast, beginning with **Cancún**. Known around the world for its beaches (although how good the beach is in Cancún depends very much on *where* the beach is), hotels, nightlife, and status as a premier Caribbean escape, the city is divided between the Vegas-like *zona hotelera,* or hotel zone, and the city center. A short maritime hop from Cancún lies **Isla Mujeres**, a more rustic destination for those who want to escape the mega-resort experience. **Isla Holbox**, north of Cancún, isn't technically listed as part of the Riviera Maya (but then, that matters little to tourists) but is even smaller and more rural than Isla Mujeres. Holbox also gets annual visits from a very special, and very large, guest: the whale shark.

From Cancún, the Riviera stretches down to **Puerto Morelos**, a laid-back fishing community with a landmark leaning lighthouse and a cluster of hotels. **Playa del Carmen** has become a worthy sister town to Cancún and boasts its fair share of all-inclusive resorts, restaurants, bars, and clubs. **Cozumel**, a short boat ride from Playa, provides a different escape and a change of pace, much like Isla Mujeres; it's also one of the most popular dive destinations in the world. Near Playa you'll also find **Xcaret**, a huge aquatic park perhaps best described as Maya Disney and Sea World.

South of Playa, the Riviera continues past two small towns—**Puerto Aventuras**, a luxury residential neighborhood and marina, and **Akumal**, a quiet beachfront resort community—to the modern town and ancient coastal city of **Tulum**. Between Akumal and Tulum lies **Xel-Ha**, the region's other significant aquatic park, built around a spectacular inlet. Beginning with Tulum, the vibe along the Riviera changes, becoming more relaxed, less crowded, and far less commercial. This is the Costa Maya. **Felipe Carrillo Puerto**, the southernmost town along the strip, has a colloquial charm and an interesting history: the city was founded by

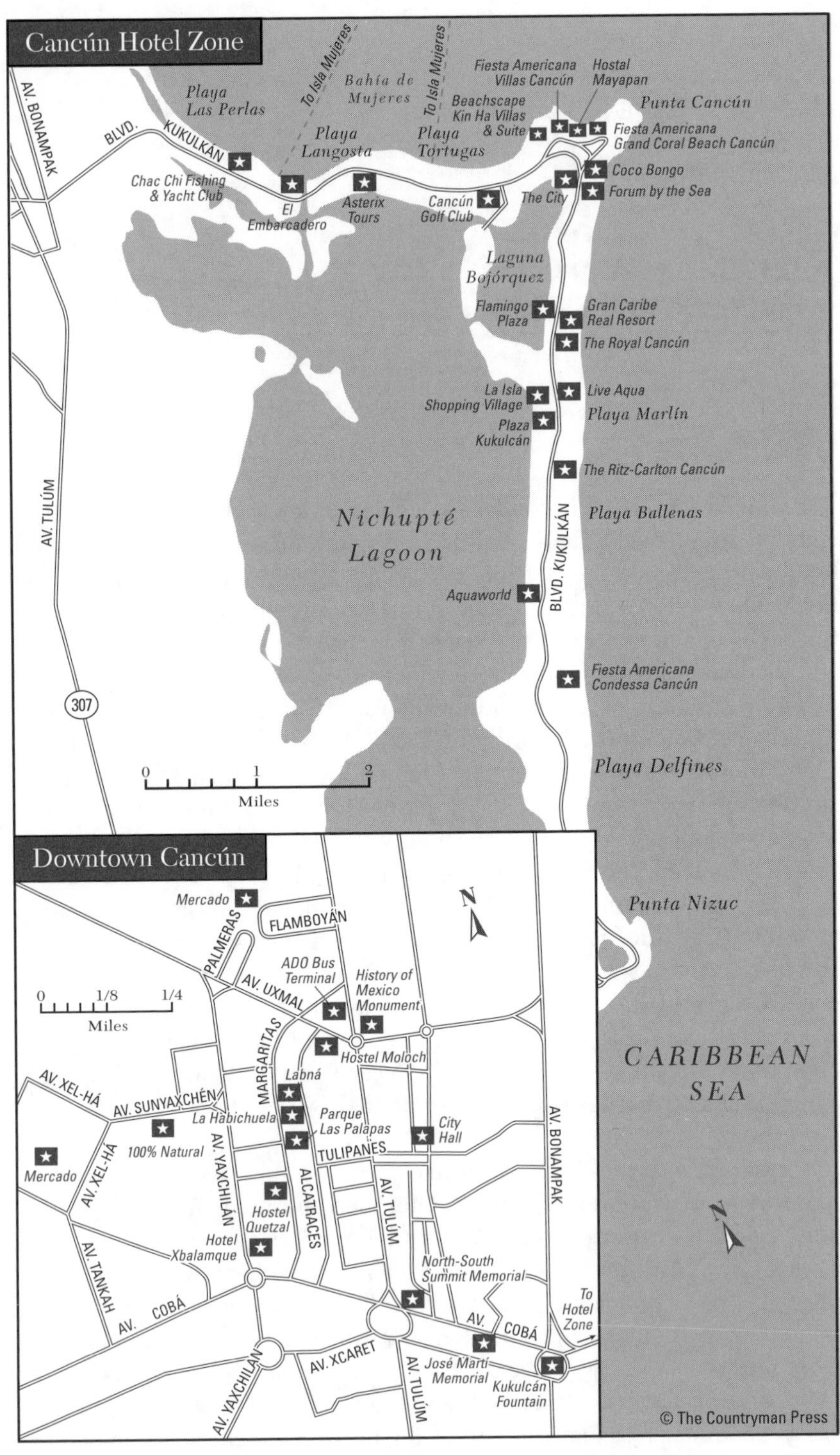

Cancún Hotel Zone
AV. BONAMPAK
Playa Las Perlas
To Isla Mujeres
Bahía de Mujeres
To Isla Mujeres
Fiesta Americana Villas Cancún
Hostal Mayapan
Punta Cancún
Beachscape Kin Ha Villas & Suite
Fiesta Americana Grand Coral Beach Cancún
BLVD. KUKULKÁN
Playa Langosta
Playa Tortugas
Coco Bongo
Chac Chi Fishing & Yacht Club
El Embarcadero
Asterix Tours
Cancún Golf Club
The City
Forum by the Sea
Laguna Bojórquez
Flamingo Plaza
Gran Caribe Real Resort
The Royal Cancún
La Isla Shopping Village
Live Aqua
Plaza Kukulcán
Playa Marlín
The Ritz-Carlton Cancún
Nichupté Lagoon
BLVD. KUKULKÁN
Playa Ballenas
AV. TULÚM
Aquaworld
Fiesta Americana Condessa Cancún
307
Playa Delfines
0 1 2
Miles
Downtown Cancún
Mercado
FLAMBOYÁN
PALMERAS
N
Punta Nizuc
ADO Bus Terminal
History of Mexico Monument
AV. UXMAL
0 1/8 1/4
Miles
MARGARITAS
Hostel Moloch
CARIBBEAN SEA
AV. XEL-HÁ
AV. SUNYAXCHÉN
Labná
La Habichuela
Parque Las Palapas
City Hall
100% Natural
TULIPANES
AV. BONAMPAK
Mercado
AV. XEL-HÁ
AV. YAXCHILÁN
ALCATRACES
AV. TULÚM
N
Hostel Quetzal
Hotel Xbalamque
AV. TANKAH
North-South Summit Memorial
AV. COBÁ
To Hotel Zone
AV. COBÁ
AV. XCARET
José Martí Memorial
Kukulcán Fountain
AV. YAXCHILÁN
AV. TULÚM
© The Countryman Press

THE LEANING LIGHTHOUSE OF THE FISHING VILLAGE OF PUERTO MORELOS

Maya during the Caste War. South of Felipe Carrillo Puerto, two Maya archaeological sites bear mentioning: **Kohunlich** and **Dzibanché** make great road trips from either the Riviera or from neighboring Campeche (both sites are much closer to Campeche's major ruins than they are to Tulum and Cobá).

* Archaeological Sites

The archaeological sites covered below are open daily 8–5 and charge only a nominal entrance fee.

Cobá

GETTING THERE The city-state of Cobá lies 104 miles southwest of Cancún. From here, Puerto Morelos or Playa, drive south to Tulum along Highway 307 and you'll see signs for the road to Cobá. It's about 40 miles from here to the site, along a serviceable road punctuated by speed bumps. When you approach the town of Cobá, you'll reach a crossroads with turnoffs to Nuevo Xcan, Valladolid, and Cobá. Follow the latter route to the ruins.

While Tulum is the more beautiful of the two, my favorite archaeological site in the Riviera Maya is Cobá. It's also a complete contrast from the manicured preservation of the Riviera's other major site. Where Tulum and Chichén bear the unmistakable mark of reconstruction and restoration, many structures in Cobá lie in much the same state as the

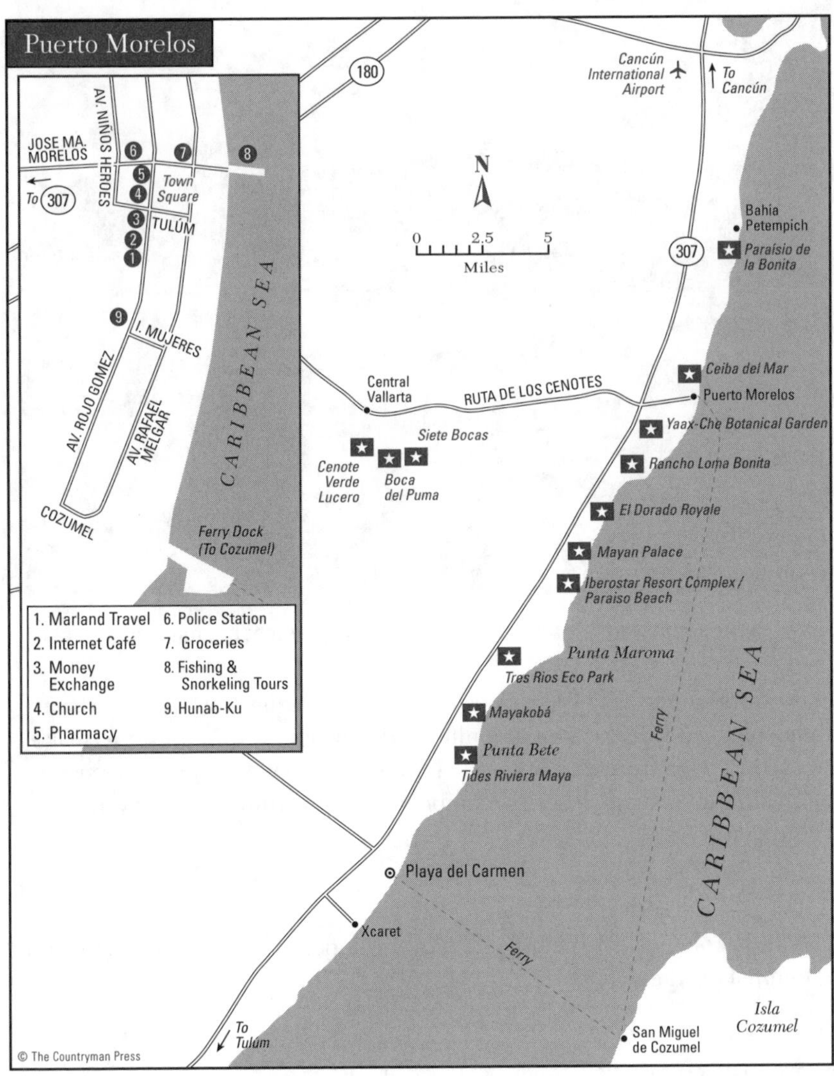

conquistadors found them. Nestled deep in the jungle, the city is spread out over 43 square miles (the majority still hidden in the brush), and was at its zenith one of the largest in the peninsula, housing a population of 70,000 to 100,000 inhabitants.

Cobá reached its height between AD 800 and 1100. Although it predates Chichén Itzá (and was a contemporary of Palenque and Calakmul), there existed an important link between the two metropolises. A 62-mile *sacbe*, or road, stretches from Cobá to Yaxuná, near Chichén. It's one of a large network of roads that links this city to the coast and other parts of the

Maya realm, confirming its status as a commercial center of great vitality. In short, in the late Classic period, this was the dominant city and the economic powerhouse of the Yucatán peninsula. And it's a fascinating place to explore today.

As it is dispersed across a large area, the site is divided into a number of groups. The first and the closest to the entrance is the Cobá Group. With 43 structures, a Grand Plaza, a ball court, and numerous *sacbeob* and stelae, this is the largest group in the site. The large pyramid fronted by a stela in the plaza is the **Iglesia** (Church). Reaching almost 80 feet high, it comprises nine round-cornered layers built over several construction phases. To the right lies the **Ball Court**. You'll also note several broken stelae in this group, and around Cobá. A local guide told me that the stela were deliberately broken when a reigning governor died, to release the spirits depicted on them.

Beyond the ball court, a broad path leads deeper into the city. There's a kiosk where you can rent bikes or three-wheeled bicycle taxis. I highly recommend either option, as it makes the experience of visiting Cobá

LA IGLESIA AT COBÁ

EL CASTILLO IS THE LARGEST BUILDING IN COBÁ.

quicker and more enjoyable. If you walk, be prepared for a lengthy trek if you want to see the entire site.

Follow the well-labeled signs along the path to reach the other groups in this city. The most impressive is the **Nohoch Mul** (Big Mound) **Group**, and its massive pyramid, **El Castillo** (The Castle). The largest structure in Quintana Roo measures 138 feet in height. Dedicated to Kukulcán, it's also the second-largest building in all of the Yucatán, eclipsing anything at Uxmal and Chichén and falling short only to Estructura II in Calakmul. Enjoy the rigorous climb to the top for commanding views and a fresh breeze on a hot day. The temple at its peak, which dates to the Postclassic period, features the figure of a descending god, representing the setting Sun. Also in this group is **Building X**, in front of which stands **Stela 30**, the best preserved of all the stelae at Cobá.

On your way back, stop by **Group D**, which contains the **Conjunto Las Pinturas** (Paintings Complex). This group corresponds to the twilight of Cobá and the last years of its occupation. You can climb to the top of **Building 1** to see the remains of its painted frieze and lintel.

A bit removed from the main trail is the **Macanxoc Group**, which must have been an important civic center. The group is rich in stelae, of which there are eight, and monolithic altars; in particular, Stela 1 is remarkable: Sculpted on all four sides, a rarity in the Maya world, it boasts an astounding 313 glyphs. Inscribed on Stela 1, incidentally, is a date which has consumed our popular culture and made Maya prophecies notorious around the world: 2012.

Dzibanché

GETTING THERE Dzibanché lies roughly 3 and ½ hours south of Tulum. Take highway 307 to its end at Highway 186, which leads from Chetumal to Escárcega. Turn right, and at kilometer 58 you'll see a sign for Dzibanché/Morocoy. Turn right again and drive just under 14 miles to reach the ruins. As with Kohunlich, Dzibanché lies outside the Riviera Maya but makes for an easy day trip by tour bus or car.

A civic and ceremonial center, Dzibanché flourished between AD 300 and 1200. The site gets its name, which means "Carved in Wood," from the inscribed wood lintel at **Temple VI**. Also important here are **Temples 1** and **2** and the **Small Acropolis**, all examples of Petén architecture. In Temple 1, or Temple of the Owl, archaeologists discovered a well-preserved tomb, evidently built for a Maya VIP. Among the offerings found here was a vessel with a sculpted owl on its lid, giving the building its name.

Temple 2, or Temple of the Cormorants, is the tallest building in Dzibanché. Climb the stairs north of the temple and you'll come to the

Plaza de Xibalbá (named for the lord of the Maya Underworld). Among the other structures of note here are **Building 14**, which has at its base an ornamentation of little drums, and **Building 13**, or Building of the Captives, named for its carvings of various captives in submissive positions.

Just over a mile to the north of Dzibanché lies **Kinichná**, a smaller site that was once a suburb or satellite of the civic center. The **Acropolis** here appears to honor the larger city.

Kohunlich

GETTING THERE To get to Kohunlich, follow the path to Dzibanché along the Chetumal/Escárcega highway. Drive past the turn for Dzibanché and in just over a mile, you'll see a sign for Kohunlich. Turn left and drive roughly 6 miles to reach the site.

Located closer to Belize than Cancún, Kohunlich is the most outstanding site in the Costa Maya. The large city was inhabited throughout the Classic period and may have been occupied until as late as AD 1200. It includes three public plazas, an acropolis, palace, ball court, and three temples. But Kohunlich gets its fame from the six colossal stucco masks and carved moldings found in the **Temple of the Masks**. Flanking a large staircase, the masks lie under a thatched roof and all face the sunset; archaeologists originally believed them to be representations of Kinich Ahau, the Sun god. That theory has changed, and researchers now believe they portray members of the city's ruling dynasty. Each mask is framed by another, anthropomorphic mask of the fanged god of the Underworld.

THE TEMPLE OF THE MASKS AT KOHUNLICH

Mexico Tourism Board

Beyond the Temple of the Masks, the impressive **North Palace** merits exploring. Home to an important ruler, the massive, raised patio of the foundation rests atop the ruins of a former building, which leads to a courtyard and a residential area once home to the city's elite. Kohunlich also boasts some of the oldest ball courts in the state.

Part of the wonder of visiting this site is its jungle setting amid wild flora and fauna. However, to stress home the fact that many Maya cities do not carry their original names, "Kohunlich" sounds native enough but actually comes from the English language; it's an interpretation of "Cohune Ridge," named for the cohune palms that grow here.

Tulum

GETTING THERE Tulum marks the southern end of the Riviera Maya, and is an easy two-hour drive from Cancún along Federal Highway 307.

In 1518, Spaniard Juan de Grijalva was on an expedition along the coast of the Yucatán peninsula when he spied a city overlooking the sea; he called it "as big as Seville," and said its tower was taller than any he had seen before. That great city was most likely Zama, which means "Where the Sun is Born." The name was later changed to Tulum, which means "Wall."

Tulum's fame stems from its spectacular location. Perched on the coast, the fortress city, with a natural port on the shores of the dazzling Caribbean Sea, has been immaculately groomed and restored. Tulum dates to the sixth century but rose to prominence in the Postclassic era

PERCHED ON THE COAST, TULUM OFFERS PANORAMIC VIEWS AS WELL AS A BEAUTIFUL BEACH.

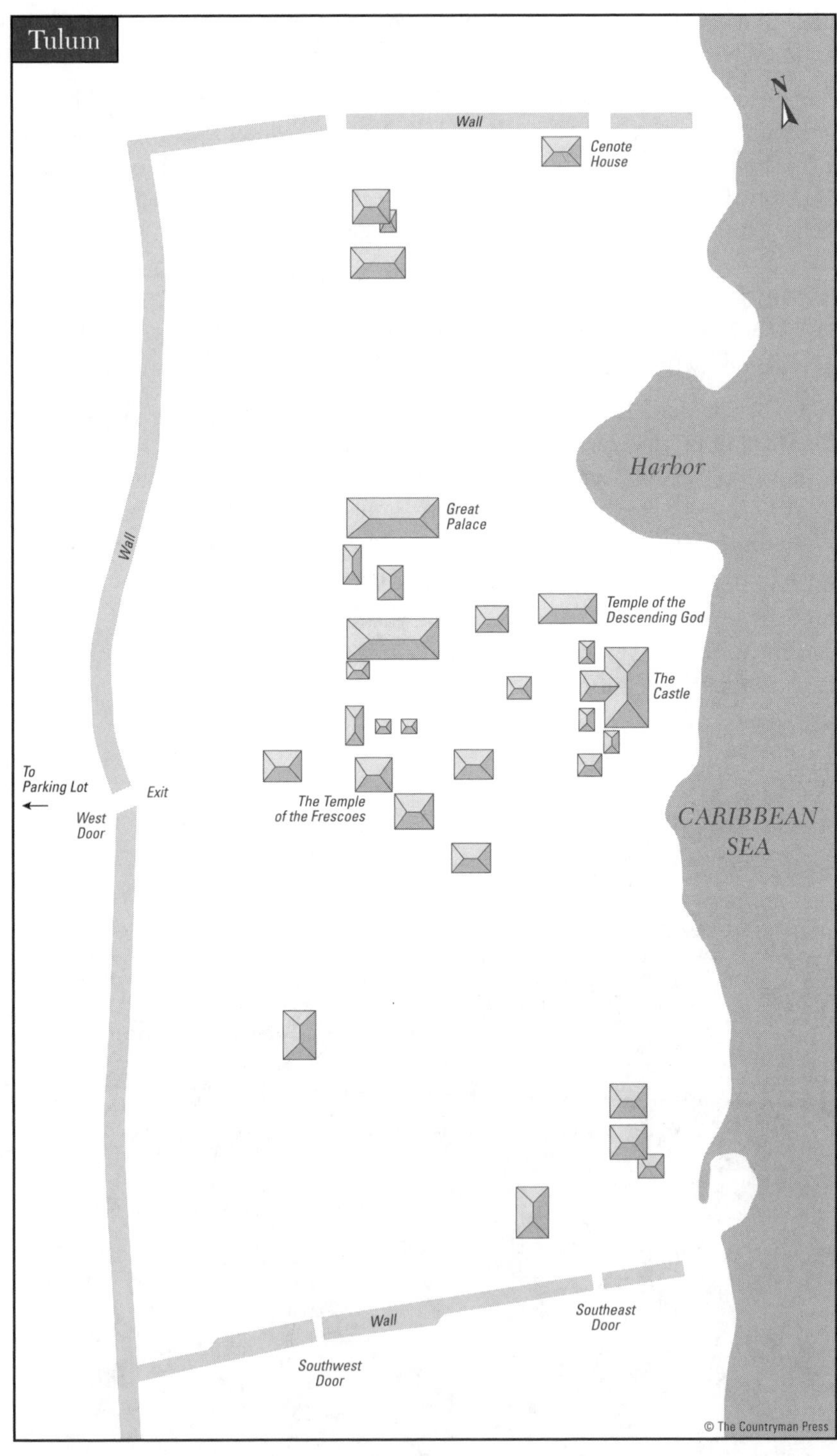

Tulum
N
Wall
Cenote House
Harbor
Great Palace
Wall
Temple of the Descending God
The Castle
To Parking Lot
Exit
West Door
The Temple of the Frescoes
CARIBBEAN SEA
Wall
Southeast Door
Southwest Door
© The Countryman Press

(AD 1200–1400), when its population numbered around 6,000 and it served as a commercial center that linked the Maya world and Mexico with Central and South America.

Among the numerous temples here you'll find the recurring image of one deity: the Descending God, who represents Venus, the setting Sun, and the honey bee. Venus was a critical figure for the Maya, a bringer of both bad luck and war. He can be found in Tulum's tallest temple, **El Castillo**. A small (compared to the immense pyramids found elsewhere in this land) but imposing structure with commanding coastal views, it was built over several phases. Note the two serpent columns at the entrance of the upper temple, which creates three entrances into the building.

Of course, you'll also find the deity at the **Temple of the Descending God.** In addition to lending credence to the belief that Tulum was the center of this cult, the temple produces an astrological-archaeological phenomenon during the summer solstice, when a needle point carved into the structure emits a laser beam of sunlight across the plaza. In the **Temple of the Frescoes** opposite the Castillo, you'll find the Descending God yet again. The painted figures within represent Chaac and Ixchel, goddess of medicine and birth.

Tulum also holds numerous residential buildings for the city's ruling class. Among these are the **House of the Halach Uinich** (the name given to the governor), **House of the Chultún** or *cenote* (to secure drinking water, most Maya cities were built near *cenotes*), and **House of the Columns**, among the more complex structures in the city.

Architecturally imperfect (note the sloping walls and irregular surfaces), Tulum is also something of a melting pot. Maya vaults, Toltec and Mixtec influences, friezes, and stucco can all be found here, along with regional East Coast architectural elements.

Don't forget your bathing suit when you visit the city. You can enjoy the beach and deliciously temperate Caribbean waters, and that thin ribbon of white surf just a short distance away from the beach marks the second-largest reef in the world.

✷ Lodging

As you can imagine, you have no shortage of lodging options in the Riviera. Just about every major (and several minor) hotel and resort chains can be found along Mexico's most popular coast. With so much to choose from, in this chapter I decided to focus on local hotels, or locally owned properties (the Ritz, for example, is owned by a Mexican).

Cancún has a hotel for every budget and taste. The premier destination here is the Zona Hotelera, the beachfront strip home to the glitzi-

TEMPLE OF THE FRESCOES AT TULUM

est resorts. Among these, I absolutely loved the **Live Aqua**. The hotel opened five years ago, but thanks to a two-year hiatus because of Hurricane Wilma, still has that new-hotel smell. Or maybe that's the aromatherapy scents piped into the lobby. Sleek and stylish, you can tell you're in a luxury resort as soon as you roll up and see the two white Rolls-Royces parked outside.

The Aqua's mission is to awaken the senses, and it does so with your choice of five aromas in the opulent guest rooms; balconies with beach and Caribbean views from every room; three outstanding restaurants led by Michelle Bernstein's **MB**; seven pools all at a different temperature; and an elite-class spa. The staff is outstanding, welcoming every guest with hands crossed over heart, a bow, and a Mayan greeting: "*In laakech,*" which means "I am you, you are me."

The aforementioned **Ritz-Carlton Cancún** is a surprisingly inconspicuous hotel. Removed from Boulevard Kukulkán, it offers an oasis of privacy, comfort, and luxury. Owner Enrique Molina wanted to re-create the feel of an elegant *casona,* or mansion, and much of the décor comes from his personal collection. The Ritz has a whopping staff of 550, ensuring an incredible customer service experience, and guests have brought their sons and grandsons back year after year.

The Ritz offers ocean views from every room; the only seafront restaurant to earn AAA Five Diamond status; the top-ranked spa among all Ritz properties; and an outstanding culinary center, with classes by Chef Rory Dunaway in a state-of-the-art Viking kitchen. Under his expert guidance, I put together a six-course Tuscan meal which, if I do say so myself, was exceptionally sophisticated.

Real Resorts has two terrific properties in Cancún. **The Royal Cancún** is the ultimate destination for adults. An all-inclusive, adults-only, all-suite property, it has some of the nicest guest rooms in the city, each sporting an oversize whirlpool bathtub. You can even get a swim-up suite with exclusive private pool access to your room. With six gourmet restaurants offering a variety of

MAKING A TUSCAN DINNER WITH CHEF RORY DUNAWAY AT THE RITZ-CARLTON CULINARY CENTER

cuisine, you won't get bored dining here, and the frequent live acts in the lobby provide a fun place to meet and mingle. The Royal gave me one of the most comfortable stays I had in Mexico, and I'd happily return.

Families will enjoy the next-door **Gran Caribe Real Resort**, a notch below the Royal but still a five-star property. The kids will love the Oki Splash playground and pool, complete with a miniature a pirate ship. Several guest rooms can comfortably accommodate a family of five, and the full-service spa, fitness center, and pool offer a separate space for adults.

The Fiesta Americana chain has a number of properties in the city. Leading the pack is the all-suite **Fiesta Americana Grand Coral Beach Cancún**, the only hotel to consecutively earn Five Diamond status since 1995. There's a lot to recommend this hotel: It's located on Punta Cancún, the northern end of the beachfront, facing Isla Mujeres; and this stretch boasts the finest beaches in Cancún, as Isla Mujeres acts as a barrier island against the ravages of hurricanes. Beyond its powder-fine sands, the hotel has a lovely amorphous pool that snakes its way around three pool bars. Located near the convention center, the hotel caters especially to groups, with a separate lobby and the first three floors reserved for group travel. It's also got a terrific Fiesta Kids' Club for families. Along with

THE POOL AT THE FIESTA AMERICANA CORAL BEACH CANCÚN

the Ritz, this is the only hotel in Cancún to boast a Five Diamond restaurant, **Le Basilic**, for multiple years. It's one of five restaurants on the property, including **Viña del Mar**, which features a fantastic buffet breakfast with live cooking stations and Mexican specialties. The hotel boasts the largest rooms in Cancún, and if you feel like an upgrade, the Grand Club gives you access to an upscale lounge with snacks, a private bar, and panoramic views.

Fiesta Americana Condesa Cancún is a pleasant and more moderate option. Its giant *palapa* roof is a fixture on the hotel strip, and its 500 rooms rank it among the largest properties in the city. The hotel has a no-spring-breakers policy, making it a good choice for families; and even during a busy season, its two-level pool (the higher level climatized) and three Jacuzzis weren't overly crowded. Their Fiesta Kids' Club features a Disney theme, and the Miluna Spa has an extensive menu of 150 treatments. It's a great deal for a hotel that has enjoyed Four Diamond status for 20 years straight.

Fiesta Americana Villas Cancún, also located on Punta Cancún, is the most affordable of the three, and provides excellent value for the money. It also includes a Fiesta Kids Club, a beautiful pool surrounded by leafy vegetation, and guest rooms with ample space, a kitchenette or more, and balconies.

Staying on Punta Cancún, **Beachscape Kin Ha Villas & Suites** is a laid-back, three-story hotel that claims the largest suites in the city. The décor is simple yet comfortable, and the property features perhaps the single best stretch of white sand beach in all of Cancún.

Away from the hotel zone in Cancún's city center, hotels tend to be cheaper and more basic. If you're into Maya archaeology, the elaborate façade of **Hotel Xbalamque** will give you a chuckle, but you can't deny it has character, and a great location on central Yaxchilán Avenue. The rooms, in bright Mexican colors, are cozy, and the grotto pool, *temazcal*, and massage services are more than you'd expect from a budget hotel.

If it's a hostel you're looking for, Cancún has plenty. **Hostel Quetzal** is among the best, thanks to its homey vibe, clean rooms, great food, and friendly hosts. **Moloch Hostel**, located near the bus terminal and Avenida Yaxchilán, is about 10 minutes from the beach and offers a mix of private rooms, mixed and separate dorms, a small terrace, and free continental breakfast. And for those who want to be close to the beach, the rather kitschy **Hostal Mayapan** is the first and only hostel in the Zona Hotelera.

North of Cancún (25 miles from the airport) in Playa Mujeres are two exceptional properties: the all-inclusive **Excellence Playa Mujeres** and **La Amada**. Removed from the hustle of more touristy areas, Excellence is well named; it aptly describes the luxurious suites (with private Jacuzzi and private Hydro Spa pool on the terrace of the junior suites); fantastic private beach; seven pools with pool bars and hammocks kissing the water; and eight terrific restaurants. Guests can enjoy a range of activities, live shows, and concerts throughout the week. The state-of-the-art Miilé Spa (with two spa suites) is a true oasis with an 18-step hydration program offering total relaxation.

The five-star La Amada, located near Excellence, is a stylish new property decorated in a South Beach palette of soft white and natural tones. The contemporary guest rooms are large and come with a Jacuzzi (and a cool feature called an X Box to dispose of your room service leftovers). Last but not least, the resort's spa is breathtaking and includes a state-of-the-art fitness center.

If you prefer something more rustic, **Isla Mujeres**, a ferry ride from Cancún, offers a variety of lodging options. On the high end, **Hotel Villa Rolandi** is a five-star property with 35 spacious, oceanfront rooms in an intimate setting. Another luxury option is **Villa Vera**, which features 22 huge suites each with a hydromassage tub and a porch strung with hammocks. A Raintree Vacation Club Resort, Villa Vera is ideal for longer stays. Its access to the lagoon also makes it popular with the yachting crowd.

THE EXCELLENCE PLAYA MUJERES LIVES UP TO ITS NAME.

My favorite boutique hotel on Isla Mujeres is **Hotel Secreto**, an aptly named gem so hidden it doesn't even have a sign. An architecturally modern and sumptuous property, its nine rooms, stunning infinity-edge pool and sense of complete escape is unmatched. **Casa IxChel** is a romantic, cozy place on a quiet stretch of beachfront. Its ten rooms are all different and each has its charm; some also have a kitchenette and Caribbean views. The upper deck has a pool, Jacuzzi, restaurant, and access to the beach (which on this side of the island is a good deal rockier than elsewhere). Finally, **Bucaneros** is a warm and friendly family-run institution on central Avenida Hidalgo, with basic but comfortable rooms, an excellent restaurant, and nifty incentives if you prepay.

On Isla Holbox, don't miss **Casa Sandra**, a serene boutique hotel owned by artist and author Sandra

Pérez Lozano. Its 12 rooms face the sea and offer a sense of get-away-from-it-all comfort. The staff is exceptional and the hotel defines "island retreat." Travelers on a tighter budget should take a look at **Xaloc Resort**, which offers rustic bungalows and suites set in a leafy enclave just steps from the beach.

In **Puerto Morelos**, I'm a big fan of **Amarte Maroma**, which combines gourmet dining, an art gallery, and pleasant cabana-style accommodations just off the highway between Cancún and Playa. The hotel is located in a lush garden setting but offers free shuttle service to one of the most pristine beaches on this coast. In addition, their beachfront villas are beautifully furnished residences with private pools and enough room to give the family a private, exclusive getaway. Even more secluded,

CASA SANDRA IS THE ULTIMATE ISLAND RETREAT ON ISLA HOLBOX.

Ceiba del Mar has drawn rave reviews and awards for years, thanks to its exceptional setting on the beach; warm and inviting guest rooms and suites featuring

HOTEL SECRETO AT ISLA MUJERES

THE BEACHFRONT VILLAS AT AMARTE MAROMA

local hand-crafted furnishings; gourmet dining; and an aromatherapy spa that uses its own line of organic products.

Playa del Carmen is a relatively upscale area, and its hotels and resorts reflect its status. **The Tides Riviera Maya**, located just outside Playa in the village of Playa Xcalacoco, offers 30 villas and over 1,000 square feet of luxurious space to spread out in, including a terrace equipped with hammocks, an award-winning spa, and exclusive majordomo service. It's consistently rated as one of Playa's most exceptional properties.

Of the sprawling resorts you pass by as you travel the highway, **Hacienda Tres Rios** ranks among my favorites. A large property in an incomparable natural setting, the resort lets you get on the beach or kayak to the mouth of a river for a refreshing dip. The entire property is built on stilts to allow for natural river flow, and the environment is beautifully integrated into the property. Because of its careful preservation efforts, the hotel has been accredited the most sustainable resort worldwide by Green Globe International. Oh, and the all-suite hotel provides large, comfortable accommodations equipped with every modern amenity, a full-service spa, and an all-inclusive plan.

In the heart of Playa, check out the **Real Playa del Carmen** on Avenida 5. The four-star resort in a tropical garden setting offers access to a private beach and can be booked as an all-inclusive or European plan hotel. If you'd rather splurge and be right on the beach, the furniture and décor at the **Gran Porto Real del Carmen Resort & Spa** recalls an opulent Mexican hacienda and provides all-inclusive indulgence. Also, **Playa Maya**, right on the beach, offers spacious accommodations in a luxury residential setting for bargain rates. Although it's meant for weekly rentals, they have availability and rates for three days or less.

Finally, **Tulum** has a laid-back, small-town vibe that lends itself to more intimate properties. Check out **Don Diego de la Selva**, a charming hotel with 10 rooms and bungalows, a lovely pool, and excellent food (continental breakfast and dinner) at bargain rates. Even more romantic is **Cabanas La Luna**, a self-proclaimed fairy tale come true. The boutique hotel consists of seven cabanas, two in the garden and the rest on the beach, and the four-bedroom Villa Zanzibar perfect for a group or a family. With their rustic décor (bamboo roofs and mosquito nets), the cabanas have a bit of Robinson Crusoe on the beach to them, but that's their charm.

✷ Dining

Dining options in this area range from your neighborhood fast-food chains to taco stalls to world-class cuisine from international celebrity chefs.

In Cancún's Zona Hotelera, many of the best restaurants have nothing to do with Mexican cuisine. Among hotel restaurants, the most outstanding are **MB** at Live Aqua, **Le Basilic** at the Fiesta Americana Grand Coral Beach Cancún, and **Fantino** at the Ritz-Carlton. MB occupies a separate space on the ground floor and boasts a creative, eclectic menu that changes every three to six months. If they have it, try the watermelon Greek salad, shrimp *tiradito* with popcorn, and fillet with kimchee.

The more formal Le Basilic presents French-Mediterranean specialties in an elegant setting

HACIENDA TRES RIOS IN PLAYA DEL CARMEN

FANTINO AT THE RITZ-CARLTON CANCÚN

accompanied by live classical music. The ever-changing menu relies on local ingredients, and the French truffles at the end of the meal are a nice touch. And Fantino (its name is Italian for "jockey") continues the Mediterranean theme. A beautiful space featuring two ceiling frescoes, the restaurant dishes out one of the best tasting menus in the city, with such dishes as crayfish and mascarpone dumplings and escargot lasagna.

Sticking to Europe, **Casa Rolandi** is among the most popular spots in the Zona Hotelera. The Italian menu includes an excellent homemade cheese tortellini with veal au jus and truffle oil, and a tender octopus carpaccio. The restaurant, resembling a Mediterranean villa, welcomes both casual and formal attire.

However, if it's Mexican cuisine you're after, my advice is to head to Cancún Centro. For sophisticated Mexican dining, **La Habichuela** (named for the popular red bean) ranks among the most touted local eateries in the city since 1977. Call ahead to reserve a table in the Maya garden, and try their most famous dish: the Cocobichuela (at last count, more than 447,000 satisfied customers), comprising lobster and shrimp cooked in curry sauce topped with tropical fruits and presented in a coconut shell. Next door, **Labná** offers Yucatecan specialties in a large, high-ceilinged hall modeled after the famous false Maya arch. Labná is the place to sample *poc chuc,* turkey in *escabeche,* and *papadzules,* among other regional classics. You can also go for the daily buffet and sample them all.

One of my favorite restaurants in the city is neither expensive nor fancy. **100% Natural** is exactly that: health-conscious, offering fresh ingredients, flavorful salads, sandwiches, breakfast fare, and fantastic fresh juices and shakes (*licuados*), among other more local specialties. There are locations all over Mexico, including one in Playa del Carmen.

I'm a huge fan of eating in *mercados,* or markets, and downtown Cancún has two of them. **Mercado 28** is the more tourist-friendly, and home to **El Cejas**, a large cafeteria-style eatery serving fresh seafood cocktails, ceviches, and coconut-crusted shrimp.

THE TIKINXIK ESPECIAL AT LA CASA DEL TIKINXIK

Next to the ruins of Cobá, **Ki-Janal** offers a large menu of salads, pastas, Mexican and Yucatecan food (including a tasty *pollo pibil*), with some continental dishes thrown in. Also just outside the gate, look for "El Marqués de Cobá" who trots out here every day with his cart selling *marquesitas,* which are crunchy tortillas stuffed with your choice of fillings, such as manchego cheese or Nutella.

Isla Mujeres has a delicious specialty called *pescado tikinxik,* a thick fillet of fish grilled with onion and achiote, among other seasonings. The best I had was **La Casa del Tikinxik** at Playa Lancheros, the only place on the island to get the "Tikinxik Especial." Another good spot for the famous fish dish, along with grilled mackerel, grouper, and barracuda, is **Playa Tiburón**. **Bucaneros**, a family-run restaurant and hotel since 1965, also serves up *tikinxik,* along with excellent salads, pizzas, fresh tropical drinks, and juices.

Holbox Island's restaurants fit right into its rustic ambience, although some are a bit pricier than you'd expect (and none take credit cards). **La Isla del Colibri** (Island of the Hummingbird) is a terrific low-key option, a colorful pink corner house chock-full of folk art. The menu is predominantly a variety of shrimp and fish

LA ISLA DEL COLIBRI IN ISLA HOLBOX

dishes; try the *filete a la diabla,* a fillet of fish with a chile de árbol hot pepper sauce. Across the plaza, **Restaurante & Pizzería Edelyn** is known primarily for its lobster pizza. I can't say it was my preferred way to enjoy lobster, but it's not a bad alternative to pepperoni.

Puerto Morelos, like many towns along the coast, specializes in seafood. Of these, **La Petita**, in a small green house, is a rustic favorite for its ceviches and simply grilled whole fish (only the fish and conch are local). Even if you're not staying here, the **Pavo Real** restaurant at Amarte Maroma offers an elegant alternative to the neighborhood's casual seaside eateries. With such dishes as a *cappuccino de langosta* (lobster "cappuccino" bisque with a creamy foam); a delicate scallop ceviche with mango, chile habanero, avocado, and plantain chips; and duck Magret in a port wine and hibiscus flower sauce, the Mexican-French fusion menu is excellent.

In Playa del Carmen, check out **La Bodeguita del Medio**, a Cuban institution that serves authentic albeit pricey Cuban cuisine in a funky setting with patrons' signatures scrawled on the walls and mementos of Havana's glory days. Ask for a Bodeguita passport with information about the restaurant, and take a look at the "Five Things to do in La Bodeguita" coaster. The cuisine, which includes *ropa vieja* (shredded beef with peppers) and grilled mahi-mahi in a peppermint mojito sauce, comes in large portions designed to be shared. Live music, a gift shop, and a cigar bar round out the experience.

Yaxché offers Maya cuisine, primarily of Yucatecan roots. Dishes include *poc-chuc,* duck-filled *kuts tacos,* and *tsotobilchay* (Maya-style tamales, stuffed with *chaya,* boiled eggs, and pumpkin seeds, wrapped in a plantain leaf and smothered with tomato sauce).

For excellent *tacos al pastor* (marinated pork sliced off the spit), *chilaquiles,* and other typical Mexican fare, **Carboncitos** is the place to go. Leave space for the Mexican-style cannoli, a deep-fried tortilla coated with cinnamon, stuffed with a chocolate brownie, and served with chocolate sauce and vanilla ice cream.

Finally, for an excellent meal in Tulum, try a little **Hechizo**, which serves gourmet fine dining cuisine (a mix of Mexican and eclectic continental) in a leafy garden setting.

✷ Don't Miss

You don't need me to tell you this is a fun place. Cancún and the Riviera Maya have world-famous nightlife, golden beaches, enough tour companies to service a small country, all manner of adventures and excursions, and world-class events.

Downtown and Isla Cancún

There are two sides to Cancún: the grittier, more urban downtown city center and the manicured island strip, where the sprawling hotels squeeze out virtually every inch of available beachfront. The two sections offer completely different environments.

Isla Cancún is the ritzy tourist zone, and Boulevard Kukulcán is its main thoroughfare. This road passes resorts (many of them a healthy walk from the boulevard), upscale restaurants, numerous shopping malls, and some of the city's most popular nightlife. **La Isla Shopping Village** and the **Forum by the Sea** are among its larger centers, boasting numerous stores, restaurants, bars, and clubs.

Nightlife options start with the ever-popular **Coco Bongo**, which is more theme show and Cirque du Soleil than nightclub. Club-goers will probably prefer **The City**, Cancún's ridiculously large nightclub that welcomes A-listers, MTV parties, and hip hordes. Fergie, Akon, and DJ Tiësto are merely the tip of the celebrity iceberg to frequent the club. This City never sleeps, with an active beach club and terrace bar during the day. On the other hand, if you'd rather bar-hop, there's no better way to go than the **Cancún Party Hopper Bar Crawl**, which begins at 9 and gives you seven hours at three clubs in VIP style (no lines and VIP tables). Given that clubs here are expensive, the cost of the bar crawl is a good deal.

In Cancún Centro, **Avenida Yaxchilán** and its environs forms the main restaurant and bar strip, but the ambience is far more casual, unpretentious, and bohemian. Numerous eateries serve basic Mexican fare, ranging from tourist traps to culinary standbys such as Labná and La Habichuela, and low-key clubs and bars abound. **Parque Las Palapas**, just east of Yaxchilán on Calle Gladiolas, is an open space where you can snack at the food stalls, mingle with locals, and check out live bands and shows on weekend evenings.

Downtown is also home to **Mercado 28** and **Mercado 23**, the two large markets that invite you to test your bargaining chops on all kinds of trinkets, souvenirs, clothes, and shoes. Mercado 28, accessible by buses R2 and R15, is the more tourist-friendly spot, while **Mercado 23**, accessible by bus R1, has a notorious reputation for attracting a rougher crowd, but locals will tell you this is the better place for good deals.

A KNIFE-SHARPENER PLIES HIS TRADE AT MERCADO 23.

Playa del Carmen

A sleepy village for decades, Playa is now a booming community that still retains a small-town ambience. Avenida Juárez is the main road, but the pedestrian-only half of Avenida 5—steps from the beach—takes you to the heart of the commercial and tourist strip. Plaza Paseo del Carmen, near the ferry port, is a nice area to roam, with shops ranging from cheap souvenirs to high-end jewelry. To the south is Playacar, an all-inclusive golf resort bordered by high-end residences, hotels and restaurants.

TOURS AND EXCURSIONS

Tour companies abound along the coast, and many offer the same basic tours and services (including hotel pickup and dropoff). A fantastic resource that will alleviate you of the task of digging through them to find the right one is **México Adventourist**, where you'll find a variety of tours and packages.

I took the Mayan Encounter tour with **Alltournative**, which proved to be a full day of fun. The tour combined a trip to Cobá with a visit to a Maya community (and a

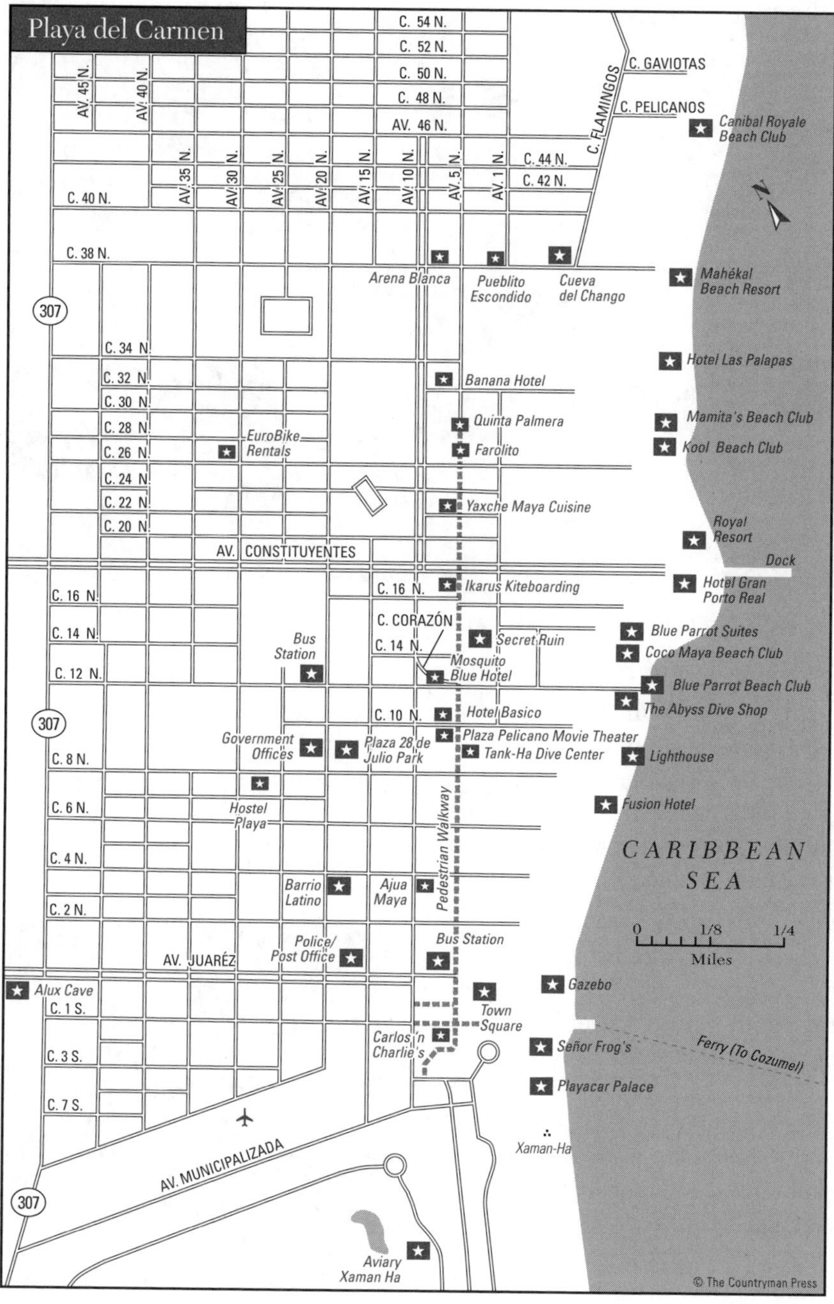

Playa del Carmen
C. 54 N.
C. 52 N.
C. 50 N.
C. 48 N.
AV. 46 N.
AV. 45 N.
AV. 40 N.
C. GAVIOTAS
C. PELICANOS
C. FLAMINGOS
Canibal Royale Beach Club
C. 44 N.
C. 42 N.
AV. 35 N.
AV. 30 N.
AV. 25 N.
AV. 20 N.
AV. 15 N.
AV. 10 N.
AV. 5 N.
AV. 1 N.
C. 40 N.
C. 38 N.
Arena Blanca
Pueblito Escondido
Cueva del Chango
Mahékal Beach Resort
307
C. 34 N.
Hotel Las Palapas
C. 32 N.
Banana Hotel
C. 30 N.
C. 28 N.
Quinta Palmera
Mamita's Beach Club
EuroBike Rentals
C. 26 N.
Farolito
Kool Beach Club
C. 24 N.
C. 22 N.
Yaxche Maya Cuisine
C. 20 N.
Royal Resort
AV. CONSTITUYENTES
Dock
C. 16 N.
Ikarus Kiteboarding
Hotel Gran Porto Real
C. CORAZÓN
C. 14 N.
Bus Station
Secret Ruin
Blue Parrot Suites
Coco Maya Beach Club
C. 12 N.
Mosquito Blue Hotel
Blue Parrot Beach Club
C. 10 N.
Hotel Basico
The Abyss Dive Shop
Government Offices
Plaza 28 de Julio Park
Plaza Pelicano Movie Theater
Tank-Ha Dive Center
C. 8 N.
Lighthouse
C. 6 N.
Hostel Playa
Fusion Hotel
Pedestrian Walkway
CARIBBEAN SEA
C. 4 N.
Barrio Latino
Ajua Maya
C. 2 N.
0
1/8
1/4
Miles
Bus Station
Police/ Post Office
AV. JUARÉZ
Alux Cave
C. 1 S.
Gazebo
Town Square
Carlos 'n Charlie's
C. 3 S.
Señor Frog's
Ferry (To Cozumel)
C. 7 S.
Playacar Palace
Xaman-Ha
AV. MUNICIPALIZADA
Aviary Xaman Ha
© The Countryman Press

THE MAYAN ENCOUNTER TOUR WITH ALLTOURNATIVE

hearty and tasty lunch cooked by local women), a swim in a submerged *cenote* after a blessing from a shaman, a brief kayak trip, and a zip line across a ravine. As a huge plus, our guide was phenomenal.

I also highly recommend **Río Secreto**, an awe-inspiring journey to an underground river in a protected natural reserve. Accompanied by a guide and equipped with miner's helmet, wetsuit, life jacket and water shoes, we had a blast exploring this underworld of stalagmites and stalactites, tiny fish and shallow natural pools, cramped spaces and cavernous halls.

Finally, I loved the **Cobá Sunset Tour**, a popular excursion offered by various companies. The trip begins with a biking tour of Cobá, followed by lunch and a visit to a nearby Maya community and a pottery workshop where Maya

LEARNING TO RAPPEL WITH ALLTOURNATIVE'S MAYAN ENCOUNTER TOUR

children display their craft and wares. The day ends with a walk down to a dry cenote where excerpts from the *Popol Vuh* and the *juego de pelota* are reenacted by players in traditional regalia. After visiting so many ball courts, this was a great chance to see the game up close. Among the operators offering this excursion are **Playa Del Carmen Tours** and **Best Day Travel**, both reputable and efficient operators that also offer many other tours and packages.

Finally, Cancún and Playa serve as gateways to the archaeological sites of the Yucatán. Trips to Chichén Itzá, Ek' Balam, Uxmal, and other sites are offered by numerous tour companies. Again, México Adventourist is a terrific resource to schedule these side trips.

Dolphin swimming is a popular activity here, and **Dolphin Discovery** and **Delphinus** specialize in it. The latter offers dolphin swims and treks at numerous locations in Cancún and the Riviera Maya. Dolphin Discovery has facilities in the Riviera Maya, Cozumel, and Isla Mujeres.

The Riviera is a boating and fishing paradise, with several tour companies catering to the sport. In Cancún, the **Chac Chi Fishing & Yachting Club** and marina

Israel Kumul is one of the most upbeat and positive people I've ever met. But that's only part of what makes him, and his company, **México Adventourist**, such a good resource for anyone who's coming to this part of the world. Israel doesn't run tours himself; rather, he coordinates them through a network of local companies.

This means two things for customers in search of a fun day out. First, you're going to get a reputable company that offers a good product; Israel does his research and he knows the territory. Second, you've got a tour concierge at your service. On my last trip, I gave Israel a seven-day calendar and told him what I was interested in. In two days, he filled it with exactly what I wanted. Whether you want to zip line across a ravine in the jungle, swim with dolphins, visit a Maya city, or a variety of other activities, he'll put it all together for you.

Best of all, you don't pay extra for his services. Israel arranges his commissions directly with the tour companies, so the price you pay is the same you'd pay by going directly to the source. He simply cuts out all the effort. Israel also offers several pre-packaged tours on his Web site. No wonder he's top-rated on Trip Advisor and gets rave reviews from his customers. Me included.

is one of the cheaper outfits for deep-sea fishing excursions. **Aquaworld** offers a huge menu of game fishing, boating, tours, scuba diving, and snorkeling tours in Playa, Cancún, and Cozumel. If you prefer smaller, local operators, three options are **Cooperative de Servicios Turísticos de Puerto Morelos** in Puerto Morelos, **Capt. Rick's Adventures** in Puerto Aventuras, and the **Cooperativa Isla Bonita** in Isla Mujeres.

And finally, this is a hugely popular diving destination, with a plethora of dive centers. **Aquaworld**, **Reef Quest Divers** in Playa del Carmen, **Aquanauts Dive Adventures** in Puerto Morelos, and **Mexidivers** in Tulum are all reliable options.

A VENDOR OFFERS A TASTE OF LOCAL HONEY AT THE MAYA VILLAGE IN XCARET.

PARKS AND RESERVES

Xcaret and Xel-Ha. These are the Riviera's two most popular nature parks, and both offer enough activities and sights to warrant at least a full day visit. Xcaret has a smorgasbord of aquatic, natural, zoological, and cultural activities. Aquatic fun ranges from swimming with dolphins to snorkeling and snuba, beaches, pools, and rivers (both subterranean and overground). Animal exhibits include turtles, tapir, deer, manatees, bats, jaguars, spider monkeys, and tropical birds. The park also has jungle trails, small archaeological sites, a coral reef aquarium, and cultural exhibits such as *papantla* flyers (a traditional dance in which four dancers twirl, suspended upside down from a rope tied to a pole, to the accompaniment of flute and drums), ball game reenactments, and the Xcaret Mexico Espectacular show.

My favorite experience here was the Maya village, a re-creation of an ancient Maya community. I was given a handful of cocoa beans which I could use to "purchase" items (I used my cash to get my picture taken with a snake and macaw). The Maya cemetery is also an interesting place to check out.

Mexico Tourism Board

SWIMMING WITH DOLPHINS AT XCARET

Xel-Ha is the world's largest natural aquarium. You almost can't leave here without snorkeling your way through its numerous environs: lagoon, caves, *cenotes*, inlet, and river. The experience of snorkeling in a natural aquarium teeming with rays, parrot fish, angel fish, and myriad other denizens of the sea is unforgettable. Float along a lazy river on an inner tube, take a leap of faith from the Cliffs of Courage, test your balance on the floating bridge, swim with dolphins, or try your hand at snuba. These are just some of the activities you can enjoy at this maritime wonderland. **Xplor** is one of the newer attractions in the Riviera, an ecotourism park that offers rafting and swimming in a subterranean river, zip lines, and amphibious vehicle jungle treks.

A few miles south of Tulum, the **Sian Ka'An Biosphere Reserve** is the largest protected land in the Mexican Caribbean, occupying 1.3 million acres, almost one third of the Caribbean coast of Mexico. Although large portions are off limits to casual tourists, you can still visit this pristine natural environment, which is quite the opposite of the parks above. *Sian Ka'an* is Mayan for "Where the Sky Is Born," and the reserve holds at least 23 small archeological sites. You can come here on your own to enjoy kayaking, birdwatching, and tours to the reserve's spectacular lagoons and reefs run by local fishermen (or coordinated through the **Centro Ecologico Sian Ka'an**), or schedule a day trip with **Community Tours Sian Ka'an**.

About 20 miles north of Isla Mujeres, **Isla Contoy** is a national park and the oldest protected area in the state. Accessible only via licensed tours, the island prohibits fishing or touching the coral (a general rule in these parts), and you can't wear sunscreen on your visit. The pristine island is home to the largest colony of brown pelicans on Mexico's coast. Chac Chi and **Asterix Tours** run tours here.

Parque Nacional Isla Mujeres Cancún Nizuc is in fact three protected areas off the coasts of Isla Mujeres, Punta Cancún, and Puerto Morelos. The Isla Mujeres section contains reefs teeming with fish; off Punta Cancún, divers can visit two sunken Mexican naval vessels and the Chitales reef; and Punta Nizuc offers shallow water reefs ideal for snorkeling. Nizuc is also the northern tip of the **Gran Arrecife Maya** (Great Maya Reef), the largest reef in the Western Hemisphere.

Cozumel

GETTING THERE There are international flights to and from Houston, New York, Atlanta, Charlotte, Denver, Dallas, and Chicago to Cozumel International Airport. From Cancún, MayaAir runs six daily, 15-minute flights to the island. And from Playa del Carmen's Terminal Maritima, two different ferries run routes to Cozumel daily from 6 AM to 10 PM.

Cozumel (Land of the Swallows) was a sacred sanctuary and holy shrine to the goddess Ixchel. The Maya made annual pilgrimages here, a ritual journey repeated annually in a must-see spectacle called **Travesía Sagrada.**

THE BEACHES OF COZUMEL

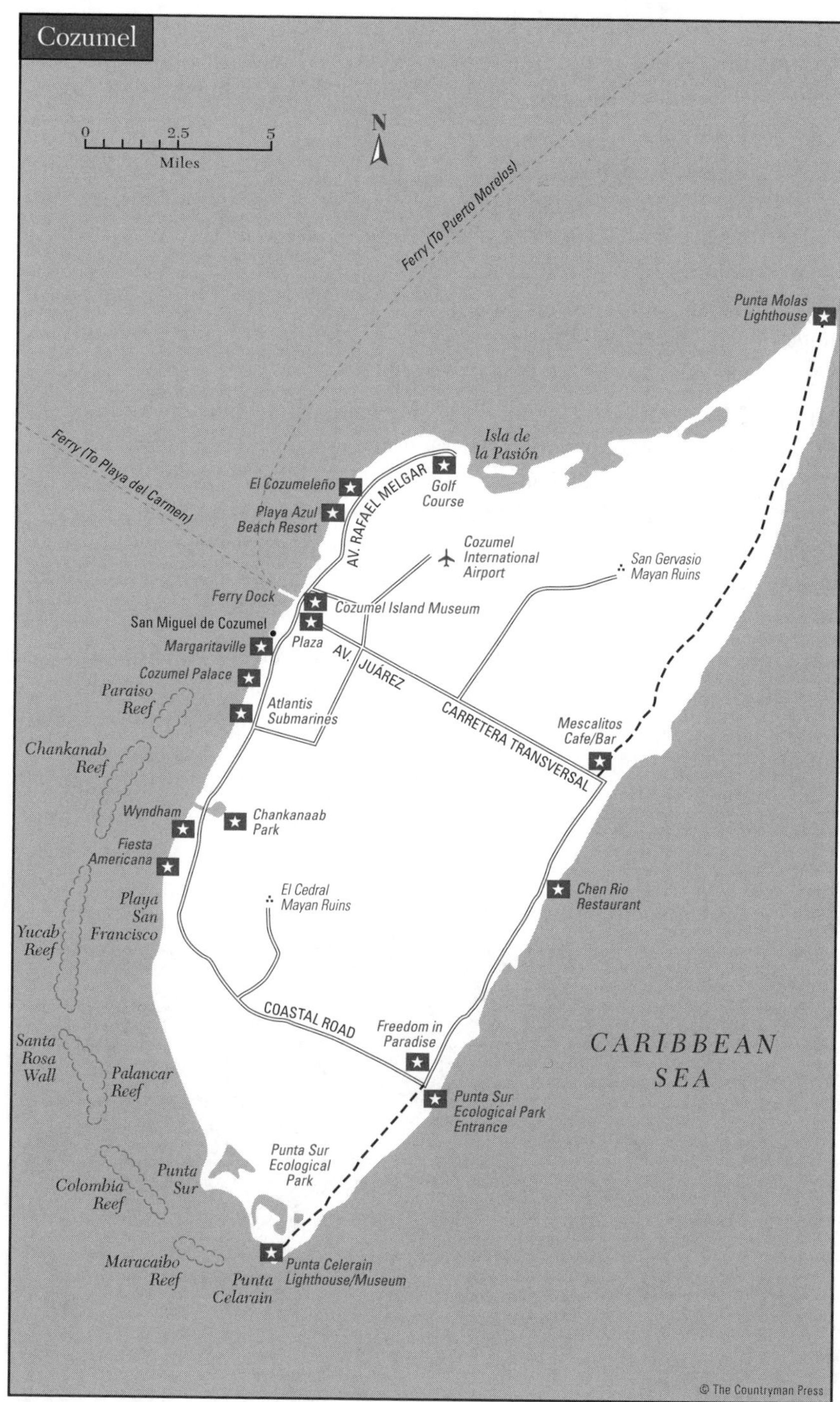

MXAztecFGi1_Cozumel

Today, the island's chief draw is its diving and snorkeling. There are tons of reputable outfits on the island, and a good resource for tourists is Cozumel-Diving.net (http://cozumel-diving.net/), an online guide to local dive shops and destinations.

Faro Celarain Eco-Park. Located on the southern end of the island and named after the Celarain lighthouse, which you can climb for spectacular views, this park has fabulous beaches. You can also visit El Caracol, a squat structure of Maya origins that may have served as a rudimentary lighthouse (you can see traces of navigational symbols on the façade) and check out its crocodile observation deck. The park runs turtle expeditions as well as kayak trips in the mangrove lagoon.

Parque Chankanaab. Cozumel's ecological park, Chankanaab ranks among the island's most popular attractions. While it has a botanical garden and a faux archaeological zone with replicas of numerous Maya structures and sculptures, Chankanaab's best asset is underwater, where its coral reef and sunken treasures (including a ship, cannon, and sculptures on the sea floor) await divers and snorkelers. The park also offers dolphin swims and sea lion shows.

San Gervasio lies off the main road, Carretera Transversal, crossing through Cozumel from the main town to the east coast. The ruins are small in size and scope (puny, in fact, compared to Cobá or Tulum), but important in the Maya world. This ceremonial center and sanctuary to Ixchel—the goddess of fertility, childbirth, and the moon—dates from the early Classic to the late Postclassic period. The most iconic structure here

EL CARACOL AT FARO CELARAIN ECO-PARK

is the 5-foot-tall arch, which forms the main entrance to the Plaza Central. The tallest building at San Gervasio is Ka'na Nah (Tall House), which was probably the principal center of worship. You might be more impressed with the quantity of lizards at the site than the site itself, but it makes for a fun trip while you're on the island.

Isla Mujeres

GETTING THERE From Puerto Juárez, you have the choice of taking the **Magaño Express Ferry** or, for the same price, the newer **Ultramar first-class boat**. You can also catch an Ultramar ferry from Playa Tortugas in Cancún's Zona Hotelera. There's also a car ferry, but tourists have no reason to bring a car to Isla.

Isla Mujeres attracts a loyal following of tourists who prefer a less intense environment. A pirate refuge for centuries, Isla now lends itself to puttering around in golf carts, dining in rustic beachfront eateries, and enjoying the homey hospitality of the locals. You can find beautiful beaches here, along with marinas, mangrove lagoons, and tropical foliage. Like Cozumel, Isla has several much-loved diving spots. A comprehensive resource for divers who want to explore its coasts is **Dive Isla** (http://mayanparadise.net/isladiveguide/).

PLAYA NORTE AT ISLA MUJERES

Isla Mujeres Town. The island's only town, where the ferries dock, is a colorful and (compared to the rest of the island) lively area. The main thoroughfares are Avenidas Rueda Medina, or *malecón,* which runs along the water, Hidalgo, and Guerrero. Here you'll find clusters of bars, shops, restaurants, and small hotels. At the town's northernmost tip is **Playa Norte**, a broad swath of dazzling white sand where you can rent beach chairs, order drinks, and enjoy the tranquil calm of azure waters.

Garrafón. Isla Mujeres's eco-park features an abundance of activities. As it's owned by Dolphin Discovery, you naturally have dolphin swims here, along with zip lines over the sea, a gorgeous pool

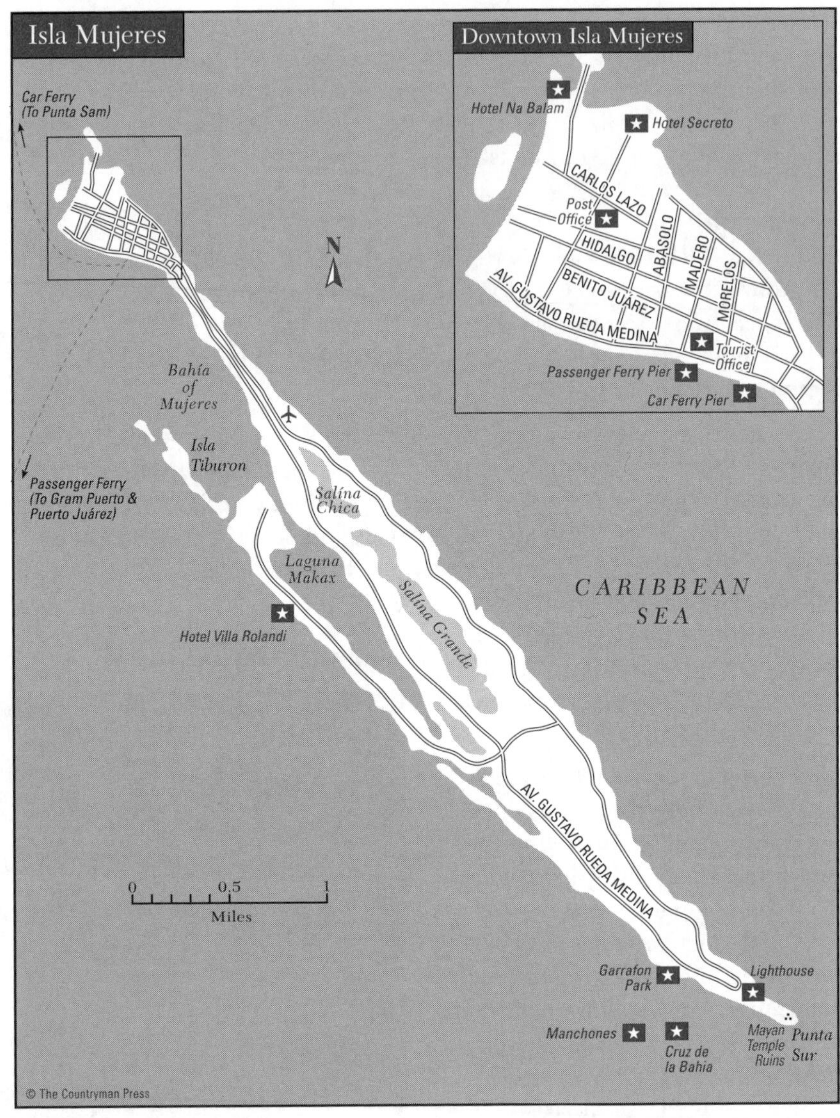

facing the Caribbean, kayaking, and some of the best snorkeling spots on Isla. The park also includes traces of a small temple to Ixchel and a sculpture garden on the southern promontory of the island. This part of the park is where the rising sun first shines on Mexican soil.

A small park with more iguanas than visitors, **Hacienda Mundaca** is a leafy refuge surrounding what's left of the home of pirate and slave trader Fermín Antonio Mundaca, who escaped to this island in 1858 and fell in love with a local woman known as "La Trigueña" for her blond hair.

GARRAFÓN PARK

Despite his best efforts, which included building the hacienda, she married someone else, and the good pirate died of grief.

Tortugranja. My favorite attraction on Isla, this small turtle farm and conservation center is dedicated to the survival and prosperity of loggerhead, hawksbill, and green sea turtles. It's been here for more than 40 years, and annually releases mature turtles to the sea in June and July. You can see baby turtles in wading pools, learn about the staff's conservation efforts, and from July to September, catch baby turtles poking out of their nests at night on the farm's beach.

Isla Holbox

GETTING THERE From Cancún, take Highway 180 toward Valladolid. As you approach the town of Nuevo Xcan, you'll see a crossroads at El Ideal. Turn north on the state road to Chiquilá. Once you get to this small town on the coast, park in the secure parking lot and take the ferry to Holbox. The ferry runs continuously until 5-6 PM, but if you don't feel like waiting, there are local boats at the pier willing to shuttle you across. The tip from Cancún takes about three hours. You can also catch a bus from Cancún to Chiquilá; the ferry will wait for the arrival of the bus. Some hotels coordinate VIP transfers from the airport to the island.

There may be little of the Maya in Isla Holbox (Black Hole), but it's a special place just off the northeastern corner of the Yucatán peninsula. The island's claim to fame is the whale shark. From May to September, over 100 of these gentle giants congregate near the island, and boats from the island shuttle tourists out in droves to swim with them.

A RESIDENT AT THE TORTUGRANJA

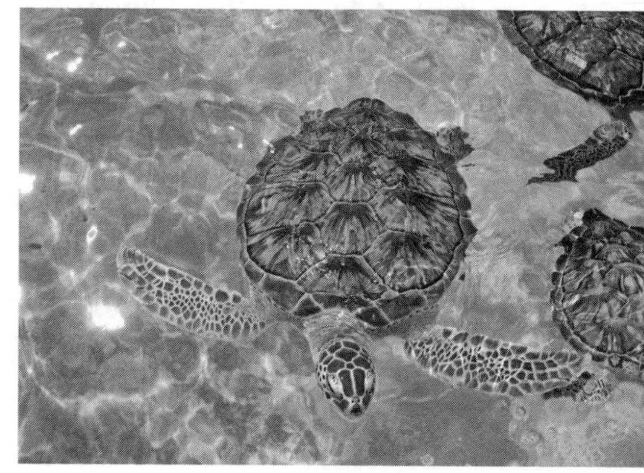

Even if you don't come here during whale shark season, the island has an edge-of-the-world serenity

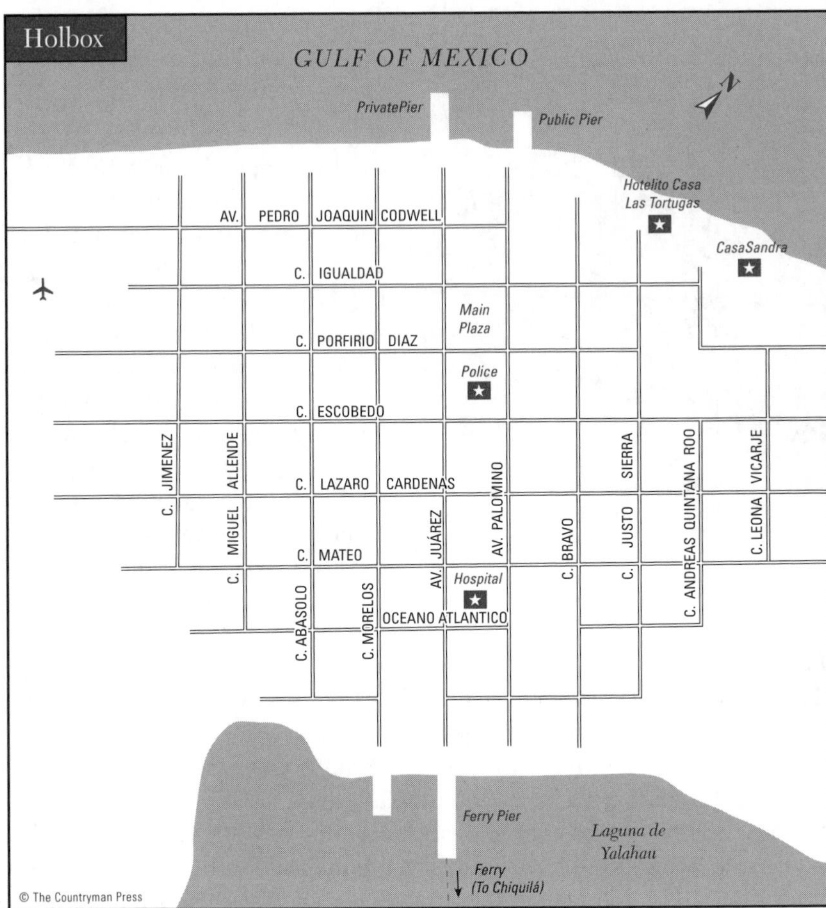

to it. Its sandy roads are designed for golf carts and little else, and as you head out toward Punta Mosquito, you'll come across idyllic beaches where the principal activity is collecting shells.

You can take a tour of Chichén Itzá, Ek' Balam, Tulum, and other archaeological sites from Holbox, but my recommendation is to visit those destinations, and then come here to disconnect and recharge. But if you do come, bring cash. Nobody accepts credit cards except Casa Sandra, and there are no banks or ATMs.

Turística Moguel. Yoni Moguel is one of Holbox's principal tour operators, offering whale shark tours (in season), fly-fishing, golf cart rentals, and more. His "Tour Clásico" provides a great introduction to Holbox. The Classic Tour (also offered by other operators) lasts three hours and has four stops around Holbox: Pajaros Island, a bird sanctuary where you

ON THE WAY TO PUNTA MOSQUITO, ISLA HOLBOX

can see flamingos, pelicans, and cormorants from an observation tower; Punta Mosquitos, the eastern tip of the island; the Yalahau Lagoon, where you can swim in a sweetwater *ojo de agua,* or natural bubbling spring; and the tiny Isla Pasión. You're almost guaranteed to spot dolphins on the tour.

Travesía Sagrada

I have to give special attention to the **Travesía Sagrada** (Sacred Journey). This annual spectacle honors and re-creates an ancient rite: the journey of Maya warriors to the island of Cozumel to consult with the oracle at the shrine of Ixchel. Held in May, the *travesía* takes place over three days.

The event begins at Xcaret with a nocturnal ceremony to honor the goddess. At dawn on the second day, teams of volunteer rowers who have trained twice a day for months climb into 150 traditional canoes—rustic wooden contraptions, nothing like a modern canoe—and, with a roar, begin the arduous journey to Cuzamil (the original name for Cozumel). On the third day, the rowers return to Playa del Carmen to the cheers of thousands, where they receive the blessings and honor of Maya priests. A closing ceremony concludes the sacred journey.

The rowers are exhausted by the end of their trials, but the feeling of exultation and accomplishment can be seen on every face as they come ashore. One of them described his experience as a union of mind, body, and heart. Full details and schedules of this beautiful and moving event can be found at www.travesiasagrada maya.com.mx.

AFTER COMPLETING THE TRAVESÍA SAGRADA, AN EXULTANT PARTICIPANT STANDS TALL.

A WEEKEND IN THE RIVIERA

On a weekend trip, the archaeological sites and parks should be your focus. Cobá and Tulum can be visited on the same day if you're driving, but tours typically don't cover both sites together.

Relax on your first day: settle into your hotel, hit the beach, and explore **Playa** or **Cancún**. Devote Day 2 to a tour such as **Alltournative**'s Maya Encounter or Cobá Sunset, as this gives you a chance to experience several of the region's cultural and natural highlights. If tours aren't your thing, rent a car and head out to **Cobá**, have lunch at **Ki-Janal**, and explore the beaches along the Riviera. On your third day, keep your bathing suit handy and combine a visit to **Xcaret** with a trip to **Tulum**.

✷ Local Knowledge

Cancún and the Riviera Maya are among the most accessible and visitor-friendly destinations in Mexico, if not all of Latin America. A good introduction to this part of Mexico can be found at www.rivieramaya.com. Another excellent resource is www.riviera maya.travel. The lifeblood of this coast is tourism, and everyone who lives and works here knows it.

The high season runs roughly from December to April, with another spike in August. May through October is the official rainy season, with hurricane season running from August to October.

The coast is a safe destination where English is commonly spoken; however, the downside is scams and ripoffs. Offers for special gifts if you listen to a time-share speech, private boat shuttles to Isla or Cozumel because "the ferry isn't working today," and unnaturally exorbitant taxi fares (Cancún already trots out the most expensive taxi fleet in Mexico) are just the tip of the unfriendly iceberg. The bottom line: If something sounds too good to be true, or even vaguely suspicious, walk away.

Driving around the Riviera Maya is quite easy: the entire coast is accessible from Highway 307, which is a wide, well-maintained road with clearly labeled signs. You can also rely on the ADO bus line (www.ado.com.mx) to take you to the Riviera's most popular destinations.

Cancún

The city has numerous Web sites replete with handy information for tourists; www.cancun.travel is the official travel Web site for the city. Other sites include www.cancun .com, www.cancunmx.com, and www.go2cancun.com. There's also a state tourism office on Boulevard Kukulcán Km. 9, 1st Floor, Hotel Zone (998-881-9000), open weekdays 9–8.

When in Cancún, take full advantage of the excellent bus system, which covers every area of the city, is cheap, and efficient. Taxis are ubiquitous and fares are set by zone, but they'll quickly drain your wallet if you're on a budget.

A brief word on street addresses, which are rather lengthier than you'd expect. In Cancún City, you'll find that addresses list the building lot, the *manzana*, or block, as well as the *supermanzana*, or cluster of blocks. In the Contacts section, I've abbreviated these as L., Mza., and SM. Consulates in Cancún include:

- **Canada**, 998-883-3360, 800-706-2900 for emergencies, Plaza Caracol 3rd Floor Loc. 330, Hotel Zone. Open Mon.–Fri. 9–3:30.
- **Great Britain**, 998-881-0100, 998-109-0286 (for

EXTENDED STAY

Cancún and Playa make a great home base from which to explore the archaeological sites of the Yucatán. During an extended stay, you can explore the peninsula at your leisure and enjoy more of the Riviera's many treasures. Here are ten things I would recommend doing on a longer vacation:

1. Visit **Tulum**.
2. Visit **Cobá**.
3. If you've never seen them, take a trip or tour to **Chichén Itzá**, **Uxmal**, or **Ek' Balam**.
4. Spend a day at **Xcaret**, **Xel-Há**, or **Xplor** (you can also buy a three-park ticket and enjoy all of them).
5. Take a road trip to **Kohunlich** and **Dzibanché**.
6. Visit **Isla Mujeres**, with a trip to **Garrafón**.
7. Visit **Cozumel**, with a trip to **San Gervasio**.
8. Go diving or snorkeling at least once.
9. Take a subterranean river adventure at Río Secreto.
10. Plan for a few days in Holbox and, if they're around, swim with the whale sharks.

emergencies) Hotel Royal Sands, Boulevard Kukulcan Km. 13.5, Mon.–Fri. 9–2:30.

- **United States**, 998-883-0272, Plaza Caracol 2, 3rd floor, Hotel Zone. Open Mon.–Fri. 9–1.

Hospitals in Cancún include:

- **Hospital Americano**, 998-884-6133, Calle Viento 15. Cancún Centro
- **AMAT Hospital**, 998-887-4422, Calle Nader 13, Cancún Centro
- **Hospiten**, 998-881-3700, Avenida Bonampak, Cancún Centro

Cozumel

Online resources for Cozumel include www.islacozumel.com.mx, www.cozumel.net, and www.cozumelmycozumel.com. The rainy season in Cozumel extends from June to October, but the weather can get very windy from October to December. There's a tourism office (987-872-7585) on Calle 2 Norte between Avenidas 10 and 15.

Isla Mujeres

The most comprehensive information on Isla Mujeres is at www.isla-mujeres.net. There's a tourism office on the island at Avenida Rueda and Muelle Fiscal (998-887-0307). The island only has one bank, an HSBC, across from the ferry docks, but there are plenty of places to change your dollars. You can call a taxi at 998-877-0066.

✷ Contacts

100% Natural 998-884-0102, Avenida Sunyaxchen, L. 62 and 64, Mza. 6, Sm. 25, Colonia Centro, Cancún, Q. Roo 77500. In Playa del Carmen: 984-873-2242, Avenida 5 between Calles 10 and 12, Playa del Carmen, Q. Roo, 77710. www.100natural.com. Open daily 7 AM–11 PM. $–$$.

Alltournative 800-507-1092 (within the U.S.), 984-803-9999, Avenida 5 between Calles 12 and 14, Playa del Carmen, Q. Roo, 77710, and Highway 240 Chetumal–Puerto Juarez Colonia Chemuyil, Tulum, Q. Roo 77780. www.alltournative.com. $$$–$$$$.

La Amada 998-872-8730, 888 6192 6232 (within the U.S.), 800-002-6232 (within Mexico), Condominio Playa Mujeres, Q. Roo 77400. www.laamadahotel.com. $$$$.

USEFUL NUMBERS

ADO: 998-884-5542
Tourist Police: 998-885-2277
Police: 998-884-1913
Consumer Protection Agency: 998-884-2634
Emergency: 066
Fire Department: 998-884-1202
Red Cross: 998-884-1616
Radio taxi: 998-840-0651

Amarte Maroma 998-872-8244, Highway 307 Km. 51, Solidaridad, Q. Roo 77710. http://amartemaroma.com. $$–$$$$.

Aquanauts Dive Adventures 998-206-9365, Hotel Carmen Hacienda, Suite No. 107, Avenida Rafael E. Melgar, Puerto Morelos, Q. Roo 77580. Tours depart 6–11:30 AM. www.aquanautsdiveadventures.com. $$$–$$$$.

Aquaworld 877-730-4054 (within the U.S.), 998-848-8327, Boulevard Kukulcán Km. 15.2, Cancún, Q. Roo 77500. www.aquaworld.com.mx. $$$–$$$$.

Asterix Tours 998-886-4847, Scuba Cancún Marina, Boulevard Kukulcán Km. 5.5. Tours depart daily at 9 AM. www.contoytours.com. $$$.

Le Basilic 998-881-3200, at the Fiesta Americana Grand Coral Beach Cancún, Boulevard Kukulcán Km. 9.5, Cancún, Q. Roo 77500. www.fiestamericana.com. Open Mon.–Sat. 6:30 PM–11 PM. $$$.

Beachscape Kin Ha Villas & Suites 866-340-9082 (within the U.S.), 800-640-6288 (within Mexico) 998-891-5400, Boulevard Kukulcán Km. 8.5, Cancún, Q. Roo 77500. www.beachscape.com.mx. $–$$.

Best Day Travel 800-593-6259 (within the U.S.), 800-BEST-DAY (within Mexico), 998-287-3674, Avenida Bonampak L. 7, Mza. 2 Sm. 10, Cancún, Q. Roo 77500. www.bestday.com. $$–$$$$.

La Bodeguita del Medio 984-803-3950, Avenida 10 Sur S/N, local 46 de Plaza Paseo del Carmen, Playa del Carmen, Q. Roo 77710. Open daily 11 AM–2 AM. www.labodeguitadelmedio.com.mx. $$–$$$.

Bucaneros 998-877-1222, 772-646-0317 (within the U.S.), 800-227-4765 (within Mexico), Avenida Hidalgo No. 11, Centro, Isla Mujeres, Q. Roo 77400. www.bucaneros.com. Call 998-877-0126 for the restaurant. Restaurant open daily 7 AM–11 PM. $.

Cabanas La Luna 818-631-9824 (within the U.S.), Carretera Tulum-Boca Paila Km. 6.5, Quintana Roo, Tulum 77789. www.cabanaslaluna.com. $$–$$$.

Cancún International Airport 998-848-7200/886-0322, Carretera Cancún-Chetumal Km. 22, Cancún Q. Roo 77500. www.cancun-airport.com.

Cancún Party Hopper Bar Crawl departs from the Congo Bar at Plaza Forum, Boulevard Kukulcán Km. 9, Hotel Zone. www.cancunpartyhopper.com. $$$. Crawl departs Mon.–Sat. at 9 PM and runs until 4 AM.

Capt. Rick's Adventures 888-449-3562 (within the U.S.), 984-873-5195, 984-873-5387. Puerto Aventuras Marina, Q. Roo. Open daily 8–7. $$$$.

Carboncitos 984 873 1382, Calle 4 and Avenida 5, Playa del Carmen, Q. Roo 77710. Open daily 7:30–11. $.

La Casa del Tikinxik 998-274-0018, Playa Lancheros, Carretera a Garrafón Km. 4.6, Isla Mujeres, Q. Roo 77400. Open daily 10–6. $–$$.

Casa IxChel 998-888-0107, Avenida Martinez Ross Mza. 98 L. 5, Salina Chica, Isla Mujeres, Q. Roo 77400. www.casaixchelisla.com. $–$$$.

Casa Rolandi 998-883-2557, Boulevard Kukulkán Km. 8.5, in Plaza Caracol, Zona Hotelera, Cancún, Q. Roo 77500. Open daily 1–11:30. www.rolandi.com. $$–$$$.

Casa Sandra 984-875-2171, Calle Igualdad, Lázaro Cárdenas, Playa Norte, Isla Holbox, Q. Roo 77310. www.casasandra.com. $$$.

Ceiba del Mar 998-872-8063, 877-545-6221 (within the U.S.), 800-426-9772 (within Mexico), Costera Norte, L. 1 Mza. 26, Sm. 10, Puerto Morelos, Q. Roo 77580. $$–$$$$.

El Cejas 998-887-1080, Mercado 28 (take Avenida Tankah to Avenida Xel-Ha), Colonia Centro, Cancún, Q. Roo 77500. Open daily 10–8. $–$$.

Centro Ecologico Sian Ka'an 984-871-2499, Highway 307 Cancún-Tulum, No. 68 Tulum, Q. Roo 77780. http://cesiak.org. Open daily 9–5.

Chac Chi Fishing & Yacht Club 998-849-5414, Km. 3.2, Zona Hotelera, Cancún, Q. Roo 77500. www.chacchimarina.com. Departures daily 7 and 2. $$$$.

The City 998-848-8380, Boulevard Kukulkán Km. 9.5, Zona Hotelera, Cancún, Q. Roo 77500. www.thecitycancun.com. Open 10:30–late. $$.

Coco Bongo 998-883-5061, Forum by the Sea No. 30, Boulevard Kukulkán Km. 9.5, Zona Hotelera, Cancún, Q. Roo 77500. www.cocobongo.com.mx. Open daily 10:30–3:30. $$.

Community Tours Sian Ka'an 984-871-2202, Avenida Tulum S/N between Beta Norte and Orion, Tulúm, Q. Roo 77780. http://siankaantours.org. $$$–$$$$.

Cooperativa Isla Bonita 998-134-6103, Avenida Rueda Medina, Terminal Marítima API, Isla Mujeres 77400. www.cooperativaislabonita.com. $$$–$$$$.

Cooperative de Servicios Turísticos de Puerto Morelos 998-206-9183, at the Principal Pier in Puerto Morelos, Q. Roo 77710. Tours leave daily at 8:30. $$.

Delphinus 998-206-3304, 888-526-2230 (within the U.S.), 800-335-3461 (within Mexico), numerous locations. www.delphinus.com.mx. $$$$.

Dolphin Discovery 866-393-5158 (within the U.S.), 998-193-3360, numerous locations in the Riviera Maya. www.dolphindiscovery.com. $$ to use their facilities, $$$$ for swims.

Don Diego de la Selva 984-114-9744, Calle Tulum, L. 3, Mza. 24 Tulum, Q. Roo 77780. www.dtulum.com. $.

Excellence Playa Mujeres 866-540-2585 (within the U.S.), 998-872-8600, Prolongación Bonampak, S/N, Punta Sam, L. Terrenos 001 Mza. 001 Sm. 003, Zona Continental de Isla Mujeres, Q. Roo 77400. www.excellence-resorts.com. $$$$.

Fantino The Ritz-Carlton Cancún, 998-881-0808, Retorno del Rey No. 36, Zona Hotelera, Cancún, Q. Roo 77500. Open Tue.–Sat. 7 PM–11. www.ritzcarlton.com/cancun. $$$$.

Faro Celarain Eco-Park 987-872-2940/8462, southern end of Carretera Sur, Cozumel, Q. Roo 77600. www.cozumelparks.com. Open daily 8–4. $$, $$$ for turtle-watching and kayak trips.

Fiesta Americana Condesa Cancún 998-881-4255, Boulevard Kukulcán Km. 16.5, Cancún, Q. Roo 77500. www.fiestamericana.com. $$–$$$.

Fiesta Americana Grand Coral Beach Cancún 998-881-3200, Boulevard Kukulcán Km. 9.5, Cancún, Q. Roo 77500. www.fiestamericana.com. $$$$.

Fiesta Americana Villas Cancún 998-881-1400, Boulevard Kukulcán Km. 8.5, Cancún, Q. Roo 77500. www.fiestamericana.com. $–$$.

Forum by the Sea 998-883-4426, Boulevard Kukulcán Km. 9, Zona Hotelera. www.forumbythesea.com.mx. Open 10 AM–11 PM, bars and clubs until 5 AM. $–$$$$.

Garrafón 866-393-5158 (within the U.S.), 800-727-5391 (within Mexico), 998-193-3360, Carretera Garrafón Km. 6, L. 12, Mza. 41, Sm. 9 Punta Sur, Isla Mujeres, Q. Roo, 77400. www.garrafon.com. Open daily 10–5. $$–$$$.

Gran Caribe Real Resort 800-760-0944 (within the U.S.), 800-216-5500 (within Mexico), 998-881-7340/7341, Boulevard Kukulcan Km. 11.5, Cancún, Q. Roo 77500. $$$.

Gran Porto Real Playa del Carmen Resort & Spa 984-873-4000, 800-760-0944 (within the U.S.), 800-216-5500 (within Mexico), Avenida Constituyentes No. 1, Playa del Carmen, Q. Roo 77710. $$–$$$.

La Habichuela 998-884-3158, Calle Margaritas 25, Colonia Centro, Cancún, Q. Roo 77500. Open daily noon–midnight. www.lahabichuela.com. $$$.

Hacienda Mundaca Carretera Garrafón Km. 3.5, Isla Mujeres, Q. Roo, 77400. Open daily 9–5. $.

Hacienda Tres Rios 984 877-2400, 998-287-4115, 800-494-9173, Cancún-Tulum Highway, Km. 54, Tres Ríos, Riviera Maya, Q. Roo 77760. www.haciendatresrios.com. $$–$$$$.

Hechizo 984-879-5020, Km. 10, Carretera Tulum-Punta Allen, Tulum, Q. Roo 77780. http://hechizotulum.com. Open Tue.–Sun. 6:30 PM, 7:30 PM, and 8:30 PM seatings. $$$.

Hostal Mayapan 998-883-3227, Boulevard Kukulkán Km. 8.5 Zona

Hotelera, Cancún, Q. Roo 77500. www.hostalmayapan.com. $.

Hostel Quetzal Calle Orquideas No. 10, Cancún, Q. Roo 75505. $.

Hotel Secreto 998-877-1048, Sección Rocas, L. 11, Isla Mujeres, Q. Roo 77400. www.hotelsecreto.com. $$$.

Hotel & Suites Chac Chi 998-877-0269, Avenida Rueda Medina, Colonia Electrisistas, Isla Mujeres, Q. Roo, 77400. www.hotelchac-chi.com. $$–$$$.

Hotel Villa Rolandi 998-999 2000, 800-525-4800 (within the U.S.) Fracc. Laguna Mar, Sm. 7 Mz. 75 L. 15 y 16, Carretera Sac-Bajo, Isla Mujeres, Q. Roo 77400.

Hotel Xbalamque 998-884-9690/887-3055, Avenida Yaxchilán No. 31, Sm 22, Mz.18, Cancún Q. Roo 77500. www.xbalamque.com. $.

La Isla del Colibri 984-875-2162, Plaza Mayor, Isla Holbox, Q. Roo 77310. Open daily 8 AM–11 PM. $–$$.

La Isla Shopping Village 998-883-5025, Boulevard Kukulkán Km. 12.5, Zona Hotelera, Cancún, Q. Roo 77500. Open daily 10–10. $–$$$$.

Ki-Janal No phone number, located at the archaeological site of Cobá, Q. Roo. Open daily 8 AM–7 PM. $–$$.

Labná 998-892-3056, Calle Margaritas No. 29, Colonia Centro, Cancún, Q. Roo 77500. Open daily noon–10. www.labna.com. $–$$.

Live Aqua 866-931-AQUA, 998-881-7600, Boulevard Kuculkán Km. 12.5, Cancún, Q. Roo 77500. www.feel-aqua.com. $$$$.

THE RIVIERA MAYA IS A POPULAR DIVING DESTINATION.

Mexico Tourism Board

MB At the Live Aqua, 866-931-AQUA, 998-881-7600, Boulevard Kuculkán Km. 12.5, Cancún, Q. Roo 77500. Open daily 6:30 PM–11 PM. www.feel-aqua.com. $$$$.

Mercado 23 On Avenida Tulum north of the ADO Bus Station, Sm. 23, Cancún Q. Roo 77500. Stores open generally 8–6 daily. $–$$$$.

Mercado 28 Avenida Sunyaxchen and Xel-Ha, Sm. 28, Cancún Q. Roo 77500. Stores open generally 8–6 daily. $–$$$$.

México Adventourist 998-802-3388, Cancún, Q. Roo 77535. www.mexicoadventourist.com. $$–$$$$.

Mexidivers 984-807-8805, 984-807-8871, Carretera Tulúm–Boca Paila, Km. 5, Hotel Zamas, Tulum, Q. Roo 77780. www.mexidivers.com. Tours depart at 8 AM. $$$$.

Moloch Hostel 998-884-6918, Calle Margaritas No. 54, Mza. 25, Sm. 22, Cancún, Q. Roo 77500. $.

Parque Chankanaab 987-872-2940, Carretera Sur Km. 9, Cozumel, Q. Roo 77600. Open daily 8–5. www.cozumelparks.com. $–$$.

Pavo Real 998-872-8244, at Amarte Maroma, Highway 307 Km. 51, Solidaridad, Q. Roo 77710. http://amartemaroma.com. Open Mon.–Sat. 6 PM–11. $$$.

La Petita Avenida Rafael Melgar off the main plaza, Puerto Morelos, Q. Roo 77710. Open daily 11–8. $–$$.

Playa del Carmen Tours 866-728-1438 or 866-471-4157 (within the U.S.), 800-822-4577 or 800-832-3632 (within Mexico), www.playadelcarmentours.com. $$$–$$$$.

Playa Maya 888-866-2988 (within the U.S.), 984-803-2022, Zona FMT between Calles 6 and 8 Norte, Playa del Carmen, Q Roo 77710. www.playa-maya.com. $$–$$$$.

Playa Tiburón 998-219-9921, Fracc. Laguna Mar, Carretera Sac-Bajo No. 17, Isla Mujeres, Q. Roo 77400. Open daily 10–10. $–$$.

Real Playa del Carmen 984-873-4350, 800-760-0944 (within the U.S.), 800-216-5500 (within Mexico), Avenida 5 between Calles 34 and 38, Playa del Carmen, Q. Roo, 77710. www.realresorts.com. $$–$$$$.

Reef Quest Divers 984-117-3597, Blue Parrot Beach Club, Calle 12 and Playa, Playa del Carmen, Q. Roo 77710. www.reefquestdiversmexico.com. Departures at 9 and 2 daily, snorkeling trips depart at noon. $$$$.

Restaurante & Pizzería Edelyn 984-875-2024 Calle Palomino S/N, Holbox, Q. Roo 77310. Open daily 11 AM–midnight. $–$$.

Río Secreto 984-877-2377, 800-985-2664 (within the U.S.), 800-212-8897 (within Mexico), Carretera Federal Chetumal–Puerto Juárez. L. 4, Mz. 122, Local 12, Playa del Carmen, Q. Roo 77710. Tours at 9, 11, 1, and 2. www.riosecretomexico.com. $$$.

The Ritz-Carlton Cancún 998-881-0808, Retorno del Rey No. 36, Zona Hotelera, Cancún, Q. Roo 77500. www.ritzcarlton.com/cancun. $$$$.

The Royal Cancún 800-760-0944 (within the U.S.), 800-216-5500 (within Mexico), 998-881-7340/7341, Boulevard Kukulkán, Km. 11.5, Hotel Zone, Cancún, 77500. www.realresorts.com. $$$$.

The Tides Riviera Maya 984-877-3000, 800-578-0281, Playa Xcalacoco Frac. 7, Q. Roo 77710. www.tidesrivieramaya.com. $$$$.

Tortugranja 998-888-0705, Sac Bajo Km. 4, Carretera a Garrafón, Isla Mujeres, Q. Roo 77400. Open daily 9–5. $.

Turística Moguel 984-875-2028, 984-114-9921, Holbox Island, Q. Roo 77310. www.holboxislandtours.com. $$–$$$$.

Ultramar 998-881-5890, Avenida López Portillo, L. 6, Mza. 5, Sm. 84, Puerto Juárez, Cancún, Q. Roo 77500. www.granpuerto.com.mx. Boats run from 5 AM–10 PM. $–$$.

Villa Vera 998-287-3340, 800-987-4941 (within Mexico), 877-445-3104 (within the U.S.) Puerto de Abrigo S/N, Colonia Electristas, Isla Mujeres, Q. Roo 77400. www.raintreevacationclub.com. $$$–$$$$.

Xaloc Resort 984-875-2160/54, C/ Chacchi S/N esq. Playa Norte, Isla Holbox, Q. Roo 77310. www.holbox-xalocresort.com. $–$$.

Xcaret 998-883-3143, 998-883-0470, 984-206-0038. Highway Chetumal-Puerto Juarez Km. 282, Solidaridad, Q. Roo 77780. Open daily 8:30 AM–9 PM. www.xcaret.com. $$–$$$.

Xel-Ha 998-884-7165, Highway Chetumal-Pto. Juárez, Km. 240 Locals 1 y 2 módulo B., Xel-Há, Q. Roo 77710. www.xelha.com. Open daily 8:30–6. $$–$$$$.

Xplor 800-00-XPLOR, 998-849-5275, Federal Highway 307 Km. 282 Solidaridad, Quintana Roo 77710. Open Mon.–Sat. 9–5. www.xplor.travel. $$$.

Yaxché 984 873 3011, Avenida 5 and Calle 22, Playa del Carmen, Riviera Maya, Q. Roo 77710. www.mayancuisine.com.

Mexico City: The Aztec Stronghold

8

MODERN MEXICO CITY

INTRODUCTION

Mexico City, the ancient Aztec capital of Tenochtitlán, is today known as the Distrito Federal (Federal District), or simply, El D.F. (pronounced "El De Efe"). The city is a massive, chaotic sprawl, full of great wonder, even greater crowds, and a wonderful blend of old and new. As the heart of the Aztec empire, it's one of the world's oldest cities, and has enough museums, archaeological sites, monuments, and temples to rival anything in the world's other great historic metropolises. Welcome to the crucible and soul of ancient and modern Mexico.

GETTING THERE AND GETTING AROUND *By air:* Mexico City's Benito Juárez International Airport is a large, modern, and busy facility with two terminals. From the airport, you have several options for getting into the city.

By car: Most major car rental agencies have offices in the international section of the airport, in Concourse E. Surprisingly, there is no bus service from the airport to the city, but there is the metro and the taxi. If you want to take the metro, the Terminal Area Station on Line 5 is open Monday to Friday, 5 AM–1 AM, Saturday 6–midnight, and Sunday 7–10. It's a bit of a hassle to get to, but by far the cheapest way to travel.

There is no shortage of transportation options to help you get around Mexico City. In general, I'd avoid driving, recommend only certain types of taxis, and highly advise making full use of the public transportation system, which may look daunting but is the most convenient and cheapest way to get around. Finally, for all its vastness, this is a walking city, and many parts of it are best enjoyed on foot.

By taxi and sitio*:* Taxis are the most convenient way to go to Mexico City from the airport. Travelers should only use authorized airport taxis, available directly from the terminal. Follow the GROUND TRANSPORTATION signs to the end of the terminal, and you'll see taxi counters. Buy your ticket at the window (make sure you're getting a regular sedan, not the large vans,

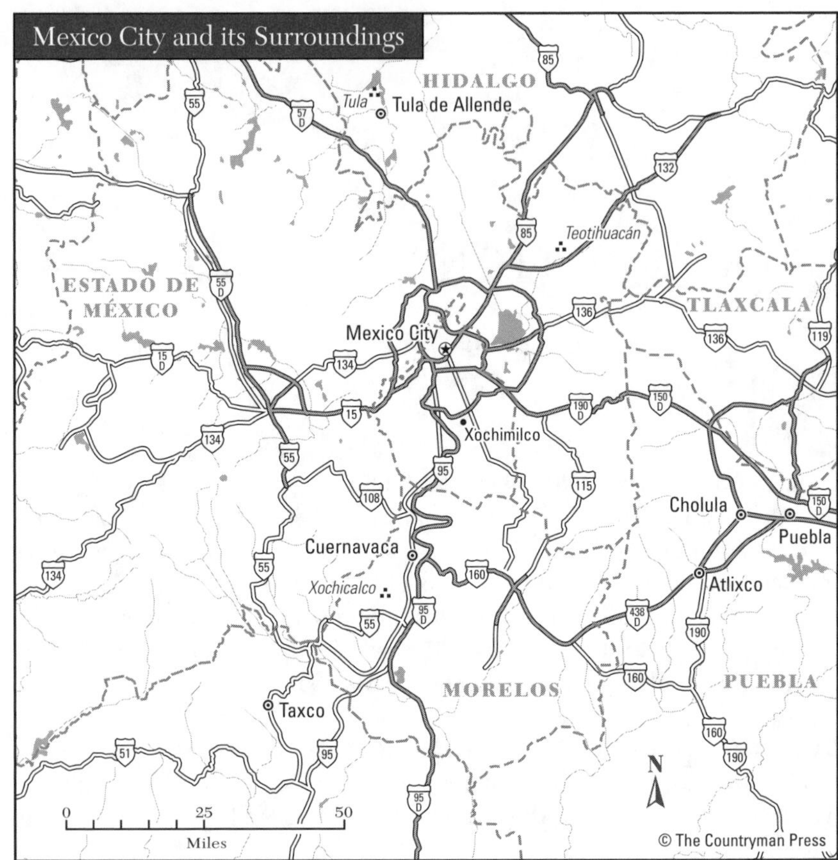

which are more expensive). The rates are based on zones, which are displayed on the window.

In Mexico City, there are taxis, and there are *sitio,* or radio, taxis. *Sitios* are the more expensive but safest mode of taxi travel. It'll help if you speak a bit of Spanish to communicate where you are and what you'll look like; and to be able to understand the operator when he or she tells you, in Spanish, what model and color of car will be picking you up. *Sitios* are expensive, but they offer the most peace of mind. Below are a few reliable operators. You can also find *sitio* taxis at designated taxi stands throughout the city.

Radio Elite 555-660-1122
Radio Taxi 555-552-1376
Servicio Elite 555-660-1060

Servitaxi 555-516-6020
Taxi Mex 555-519-7690

Your hotel can arrange a taxi for you, but expect to pay extra for the service. It's cheaper to call a *sitio* directly and have it pick you up at your hotel. If you don't have a radio taxi's number and you're in a pinch, you can flag down a maroon-and-gold checkered taxi. These metered cabs are generally considered okay, although you may end up taking the scenic route to your destination. Your last resort is the green-and-white taxi, which is hardly seen in the capital anymore. They are considered the least reliable.

If you do plan on taking something other than a *sitio* taxi, your Spanish should be good enough to hold a conversation. Also make sure the license number and ID of the driver is prominently displayed. And finally, whether you're booking a taxi via the phone or jumping into one off the street, always ask what the fare will be, even if it's an approximation. After one or two rides, you'll know when you're getting ripped off.

STATUE OF CUAUHTÉMOC IN MEXICO CITY

By metro and light rail: Mexico City's metro system (www.metro.df.gob.mx) has to be one of the most incredible bargains in urban transportation history. The cost for a one-way ticket? Two pesos. At press time, this is approximately 14 cents! The metro is also very efficient and extensive. There are 11 color-coded lines, labeled 1 through 9 and then A and B, that cover the vast majority of the city. The trains and stations are generally clean and well lit, and some stations feature beautiful murals and other works of art. Visitors are sometimes wary of what they feel is an unsafe trip underground, but the metro's main hazards are pickpockets, and tourists should keep their eyes on their valuables at all times.

During the morning and evening rush hour periods, an army of commuters descends on the trains

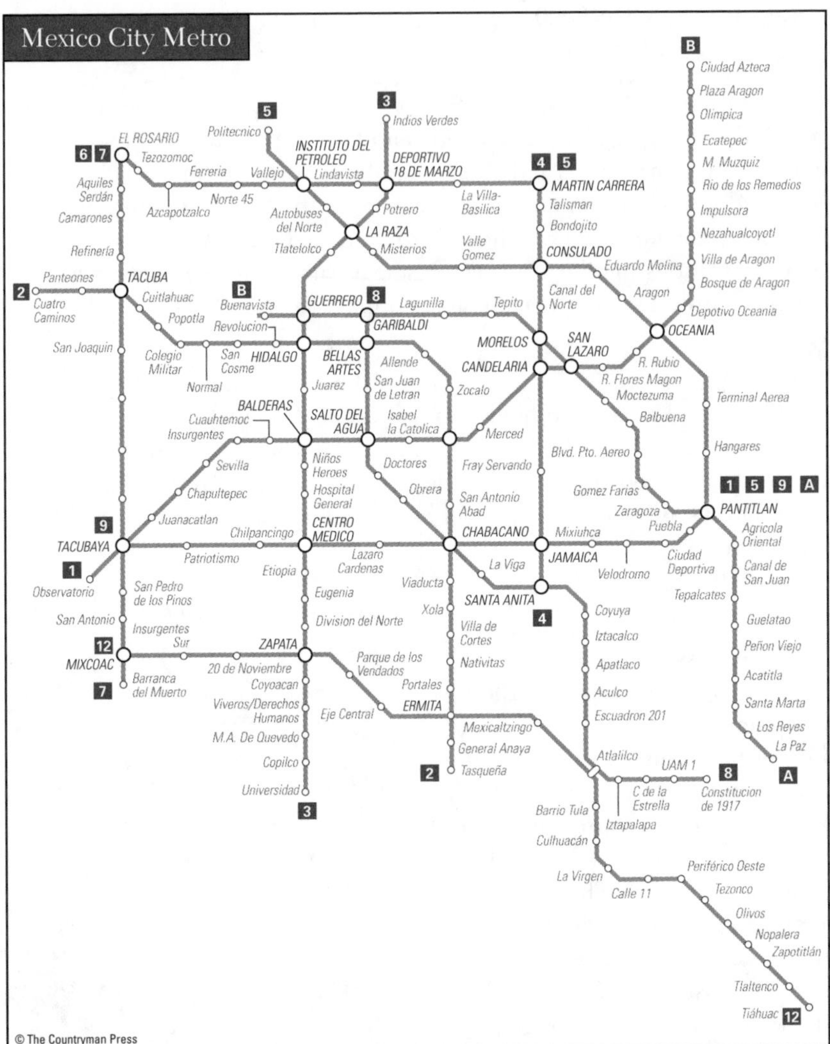

(the metro moves about five million people per day), and you'll be best served by avoiding these hours unless you enjoy being squashed. Also during peak periods, authorities will designate some cabins for women only. Women can choose to travel here or with their family and friends in the other cabins. The other interesting, and unofficial, bit of segregation that occurs is more social. At night, it is common for the last two cars on the train to be occupied by gay men and women. The metro runs weekdays 5 AM–midnight, Saturday 6 AM–midnight, Sundays and holidays 7 AM–midnight.

Beyond the metro, the *tren lígero* (light rail) extends further south from Tasqueña to Xochimilco. These trains require another ticket, but are also quite cheap.

By bus: The bus system here is terrific, whether you're enjoying coach class service to destinations outside the D.F. or heading a few blocks down the road. To get around the city, climb into a *pesero.* This fleet of small, rickety buses careen around the streets at all hours. To this day, I've been unable to unearth a bus map of the vast and complex network, but look at the posted final destinations on the window and ask the driver if he or she will be passing your stop. The bus has a maximum fare of about 50 cents. *Peseros* can be hailed at designated stops and can be found at the end of each metro line; they also have a tendency to stop just about anywhere, so if you see your destination pass by, ask the driver to drop you off. The buses might scare off tourists even more than the metro, but besides the usual threat of pickpockets and the possiblity of getting lost, they're great fun. Some *peseros* switch on disco lights and loud club music at night, making them the cheapest mobile nightlife options around.

The cleaner, newer **Metrobús** (www.metrobus.df.gob.mx) has two lines that cut through the city, with Line 1 running along Avenida Insurgentes, one of the D.F.'s main arteries. These buses travel on an exclusive lane in the middle of the road, with frequent, handicap-accessible stops. There are no *peseros* on this avenue, so this is the only bus service along it. The Metrobús can get crowded during rush hour, but it's consistent and reliable. To use the Metrobús, you'll need to purchase a card, on which you can then add money. Swipe the card at the turnstile at the bus station to get on.

To get beyond the capital city, Mexico has a fabulous bus system that offers luxury first-class service and pretty comfortable second-class service to virtually anywhere in the country. There are four major bus terminals around the city:

Terminal Central del Norte (Northern Terminal)

55-5133-2444

Avenida de los Cien Metros No. 1907

Metro: Line 5 (yellow) metro to Autobuses del Norte

Bus service to northern Mexico, including Guanajuato, Puebla, Oaxaca, Querétaro, San Miguel de Allende, and Veracruz, and to the United States.

Terminal Central del Sur (Southern Terminal)

55-5689-9745

Avenida Tasqueña No. 1320

Metro: Line 2 (blue) to Tasqueña

Also known as Terminal Tasqueña. Bus service to Cuernavaca, Morelos, Puebla, Oaxaca, Taxco, and other destinations.

Terminal Oriente (Eastern Terminal)

55-5542-0400

Calzada Ignacio Zaragoza No. 200

Metro: Line 1 (pink) or B to San Lázaro

Also known as the TAPO. Bus service to Campeche, Cancún, Puebla, Oaxaca, Tlaxcala, and Tabasco, among other destinations.

Terminal Poniente (Western Terminal)

55-5271-0038

Avenida Sur No. 122

Metro: Line 1 (pink) to Observatorio

Bus service to Guerrero, Jalisco, Morelia, Toluca, and Valle de Bravo, among other destinations.

TOURS AND TOUR GUIDES A word about tours in Mexico City: The vast majority of them require patience. Patience, that is, to travel to a prearranged gift shop on the way to your destination, where you will likely sit through a lecture on tequila production, silver smithing, or any number of other trades, and then be given the "opportunity" to buy one of their products. Many customers will hate the hour or more spent on this distraction, along with being forced to eat at designated, prearranged restaurants when they arrive at their destination.

But if you want to take a tour from Mexico City, these are necessary evils. The good news is that, while these earmarked stores are usually pricier than what you'll find in local markets and shops, they generally carry good-quality merchandise. Also, the instructional element of the stop can be insightful (on one tour I learned about the many uses of the maguey plant). And finally, you are never *required* to make a purchase. Of course, tours within the city don't have these side trips.

Much more important is the quality of the tour itself: whether the guide knows what he or she is talking about; whether he or she speaks passable English; and whether the tour itself is comfortable. I've listed these for their reliable service or their niche, themed excursions.

- **City Discovery**, 419-244-6440 (www.city-discovery.com/mexico)—A U.S.-based agency with a variety of affordable tour packages within and around Mexico City.

- **Journeys Beyond the Surface**, 59-5922-0205, 55-1497-9610 (www.travelmexicocity.com.mx) Mojdeh Hojjati offers a departure from the typical tour. She tailors cultural and educational immersions into the city, showing visitors a Mexico City they wouldn't normally see. If you're looking for a cultural experience that takes you from the confines of a tour bus and puts you on the ground, give Mojdeh a call.
- **Olympus Tours**, 55-5684-8921, (www.olympus-tours.com)—The company offers a variety of tours in and around Mexico City, including Teotihuacán.
- **Turibus**, 55-5563-6693, 55-5598-6309 (www.turibus.com.mx), Turibus runs an almost three-hour route to the major sites in Chapultepec, the Centro Histórico, Condesa and Roma in an open-roofed double-decker bus. You can get on and off at any stop throughout the day with your ticket.
- **Wayak**, 55-5518-1726, 800-823-2410 (www.hostelcatedral.com)—A budget option with tours to Teotihuacán, Lucha Libre, and free city walking tours.

MODERN MEXICO CITY

Mexico City is a tapestry of distinct *colonias*, or neighborhoods, sorted into 16 *delegaciones*, or boroughs. It will help you to organize your time and your itinerary so that your destinations lie close to one another.

Mexico City's **Centro Histórico** (Historic Center), is the cradle of the city, the nation, and before that, the empire. It was the ancient Aztec capital of Tenochtitlán, and later, the heart of New Spain. It is, in other words, a city center that has been a thriving, dominant force for over 700 years, and the entire area has been designated a World Cultural Heritage Site by UNESCO. Like most Mexican cities, the Centro Histórico revolves around the **Zócalo**, also known as the Plaza de la Constitución. Here you'll find some of the country's most important and historic landmarks, around what has to be one of the biggest flags you'll ever see.

From the Zócalo to the **Alameda Central**—a large green plaza dotted with fountains, street performers, monuments, and food vendors—exploring the city center can occupy two full days. North of the Alameda along the broad Eje Central Lázaro Cárdenas Norte you'll come to the famous **Plaza Garibaldi**, known for its abundance of mariachis. While its fame is well founded, Garibaldi is seedier and less attractive than it should be, and there are better places to enjoy mariachi music.

Chapultepec and **Polanco** are two of the city's wealthiest and prettiest neighborhoods: the Central Park and Beverly Hills of the D.F. The Bosque de Chapultepec (Chapultepec Forest) is not only the city's largest and greenest area, but also home to world-class museums. Spread over 540 acres, Chapultepec (which means "Grasshopper Hill" in Nahuatl) has a few must-visit cultural highlights, along with a zoo, amusement park, lakes, auditorium, theater district, castle, and a broad avenue dotted with beautiful sculptures. Neighboring Polanco is Mexico City's ritziest neighborhood and its main destination for fine dining, exclusive shopping, and chic nightlife. Its high-end boutique and chain hotels make it a great place to stay, but cultural offerings are slim.

Chapultepec is located about 3 miles west of the Zócalo, a straight shot

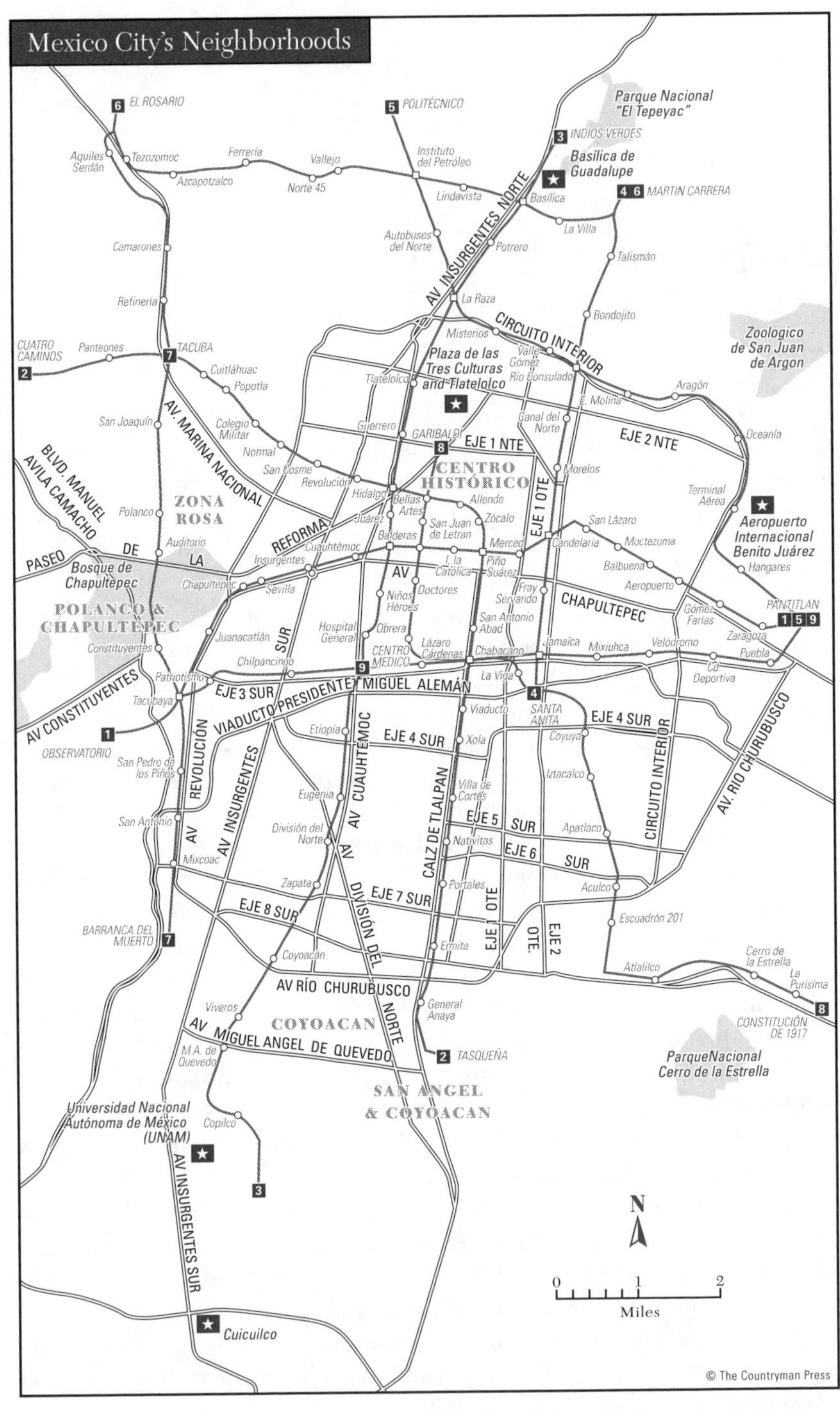
Mexico City's Neighborhoods
CENTRO HISTÓRICO
ZONA ROSA
POLANCO & CHAPULTEPEC
COYOACAN
SAN ANGEL & COYOACAN
Parque Nacional "El Tepeyac"
Basílica de Guadalupe
Plaza de las Tres Culturas and Tlatelolco
Zoologico de San Juan de Argon
Aeropuerto Internacional Benito Juárez
Bosque de Chapultepec
ParqueNacional Cerro de la Estrella
Universidad Nacional Autónoma de México (UNAM)
Cuicuilco
AV INSURGENTES NORTE
CIRCUITO INTERIOR
AV. MARINA NACIONAL
BLVD. MANUEL AVILA CAMACHO
PASEO DE LA REFORMA
EJE 1 NTE
EJE 2 NTE
EJE 1 OTE
CHAPULTEPEC
AV CONSTITUYENTES
EJE 3 SUR
VIADUCTO PRESIDENTE MIGUEL ALEMÁN
EJE 4 SUR
AV REVOLUCIÓN
AV INSURGENTES SUR
AV CUAUHTEMOC
CALZ DE TLALPAN
EJE 5 SUR
EJE 6 SUR
EJE 7 SUR
EJE 8 SUR
EJE 2 OTE.
AV. RIO CHURUBUSCO
AV RÍO CHURUBUSCO
AV DIVISIÓN DEL NORTE
AV MIGUEL ANGEL DE QUEVEDO
AV INSURGENTES SUR
6 EL ROSARIO
5 POLITÉCNICO
3 INDIOS VERDES
4 6 MARTIN CARRERA
2 CUATRO CAMINOS
7 TACUBA
8 GARIBALDI
1 5 9 PANTITLAN
9 CENTRO MEDICO
4 SANTA ANITA
1 OBSERVATORIO
7 BARRANCA DEL MUERTO
8 CONSTITUCIÓN DE 1917
2 TASQUEÑA
3
Aquiles Serdán
Tezozomoc
Azcapotzalco
Ferrería
Vallejo
Norte 45
Instituto del Petróleo
Lindavista
Basílica
La Villa
Autobuses del Norte
Potrero
Talismán
Camarones
Refinería
La Raza
Bondojito
Panteones
Misterios
Valle Gómez
Río Consulado
Cuitláhuac
Popotla
Tlatelolco
E. Molina
Aragón
San Joaquín
Colegio Militar
Normal
Guerrero
Canal del Norte
Oceanía
San Cosme
Revolución
Hidalgo
Morelos
Terminal Aérea
Bellas Artes
Allende
Polanco
Juárez
San Juan de Letran
Zócalo
San Lázaro
Auditorio
Balderas
Merced
Candelaria
Moctezuma
Cuauhtémoc
Insurgentes
I. la Católica
Pino Suárez
Balbuena
Hangares
Chapultepec
Sevilla
Doctores
Niños Héroes
Fray Servando
Aeropuerto
Gómez Farías
Zaragoza
Constituyentes
Juanacatlán
Hospital General
Obrera
San Antonio Abad
Lázaro Cárdenas
Chabacano
Jamaica
Mixiuhca
Velódromo
Puebla
Patriotismo
Chilpancingo
La Viga
Cd. Deportiva
Tacubaya
Viaducto
Etiopía
Xola
Coyuya
San Pedro de los Pinos
Iztacalco
Eugenia
Villa de Cortés
San Antonio
Apatlaco
División del Norte
Nativitas
Mixcoac
Zapata
Portales
Aculco
Escuadrón 201
Ermita
Coyoacán
Atlalilco
Cerro de la Estrella
La Purísima
Viveros
General Anaya
M.A. de Quevedo
Copilco
N
0 1 2
Miles
© The Countryman Press

THE CASTILLO DE CHAPULTEPEC RISES ABOVE CHAPULTEPEC PARK.

down **Paseo de la Reforma**. Once Reforma enters the park, it becomes a broad avenue with a tree-lined walkway in the middle lined with sculptures and statues. Beyond lies Las Lomas, one of Mexico's wealthiest residential neighborhoods.

Modeled after the Champs-Élysées and built by Emperor Maximilian as part of his rampant Europeanization of the city, Paseo de la Reforma is the city's most regal road. Punctuated by some of Mexico City's most iconic statues, fountains, and monuments, Reforma is also home to the tallest building in Latin America, the soaring Torre Mayor; the stock exchange and other finance centers; and top-class hotels and restaurants.

Directly south of Reforma, between the Monumento de la Independencia and Monumento a Cuauhtémoc, lies the **Zona Rosa** (Pink Zone). A once-hip neighborhood, the Zona has seen better days but still offers worthy dining destinations, pedestrian-only promenades, a fun market, and a well-known antiques district; it's also a popular destination for gay locals and tourists, thanks to its hopping alternative nightlife.

The bohemian residential neighborhoods of **Condesa** and **Roma** present a different side of Mexico City. They are home to leafy avenues, plazas, and parks, art deco architecture, pleasant cafés, hip restaurants, art galleries, and an eclectic mix of bars and clubs. Condesa used to be the "in" neighborhood in the city, before Mexico's elite moved on to other pastures, but it still retains its sense of former grandeur, and remains a sought-after part of the city to live in. Roma has a more blue-collar,

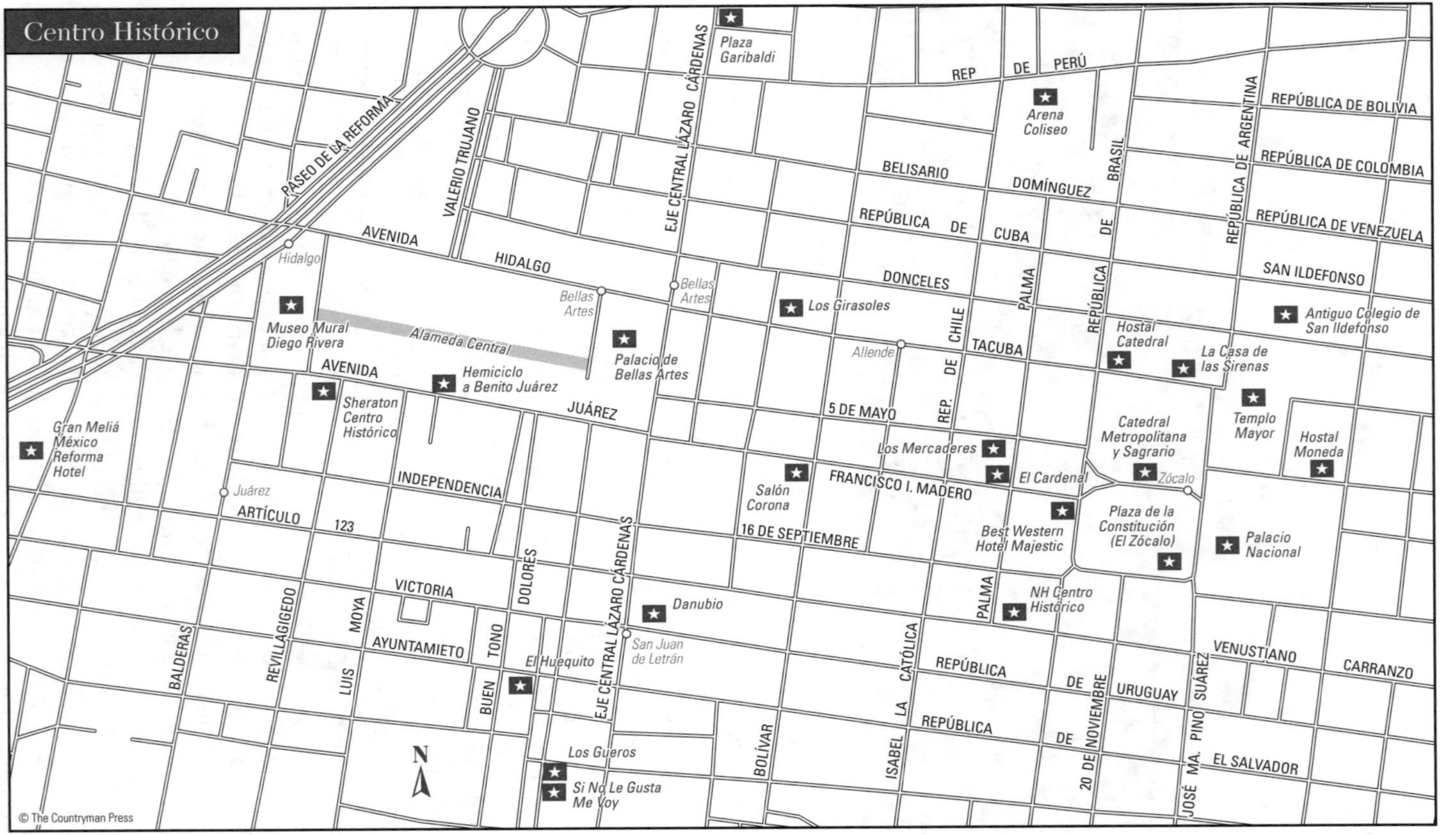

Centro Histórico
Plaza Garibaldi
REP DE PERÚ
Arena Coliseo
REPÚBLICA DE BOLIVIA
REPÚBLICA DE COLOMBIA
REPÚBLICA DE VENEZUELA
REPÚBLICA DE ARGENTINA
SAN ILDEFONSO
Antiguo Colegio de San Ildefonso
PASEO DE LA REFORMA
VALERIO TRUJANO
EJE CENTRAL LÁZARO CÁRDENAS
BELISARIO DOMÍNGUEZ
BRASIL
REPÚBLICA DE CUBA
AVENIDA HIDALGO
DONCELES
Hidalgo
Bellas Artes
Los Girasoles
Museo Mural Diego Rivera
Alameda Central
Palacio de Bellas Artes
Allende
REP. DE CHILE
PALMA
REPÚBLICA DE
TACUBA
Hostal Catedral
La Casa de las Sirenas
AVENIDA JUÁREZ
Hemiciclo a Benito Juárez
Sheraton Centro Histórico
5 DE MAYO
Templo Mayor
Hostal Moneda
Catedral Metropolitana y Sagrario
Gran Meliá México Reforma Hotel
Los Mercaderes
El Cardenal
Zócalo
INDEPENDENCIA
Salón Corona
FRANCISCO I. MADERO
Juárez
ARTÍCULO 123
16 DE SEPTIEMBRE
Best Western Hotel Majestic
Plaza de la Constitución (El Zócalo)
Palacio Nacional
VICTORIA
DOLORES
Danubio
NH Centro Histórico
MOYA
AYUNTAMIETO
TONO
San Juan de Letrán
VENUSTIANO CARRANZO
BALDERAS
REVILLAGIGEDO
LUIS
El Huequito
BUEN
CATÓLICA
REPÚBLICA DE
URUGUAY
SUÁREZ
20 DE NOVIEMBRE
BOLÍVAR
ISABEL LA
REPÚBLICA DE
PINO
Los Gueros
JOSÉ MA.
EL SALVADOR
N
Si No Le Gusta Me Voy
© The Countryman Press

undeveloped character to it. It has lovely hidden pockets and promenades, but also areas that are best avoided at night. Although these neighborhoods don't have the cultural richness of Chapultepec or the Centro Histórico, they offer a laid-back charm and hip social scene.

Dividing Condesa and Roma is **Avenida Insurgentes**, the longest avenue in Mexico and believed to be the longest road in the world. From Condesa, Insurgentes Sur leads to the cobblestone neighborhoods of **San Ángel** and **Coyoacán**. These picturesque neighborhoods well south of the city center have a character all to their own. They are well loved for their colonial-era architecture, cobblestone streets, romantic ambience, and legacy as an artists' haven, and favored by both locals and tourists seeking a more relaxed change of pace. Diego and Frida lived here; so did Leon Trotsky. Sidewalk cafes, fine restaurants, and beautiful plazas abound, and San Ángel, in particular, is also home to a thriving arts-and-crafts community.

THE FOUNTAIN OF DIANA THE HUNTRESS IS ONE OF SEVERAL MONUMENTS LINING REFORMA AVENUE.

There are only two downsides about these neighborhoods: They aren't easily accessible by the metro, and there is a scarcity of hotels. Whichever stop you get off at (Coyoacán or Viveros for Coyoacán, and M.A. Quevedo for San Ángel), be prepared to walk to get where you want to go. *Peseros* can get you closer, but you'll need to tell the driver where you're going. To avoid both, call a *sitio* taxi.

Finally, **Santa Fe** is the city's relatively new business district, located in the western part of the city. Far from the Centro Histórico, Santa Fe is accessible by Paseo de la Reforma and Avenida Constituyentes (the cheapest and best way to get here is to take a bus straight down Paseo de la Reforma). The area's architecture is unique to Mexico. With marvelously unusual, futuristic buildings with marvelously appropriate

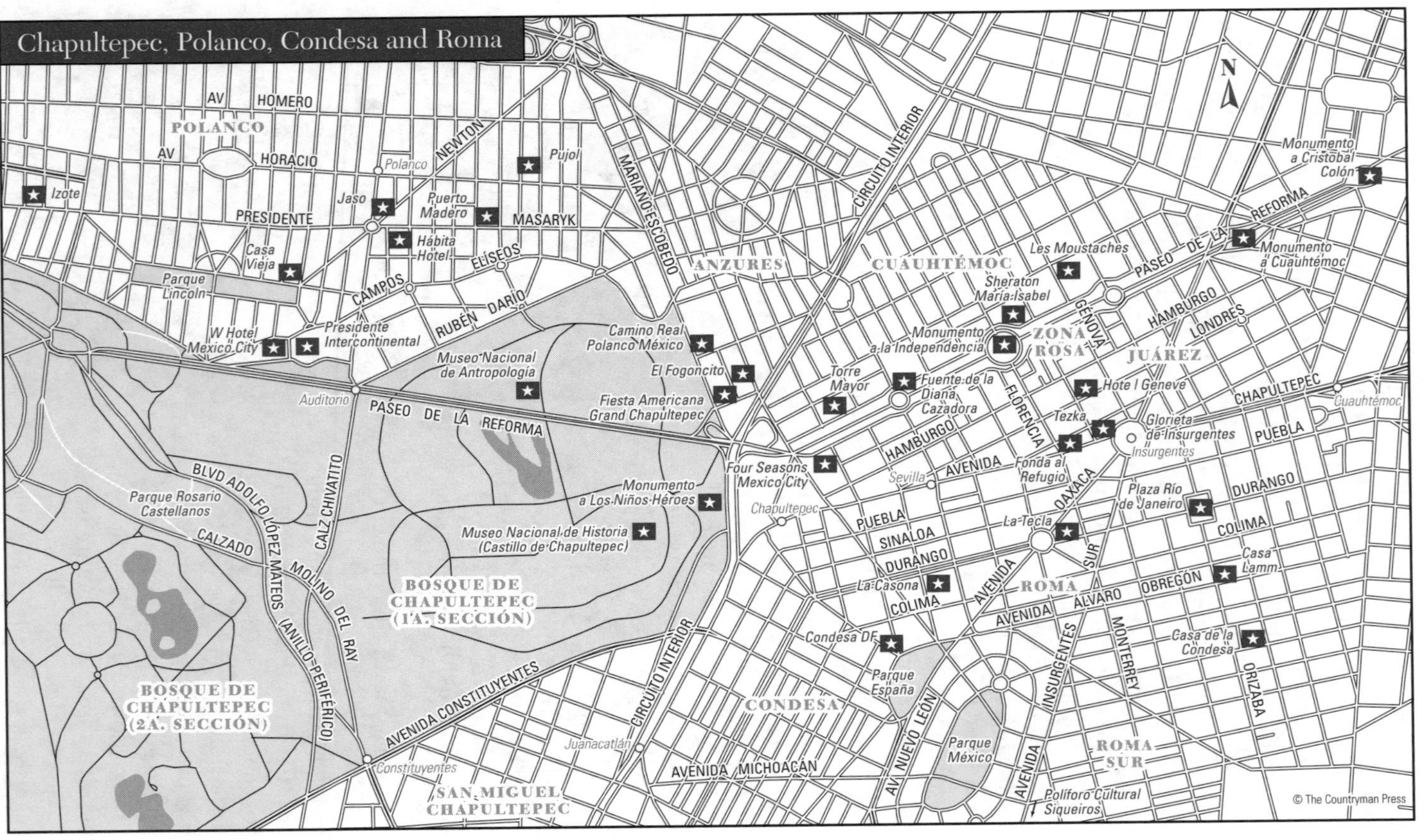

Chapultepec, Polanco, Condesa and Roma
N
AV HOMERO
POLANCO
AV HORACIO
NEWTON
Polanco
Pujol
Izote
Jaso
Puerto Madero
MASARYK
PRESIDENTE
Hábita Hotel
Casa Vieja
ELÍSEOS
Parque Lincoln
CAMPOS
RUBÉN DARÍO
W Hotel Mexico City
Presidente Intercontinental
MARIANO ESCOBEDO
ANZURES
CIRCUITO INTERIOR
CUAUHTÉMOC
Les Moustaches
Sheraton María Isabel
PASEO DE LA REFORMA
Monumento a Cristobal Colón
Monumento a Cuauhtémoc
HAMBURGO
LONDRES
GÉNOVA
ZONA ROSA
JUÁREZ
Monumento a la Independencia
Camino Real Polanco México
El Fogoncito
Fiesta Americana Grand Chapultepec
Museo Nacional de Antropología
Auditorio
PASEO DE LA REFORMA
Torre Mayor
Fuente de la Diana Cazadora
FLORENCIA
Hotel I Geneve
CHAPULTEPEC
Cuauhtémoc
Tezka
Glorieta de Insurgentes
Insurgentes
PUEBLA
HAMBURGO
Four Seasons Mexico City
AVENIDA
Fonda al Refugio
Sevilla
OAXACA
Plaza Río de Janeiro
DURANGO
Monumento a Los Niños Héroes
Chapultepec
PUEBLA
La Tecla
COLIMA
SINALOA
Museo Nacional de Historia (Castillo de Chapultepec)
DURANGO
SUR
Casa Lamm
BLVD ADOLFO LÓPEZ MATEOS (ANILLO PERIFÉRICO)
Parque Rosario Castellanos
CALZ CHIVATITO
CALZADO
MOLINO DEL RAY
BOSQUE DE CHAPULTEPEC (1A. SECCIÓN)
La Casona
COLIMA
AVENIDA
ROMA
ALVARO OBREGÓN
AVENIDA
Condesa DF
Casa de la Condesa
INSURGENTES
MONTERREY
ORIZABA
Parque España
CONDESA
BOSQUE DE CHAPULTEPEC (2A. SECCIÓN)
AVENIDA CONSTITUYENTES
CIRCUITO INTERIOR
Juanacatlán
AV NUEVO LEÓN
Parque México
AVENIDA
ROMA SUR
Constituyentes
AVENIDA MICHOACÁN
SAN MIGUEL CHAPULTEPEC
Políforo Cultural Siqueiros
© The Countryman Press

ARTISTS GATHER TO SELL THEIR WARES AT PLAZA SAN JACINTO.

nicknames (e.g., Torre Pantalón [Trouser Tower] and La Lavendería [The Washing Machine], it's a modern architectural playground. However, there is precious little here of cultural value, and its distance makes it an unappealing destination for casual tourists.

✷ Archaeological Sites

Tenochtitlán. Long ago, the leader of a wandering tribe of nomadic warriors saw a prophetic vision: an eagle perched on a cactus, devouring a snake. Following his people's legends, he and his people settled on an island in the center of a lake. The priest, Tenoch, christened this place Tenochtitlán.

The Aztec capital has been mostly consumed by the conquistadors. What remains of it is mostly located in and around the Centro Histórico, or El Centro, as most people call it. Fortunately, Cortés and his army did not entirely raze Tenochtitlán to the ground. Among the historic center's colonial treasures lie two critical remnants of the mighty Aztec capital: the Templo Mayor and Tlatelolco.

Templo Mayor. The city of Tenochtitlán revolved around a sacred compound where the most impressive structures in the Aztec realm were located. Chief among these was the Templo Mayor, or Huey Teocalli, as the Aztecs called it. This was the political, symbolic, and spiritual center of the Mexica empire. It was here where ritual sacrifices were made to the altars of Tlaloc (the rain god) and Huitzilopochtli (a Sun god and god of

THE REMAINS OF TENOCHTITLÁN, NOW THE TEMPLO MAYOR MUSEUM

war), which crowned the main pyramid (the latter's was the slightly larger of the two shrines). In typical Aztec fashion, the temple was expanded 12 times during seven major phases, with each new layer built over the older one. Construction began in 1325 and continued until it reached close to 200 feet in height at its peak in 1521. Around it, a vast complex of more than 70 buildings included the most prominent institutions of the Aztec empire.

When Cortés arrived, he and his conquistadors were awed by the majesty and artistry of this mighty city. It was at the Templo Mayor where the ill-fated Moctezuma greeted the conquistadors, and it was here where some of the bloodiest battles for domination were waged. After the Spanish victory, it was left to the vanquished Aztecs to destroy their former city and use its remains to build the new one.

Today, the Templo Mayor and its surrounding buildings lie just off the Zócalo, the central plaza of Mexico City and the second largest square in the world, after Moscow's Red Square. A walkway leads you around the ruins before leading to the outstanding museum. Of particular note is the seated figure of Chac-Mool, the messenger of Tlaloc, at the foot of his altar on the Templo Mayor; La Casa de Las Águilas (House of the Eagles), one of the most important and aristocratic buildings in the sacred center; the temple of Quetzalcóatl; the Tzompantli altar, with its 240 stone skulls arrayed in rows; and the Red Temple, known for its fine mural.

THE STONE DISK OF COYOLXAUHQUI, THE DISMEMBERED MOON GODDESS, AT THE TEMPLO MAYOR MUSEUM.

But this is only the first part of the Templo Mayor experience. After touring the ruins, enter the museum, which has an astounding collection of Aztec artifacts that best displays the beauty, complexity, spirituality, and creativity of the empire. The museum has eight halls and between 6,000 and 7,000 immaculately preserved or restored pieces. One of its most important is the massive stone disk depicting the dismembered body of Coyolxauhqui, the moon goddess, which was excavated in 1978 and spurred the major archaeological project to uncover the buried treasures of the Templo Mayor. The stone relief relates the legend of Huitzilopochtli's springing from his mother's womb in full armor and killing his sister, Coyolxauhqui. The war god cut off her limbs and threw her into the sky, where she became the moon.

The Templo Mayor is a place of incredible resonance, history, and symbolism. Although a shadow of its former self, it's a fitting symbol of the enduring Aztec spirit.

TLATELOLCO, WHERE THE LAST BATTLE FOR CONTROL OF THE NEW WORLD WAS FOUGHT

Finally, if you speak Spanish, be sure to check out the Templo Mayor Web site, among the best of any of Mexico's cultural attractions.

Plaza de las Tres Culturas and Tlatelolco. This plaza, several blocks from the Zócalo and a short walk from the Tlatelolco metro, is quintessentially Mexican. It is named for the three cultures represented in this single space: the Aztec ruins of **Tlatelolco**, the 16th-century **Ex-Convento de Santiago Tlatelolco**, and the more contemporary office building and residential complex. Tlatelolco was a twin city to Tenochtitlán and in its heyday boasted a massive, vibrant market that was at its time a wonder of the ancient world, according to the conquistadors. It was also here that the final and decisive battle for the New World was fought, when, on August 13, 1521, the Aztecs led by Cuauhtémoc fell to the hands of the Spanish. Thousands of Aztec warriors were slain in the last resistance to the conquistadors, and a plaque in the plaza commemorates the date as, "neither triumph nor defeat, but the painful birth of the mixed-race nation that is Mexico today."

The ruins of Tlatelolco dominate the plaza and are well organized for visitors, with raised walkways and bilingual plaques describing the temples and structures. Of particular interest is the Templo Calendário, decorated with niches symbolizing the days according to the Mexica calendar; the unusual circular temple to Ehécatl-Quetzalcóatl, where 41 human burials (believed to be part of a petition for rainfall during the drought of 1450–55) were excavated in 1987; and the Templo Mayor, or main temple, which, like Tenochtitlán, boasted two altars to Huitzilopochtli and Tlaloc.

AROUND MEXICO CITY

Beyond Tenochtitlán, this region boasts impressive and beautiful examples of pre-Hispanic Mexico, either within or a short distance away from its borders.

Teotihuacán

GETTING THERE Dozens of tour operators conduct tours to Teotihuacán, which can be arranged from your hotel or by contacting the company directly. These are typically full-day tours combined with another attraction such as the Basílica de Guadalupe. You can also organize a private tour through the **Secretary of Tourism** (800-008-9090). If you're driving, your quickest route is Insurgentes Norte to the Autopista México-Pachuca (Highway 85D, a toll road) out of the city. Buses leave frequently from Mexico City's Terminal Central del Norte for the site (look for the AUTOBUSES SAHAGUN sign). Make sure you get on the bus marked "Los Pirámides" and ask the driver when the last bus returns to the city (usually 6 PM). The site is open daily 9–5.

Mexico Tourism Board

THE MAGNIFICENT ANCIENT CAPITAL OF TEOTIHUACÁN IS AN EASY DAY TRIP FROM MEXICO CITY.

The ancient city of Teotihuacán is one of the most incredible ruins in all of Mexico, a UNESCO World Heritage Site, and deservedly the most popular day trip from of Mexico City. Teotihuacán, which means "Place Where Gods Were Born," was the heart of a mighty empire built by an advanced civilization that vanished into history as mysteriously as it appeared. Who the Teotihuacanos were and where they came from remains a mystery. But what they left behind was indelible evidence of their glory.

Although the area was first populated circa 500 BC, it is only around 100 BC that Teotihuacán began to take shape. It became a major center of commerce and trade, as well as a religious and spiritual capital, and its influence spread throughout Mexico. In addition to their skill as builders and craftsmen, the Teotihuacanos were proficient astrologers and scientists. By AD 600, the city had grown to be the sixth largest in the world. Just 150 years later, it was abandoned. Many believe its downfall was due to a combination of overpopulation, a growing lack of resources and water, destruction from within, and invasion from the outside. It was the Aztecs, arriving on the scene 500 years later, who gave the city and its principal structures their name. Like them, we remain in awe of Teotihuacán.

The city is remarkable for the size of its monuments (which altogether cover roughly 12 square miles) and its precise geometric layout. When you visit, be sure to take comfortable shoes, a hat, sunblock, sunglasses, and plenty of water (although this is available on site). You should also be prepared for a hike up the steep steps of the main pyramids; and finally, expect to be blown away.

Your first stop should be the **Visitors Center,** located at the southwest entrance to the ruins. Here you'll find an excellent museum that offers a great visual overview of the city, a restaurant, and restrooms.

Directly across from the Visitors Center is **La Ciudadela** (The Citadel), a massive walled square that houses the **Templo de Quetzalcóatl** (Temple of the Feathered Serpent). This is the most beautiful, though not nearly the largest, of Teotihuacán's structures. It is famed for the ornate carvings of stone serpent heads and reliefs of Tlaloc, the rain god, jutting out along one side (the sculptures along the other three sides were destroyed long ago). The detailed work, and the large number of human remains found buried here by archaeologists, attest to the temple's importance as a ceremonial center.

Calzada de los Muertos. The broad road stretching from the northern to southern ends of the city is called the "Avenue of the Dead," something of a misnomer by the Aztecs, who believed the mounds along each side were tombs. As you walk along this road, with the Temple of the Sun looming on the right and the Temple of the Moon in the distance, you'll pass several smaller structures believed to be residences and other temples.

Pirámide del Sol. The stepped Pyramid of the Sun is an awe-inspiring structure that dominates the landscape of Teotihuacán. Believed to be the third-largest pyramid in the world, it is over 700 feet wide and more than 200 feet high. During the era of the Teotihuacanos, there was a temple atop the pyramid, and it was painted red. A climb to its peak is highly recommended, and although the 250-plus steps are quite steep, the view from the top is worth it. For a slightly surreal experience, visit on the days of the winter and summer solstices, when pilgrims dressed in white scale the pyramid and stretch out their arms to receive its heightened energies.

Pirámide del la Luna. At the north end of the Avenue of the Dead stands the Pyramid of the Moon. The second-largest pyramid in the city, it offers incredible views of the Calzada de los Muertos stretched out before you. In the plaza at its base are several other important buildings, including the brightly colored Palace of Quetzalpapalotl (Quetzal-Butterfly), a mythical bird-butterfly hybrid that's painted on the walls, and the Palace of the Jaguars, where you can see a mural of jaguars.

The Ruins of Tula

GETTING THERE Tula is located 50 miles north of Mexico City in the state of Hidalgo. By car, take the Circuito Interior to Avenida Ejército Nacional Mexicano, which becomes Boulevard Manuel Avila Camacho. This road turns into the Autopista México-Querétaro (Highway 57D). Continue on this road until you come to México 126, which takes you into town. Follow the signs for Las Ruinas (The Ruins) to get to Tula. By bus, head to the Terminal del Norte and catch an Ovnibus, run by Autotransportes Valle de Mezquital (55-5567-6791, www.gvm.com.mx). These comfortable coaches make trips every half hour from 6:20 AM to 9:15 PM daily.

The legendary Toltec capital of Tula (originally Tollan) was founded around the 10th century by a high priest of the cult of Quetzalcóatl (according to legend, Quetzalcóatl himself). Although it would never reach the height of Teotihuacán, Tula was still the major capital of its era, boasting roughly 50,000 inhabitants at its zenith. It was an advanced society that knew how to build dams and canals, and spawned great artisans who worked especially with obsidian. The Toltec also played a critical role in the development of central Mexico. Many believe they were the first truly militaristic society, one that used its armies to subjugate nearby tribes. In this sense, the Toltec were the forerunners of the Aztecs.

Tula suffered a similar fate to Teotihuacán, in that it experienced a rather sudden and very final demise. However, its reign was much shorter.

Evidence points to a great fire and destruction of the city in the 12th century, and it was eventually sacked by rival tribes.

Today, its remains comprise a cluster of restored and reconstructed temples, buildings, ball courts, and four mighty statues that have made the ruins famous: *Los Atlantes* (The Atlanteans). Still, as you walk along a cactus-lined boulevard to the main plaza, you can almost imagine the metropolis that once stood here, a city of plazas and pyramids, canals and bridges, and beautiful sculptures. The site is open daily 9–5.

Jorge R. Acosta Museum. This small museum at the entrance explains the history of Tula and depicts how it must have looked in its heyday. It has a minor collection of artifacts from the site, as well as books and leaflets about the Toltec. You can hire a guide here to take you around.

El Coatepantli. A protected "Wall of Snakes," El Coatepantli is one of the most intricate carvings at Tula, and the prototype of the designs found in Aztec cities later on. The reliefs show numerous animals and human skeletons being devoured by giant rattlesnakes.

Juego de Pelota 1. One of two ball courts to be excavated in Tula, this one still has traces of the original carving in the southwest corner. Archaeologists found the remains of a warrior dressed in garments symbolic of Tlaloc, the rain god, at this site.

Pyramid B, also known as the **Pyramid of the Morning Star**, is the most famous of all of Tula's monuments. Adorned with carvings of eagles, jaguars, coyotes, and pumas, it is far more known for the four massive, solemn warrior statues standing sentry on its peak. *Los Atlantes* measure over 16 feet in height, were used to hold up the roof of a sacred temple that once stood here, and were not visible to the public. They are majestic sights, but unfortunately, three of the four are replicas; the originals were taken down due to overexposure to the elements. From the top of this pyramid you'll have a great view of the adjacent ruin, notable for its ordered rows of broken columns, called **The Burnt Palace**, which was damaged by invading tribes (probably the Aztecs).

Pirámide C. While its neighbor gets all the attention, Pyramid C is believed to be the most important religious structure in Tula. It was constructed in similar fashion to the great pyramids of Teotihuacán, showing the linkage between the two societies.

Juego de Pelota 2. This ball court is very similar in design to the one in Chichén Itzá. The platform in front of the court was known as the Tzompantli. It was here where the skulls of the decapitated were placed.

Xochimilco

GETTING THERE The most direct way to get here is by taxi. If you're driving, hop on the Anillo Periférico highway to Prolongación División del

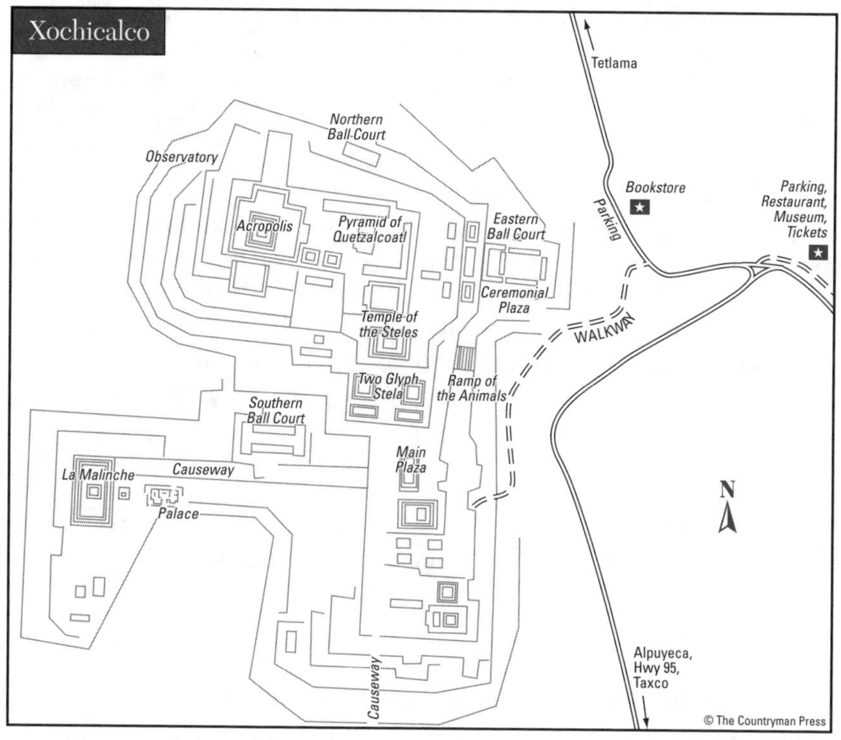

Norte, which will take you into the city center and the piers. However, public transportation is by far the cheapest and often quickest option. Take the Metro line 2 to Tasqueña, and then board the *tren lígero* to Xochimilco.

Xochimilco (which means "Place of the Flower Beds" in Nahuatl), is a borough of Mexico City located to the south, where a wonder of ancient technology can transport you back in time to the era of the Aztecs. This area, designated a UNESCO World Heritage Site, is famed for its network of canals that wind through floating artificial islands called *chinampas*. These were creative solutions devised by a migrant tribe called the Xochimilcas, who lived here between the 10th and 14th centuries. The *chinampas* were constructions of reed, soil, and wood that helped the natives farm the earth of Lake Xochimilco. The project was so successful that, before long, a vast network of islands covered the lake, forming canals between them. It is through these canals that you can journey today, the last remnants of what the lakeside towns of ancient Mexico once looked like.

I've heard the floating islands of Xochimilco often referred to as the "Venice of Mexico." Insofar as you get to climb aboard a boat and be punted along canals, I agree. But I still find the comparison inaccurate. That's no knock on Venice; it's a beautiful city. Xochimilco, on the other hand, is a marvel of ancient engineering and a living chronicle of pre-Hispanic life.

It's also tremendous fun to board one of the brightly colored *trajineras*, or boats, (you can join as part of a group or reserve one for yourself) and let the boatmen shunt you around. As you enjoy the ride and the greenery around you, other boats will pull up alongside with vendors selling delicious food (enchiladas, moles, and other standard fare) and with mariachi bands ready to play for a nominal tip. To really enjoy the tranquility of your surroundings, go during the week.

Xochicalco

GETTING THERE Xochicalco is located about 76 miles from Mexico City, just off Highway 95 toward Acapulco. Open daily 9–5, observatory 10–5. $.

TRAJINERAS STAND READY TO GIVE YOU A TOUR OF XOCHIMILCO.

XOCHICALCO ROSE TO POWER AFTER THE FALL OF TEOTIHUACÁN.

The sprawling ruins of Xochicalco are one of the wonders of Mexico. Xochicalco ("House of Flowers" in Nahuatl) was a vast, walled city-state from AD 700 to 900. Interestingly, its rise to power occurred right after the fall of Teotihuacán and just before the ascent of Tula. As with other ancient strongholds, historians aren't completely sure why Xochicalco fell, but the prevailing theory is that it was destroyed from within.

Built on a series of adjacent hilltops, the city must have been an astounding sight during its zenith, but it is both formidable and fascinating even now—and that's with only about 15 percent of the ruins excavated. Visiting Xochicalco requires a full day, and you can opt to drive there yourself or take a tour. The tour will provide a lot more information, although the ruins themselves have plaques explaining the main structures.

Begin your day with a trip to the Museo de Sitio de Xochicalco. This solar-powered building is a pioneer of eco-technology, employing natural refrigeration and heating, and offers panoramic views of the ancient city. Every night at 7 PM from May to October, this is the place to catch Xochicalco's light and sound spectacle. The museum houses relics and artifacts excavated from the city, with beautifully preserved pieces highlighting the exhibits. Chief among these is the *Señor de Rojo* (Red Man), a powerfully symbolic sculpture bathed in vermillion to give it its distinctive red hue.

After, drive or walk to the entrance of the site and enjoy the steep walk up to its main buildings. The vastness of the ceremonial center will give you an idea of the city's former splendor. The most notable and intricate structure here is the Pirámide de la Serpiente Emplumada (Pyramid of the Feathered Serpent), where you'll find carvings and reliefs of twisting serpents, the symbol of Quetzalcóatl. The temple was reconstructed in 1909 by Don Leopoldo Batres. Nearby, keep your eyes on the floor for the "Animal Ramp." A marvel in its time, this stone pathway to the main plaza was carved with animal reliefs.

The other treasure of this city lies beneath the surface: The ancient observatory. Xochicalco was a religious and economic powerhouse (it controlled the obsidian trade throughout Mexico), but it was also an important astronomical center. In AD 743, the first pre-Hispanic astronomical congress was held here, with scientists from all over Mesoamerica attending. (The gathering is chronicled in reliefs on the walls of the Pyramid of the Feathered Serpent.) It was here that, after a total eclipse, all Mesoamerican calendars synchronized.

Today, the practices of the ancients are preserved, thanks to a pre-Hispanic solar observatory still used to track the motion of the sun. A trip to this underground chamber is a must if you're visiting from the end of April to August 15, when you'll see a beam of sunlight shining through a rough-hewn opening, with a (modern-day) expert on hand to plot its course. During the equinox, when the sun is at its zenith, the entire chamber is brilliantly lit.

✷ Lodging

The Centro Histórico has plenty of budget-friendly options, starting with its youth hostels. **Hostal Moneda** is a perennial favorite with backpackers and budget travelers. It can house you for as little as $10 if you're willing to share, and for not much more if you want a private room (rates include breakfast and Internet access). Throw in a great location a block away from the Zócalo, the terrace bar, a tour company on premises, and cheap airport pickup service, among other amenities, and it's easy to see why this hostel stays busy.

At **Hostel Catedral**, lodging starts at prices cheaper than lunch at many restaurants, if you don't mind a bunk bed, and costs not much more for a private room. Amenities include an on-site cybercafé, a rooftop bar with awesome views of the Centro Histórico, breakfast included, free daily walking tours, and a host of activities from poker nights to movie nights. There's an on-site, cheap, and reliable tour company. And its location right behind the cathedral is ideal.

For value hotels in the Centro, the **Best Western Hotel Majestic** has an enviable location right on the Zócalo, equally enviable setting in a seven-story colonial building, and a rooftop restaurant with terrific views. I wish the rooms carried through some of the grandeur of the ornate baroque-style lobby, but for the price they're not a bad deal, and children under age 12 stay for free. Nearby, the **Holiday Inn Zócalo**, located in a colonial building next to the Zócalo, offers affordable accommodations in minimal but clean and well-kept style (the old-fashioned photos of the city in the rooms are a nice touch). The suites are a bargain, given the extra space and large bathrooms. The hotel also has meeting and business facilities, a rooftop restaurant with lovely views, a sauna, and—a highly convenient feature—on-site washers and dryers for guest use.

One of my favorite choices in the Centro is the **NH Centro Histórico**. Located just a block away from the Zócalo, its minimalist Asian-themed contemporary décor is unpretentious and comfortable. Amenities include a business center, meeting rooms, a gym, and a restaurant with daily buffet breakfast. You'll be hard-pressed to find better lodgings in a more central location at these prices.

On the other end of the budget, the **Sheraton Centro Histórico**, boasting prime location off the Alameda Central and five-star status, is the city center's most exclusive address. A tall, sleek tower, the beautiful lobby has an ample reception area, excellent Mexican restaurant and funky bar. The hotel's 457 rooms and suites are furnished in a modern style and come with a kitchenette, flat-screen TV, and work desk, among other amenities, although the charge for high-speed Internet is a little grating (you'll find this fee applies at several of Mexico's finer hotels, however). The hotel is particularly popular with business travelers, thanks to its plush business center, fully equipped gym and meeting space; it's also the only hotel in the city with an in-house convention center. There's even a heliport for the executive types.

Polanco is home to some of the city's best hotels. Named for the Royal Road that connected six missions in present-day California, the **Camino Real Polanco México** is a contemporary, eye-catching property located on the border of

THE HOLIDAY INN, CENTRO HISTÓRICO

the Chapultepec Park. The hotel is a celebration of Mexican art and style, and presents a bold face to the visitor, with a funky swirling and sloshing fountain outside the ultramodern red, white, and yellow building. The lobby is a sleek and stylish multilevel space headlined by a Rufino Tamayo mural. The rooms, from single bedrooms to two-floor suites, are spacious and continue the hotel's bright color palette and modern décor. Public spaces include a large open-air pool, two funky lounges, and a range of restaurants that have little to do with its Mexican roots but offer world-famous names: Le Cirque and the China Grill.

The **Fiesta Americana Grand Chapultepec**, the flagship property of the Fiesta Americana chain, is a tall glass and steel tower that rises above Chapultepec Park. Distinctive for its round turret and fantastic views of the forest and Chapultepec Castle, it caters especially to business professionals but is a top-class choice for any traveler. The hotel has a full service spa and fitness center, and some rooms even come with an exercise bike. Rooms and suites are tastefully decorated, with plenty of space to spread out. If you can swing it, the Grand Club rooms offer panoramic views, access to a private lounge with complimentary daily American breakfast, nightly snacks and non-alcoholic drinks, and butler service.

Among Mexico City's more luxurious small hotels, **Casa Vieja** is indeed an "Old House," located on a quiet, leafy street in Polanco. A visit here is an immersion into Mexican art and folklore. The handsome, ivy-draped 19th-century

THE ROOFTOP POOL DECK IS ONE OF THE COOLEST SPOTS AT HÁBITA HOTEL.

mansion has just ten suites, each inspired by a Mexican artist (except for Lola, named for the founder of Casa Vieja). The rooms are all painted in bright colors and come with plush beds and full kitchen with bar stool and counter. However, it is one of the pricier lodging options around, even in posh Polanco.

Sticking to luxury boutique, **Hábita Hotel** is one of the hippest addresses in Mexico City. The definition of minimalist chic, it's a deceptively simple and luxurious hotel. You could walk by without ever noticing it, and even the lobby is almost nonexistent, as the restaurant takes up most of the ground floor. The rooms are large and aesthetically bare, but the effect works with the hotel's theme. Of course, amenities such as flat-screen TVs, DVD players, direct high-speed Internet dataports, low-to-the-ground beds with plush mattresses, and stylish bathrooms help. The 36 rooms and suites make this a small, intimate oasis of cool in the heart of Polanco. The rooftop has a small gym next to a secluded Jacuzzi tub; a small but artfully designed open-air heated pool along one edge, with comfy chaise longues for sunbathers; and a cool lounge.

Polanco has a luxury hotel row along Campos Elíseos. My favorites here are the **Presidente Intercontinental** and the **W Hotel Mexico City**. The large and impressive Intercontinental offers guests well-appointed accommodations (the suites are an opulent upgrade), and a range of world-class dining, including French and Chinese fine dining restaurants that rank among the city's best. The large, split-level lobby is practically a destination unto itself, with a piano bar, British Tea Room, travel agent, tour company, ATM, florist, and newsstand, among other services.

The W Hotel Mexico City was the first W in Latin America, and continues the brand's ultra-hip, ultra-stylish philosophy. The 237-room hotel splurges on its guests as much as they need to splurge to afford a room here. The rooms follow the latest contemporary fashion, with custom-built iPod docking stations, multijet showers (many with large soaking tubs), separate workspace, and in-room hammocks. The W has two very happening lounges, a nightclub on the terrace, a superb restaurant (Solea) and one of the best spas in Mexico City. All in all, it's one of the most polished and trendy addresses in the city.

In hip Condesa, three hotels stand out. The **Condesa DF** is among my favorite hotels in the city. The vintage car parked outside the stately mansion at the corner of a leafy park in a quiet cul de sac disguises the splashy modern interior. Then you walk in and notice the aquamarine-colored walls, contemporary furnishings, and the fashion-forward clientele, and you'll realize why this place gets so much well-deserved hype. Set around a triangular atrium, the 40 rooms (16 of them suites with patios) aren't overly spacious, but they are stylish, with iPod docks, flat-screen TVs, plush beds, wooden screens, and contemporary furnishings. The hotel also has an excellent eclectic restaurant (with breakfast included), a relaxed rooftop bar, steam room, and hot tub.

A soft pink 19th-century mansion, **La Casona** exudes old-fashioned charm. Each of the 29 rooms is unique and tastefully decorated. Many have warm floral patterns, and the writing desk in the corner is a welcome perk for a writer.

LA CASONA, A BOUTIQUE PROPERTY IN A 19TH-CENTURY MANSION

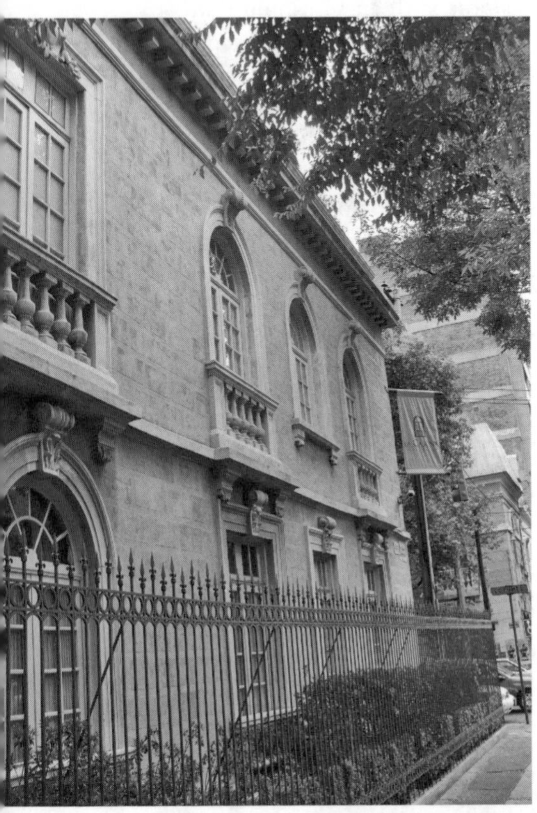

Casa de la Condesa offers bargain lodging for those in town for an extended stay. The furnished apartments include a fully equipped kitchen, separate bedroom and living areas; amenities include laundry service, daily housekeeping, and 24-hour concierge.

Finally, Paseo de la Reforma offers numerous options in a central location. Sitting atop the pack as Mexico City's top-ranked hotel is the **Four Seasons Mexico**. Its understated, almost hidden façade and neoclassical European architecture are designed to blend in with the style and elegance of Reforma's original design. In fact, this building was built specifically to be a Four Seasons hotel in 1994. It's the only AAA 5-Diamond rated hotel in the city, and it's been given the distinction for 13 years running. Most of the tastefully decorated rooms face the handsome courtyard and have luxury amenities, including LCD flat-screen TVs, bathrooms with bathtub and separate shower, and L'Occitane bath products. The hotel's celebrity and VIP guests can enjoy a private elevator directly from the garage to the eighth floor, to the hotel's executive suites. And the grand Presidential Suite has a royally furnished parlor that by itself comprises three guest rooms.

The **Embassy Suites Mexico City–Reforma**, located in an elegant glass tower steps from the Monumento a Cristobal Colón, offers all-suite comfort and room to spread out. Each suite has smart, contemporary furnishing with a separate bedroom, 32-inch flat-screen TV, high-speed Internet access, Italian bed linens, and bathrooms outfitted with marble accents. Guests also receive a complimentary gourmet breakfast and a manager's reception every evening.

The **Gran Meliá Mexico Reforma Hotel** occupies a commanding spot just a block after Reforma leaves the Alameda Central. An AAA 4-diamond hotel, it has close to 500 rooms furnished in a sophisticated European style. One of the better spas in the city, it includes a gym and an indoor heated pool enclosed in a solarium.

A more affordable option is the **Sheraton María Isabel**, which offers inviting and spacious rooms, prime location, and **Bar Jorongo**, one of the best places to see mariachis in the city. The hotel sports a fully equipped business center, outdoor heated pool, small but well-stocked fitness center, and tennis courts. The staff is excellent and the *USA Times*, a brief compilation of the world's newswires delivered daily to your door, is a nice service.

Finally, **Hotel Geneve** is a venerable stalwart in the heart of the Zona Rosa. The place has the look of an old European luxury property, and the fabulous library, complete with rolling ladders, chandelier, and portraits, is my favorite spot in the hotel. The rooms aren't quite as glamorous, but they have detailed wood furniture from the same era and include wireless Internet, cable TV, in-room safe, and mini bar. The Geneve has plenty of character and charm at a great price.

THE GRAN MELIÁ MEXICO REFORMA HOTEL COMMANDS AN EXCELLENT LOCATION ON REFORMA AVENUE.

✱ Dining

From its taco stands to its gourmet Mexican dining, I simply love dining in the D.F. In the Centro Histórico, one of the best bets near the Zócalo is **La Casa de las Sirenas** (House of the Mermaids), which offers a hard-to-beat combination of location, setting, ambience, and excellent cuisine. Occupying a three-story colonial mansion, the restaurant is divided into three distinct spaces: the ground floor tequila saloon (which stocks over 200 varieties of the spirit), a second level bar and indoor dining hall, and an open terrace on the third floor overlooking the back of the cathedral. On a sunny day, this is one of the best places in the city center for a respite from active sightseeing.

MOLE AND *MOLCAJETE* AT CASA DE LAS SIRENAS

Try their delicious *molcajete,* a combination of meat, white cheese, and *nopales* served in a stone bowl for which the dish is named; and their tortillas, pounded in constant supply by a lady in the corner tortilla stand. If you want a lighter meal, go for the *ensalada hortaliza* salad made with goat cheese, lettuce, spinach, avocado, and basil.

For seafood, **Danubio** is a terrific choice, equally popular with tourists, business professionals, and politicians. Check out the many framed autographs and personal messages from celebrity clients over the years, including former president Vicente Fox, author Carlos Fuentes, and my personal favorite, Gabriel García Márquez. Danubio's old-fashioned, well-heeled charm is carried through by the formal and courteous staff. For a light meal, try the excellent *sopa verde con mariscos,* a savory *peregil* (similar to cilantro)-infused soup brimming with chunks of haddock, shrimp, and clams. Their grilled crayfish (*langostinos*), lobster Thermidor, and fish dishes are all highly recommended.

El Cardenal has long been considered one of the best restaurants in the Centro, with a menu that celebrates the full range of Mexican regional specialties. If you want something typical, try the much-loved *gusanos de maguey* (fried cactus worms) wrapped in cheese, the *caldo Xóchitl* (a broth made with shredded chicken, rice, chiles, avocado, and tortilla strips), or *escamoles* (ant eggs). If they're in season, the *chiles en Nogada* (a Puebla specialty made with chiles stuffed with a mix of pork, beef, olive, almonds and raisins) is a must-try. There is another branch of the restaurant in the lobby of the Sheraton Centro Histórico.

For an authentic pre-Hispanic dining experience, head straight to **La Fonda de Don Chon**, the city's most well-known Aztec restaurant. For all its fame (or perhaps notoriety), it's an unpretentious place where you can dine on such delicacies as *gusanos de maguey*, fried grasshopper, roast armadillo, and venison.

Los Girasoles, a large, convivial restaurant overlooking Plaza Manuel Tolsá, has flavorful cuisine and innovative specials. The menu celebrates classic dishes from every region, and throws in a few nouveau Mexican creations such as duck tacos, tamarind mole, and chicken breast stuffed with plantain and rice. Even the tortilla chips served tableside are a cut above the norm.

Another favorite spot is **Los Mercaderes**, a modern Mexican bistro serving classically Mexican cuisine. Its gourmet breakfasts are a must to start your day if you're staying in the area. The *sopa de médula* (marrow soup), a tomato-infused broth with *flor de calabaza* and *nopales,* is a tasty introduction to the menu, and the selection of filets and duck cooked in a pear chipotle sauce are terrific. Vegetarians should pounce on the *chile hojaldrado,* a house specialty of chile poblano stuffed with goat cheese and nuts.

Polanco has so many terrific restaurants that I highly recommend a trip to this neighborhood just for the food. I'll start with my three favorite restaurants. As long as the supremely talented Patricia Quintana is cooking at **Izote**, it will stand as one of the most acclaimed restaurants in the city. Her approach is a mix of passion, tremendous knowledge of her country's culinary roots, personal philosophy, and deep respect for the soul of Mexican cooking. The two-page menu, plus added daily specials, is thoughtfully composed and worthy of your three-course attention. Start with the excellent tamale tasting plate, and follow up with the *mole de Oaxaca* with duck or, if it's on the menu, the smoky, cocoa-crusted steak with a hibiscus mole. For a top-flight restaurant, prices are remarkably affordable.

ENRIQUE OLIVERA LEADS THE VANGUARD OF MODERN MEXICAN CUISINE.

Enrique Olivera

Pujol is a transcending experience. The creation of chef Enrique Olivera—one of the boldest and most creative culinary minds in the country—the restaurant is an exercise in *cocina del autor*, or author's cuisine. The food at Pujol is pure Mexican with an element of whimsy and inspiration from its author. It keeps changing, according to season, ingredient, and the chef's design, which makes the tasting menu here a spur-of-the-moment culinary voyage. I began mine with a rich, out-of-the-box, "cappuccino" of *flor de calabaza* with coconut milk foam. From there, I continued with *chapulines* (grasshoppers) fried in lemon, butter and salt, served with tortillas, guacamole, and radish; a succulent local trout prepared with wild mushrooms, chile pasilla, and baby *elote* (corn) in a roasted onion sauce; and a deconstructed lime pie made with a meringue that took 24 hours to perfect. In short: Mexican cuisine at its most refined.

Rounding out my top three is **Jaso**, a sleek bistro nestled in a quiet street and barely visible from the road. The menu is eclectic, focusing on a rich balance of flavor, and prepared with *sous-vide*, foams, and other cutting-edge techniques. Chef Jared puts forth some brilliantly unorthodox flavor combinations such as *garra de león* (lion's mane), or scallops arranged around a cauliflower purée; chicken breast cooked in milk curd with a sweet pea ravioli, black truffle butter and manchego cheese; or the cooked-to-perfection salmon in eel sauce and broccoli purée. With over 500 labels of wine, an outstanding and knowledgeable staff, and a modern, chic décor, Jaso never disappoints.

Mexico City is full of Argentinean steakhouses, but my favorite has to be **Puerto Madero**. Located in a stately two-story space, the restaurant is revered for its steaks, large sides (including an interesting take on French fries), and tempting seafood items (try the salmon or the octopus). This neighborhood is also home to one of the best Chinese restaurants I know. **Zhen Shanghai**, at the Presidente Intercontinental, delivers flawlessly executed, flavorful and authentic Cantonese cuisine. Four different chefs man the steam, wok, dim sum, and barbecue stations. The star of the menu is the Peking duck, served two ways: prepared tableside (a chef was brought in from China to teach the staff exactly how to slice the skin), with the skin served in crepes, and folded into lettuce wraps. The plump jumbo shrimp with fresh vegetables is another fine choice.

For a more affordable meal in Polanco, **El Bajío** is an excellent option. The colorful and homey restaurant is an offshoot of the original in the northern part of the city, where Chef Carmen Ramírez, known as "Titita," has achieved legendary fame. This branch is a modern space with an open kitchen, dominated by Mexican décor that includes a wall of handwoven bowls. The menu is Mexican home cooking, with tacos, tostadas, gorditas, quesadillas, an excellent variety of soups, and other typical fare. Two bestsellers are the pork and *chicharrón* (fried pork skin) meatballs, and Titita's fine mole with chicken.

The Condesa and Roma neighborhoods are home to numerous bistros. Among the most sophisticated is **Casa Lamm** in Colonia Roma. Housed in the Casa Lamm Cultural Center, a 1911 mansion, the restaurant is set off in a modern, high-ceilinged, open-air space with glass walls, on a wooden deck built over a shallow pool of water. The overall effect is quite incongruous from the rest of the mansion, but also quite pleasant. The menu is international with Mexican flavors thrown in.

Ligaya is my favorite restaurant in the Condesa, in part because of the ambience. The former house of owner Gonzalo Serrano's family, the restaurant retains its charm and intimate atmosphere; it has purposely been left as it was to give the semblance of a home (there's even a working doorbell outside), with a dedicated kids' room on weekends. At the same time, the décor is done in a chic style, with grass carpeting the main dining room, plenty of greenery inside and on the terrace, and frequent art expositions. All this good taste translates to the eclectic menu, which has strong Mexican influences. Try the crunchy and tasty tostada with avocado and tuna, and red snapper cooked in an orange butter sauce. To finish off your meal, go for their trademark Milky Way cake.

Contramar is a popular neighborhood spot that attracts fans from all over the city. The open kitchen, thatched roof, and handwoven basket lamps give it an informal, down-home vibe, and seafood is its star. The restaurant keeps limited hours, and it's common to find lines outside for a chance to enjoy the excellent *pescado a la talla* (a delicious whole grilled fish dish), *mejillones al chipotle* (mussels in chipotle sauce) or fresh peel-and-eat shrimp.

Among my favorite restaurants in Roma, **La Tecla** specializes in *alta cocina Mexicana,* or refined Mexican cuisine. It's an unpretentious spot with rustic décor, friendly service, and above all, great food. Start your meal with a bowl of *flor de calabaza* soup with *elote, rajas,* and mushrooms, and move on to their signature steak with Roquefort and *cuitlacoche.* For dessert, a popular classic is the crepes with *cajeta* (caramel) and nuts.

In Paseo de la Reforma and Zona Rosa, **Fonda el Refugio** is a tourist favorite dedicated to traditional Mexican cuisine. The free guacamole and handmade tortillas are just the beginning of the goodies at the Fonda. From *gusanos de* *maguey* to *escamoles,* you'll find exotic Mexican delicacies as well as seasonal dishes such as *chiles en nogada* and *romeritos* (an omelet made with the herb *romerito* and dried shrimp, a classic Christmas meal). Less adventurous palates will enjoy the moles, enchiladas, and other popular fare.

Set in an elegant white mansion, **Les Moustaches** ranks among the best French restaurants in the city. You'll find a few Mexican twists to the predominantly French menu, such as abalone in a chipotle cream sauce. But purists will prefer the *escargot provençal,* foie gras, and French onion soup. Other favorites include the salt-crusted rack of lamb, *sole Veronique* (baked in hollandaise sauce with skinned grapes), or duck in Dubonnet sauce. The service is outstanding, among the best in the city.

LES MOUSTACHES OFFERS CLASSIC FRENCH FINE DINING.

Tezka, founded in 1994 by famed Michelin three-star chef Juan Mari Arzak, celebrates the culinary traditions of Spain's Basque Country with creative and artistic cuisine. The menu blends in Mexican touches and changes frequently. If they have it, opt for the homemade duck ham salad and *atún ajillo y sandía,* a fillet of tuna molded into a tower, served with a square cake of what you'll swear is watermelon, but is actually potato. As a final touch, the tower is filled with a light watermelon dressing. There's a reason Tezka has won the Five-Star Diamond award seven years in a row.

San Ángel and Coyoacán are home to fine neighborhood eateries. **Capicua** is a lively tapas bar and restaurant where the ambience, cuisine, and superlative staff combine to make it an excellent choice in San Ángel. The tapas range from traditional Spanish—Serrano ham (true pork connoisseurs will be delighted to learn that Capicua has true Iberian ham, made from free-range, semiwild, acorn-fed pigs), *octopus a la Gallega,* and *morcilla,* or blood sausage—to creative Mexican and fusion, such as *arrachera* steak with beans and chiles on toast and tuna tartare with avocado served on tostadas.

SAKS occupies prime space in a converted mansion in San Ángel's Plaza San Jacinto. I've never had a bad meal here, and have always appreciated their focus on healthy, flavorful food delivered *lo más natural,* or the most natural way, with organic, fresh ingredients. The sidewalk seating and courtyard are especially pleasant.

TACO CORNER

You can't walk three blocks without running into a taqueria in Mexico City. While a few (especially those in the subway) are best avoided, most offer cheap and tasty meals. The ones below are my favorites.

EL CALIFA "The Caliph" offers ludicrously long hours, home delivery, and tacos and other bites of a higher quality than sold by many of its competitors.

LOS GUEROS This tiny spot in a nondescript part of the city center is known for one thing: succulent *tacos de cabeza de res* (tacos made from the meat from the head of the cow). Don't let that freak you out; they're delicious.

EL HUEQUITO A D.F. institution, this hole in the wall (literally "the little hole") has been around for 50 years. The proprietor has a Soup Nazi approach to his work, but he slaps together a mean *taco al pastor* (marinated pork sliced off the spit); for a few extra pesos, you can order a double portion of meat.

EL FOGONCITO While this is a chain, it's harder to find than some more ubiquitous franchises, and in my opinion, it's better than the rest. Their secret ingredient is Gouda cheese, which they use in tacos (*barbacoa* with *nopales* and cheese is a personal favorite) and their *chicharrón de queso* (crispy-fried wafer-thin cheese).

SALÓN CORONA Many feel this place is a must-do while you're in the Centro. It combines the ambience and color of a cantina with cheap beer on tap, and delicious tacos.

SI NO LE GUSTA ME VOY I love this place for many reasons. The name, for one: "If you don't like it, I'm going." They mean it, too; if you don't like their food . . . but you will. Their steak and potato tacos are to die for, and so are their *longaniza* (sausage) and pork combos.

Sublime cuisine in an artful presentation makes **Paxia** a destination for gourmets and gourmands. Start your meal with a Paxia original, called their *lotería* (lottery), which is a tasting menu of tequilas and mezcales, beautifully presented in a wooden setting made just for the restaurant. The menu is pure Mexican, but in a nod to nouveau cuisine, Chef Daniel Ovadía adds an ever-changing selection of specials that reinterpret traditional recipes. Take his version of the classic *budín Azteca,* a savory *mille feuille* tart with chicken, tortilla, butter, and mushrooms. Chef Ovadía substitutes duck for chicken, black truffle for mushroom, and foie gras for butter, creating a sumptuous, decadent dish.

✷ Don't Miss

As the largest city in Latin America, the D.F. offers a virtually endless list of things to do and see. In the Centro Histórico, the **Zócalo** offers plenty beyond the Templo Mayor. The heart of Mexico is all the more dramatic for its complete absence of greenery or adornment, and its absolutely massive Mexican flag. Political rallies and speeches are often held here, and costumed Aztec dancers frequently perform in the plaza.

The most impressive structure in the plaza is the **Catedral Metropolitana** (Metropolitan Cathedral). The largest cathedral in the Americas is a monumental work of architecture and symbolism. When the Spanish conquered Tenochtitlán in 1521, they chose this site as their first place of worship. A chapel, the first in the New World, was constructed in 1524 from the ruins of Aztec temples, marking not only a symbolic but a physical transfer of spiritual power. The modest structure was soon taken down as plans for the cathedral began in the late 1500s. Its construction took shape over two centuries, and even today it's rare to see it without a scaffolding, as its restoration is a never-ending effort. This is also due to the fact that, like other buildings in Mexico City that are built on its soft subsoil, the church has partially sunk into the ground.

The cathedral is a showcase for no less than five architectural styles: the 17th- century detailed baroque principal façade of the main church and Churrigueresque façade of the adjoining Sagrario Chapel; the 18th-century neoclassical bell towers and the 19th-century dome, the work of Manuel Tolsá; the earlier Renaissance style of the other façades; and the Gothic churches popular in colonial Spain. Inside, there are enough artistic and architectural gems to warrant a guided tour: take note especially of the towering, ornate baroque altarpiece in the central Altar of the Kings; the Capilla de San Felipe (Saint Philip's Chapel), wherein lie the remains of Emperor Agustín de Iturbide; the baptistery and baroque hallway of the adjacent

THE SAGRARIO CHAPEL AT THE CATEDRAL METROPOLITANA

tabernacle; and the two 18th-century organs, among the largest on the continent.

On the east side of the Zócalo, the **Palacio Nacional** is an impressive building made of a red stone called *tezontle* and quarry, The official residence of the president, this 17th-century building was built over an earlier palace that housed Hernán Cortés and, before him, Moctezuma. Above the central door, note the Bell of Dolores that was rung by Miguel Hidalgo in 1810 as he declared Mexico's independence. (The bell was rung in the town of Dolores in Guanajuato but brought to the palace by Porfirio Díaz, who began the tradition of the *grito,* when the president rings the bell each year on September 15.) Be sure to visit the Diego Rivera murals on the upper floors, including a series that depicts Mexico's history from the Aztecs to the American invasion in the 19th century.

Near the Zócalo lies the **Antiguo Colegio de San Ildefonso**, one of the most important and historic centers of art and education in the country. This was where the Mexican muralist movement was born, and here you'll find works by its most celebrated masters before they were famous, including Diego Rivera, Jean Charlot, Fernando Leal, Davíd Alfaro Siqueiros, and José Clemente Orozco. In particular, take a look at Rivera's remarkable *La Creación* in the amphitheater; Orosco's *Cortés y La Malinche,* showing the conquistador and his consort naked, holding hands; and Charlot's stark depiction of the massacre in the Templo Mayor.

A few blocks west of the Zócalo, the **Alameda Central** is a broad, open plaza that served as a *tianguis,* or traditional market, in the days of Tenochtitlán. The Spanish turned it into a public square, and converted one end to El Quemadero, where infidels captured by the Spanish Inquisition were publicly burned at the stake. Today, the Alameda is one of the most pleasant of Mexico City's parks, a refreshing green space in a densely packed urban center, with fountains, sculptures, and vibrant life from street performers to children's puppet theaters to street vendors.

Among its fountains and monuments, none is more impressive than the **Hemiciclo a Benito Juárez**, a wide semicircle of marble columns flanking a statue of one of Mexico's most beloved leaders. Also keep an eye out for the *policías charros,* the mounted police in sombrero and full cowboy regalia, who monitor the park. The Alameda is bordered by the exquisite **Palacio de Bellas Artes**, one of the city's most iconic and beautiful buildings; the **Museo Franz Mayer** of Mexican and European colonial art; and the spectacular **Museo Diego Rivera Mural**, all worth a visit. The Palacio bears special mention as the home of the **Ballet**

THE STUNNING PALACIO DE BELLAS ARTES

Folklórico, a collage of regional folk dances from all over Mexico and from different eras, including ritual Aztec dances and mariachis.

From the Centro Histórico, Paseo de la Reforma takes you to **Chapultepec Park**, an immense green expanse divided into three sections. Focus on the first, which is closest to Mexico's main tourist sights and contains the city zoo, five museums, a palace, and a moving monument. Of all the attractions here, the most important and impressive is the **Museo Nacional de Antropología**, one of the top museums in the world.

Anyone interested in Mexico's Maya and Aztec past will want to make a pilgrimage to this place, which boasts a collection of prehispanic art and artifacts so vast (more than 10,000 original pieces), well organized and breathtaking that one visit will never be enough. It's such an extensive chronicle of indigenous history and society that you would do well to watch the introductory video in the main entrance, and then map out the rooms and cultures you want to focus on when you enter. Whichever you pick, you will see some of the best examples of pre-Columbian art in the world. The museum is bilingual, but I recommend investing in a headset to enjoy the experience in greater comfort. Of all the museums in Mexico, this one should be at the top of your list.

The park's other highlight is **Castillo de Chapultepec** (Chapultepec Castle). Perched atop a hill with commanding views of the city, the original castle was built

THE MUSEO NACIONAL DE ANTROPOLOGÍA IS A MUST-VISIT DESTINATION FOR ANYONE INTERESTED IN MEXICO'S ANCIENT CULTURES.

between 1785 and 1787 by the viceroy of New Spain. It was a military academy after the War of Independence, and the sight of the infamous battle of 1847 during the Mexican-American War, when the Niños Héroes (Child Heroes) fought to their death in defense of their country. When Maximilian became emperor, he and Carlota made it their home, infusing it with a European identity it retains to this day. After his unfortunate departure, it became the official residence of Mexican presidents until 1932 before being converted into a museum by Lázaro Cárdenas in 1939. To get here, you can either enjoy the mildly strenuous uphill walk or, for a nominal fee, take a train to the gate. The castle is separated into two exhibits. The former military school now houses the national history museum and contains a wealth of art, artifacts, and historical records dating from the 1500s and the clash of two civilizations. In particular, note the outstanding murals by Davíd Alfaro Siqueiros depicting the violent transition from the dictatorship of Porfirio Díaz to the revolution. Also, at the main entrance to the museum, look up for a moving mural of the last of the *niños héroes* falling to his death, wrapped in a flag. The other part of the museum is the Alcázar, the palatial residence of Maximilian and Carlota, where opulent 19th-century furnishings can be viewed in different rooms.

From the foot of the castle, walk east to the **Monumento a los Niños Héroes**, a dramatic memorial of six white columns arrayed in a semicircle around a marble statue. The monument commemorates a pivotal moment in the Mexican-American War, when U.S. troops marched into Mexico City and engaged a battalion of Mexican soldiers at Chapultepec Castle. On September 13, 1847, when an American victory was all but assured, six young cadets aged 13 to 19 chose to give their lives to the republic rather than surrender. The last of them is believed to have wrapped his body in a Mexican flag and thrown himself from the castle of Chapultepec, to his death.

South of the Centro Histórico, **Coyoacán** and **San Ángel** are scenic neighborhoods where artists and intellectuals have long made their homes. Today, locals and tourists alike enjoy its quaint bohemian charm.

The heart of Coyoacán is **Plaza Hidalgo**, a picturesque *zócalo* with a second, adjacent plaza called Jardín Centenario. This is a lovely area to visit, with its bubbling fountain of frolicking coyotes, a 19th-century kiosk, the colonial-era municipal hall (which used to be one of Cortés's palaces), and the 16th-century Templo de San Juan Bautista, a former Dominican convent, framing the square. Around the plaza, a network of streets wind through the neighborhood, whose tucked away mansions and country homes include the former residence of La Malinche, the interpreter and consort of Hernán Cortés, on Higuera Street; the home (on Londres Street) and garden (on Higuera Street) of Frida Kahlo; and, further out, the former home of Leon Trotsky. The plaza is usually a hub of activity, especially on weekends, when vendors gather and people come to take in the atmosphere.

Smaller and quainter than Plaza Hidalgo, **Plaza San Jacinto** in

A ROOFTOP MURAL AT CASTILLO DE CHAPULTEPEC DEPICTS THE DEATH OF THE LAST OF THE NIÑOS HÉROES.

San Ángel is an oasis of colonial architecture, fine arts, craft, and furniture shops, and a bustling Saturday arts market called Bazar Sábado that's among the best in Mexico. With its boutiques and restaurants, the plaza makes for a pleasant day out. Two buildings of note here are the San Ángel cultural center, which looms over one corner, and the church of San Jacinto.

Among the many cultural offerings here, **Museo Frida Kahlo** is the most visited. One of Mexico's most internationally celebrated artists, Magdalena Carmen Frida Kahlo y Calderón has become a global icon of bold art and individual spirit. Kahlo's life was marred by physical and emotional pain, not least of which was the widespread belief (which lasts to this day) that she had little real talent and owed everything to her more renowned husband, Diego Rivera. Her work certainly reflects her emotions: dark, defiant, vibrant, and self-reflective. The bright blue house where she was born is a microcosm of her life, showcasing her personal items, paintings, letters, and work. I particularly liked the room of letters, which contains Diego and Frida's correspondence with friends and notable personalities of the day.

A PAINTING OF DOLORES DEL RIO AT THE HOUSE AND STUDIO OF DIEGO AND FRIDA

Fans of the couple will also want to visit the **Museo Casa–Estudio de Diego y Frida Kahlo.** The two unusual modern buildings were the studio and workshop of Rivera, where he lived with wife from the early '30s until his death in 1957. Among the works on display are a beautiful portrait of his friend Dolores del Rio, which occupies a prominent place in his studio, and a collection of large papier-mache folkloric figures.

To round out the three most famous residents in the neighborhood, the **Museo León Trotsky** honors Trotsky's time in Mexico. Given his persecution at the hands of Stalin, it's not surprising that he turned his house into a small fortress, with watchtowers, steel doors, and round-the-clock guards. Unfortunately, his security measures failed; in 1940, he was murdered (stabbed with an ice pick) by a Stalinist agent. The room where Trotsky died has been left intact, and the museum contains many of his personal affects.

A bit of a trek from the city center, the **Basílica de Guadalupe** is the holiest shrine in Mexico and the second-most visited Catholic Church in the world after St. Peter's in the Vatican. But the numbers alone don't tell its story. This the epicenter of the Catholic faith in Mexico; it was here that the image of the "Virgen de Guadalupe," the most precious and revered symbol of faith in the country, was first seen in the 16th century by a humble indigenous man named Juan Diego. La Virgen is omnipresent in modern Mexico, and instrumental to the church's conversion of the indigenous natives, who revered the feminine and found, in La Virgen, a figure worthy of their adoration. And it was from this place that her message spread.

Today, the site of the miracle is a large complex made up of several structures. The old basilica (itself the second one built here; the first is located up the hill) has a notable tilt and has been the source of near continuous restoration for years. Inside is a religious art museum. Next to it, the massive, newer construction was inaugurated in 1976 to handle the

THE BASÍLICA DE GUADALUPE MARKS THE EPICENTER OF THE CATHOLIC FAITH IN MEXICO.

enormous masses of pilgrims who flocked to the site each year. Designed to resemble a pilgrim's tent, or the Virgin's cloak, it can hold up to 10,000 people, with the atrium capable of holding 50,000. It also houses, ensconced behind the altar and safely protected behind a sheet of bulletproof glass, the most sacred religious artifact in all of Mexico: the image of the Virgin imprinted on the cloak of Juan Diego in 1531. Visitors can take a short conveyer-belt ride behind the altar to view the image.

On December 12, Mexico celebrates the Día de Nuestra Señora de Guadalupe (Day of Our Lady of Guadalupe), commemorating the day Juan Diego saw the vision of the Virgin. Come early if you want to see the plaza come alive with the press of millions of worshippers.

And finally, what would a trip to Mexico City be without a night of **Lucha Libre** (literally "Free Fight"), or wrestling. Sure, it's fake, but it's also a tremendously campy, colorful, and entertaining spectacle, one with an immensely popular following. The image of the masked and costumed Mexican wrestler is well known beyond Mexico, but here they are part of the social fabric. Famous *luchadores* are practically saints—one of the most famous is *El Santo* (The Saint) whose son also got into the business under the catchy name Hijo del Santo (Son of the Saint). Filled with theatrics, flying bodies, and bloodthirsty crowds, it makes for a fun night out. There are two Lucha Libre arenas—the **Arena Coliseo** and **Arena México.** Neither are in the greatest part of town, so if you go, take a *sitio taxi.* Of the two, Arena

TRY TO CATCH A NIGHT OF LUCHA LIBRE WHILE YOU'RE IN MEXICO CITY.

A WEEKEND IN MEXICO CITY

Spend your first day in the Centro Histórico. I recommend the following walking tour.

1. Start in the **Zócalo**, where you can visit the **Catedral Metropolitana, Palacio Nacional**, and **Templo Mayor**. These sites will easily occupy you up to lunch. Then head to Calle República de Guatemala, just behind the cathedral, where you can enjoy lunch on the terrace at **La Casa de las Sirenas**. Afterward, walk another block away from the Zócalo to Justo Sierra Street and turn right to reach the **Antiguo Colegio de San Ildefonso**.

2. Retrace your steps to República de Guatemala, turn right and walk west. The road becomes Calle Tacuba, which is lined with colonial-era buildings. Tacuba will lead to the **Alameda Central** and the gorgeous **Palacio de Bellas Artes, Hemiciclo a Benito Juárez**, and **Museo Mural Diego Rivera**.

3. After a full day of cultural highlights, freshen up at your hotel before dinner. One recommendation is to head to Paseo de Reforma and **Les Moustaches** for an elegant French dinner. If you want to stick to Mexican cuisine, try **La Fonda el Refugio** in the Zona Rosa. Either option gives you the chance to see Paseo de Reforma's monuments lit up at night. After dinner, you can head to the Sheraton María Isabel and **Bar Jorongo**, to watch the mariachis, or enjoy the **Ballet Folklórico** at the Palacio de Bellas Artes.

On Day Two, take a tour (just about every tour company operating in Mexico offers one) to **Teotihuacán**, a full-day excursion, followed by dinner at a restaurant in Polanco. And finally, spend Day Three in Chapultepec Park, focusing on the spectacular **Museo Nacional de Antropología**. For lunch, take a taxi to nearby **El Fogoncito** if you want to enjoy tacos and other street-food staples.

México is the more famous and venerated Lucha institution.

✱ Local Knowledge

CLIMATE Generally, Mexico City has a wonderfully temperate climate. There is a rainy season that runs from April to October. Rain is sporadic, and many times of the "flash flood" variety: strong downpours that appear suddenly and vanish after a short but thorough soaking. The rainy season also overlaps with the hottest months of the year in April and May. The dry season runs from mid-October to April, and includes a mild winter from December to February, when it's brisk enough to require warm clothes but nothing too extreme. The fall hurricane season doesn't do much damage here, generally producing overcast days and strong rains, with occasional flooding.

It's not uncommon to walk around in a T-shirt and jeans during the day, return to your hotel at night, and change into a nice pair of trousers and a warm sweater. Part of this is the weather and part is style. Mexicans in the D.F. dress well and conform to a certain standard when stepping out at night. At most restaurants, the shorts-and-Hawaiian-shirt getup will have you sticking out like the worst kind of gringo. In fact, it's rare to see Mexico City men and women wearing shorts, even on the hottest days.

My other piece of advice is to leave the valuables at home. It's no secret that there is crime in Mexico City, and wearing flashy jewelry isn't the wisest move when you're out on the town.

EXTENDED STAY

Keep to the itinerary above, which covers the best of Mexico City. In addition, make sure to visit **Xochimilco**, a wonderful day out in a pre-Columbian land of canals and waterways. Reserved the weekend for the quaint neighborhoods of **Coyoacán** and **San Ángel** and its Saturday Bazaar. Finally, spend a day in **Xochicalxo**, make a pilgrimage to the **Basílica de Guadalupe**, and don't forget one night of **Lucha Libre** before you leave.

ALTITUDE AND POLLUTION Pollution in Mexico City is another hotbed issue, but things have gotten better in the last few years. Sure, there is still a layer of smog to contend with, and pollution limits can exceed acceptable levels as measured by the Mexico's Metropolitan Index of Air Quality (IMECA). But the city is in the midst of an ambitious environmental cleanup program targeting air quality and emissions. If you want to know how clean the air is on any given day, check the Web site of the city's Atmospheric Monitoring System at www.sma.df.gob.mx/simat/. The IMECA scale is as follows:

- 0–50: Good
- 51–100: Regular
- 101–150: Bad
- As long as it's between 0 and 150, you need not worry.
- 151–200: Very Bad
- Over 201: Extremely Bad
- As you can imagine, these are not good levels of air quality, and if the levels push beyond 201, the city is likely to take action.

Altitude plays a big role in influencing the weather. Mexico City is at an elevation of over 7,000 feet above sea level, which leads to cool nights throughout the year. Still, the weather is generally very agreeable during the day. Altitude sickness affects some travelers more than others. Many people won't notice much of a change; some may just find the air a little thin; while others can experience headaches, dizziness, shortness of breath, fatigue, or worse if they have heart- or lung-related medical problems. The latter should consult with a doctor before flying to Mexico City. If you do feel any of the above symptoms, don't exercise, drink plenty of fluids, stay away from alcohol, and wait it out. Your body will adjust.

✷ Special Events

Festival de Mexico en el Centro Histórico. Held in March–April, the festival (http://festival.org.mx) celebrated its 26th year in 2010. Spanning almost three weeks, it brings hundreds of thousands of people to more than 60 locations in the Centro Histórico, and features a variety of events.

El Grito and Mexican Independence Day. Hundreds of thousands of people, wearing the colors of the flag or traditional dress, and packing flags, shaving cream, and an exuberant excess of national spirit, gather at the Zócalo on the night of September 15 to see the president appear on the balcony of the National Palace and give the *grito* (shout). Echoing, but not quite repeating, the words of Miguel Hidalgo, the shout is:

"*¡Viva México!* "Long live Mexico!"

¡Viva los héroes de la patria! "Long live the heroes of the motherland!"

¡Viva la república! "Long live the republic!"

The jubilant horde screams along and then fireworks erupt around the plaza. This is Mexico's most important national holiday, and nobody celebrates it with more passion and pomp than Mexico City.

Noche de Alebrijes. (www.map.df.gob.mx) In October/November, this procession of *alebrijes*, or half-animal, half-demonic creatures of fantasy, runs from the Zócalo to the Alameda via Cinco de Mayo, and down Paseo de la Reforma.

Días de los Muertos (Days of the Dead). My favorite event in

USEFUL NUMBERS

Emergency and Police: 060 (911 will work from cell phones)

Red Cross: 065

Fire Department: 068

LOCATEL (missing persons): 52-5658-1111

National 24-Hour Tourist Helpline: 800-987-8224 (within Mexico), 55-5089-7500

Tourist Security: 800-007-7100 (within Mexico), 55-5250-23/0493/0027/0151/0292/0589

Tourist-Aid Police: 52-5250-8221

Tourist Legal Assistance: 55-5625-8153

Federal Highway Police: 52-5677-2227

PRACTICAL INFORMATION

Country Code: 52

Mexico City Area Code: 55 (*Note: all phone numbers in Mexico City are 8 digits long, beginning with 5. If you see a 7-digit number, add the 5 before dialing it)*

Operator-assistance: 020 (domestic long distance), 040 (domestic directory assistance), 090 (international long distance)

Altitude: 7,240 feet above sea level

Climate: Annual average of 64F

Time Zone: Mexico City is at GMT–6, or 1 hour behind Eastern Standard Time (dial 030 for the official time)

Hours of Operation: Shopping centers and other commercial businesses open daily 9–8

Banks: Open Mon.–Fri. 9–4

Museums: Open Tue.–Sun. 9–5, with free admission on Sun.

Public Transportation: Operates from 5 AM–midnight.

Mexico, the Days of the Dead are celebrated on November 1 and 2. At the Zócalo, the two-day celebration features a Halloween-like gathering of skulls and elaborate altars to honor the deceased.

There are many customs associated with the event, including offering food to the dead, ordering sugar skulls from local bakeries imprinted with the names of family members (alive and deceased),

TOURIST INFORMATION

Infotur: Offers maps, information, and literature in English and Spanish by the Ministry of Tourism, 888-401-3880 (within the U.S.), 800-987-8244 (within Mexico)
55-5208-1030, Presidente Masaryk 172, ground floor, Chapultepec Morales, Miguel Hidalgo, Mexico City, open Mon.–Fri. 8–6, Sat. 10–3

Sectur (Ministry of Tourism): Mexico's Tourism Board has an excellent national portal for tourists called www.visitmexico.com, or you can all 800-44-MEXICO from the United States. Mexico City's Ministry of Tourism also has a useful and detailed online resource at www.mexicocity.gob.mx, and can be reached at 800-008-9090 (within Mexico). In addition, look for these tourist information booths throughout the city:

Benito Juárez International Airport: 55-5786-9002, National Arrivals Terminal, open daily 7–9

TAPO Bus Terminal: 55-5784-3077, open daily 9–6

Terminal Central Del Sur (Tasqueña Bus Terminal): 55-5336-2321, open daily 9–6

Centro Histórico: 55-5518-2799, at the Alameda Central in front of the Palacio de Bellas Artes, open daily 9–6; 55-5518-1003, at the Zócalo by the cathedral, open daily 9–6

Chapultepec-Polanco: 55-5286-3850, Paseo de la Reforma in front of the Museo Nacional de Antropología, open daily 9–6; 55-5208-1030, Paseo de la Reforma at the Angel de la Independencia Plaza, open daily 9–6

Other useful Web sites: www.tiempolibre.com.mx, www.mexicofile.com, www.inside-mexico.com, www.mexicocitylife.com

Useful magazines: *Dónde Ir* (Spanish), *Chilango* (Spanish), *Explore México* (Bilingual)

and parades of iconic skeletal figurines and altars.

Christmas and Three Kings Day. If you're here during the Christmas season, visit the Alameda Central, which is decorated with Santa Claus displays, festive lights, and decorations. After December 25, the focus changes to the Three Kings, who are generally more important than Santa throughout the Latin world.

✷ Contacts

Antiguo Colegio de San Ildefonso 55-5702-6378, 5795-5922, Justo Sierra 16, Colonia Centro, Mexico, D.F. www.san ildefonso.org.mx. Open Tue.–Sun. 10–6. $. **Metro: Zócalo.**

Arena Coliseo 55-5526-1687, República de Perú 77, Colonia Centro Histórico, Mexico City, D.F. www.cmll.com, www.ticket master.com.mx. Fights scheduled Tue. at 8 and Sun. at 5. **Metro: Garibaldi.**

Arena México 55-5588-0508, Dr. Lavista 197, Colonia Doctores, Mexico City, D.F. www.arena mexico.com.mx, www.ticketmaster .com.mx. Fights typically scheduled Tue. at 7:30 and Fri. at 8:30. **Metro: Cuauhtémoc.**

El Bajío 55-5281-8246/45, Alejandro Dumas 7, Colonia Polanco, Mexico City, D.F. Open Mon.–Sat. 8–11, Sun. 9–10. $–$$. **Metro: Auditorio.**

Ballet Folklórico 55-5512–2593, 5130-0900, Corner of Eje Central Lázaro Cárdenas and Avenida Juárez at the Palacio de Bellas Artes. www.bellasartes.gob.mx. Performances run Wed. at 8:30 and Sun. at 8:30 and 9:30. $$$–$$$$. **Metro: Bellas Artes.**

Basílica de Guadalupe 55-5577-6022, Plaza de las Américas 1, Colonia Villa de Guadalupe, Mexico City, D.F. www.virgende guadalupe.org.mx. Open daily 6–9. Free, $ for the museum. **Metro: La Villa-Basílica.**

Best Western Hotel Majestic 55-5521-8600, Avenida Madero No. 73, Colonia Centro, Mexico City, D.F. www.bestwestern.com. $–$$. **Metro: Zócalo.**

El Califa 55-5271-7666/6285, Altata 22, Colonia Condesa, Mexico City, D.F. Open daily noon to 5 AM. $. **Metro: Chapultepec.**

Camino Real Polanco México 55-5263-8888, Mariano Escobedo 700, Colonia Anzures, México D.F. www.caminoreal.com. $$$–$$$$. **Metro: Chapultepec.**

Canals of Xochimilco 5676 8879, 5673-7890, Embarcadero (Pier) Fernando Celada, Avenida Guadalupe I. Ramírez, Xochimilco. Open daily, generally between 9 and 8. $$. **Metro: Xochimilco (Light Rail).**

Capicua 55-5616-5211, 5616-4600, Avenida de la Paz 14, Colonia San Ángel, Mexico City, D.F., www.capicua.com.mx. Open Mon.–Sat. 1–1, Sun. 1–6. $$–$$$. **Metro: M.A. de Quevedo.**

El Cardenal 55-5521-3080, 5521-8815, Palma 23, Colonia Centro, Mexico, D.F. Open daily 8:30–7. $$–$$$. **Metro: Zócalo.**

Casa de la Condesa 55-5574-31-86, 5584-3089, Plaza Luis Cabrera 16, Colonia Roma Sur, México City, D.F. www.extendedstay mexico.com. $–$$. **Metro: Insurgentes.**

La Casa de las Sirenas 55-5704-3345, República de Guatemala No. 32, Colonia Centro, Mexico, D.F. Open Mon.–Thu. 1–11, Fri. and

Sat. 1–2. www.lacasadelassirenas .com.mx. $–$$$. **Metro: Zócalo.**

Casa Lamm 55-5514-8501, 5514-8504, Álvaro Obregón 99, Colonia Roma, Mexico City, D.F, www .lamm.com.mx. Open Mon.–Fri. 8 AM–3 AM, Sat. 9 AM–3 AM, Sun. 9 AM–5 PM. $$–$$$. **Metro: Insurgentes.**

Casa Vieja 55-5282-0067, Eugenio Sue 45, Colonia Polanco, Mexico, D.F. www.casavieja.com. $$$–$$$$. **Metro: Polanco.**

La Casona 55-5286-3001, 800-5CASONA, Durango 280, Colonia Roma, Mexico City, DF. www .hotellacasona.com.mx. $$–$$$. **Metro: Sevilla.**

Castillo de Chapultepec 55-5-61-9214/15, www.castillodechapultepec.inah.gob.mx. Open Tue.–Sun. 9–5. $. **Metro: Chapultepec.**

Catedral Metropolitana 55-5521-2447, 5510-0440, at the Plaza de la Constitución (Zócalo). Open daily 7–7. Free. **Metro: Zócalo.**

Condesa DF 55-5241-2600, Avenida Veracruz 102, Colonia Condesa, Mexico City D.F. www .condesadf.com. $$$–$$$$. **Metro: Chapultepec.**

Contramar 55-5514-3169, 5514-9217, Durango 200, Colonia Roma, Mexico City, D.F. Open Mon.–Fri. 1:30–6:30, Sat. and Sun. 1–6:30. $$–$$$. **Metro: Sevilla.**

Danubio 55-5512-0912, Uruguay 3, Colonia Centro, Mexico, D.F. www.danubio.com. Open daily 1–10. $–$$$. **Metro: Salto del Agua.**

Embassy Suites Mexico City–Reforma 55-5061-3000, Paseo de la Reforma 69, Colonia Tabacalera, Mexico City, D.F. www.embassysuites.com. $$–$$$. **Metro: Juárez or Revolución.**

Fiesta Americana Grand Chapultepec 55-2581-1500, Mariano Escobedo 756, Colonia Anzures, Mexico City, D.F. www.fiestaamericana.com. $$–$$$$. **Metro: Chapultepec.**

El Fogoncito 55-5531-6469, Liebnitz 54, Colonia Anzures, Mexico City, D.F. Open Sun.–Tue. noon–2, Wed. noon–3, Thu.–Sat. noon–5. $–$$. **Metro: Chapultepec.**

La Fonda de Don Chon 55-5542-0873, Regina 160, Colonia Centro, Mexico, D.F. Open Mon.–Sat. noon–6. $–$$. **Metro: Merced.**

Fonda el Refugio 55-5525-8128, 5207-2732, Liverpool 166, Colonia Juárez, Mexico City, D.F., www .fondaelrefugio.com.mx. Open daily 1–11. $$. **Metro: Insurgentes.**

Four Seasons Mexico 55-5230-1818, Paseo de la Reforma 500, Colonia Juárez, Mexico City, D.F. www.fourseasons.com. $$$$. **Metro: Insurgentes.**

Los Girasoles 55-5510-3281, Calle Tacuba No. 8, Colonia Centro, Mexico, D.F. www.restaurantelosgirasoles.com. Open Tue.–Sat.

1–midnight, Sun.–Mon. 1–9. $$–$$$. **Metro: Allende.**

Gran Meliá Mexico Reforma Hotel 55-5128-5000, 866-43MELIA (within the U.S.), Paseo de la Reforma 1, Colonia Cuauhtémoc, Mexico City, D.F. www.meliamexicoreforma.com. $$–$$$$. **Metro: Hidalgo.**

Los Gueros Lopez 93, Colonia Centro, Mexico, D.F. Open Mon.–Sat. 9–9:30. $. **Metro: San Juan de Letrán.**

Hábita Hotel 55-5282-3100, Presidente Masaryk 201, Colonia Polanco, Mexico, D.F. www.hotelhabita.com. $$–$$$$. **Metro: Polanco.**

Holiday Inn Zócalo 55-5130-5130, Avenida Cinco de Mayo 61, Colonia Centro, Mexico City, D.F. www.holidayinn.com. $–$$. **Metro: Zócalo.**

Hostal Moneda 55-5522-5803, Calle Moneda 8, Colonia Centro, Mexico, D.F. www.hostalmoneda.com.mx. $. **Metro: Zócalo.**

Hostel Catedral 55-5518-1726, 800-823-2410, República de Guatemala No. 4, Colonia Centro, Mexico, D.F. www.hostelcatedral.com. $. **Metro: Zócalo.**

Hotel Geneve 55-5080-0870, 877-657-5799 (within the U.S.), Londres 130, Colonia Juárez, Mexico City, D.F. www.hotelgeneve.com.mx. $$. **Metro: Insurgentes.**

El Huequito 55-5518-3313, Ayuntamiento 21, Colonia Centro, Mexico, D.F. Open Mon.–Sat. 9:30–10. $. **Metro: San Juan de Letrán.**

Izote 55-5280-1671/1265, Presidente Masaryk 513, Local 3, Colonia Polanco, Mexico City, D.F. Open Mon.–Sat. 1–12, Sun. 1–6. $$–$$$. **Metro: Polanco.**

Jaso 55-5545-7476, 88 Newton, Colonia Polanco, Mexico City, D.F. www.jaso.com.mx. Open Mon.–Sat. 2–11. $$$–$$$$.

Ligaya 55-5286-6268/6380, Nuevo León 68, Colonia Condesa, Mexico City, D.F., www.ligaya.com.mx. Open Tue.–Sat. 2–1, Sun. 2–5:30. $$–$$$. **Metro: Chilpancingo.**

Los Mercaderes 55-5510-3687, 5510-2213, Avenida Cinco de Mayo 57, Colonia Centro, Mexico, D.F. Open Mon.–Wed. 8–10, Thu.–Sat. 8–1, Sun. 8–8. $$. **Metro: Allende.**

Les Moustaches 55-5533-3390, 5525-1265, 800-000-7824, Río Sena 88, Colonia Cuauhtémoc, Mexico City, D.F. www.lesmoustaches.com.mx. Open Tue.–Sat. 1–11:30, Sun. 1–6. $$–$$$. **Metro: Insurgentes.**

Museo Casa–Estudio de Diego y Frida Kahlo 55-5550-1518/1189, Diego Rivera and Altavista, Colonia San Ángel Inn, Mexico City, D.F. Open Tue.–Sun. 10–6. $, free on Sun. **Metro: Barranca del Muerto.**

Museo Franz Mayer 55-5518-2266, Avenida Hidalgo 45, Colonia Centro, Mexico City, D.F. www.franzmayer.org.mx. Open

Tue.–Sun. 10–5. $, free on Tue. **Metro: Bellas Artes.**

Museo Frida Kahlo 55-5554-5999, Londres 247, Colonia El Carmen, Coyoacán, Mexico City, D.F. www.museofridakahlo.org. Open Tue.–Sun. 10–6. $. **Metro: Coyoacán.**

Museo León Trotsky 55-5658-8732, Río Churubusco 410, Colonia El Carmen, Coyoacán, Mexico City, D.F. Open Tue.–Sun. 10–5. $. **Metro: Coyoacán.**

Museo Mural Diego Rivera 55-5512-0754, across the Alameda Central on the corner of Balderas and Colón, Open Tue.–Sun. 10–6. $. **Metro: Hidalgo.**

Museo Nacional de Antropología 55-5553-6285/6554/6253, off Paseo de Reforma and Calzada Gandhi. www.mna.inah.gob.mx. Open Tue.–Sun. 9–7. $, free on Sun. **Metro: Auditorio.**

NH Centro Histórico 55-5130-1850, Palma 42, Colonia Centro, Mexico City, D.F. www.nh-hotels.com. $–$$. **Metro: Zócalo.**

Palacio de Bellas Artes 55-5512–2593, 5130-0900, corner of Eje Central Lázaro Cárdenas and Avenida Juárez. www.bellasartes.gob.mx. Guided tours Tue.–Sun. at 1 PM. Free, $ for galleries, free on Sun. **Metro: Bellas Artes.**

Palacio Nacional 55-3688-1202, eastern side of the Plaza de la Constitución. Open daily 9–5. Free. **Metro: Zócalo.**

Paxia 55-5550-8355, Avenida de la Paz 47, Colonia San Ángel, Mexico City, D.F. www.paxia.com.mx. Open Mon.–Thu. 1–11, Fri. and Sat. 1–1. $$–$$$$. **Metro: M.A. de Quevedo.**

Presidente Intercontinental 55-5327-7700, Campos Elíseos 218, Colonia Polanco Mexico City, D.F. www.intercontinental.com. $$–$$$$. **Metro: Auditorio.**

Puerto Madero 52-55-5545-6098, Avenida Masaryk 110, Colonia Polanco Mexico City, D.F. Open daily 1–1 $$$–$$$$. **Metro: Polanco.**

Pujol 55-5545-4111, 5545-3507, Petrarca 254, Colonia Polanco Mexico City, D.F. www.pujol.com.mx. Open Mon. 1–6, Tue.–Sat. 1–11. $$$–$$$$.

SAKS 55-5616-1601, Plaza San Jacinto 9, Colonia San Ángel, Mexico City, D.F. www.saks.com.mx. Open Mon.–Sat. 9–midnight, Sun. 10–9. $$–$$$. **Metro: M.A. de Quevedo.**

Salón Corona 55-5512-9007, Bolívar 22, Colonia Centro, Mexico, D.F. Open daily 9–midnight. $–$$. **Metro: Allende.**

Sheraton Centro Histórico 55-5130-5300, Avenida Juarez 70, Colonia Centro, Mexico, D.F. www.starwoodhotels.com. $$–$$$$. **Metro: Juárez.**

Sheraton María Isabel 55-5242-5555, Paseo de la Reforma 325 Colonia Cuauhtémoc, Mexico City, D.F. www.sheratonmariaisabel.com. $$–$$$. **Metro: Insurgentes.**

Si No Le Gusta Me Voy Corner of Lopez Street and Vizcaínas, Colonia Centro, Mexico, D.F.

Open Mon.–Sat. 12–6. $. **Metro: Salto del Agua.**

La Tecla 55-5525-4920, Durango 186-A, Colonia Roma, Mexico City, D.F. Open Mon.–Sat. 1:30–12, Sun. 1:30–6. $–$$. **Metro: Insurgentes.**

Templo Mayor 55-5542-4943, 5542-4784, Seminario 8, Colonia Centro, Mexico City, D.F. www.templomayor.inah.gob.mx. Open daily 9–5. $, free on Sun. **Metro: Zócalo.**

Tezka 55-9149-3000, Amberes 78, Colonia Juárez, Mexico City, D.F. www.tezka.com.mx. Open Mon.–Fri. 1–5 and 8–11, Sat. 1–5. $$$–$$$$. **Metro: Insurgentes.**

Tlatelolco 55-5583-0295, Eje Central Lázaro Cárdenas and Avenida Ricardo Flores Magón, Colonia Nonoalco-Tlatelolco, Mexico City, D.F. Open daily 8–6. Free. **Metro: Tlatelolco.**

W Hotel Mexico City 55-9138-1800, Campos Elíseos 252, Colonia Polanco Mexico City, D.F. www.whotels.com/mexicocity. $$$–$$$$. **Metro: Auditorio.**

Zhen Shanghai 55-5327-7756, Campos Elíseos 218 at the Presidente Intercontinental, Colonia Polanco Mexico City, D.F., www.intercontinental.com. Open daily 1–1. $$$–$$$$. **Metro: Auditorio.**

A TRAVELER'S DICTIONARY

Basic Spanish

BARE NECESSITIES

Yes—*Sí*

No—*No*

Please—*Por favor* (a slangy version is *¡porfa!*)

Thank you—*Gracias*

Thank you very much—*Muchas gracias*

You're welcome—*De nada*

I don't know—*No sé*

I'm sorry—*Lo siento*

Good—*Bueno*

Better—*Mejor*

Bad—*Malo*

Worse—*Peor*

Okay/Fine—*Está bien*

And—*Y*

But—*Pero*

English—*Inglés*

Spanish—*Español*

I don't speak Spanish—*No hablo español*

I don't speak Spanish well—*No hablo bien el español*

I don't understand Spanish—*No entiendo español*

Do you speak English?—*¿Usted habla inglés?* (formal)/*¿Hablas inglés?* (informal)

Is English spoken here?—*¿Se habla ingles aquí?*

How do you say . . . *¿Cómo se dice . . . ?/*

Where is . . . ?—*¿Dónde está . . . ?*

How much is . . . ?—*¿Cuánto es . . . ?/ Cuánto cuesta . . . ?*

I want . . .—*Yo quiero . . .*

Excuse me?—*¿Perdón?*

Excuse me (to get by)—*Perdóneme*

Excuse me (to ask a question/get attention)—*Discúlpeme* (Mexicans also say *¿mande?* or, informally, *¿cómo?*)

GREETINGS AND GOODBYES

Hello—*Hola*

Good morning—*Buenos días*

Good afternoon—*Buenas tardes*

Good evening—*Buenas noches*

How are you?—*¿Cómo estás?* (informal)/*¿Cómo está?* (formal)

How are you (informal)?—*¿Que tal?*

Good/Very good, thanks—*Bien/Muy bien, gracias*

And you?—*¿Y usted?*

Pleased to meet you—*Mucho gusto*

Goodbye—*Adiós*

See you later—*Hasta luego*

See you soon—*Hasta pronto*

Be seeing you—*Nos vemos*

Take care—*Cuidate*

Have a good day—*Que tenga un buen día*

Hope all goes well for you—*Que le vaya bien*

NUMBERS

0—*Cero*

1—*Uno/Una*

2—*Dos*

3—*Tres*

4—*Cuatro*

5—*Cinco*

6—*Seis*

7—*Siete*

8—*Ocho*

9—*Nueve*

10—*Diez*

11—*Once*

12—*Doce*

13—*Trece*

14—*Catorce*

15—*Quince*

16—*Dieciseis*

17—*Diecisiete*

18—*Dieciocho*

19—*Diecinueve*

20—*Veinte*

30—*Treinta*

40—*Cuarenta*

50—*Cincuenta*

60—*Sesenta*

70—*Setenta*

80—*Ochenta*

90—*Noventa*

100—*Cien*

150—*Ciento cincuenta*

200—*Doscientos*

500—*Quinientos*

1,000—*Mil*

1,000,000—*Un millón*

DAYS AND MONTHS

Monday—*Lunes*

Tuesday—*Martes*

Wednesday—*Miércoles*

Thursday—*Jueves*

Friday—*Viernes*

Saturday—*Sábado*

Sunday—*Domingo*

Day—*Día*

Today—*Hoy*

Tomorrow—*Mañana*

Yesterday—*Ayer*

Day after tomorrow—*Pasado mañana*

Day before yesterday—*Antes de ayer*

The next day—*El día siguiente*

Week—*Semana*

Month—*Mes*

Year—*Año*

TIME

Time—*Tiempo*

Hour—*Hora*

Minute—*Minuto*

Second—*Segundo*

What time is it?—*¿Qué hora es?*

It's one o'clock—*Es la una*

It's two o'clock—*Son las dos*

It's three o'clock in the afternoon—*Son las tres de la tarde*

At nine o'clock in the morning—*A las nueve de la mañana*

At 2:30—*A las dos y media*

It's ten past seven—*Son las siete y diez*

At quarter to five—*A las cinco menos cuarto*

Noon—*Mediodía*

Afternoon—*La tarde*

Midnight—*Medianoche*

Night—*La noche*

Last Night—*Anoche*

Dawn—*La madrugada*

PRONOUNS AND TERMS OF ADDRESS

I—*Yo*

You—*Usted* (formal)/*Tú* (informal)

He/Him—*Él*

She/Her—*Ella*

We/us—*Nosotros*

They—*Ellos/Ellas*

You all—*Ustedes*

Mr.—*Señor*

Mrs.—*Señora*

Miss (young)—*Señorita*

Sir/Mr. (formal)—*Don*

Sir/Mrs. (formal)—*Doña*

FRIENDS AND FAMILY

Husband—*Esposo*

Wife—*Esposa*

Son—*Hijo*

Daughter—*Hija*

Brother/sister—*Hermano/hermana*

Father—*Padre*

Dad—*Papá*

Mother—*Madre*

Mom—*Mamá*

Grandfather/grandmother—*Abuelo/abuela*

Boyfriend/fiancé—*Novio*

Girlfriend/fiancée—*Novia*

Friend—*Amigo/amiga*

THE FIVE W'S

Who—*Quién/quiénes* (for more than one)

What—*Qué*

When—*Cuando*

Where—*Dónde*

Why—*Por qué* (*Because* is also *porque,* but it's one word instead of two)

SIZES AND AMOUNTS

Big—*Grande*

Small—*Pequeño/chico*

More—*Más*

Less—*Menos*

A lot—*Mucho*

A little—*Poco*

Nothing—*Nada*

Everything—*Todo*

GETTING AROUND

Here—*Aquí*

There—*Allá*

From . . . to . . .—*De . . . a . . .*

Road—*El camino*

Street—*Calle*

Little street—*Callejón*

Avenue—*Avenida*

Highway—*Carretera/autopista*

Block—*Cuadra*

Kilometer—*Kilómetro*

North—*Norte*

South—*Sur*

West—*Oeste/poniente*

East—*Este/oriente*

Left—*Izquierda*

Right—*Derecha*

Straight ahead—*Derecho, adelante*

Back—*Atrás*

Behind—*Detrás*

In front of—*En frente a*

Airport—*Aeropuerto*

Bus—*Autobús/bus* (In Mexico City, the small, boxy public buses are called *peseros*)

Bus stop—*Parada*

Bus terminal—*Terminal de autobuses*

Where does this bus go?—*¿A dónde va este autobús?*

Taxi—*Taxi*

What do I owe you—*¿Cuanto le debo?*

GETTING A ROOM

Do you have a room?—*¿Hay cuarto?*

Rate/tariff—*Precio/tarifa*

Room—*Habitación*

A single room—*Un sencillo*

A double room—*Un doble*

Air-conditioning—*Aire acondicionado*

Key—*Llave*

Bed—*Cama*

Bathroom/toilet—*Baño/el baño*

Shower—*Ducha*

EMERGENCIES

Help—*Ayuda*

Watch out!—*¡Cuidado!*

I need help—*Necesito ayuda*

Please help me—*Ayúdeme por favor*

Police—*Policía*

Ambulance—*Ambulancia*

Doctor—*Médico*

Firefighters—*Bomberos*

Emergency—*Emergencia*

Medicine—*Medicina*

AT THE TABLE

To eat—*Comer*

To drink—*Beber*

Restaurant—*Restaurante*

Inn/Tavern—*Fonda*

Breakfast—*Desayuno*

Lunch—*Comida*

Dinner—*Cena*

Menu—*La carta, el menu*

Plate—*Plato*

Glass—*Taza*

Knife—*Cuchillo*

Spoon—*Cuchara*

Fork—*Tenedor*

Napkin—*Servilleta*

Drinking water—*Agua pura/ potable*

Bottled water—*Agua mineral*

Bottled carbonated water—*Agua mineral con gas*

Beer—*Cerveza*

Wine—*Vino*

Juice—*Jugo*

Tea—*Té*

Coffee—*Café*

Milk—*Leche*

Straw—*Popote*

Meat—*Carne*

Chicken—*Pollo*

Fish—*Pescado*

Shellfish—*Mariscos*

Shrimp—*Camarones*

Soup—*Caldo*

Bread—*Pan*

Fruit—*Fruta*

Beans—*Frijoles*

Bon appétit!—*¡Buen provecho!*

The check—*La cuenta*

Cheers!—*¡Salud!*

ITEMS ON THE MEXICAN MENU

Antojitos—The name given to a host of finger food and snacks found at taquerias and restaurants

Birria—A stew made with lamb, goat or mutton, and chiles and dried roasted peppers, among other spices and herbs

Cajeta—Caramel

Camote—Mexican sweet potato

Cecina—A thinly sliced, salted, and cured meat that is dried in the sun before being cooked

Chapulines—Grasshoppers, typically toasted in lemon juice and garlic

Chilaquiles—Fried, crispy tortilla chips mixed with a red or green chile sauce and typically served with chicken and cheese; also a popular breakfast food

Chile—Chile peppers are the most ubiquitous ingredient in Mexican cuisine, offering a tremendous variety, cooking style (dried, roasted, ground, charred), and dating back to the earliest Mesoamerican tribes. Here are just a few of the more popular chiles you'll find in Mexican cuisine:

- Árbol—Thin, dry, and spicy
- Chilaca—A long, thin, dark green, or brown chile that ranges from mild to medium in heat; when dried, called a chile pasilla
- Guajillo—A dried, pointy, deep red chile that can be very spicy
- Habanero—A plump orange chile that is among the hottest around
- Jalapeño—One of the more famous chiles in the United States; medium to large green chiles (red when mature) that are relatively spicy and named after the town of Xalapa, where they were traditionally grown (dried and smoked jalapeños are called chipotle)
- Poblano—A typically mild, large green pepper from Puebla (when dried, it is called chile ancho)
- Serrano—A small, hot, and thin chile that is green,

red, or yellow, depending on its maturity

Chile relleno—A roasted fresh poblano pepper (sometimes ancho or pasilla peppers are used instead) stuffed with cheese, and/or meat (typically a mix of pork, raisins, and nuts), covered in egg batter and fried, and usually smothered in a tomato sauce

Chipotle—A dried and smoked jalapeño pepper

Cochinita pibil—A Yucatán specialty; slow-roasted pork that's been marinated in citrus juice and wrapped in banana leaves

Comida corrida—A cheap, "express" set menu usually featuring soup, entrée, and dessert

Cuitlacoche or *huitlacoche*—A truffle-like fungus found on corn

Elote—Roast corn

Epazote—A green, leafy herb similar to licorice

Escamoles—Ant eggs (they have a nutty taste and a soft consistency)

Fideos—Noodles

Flor de calabaza—Squash blossom

WHAT TO ORDER AT THE TAQUERIA

The first time I checked out a menu at a local taqueria, I almost got up and walked away. Except for *taco* and *enchilada*, I couldn't understand a thing. In fact, even the stuff I was familiar with, such as tacos and chalupas, were invariably different from the Tex-Mex versions I knew. And what the heck was a *huarache*? What about *alambre*? Here's a little clarification so you don't feel as lost as I once did:

Alambre—A flavorful mix of steak, bacon, onion, green pepper, and cheese

Carnitas—Braised, tender, sliced pork

Curtido—A garnish of pickled carrots and onions served at most taquerias

Chalupa—An elongated oval tortilla, resembling the *chalupas* (canoes) that give them their name, topped with shredded meat, cheese, and other ingredients

Chimichanga—A deep-fried burrito, often served with salsa and guacamole

Enchilada—A corn tortilla placed briefly in hot oil and often dipped in a chile sauce, wrapped around a filling, and baked. Enchiladas are usually garnished with more sauce and cheese; other varieties

Guajolote—Turkey (The more common *pavo* is also used)

Gusanos de Maguey—Cactus worms (typically fried with tortillas)

Huachinango—Red snapper

Jaiba—Crab

Jamaica—Hibiscus

Jícama—A type of Mexican turnip

Jitomate—Tomato

Mixiote—An oven-roasted or pit-barbecued meat dish (usually mutton, rabbit, or chicken), seasoned with pasilla and guajillo chiles and other seasonings, and wrapped the outer skin of the maguey plant

Molcajete—A variety of meats, vegetables, or cheeses cooked and presented in the stone bowl that gives the dish its name

Mole—A general name given to a variety of sauces, the most typical of which combines ground chiles with onion, charred tortilla, nuts or seeds, and unsweetened chocolate

Mollete—A Mexican take on a grilled cheese sandwich: a

include *enfrijoladas* (dipped in refried beans instead of chile) and *entomatadas* (dipped in tomato sauce).

Flauta—A corn tortilla rolled around a filling, usually shredded beef or chicken, and then deep-fried

Gordita—A thick tortilla, sometimes made with *pan árabe* (pita bread) stuffed with a filling, usually beans or spicy shredded meat and cheese

Huarache—A large, flat, oval-shaped tortilla (*huarache* literally means "sandal") topped with fried meat and chiles

Pancita—Sheep's stomach cooked with spices

Quesadillas—Corn or flour tortillas folded over a filling of cheese and sometimes other ingredients, and cooked until the cheese is melted and the tortilla is slightly crisp

Sope—Another name for *gordita*

Taco—Quite simply, a tortilla wrapped around a filling

Tacos al pastor—Tacos made with sliced roast pork marinated in adobo off a vertical spit

Tacos al carbón—A taco filled with charbroiled meat

Tacos de cabeza—Tacos made with meat from the goat's head

Tinga—Spicy, shredded pork

grilled sandwich roll stuffed with frijoles and cheese

Nopales—The fleshy oval pads of the cactus (sometimes called cactus leaves)

Pozole—A stew typically made with hominy, pork or chicken, lime, salt, chiles, onions, and avocado

Rajas—Roasted and peeled strips of poblano chile

Róbalo—Sea bass

Tamales—A pre-Hispanic classic, made from cornmeal dough (*masa*) or ground corn; often filled with meat, seafood, insects, vegetables, and other ingredients; then wrapped in a corn husk and steamed

Tlacoyo–A flat, torpedo-shaped cornmeal cake toasted and stuffed with a variety of fillings, including *flor de calabaza, huitlacoche,* or beans and cheese

Torta—A Mexican sandwich, with a choice of fillings served on a crusty white roll, also called *cemita*

WHAT TO DRINK

Aguas frescas—Literally "fresh waters," this is a blend of water, sugar, and either fruits, cereals, or seeds

Atole—A hot, thick drink made with cornmeal, crushed fruits, and sugar or honey

Barrilitos—Mexico's popular fruit-flavored soft drink brand

Jarritos—Another popular brand of fruit-flavored carbonated soft drinks

Mezcal—A liquor distilled from the agave plant (*not* tequila, which is only made from blue agave)

Michelada—A Mexican take on Bloody Mary, made with beer instead of vodka

Tequila—The classic liquor made by fermenting and distilling the sap of the blue agave plant

Pasita—A liquor made from raisins

Pulque—An alcoholic, often flavored beverage fermented from the juice of the agave plant

HOW IT'S COOKED

Adobo/adobado—Marinated in a spicy vinegar and chile sauce

A la parrilla—Grilled

A la talla—Fish rubbed with spices and grilled on a rack over hot coals

Al carbon—Charbroiled

Al pastor—Meat (almost always pork) roasted on a vertical spit, like a gyro

Al vapor—Steamed

Asado—Roasted

Barbacoa—Slow-roasted in a pit or over an open fire

Empanizada—Breaded

Encebolladao—Cooked with onions

Frito—Fried

Guisado—Stewed

Horneado—Baked

Rostizado—Roasted

A GLOSSARY OF AZTEC AND MAYA GODS

Gods of the Maya Pantheon

AH PUCH OR YUM CIMIL God of Xibalbá, the Underworld, Ah Puch can be readily identifiable by his skeletal figure and adornments made of bone. He is also depicted covered with black spots, a decomposing state, and wears a collar with eyeless sockets, a symbol of the Underworld.

CHAAC The venerable rain god, Chaac was naturally all-important to the cultivation of maize. In Uxmal's Light and Sound show, Chaac's name is repeatedly invoked in prayer for a bountiful harvest.

EK CHUAH Distinctive for his black face and elongated nose, Ek Chuah was god of commerce and cacao, but also served as a war god.

HUNAHPU AND XBALANQUE Better known as the Hero Twins, Hunahpu and Xbalanque are among the most popular figures in Maya mythology. They are both main characters in the Maya creation story as told in the *Popul Vuh,* and it is their adventures in the underworld (Xibalba) that is retold in the *juego de pelota,* or ball game. The story begins with the maize god, **Hun Hunahpu**, and his sons Hun Batz and Hun Chuwen playing ball in a ball court. The commotion they made angered the lords of Xibalbá, who commanded them to enter the Underworld and pass through a series of challenges. At the end, they were sacrificed, and the maize god's head was hung from a tree.

Then the legend gets interesting; apparently the maize god's head somehow impregnates a passing girl, daughter of one of the lords of the Underworld. She is consequently banished to the surface, where she gives birth to the Hero Twins. The brothers, in true hero fashion, rose to all kinds of Herculean challenges, among them defeating the bird-monster Wuqub

Kaquix (Macaw 7); transforming the aforementioned Hun Batz and Hun Chuwen (their half brothers) into monkey-men (who are revered among the Maya as gods and patrons of the arts); defeating a volcano; and, most importantly, vanquishing the lords of Xibalbá. Finally, after many trials (including their own death and resurrection), the twins also succeed in reviving their father, the maize god, and returning him to the Earth.

IK God of wind and hurricanes, Ik is usually shown with puffs of breath emanating from his mouth.

ITZAMNA A principal creator deity and lord of the sky, Itzamna is often depicted as an old man. He invented writing and was patron god of learning and sciences.

IXCHEL Goddess of birth and fertility, weaving, medicine, and the moon, Ixchel is easily recognizable for her headdress, which is an intertwined serpent. Her spouse was Itzamna.

KINICH AHAU The Sun god, Kinich Ahau and Itzamna may be one and the same.

KUKULCÁN God of the wind, Kukulcán was often represented as the Feathered Serpent, and was a direct import from the Toltec. The most striking examples of temples to this god can be found at Chichén Itzá.

YUM KAX God of agriculture, Yum Kax is a youthful-looking deity who personified male beauty; he is dependent on Chaac.

Aztec Pantheon

CINTEOTL An important deity, Cinteotl was the god of maize. Similar to the Maya Yum Kax, he was usually depicted as a young man with a maize headdress.

COATLICUE “She of the Serpent Skirt” was mother of the Sun, Moon, and stars. She is the Aztec counterpart of Ixchel, although she is depicted sporting a skirt made of snakes and a necklace of human hearts, hands, and skulls. Coatlicue’s face is comprised of two serpents, the result of her decapitation and sacrifice during the beginning of this age.

HUITZILOPOCHTLI The chief deity of the Aztecs, Huitzilopochtli (Hummingbird on the Left) was the Sun god and god of war; it was for the sake of his passage across the sky that the Aztecs fed him a steady diet of human sacrifice. Huitzilopochtli was the son of Coatlicue; while in her womb, he learned of his sister **Coyolxauhqui**’s plan to kill their mother.

He emerged from Coatlicue's womb fully grown and armed, and killed his sister along with hundreds of other rival siblings. He dismembered his sister and threw her head into the sky, where it became the moon. His other slain brothers and sisters became stars.

NANAHUATL The humblest of all the gods in Aztec mythology, Nanahuatl is nonetheless largely responsible for this current age. According to legend, during the creation of the fifth age, he dutifully sacrificed himself to become the sun.

OMETEOTL The Aztec belief and reverence for duality is best repretsented in Ometeotl, a bisexual god of creation. Known as both mother and father of the gods, Ometeotl lived in the 13th level of heaven, its highest plane.

QUETZALCÓATL Offspring of Ometeotl, lord of life and patron of rulers and priests, Quetzalcóatl appeared in human form as well as the famed feathered serpent. Although he first appeared in Teotihuacán, Quetzalcóatl was a chief deity of the Toltec and the Aztecs, as well as the Maya of the Postclassic era under the guise of Kukulcán. There are many legends surrounding Quetzalcóatl; in fact, the cosmic ages of the world, each of which end in a cataclysm, are all the result of the battles between Quetzalcóatl and Tezcatlipoca, who fight for dominion over each age. Quetzalcóatl did two pivotal things for the Aztecs; after the fall of the fourth age, human life perished, but Quetzalcóatl retrieved human bones from the Underworld and re-created them. He also gave humans maize, their most basic and important crop; he did this by transforming into an ant and entering the magic mountain of the gods, where the grains were kept.

TEZCATLIPOCA Offspring of Ometeotl, the black Tezcatlipoca was a sinister character, god sorcerery and war, night, death, discord, conflict, temptation, and change. He could give or take life and wealth, and his rival was the rather more popular Quetzalcóatl.

TLALOC The second-most important deity in the Aztec pantheon, Tlaloc was god of rain and thunder, and merited his own allowance of sacrifices (the Aztecs even sacrificed children to appease him and ensure rain). His temple stood next to that of Huitzilopochtli in Tenochtitlán's Templo Mayor. He is typically depicted with large, round, goggle eyes.

XIPE TOTEC God of the seasons and renewal of crops, Xipe Totec's name means "Our Lord of the Flayed One"; this deity flayed himself to feed humanity; Aztec priests would impersonate him by donning the skin of a flayed captive.

A BRIEF DICTIONARY OF MAYAN-NAHUATL-ENGLISH

While the Mayan language is composed of numerous dialects substantially different from each other, the language of the Aztecs was Nahuatl (hence the multiple words listed in Mayan below, which lean toward the Yucatec dialect). The Nahuatl tongue has given the world words like *tomato, avocado, tamale,* and *chocolate.* On the other hand, it's possible that *shark* comes from the Mayan *xoc.* Happily, both languages are still spoken and taught in Mexico today.

ENGLISH	**NAHUATL**	**MAYA**
Yes	*Quema*	*Beyó, Beey, Jaaj, Jaan*
No	*Amo*	*Ma'*
Greeting	*Niltze* (Hello)	*Bix a Belex* (Hi, how are you?) *In Laakech* (I am you, you are me)
What's your name?	*Tlen mo tokatsin?*	*Bix a K'aaba'?*
Goodbye/farewell	*Nimitsittas*	*Tak sáamal* (Until tomorrow)
Thank you	*Tlazocamati*	*Dios Bo'otik, Níib Óolal*
I/me	*Ne*	*En, In, Kin, Teen, Tin*
You	*Te, Tehwatl, Tehwatzin*	*Ech, Teech*
We	*Tehuan, Tehuantin*	*To'on*
Man	*Oquichtli*	*Xiib, Máak, Wíinik*
Woman	*Cíhuatl*	*Ch'up, Ch'uup, Ko'olel*

Child	*Telpochtli* (Boy)/ *Ichpochtli* (Girl)	*Paal, Ju'uk,' Lek Muuch*
Father	*Tahtli, Tahtzintli*	*Taat, Taatáa, Yuum*
Mother	*Nantli, Nantzintli*	*Na'*
Spouse	*Namictli*	*Éet Núup*
Son	*Pilli, Piltzintli*	*Aal*
Daughter	*Nochpochtzin* (my daughter)	*Ch'upul aal*
Brother	*Icniuhtli*	*Íits'in* (younger)
Sister	*Hueltiuhtli*	*Suku'un* (older)
House	*Calli*	*Naj, Nay, Otoch*
Lord	*Tecuhtli*	*Yuum, Nojoch Máak*
Name	*Tocaitl, Tocatzintli*	*K'aaba'*
Food	*Tlacualli*	*Janaj Janal, O'och*
Water	*Atl, Atzintli*	*Ha,' Ja'*
Corn	*Tlaolli*	*Ixi'im, Nal*
Time	*Cahuitl*	*K'iin, K'iinil*
How	*Quenin*	*Bix, Bixi' Bix Túun*
How much	*Quezqui*	*Bajun, Bajux, Buka'aj*
When	*Itquin*	*Ba'ax K'iin, Bik'ix*
Where	*Campa*	*Tu'ux*
Why	*Teica*	*Ba'ax ten*
Who	*Aquin*	*Máax, Máaxil, Máakalmáak*
Good	*Cualli*	*Ki,' Ma'alob, Uts*
Bad	*Amo Cualli*	*K'aas, K'asa'an, K'aak'as*
Sun	*Tonatiuh*	*K'iin*
Moon	*Meztli*	*Uj, Un*
Rain	*Quiyahuitl*	*Cháak, Ja,' K'áaxal ja'*

Numbers

One	*Ce*	*Jun*
Two	*Ome*	*Ka,' Ka'a*
Three	*Eei*	*Óox*
Four	Nahui	Kan
Five	*Macuilli*	*Jo'o*
Six	*Chicoace*	*Waak*
Seven	*Chicome*	*U'uk*
Eight	*Chicuey*	*Waxak*
Nine	*Chicnahui*	*Bolon*
Ten	*Matlactli*	*Lajun*

Native Animals

Jaguar	*Ocelotl*	*Báalam, Chak Mo'ol*
Hummingbird	*Huitzitzilin*	*Ts'unu'un*
Eagle	*Cuauhtli*	*Éek' Píip, Koos, I,' Ch'uuy*
Turkey	*Huexolotl*	*Úulum, tso'*
Owl	*Tecolotl*	*Kulte,' Tunkuruchu*
Dog	*Itzcuintli*	*Peek,' Ts'i, Wichu*
Cat	*Mizton*	*Miis, Ch'amak, Ch'omak*
Snake	*Coatl*	*Kaan*

SUGGESTED READING

Archaeological Mexico (English Edition), Marcia Castro Leal, Monclem Ediciones.

Archaeological Mexico: A Guide to Ancient Cities and Sacred Sites, Andrew Coe, Avalon Travel Publishing, 2001.

A Forest of Kings: The Untold Story of the Ancient Maya, David Freidel, Harper Perennial, 1992.

The Maya, Michael D. Coe, Thames & Hudson, 2005.

The Maya: The Splendor of a Great Culture, Mario Pérez Campa and Laura Sotelo Santos, Monclem Ediciones 2007.

Mayan Prophecies, Hervé Baeza Braga, Editorial Dante, 2nd ed., 2009.

Mayan Legends, Hervé Baeza Braga, Editorial Dante, 2nd ed., 2009.

Mexico: From the Olmec to the Aztecs, Michael D. Coe and Rex Koontz, Thames & Hudson, 2008.

Popol Vuh: The Definitive Edition of the Mayan Book of the Dawn of Life and the Glories of Gods and Kings, Dennis Tedlock, Touchstone, 1996.

INDEX

C

M

Q

R

S

T